Reading STREET

Program Authors

Peter Afflerbach

Camille Blachowicz

Candy Dawson Boyd

Elena Izquierdo

Connie Juel

Edward Kame'enui

Donald Leu

Jeanne R. Paratore

P. David Pearson

Sam Sebesta

Deborah Simmons

Alfred Tatum

Sharon Vaughn

Susan Watts Taffe

Karen Kring Wixson

PEARSON

Glenview, Illinois • Boston, Massachusetts
Chandler, Arizona • Upper Saddle River, New Jersey

We dedicate Reading Street to
Peter Jovanovich.

His wisdom, courage,
and passion for education
are an inspiration to us all.

Accelerated Reader

PEARSON

ISBN-13: 978-0-328-46989-5
ISBN-10: 0-328-46989-0
2 3 4 5 6 7 8 9 10 V064 14 13 12 11 10
CC1

Any Path, Any Pace

Reading STREET

CALLE de la Lectura

"Welcome to Reading Street! Bienvenidos too."

PEARSON

SCOTT FORESMAN

PEARSON

Find Your Place on Reading Street!

Who said so?

The Leading Researchers,

Program Authors

Peter Afflerbach, Ph.D.
Professor
Department of Curriculum and
Instruction
University of Maryland at
College Park

Camille L. Z. Blachowicz, Ph.D.
Professor of Education
National-Louis University

Candy Dawson Boyd, Ph.D.
Professor
School of Education
Saint Mary's College of California

Elena Izquierdo, Ph.D.
Associate Professor
University of Texas at El Paso

Connie Juel, Ph.D.
Professor of Education
School of Education
Stanford University

Edward J. Kame'enui, Ph.D.
*Dean-Knight Professor of
Education and Director*
Institute for the Development of
Educational Achievement and
the Center on Teaching and Learning
College of Education
University of Oregon

Donald J. Leu, Ph.D.
*John and Maria Neag Endowed
Chair in Literacy and Technology
Director, The New Literacies
Research Lab*
University of Connecticut

Jeanne R. Paratore, Ed.D.
Associate Professor of Education
Department of Literacy and
Language Development
Boston University

P. David Pearson, Ph.D.
Professor and Dean
Graduate School of Education
University of California, Berkeley

Sam L. Sebesta, Ed.D.
Professor Emeritus
College of Education
University of Washington, Seattle

Deborah Simmons, Ph.D
Professor
College of Education and
Human Development
Texas A&M University

Alfred W. Tatum, Ph.D.
*Associate Professor and Director
of the UIC Reading Clinic*
University of Illinois at Chicago

Sharon Vaughn, Ph.D.
*H. E. Hartfelder/Southland
Corporation Regents Professor
Director, Meadows Center for
Preventing Educational Risk*
University of Texas

Susan Watts Taffe, Ph.D.
Associate Professor in Literacy
Division of Teacher Education
University of Cincinnati

Karen Kring Wixson, Ph.D.
Professor of Education
University of Michigan

Consulting Authors

Jeff Anderson, M.Ed.
Author and Consultant
San Antonio, Texas

Jim Cummins, Ph.D.
Professor
Department of Curriculum,
Teaching and Learning
University of Toronto

Lily Wong Fillmore, Ph.D.
Professor Emerita
Graduate School of Education
University of California, Berkeley

Georgia Earnest García, Ph.D.
Professor
Language and Literacy Division
Department of Curriculum
and Instruction
University of Illinois at
Urbana-Champaign

George A. González, Ph.D.
Professor (Retired)
School of Education
University of Texas-Pan American,
Edinburg

Valerie Ooka Pang, Ph.D.
Professor
School of Teacher Education
San Diego State University

Sally M. Reis, Ph.D.
*Board of Trustees Distinguished
Professor*
Department of Educational
Psychology
University of Connecticut

Jon Scieszka, M.F.A.
*Children's Book Author
Founder of GUYS READ
Named First National Ambassador
for Young People's Literature 2008*

Grant Wiggins, Ed.D.
Educational Consultant
Authentic Education
Concept Development

Lee Wright, M.Ed.
Pearland, Texas

Practitioners, and Authors.

Consultant

Sharroky Hollie, Ph.D.
Assistant Professor
California State University
Dominguez Hills, CA

Teacher Reviewers

Dr. Bettyann Brugger
Educational Support Coordinator–
Reading Office
Milwaukee Public Schools
Milwaukee, WI

Kathleen Burke
K–12 Reading Coordinator
Peoria Public Schools, Peoria, IL

Darci Burns, M.S.Ed.
University of Oregon

Bridget Cantrell
District Intervention Specialist
Blackburn Elementary School
Independence, MO

Tahira DuPree Chase,
M.A., M.S.Ed.
Administrator of Elementary
English Language Arts
Mount Vernon City School District
Mount Vernon, NY

Michele Conner
Director, Elementary Education
Aiken County School District
Aiken, SC

Georgia Coulombe
K–6 Regional Trainer/
Literacy Specialist
Regional Center for Training and
Learning (RCTL), Reno, NV

Kelly Dalmas
Third Grade Teacher
Avery's Creek Elementary, Arden, NC

Seely Dillard
First Grade Teacher
Laurel Hill Primary School
Mt. Pleasant, SC

Jodi Dodds-Kinner
Director of Elementary Reading
Chicago Public Schools, Chicago, IL

Dr. Ann Wild Evenson
District Instructional Coach
Osseo Area Schools, Maple Grove, MN

Stephanie Fascitelli
Principal
Apache Elementary, Albuquerque
Public Schools, Albuquerque, NM

Alice Franklin
Elementary Coordinator, Language
Arts & Reading
Spokane Public Schools, Spokane, WA

Laureen Fromberg
Assistant Principal
PS100 Queens, NY

Kimberly Gibson
First Grade Teacher
Edgar B. Davis Community School
Brockton, MA

Kristen Gray
Lead Teacher
A.T. Allen Elementary School
Concord, NC

Mary Ellen Hazen
State Pre-K Teacher
Rockford Public Schools #205
Rockford, IL

Patrick M. Johnson
Elementary Instructional Director
Seattle Public Schools, Seattle, WA

Theresa Jaramillo Jones
Principal
Highland Elementary School
Las Cruces, NM

Sophie Kowzun
Program Supervisor, Reading/
Language Arts, PreK–5
Montgomery County Public Schools
Rockville, MD

David W. Matthews
Sixth Grade Teacher
Easton Area Middle School
Easton, PA

Ana Nuncio
Editor and Independent Publisher
Salem, MA

Joseph Peila
Principal
Chappell Elementary School
Chicago, IL

Ivana Reimer
Literacy Coordinator
PS100 Queens, NY

Sally Riley
Curriculum Coordinator
Rochester Public Schools
Rochester, NH

Dyan M. Smiley
Independent Educational Consultant

Michael J. Swiatowiec
Lead Literacy Teacher
Graham Elementary School
Chicago, IL

Dr. Helen Taylor
Director of English Education
Portsmouth City Public Schools
Portsmouth, VA

Carol Thompson
Teaching and Learning Coach
Independence School District
Independence, MO

Erinn Zeitlin
Kindergarten Teacher
Carderock Springs Elementary School
Bethesda, MD

Any Path, Any Pace

UNIT 5

Going Places

In this Teacher's Edition Unit 5, Volume 1

WEEK 1 • Max Takes the Train

Animal Fantasy 7–104

Differentiated Instruction **SI** **OL** **A** **ELL** ....DI•1–DI•17

WEEK 2 • Mayday! Mayday!

Nonfiction 105–210

Differentiated Instruction **SI** **OL** **A** **ELL** ....DI•18–DI•34

WEEK 3 • Trucks Roll! Rhyming Nonfiction 211–310

Differentiated Instruction **SI** **OL** **A** **ELL** ....DI•35–DI•51

Customize Literacy..CL•1–CL•31

In the First Stop on Reading Street

GO Digital!

See It!
- **Big Question Video**
- **Concept Talk Video**
- **Envision It! Animations**
- **Sing With Me Animations**

Hear It!
- **Sing With Me Animations**
- **eReaders**
- **Grammar Jammer**
- **Leveled Reader Database**

Do It!
- **Story Sort**
- **Letter Tile Drag and Drop**

UNIT 1

All Together Now

Volume 1

Carol Roth
The Little School Bus
Illustrated by Pamela Paparone

Volume 2

UNIT 2

Look at Us!

Volume 1

Volume 2

UNIT 3

Changes All Around Us

Volume 1

Volume 2

UNIT 4

Let's Go Exploring

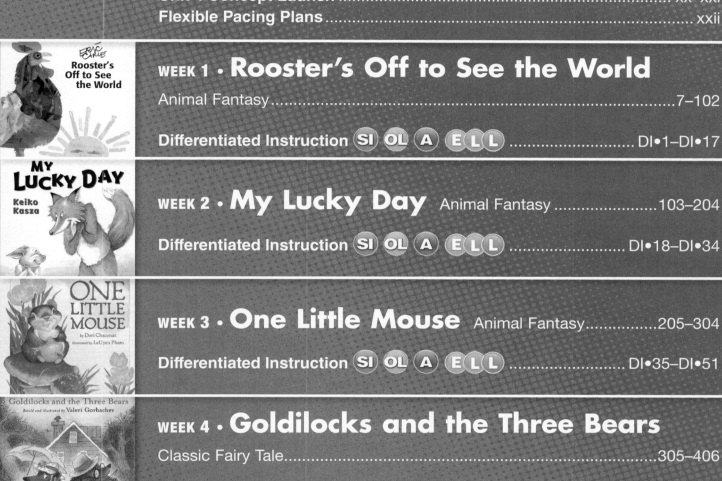

Volume 1

Volume 2

UNIT 5

Going Places

Key

- **SI** Strategic Intervention
- **OL** On-Level
- **A** Advanced
- **ELL** ELL

Volume 1

Volume 2

Putting It Together

UNIT 5

Skills Overview

	WEEK 1  **Max Takes the Train** Animal Fantasy pp. 60–71	WEEK 2 **Mayday! Mayday!** Nonfiction pp. 158–177
Question of the Week	What are different ways of going places?	What kinds of transportation help us in an emergency?
Amazing Words	*plane, jetway, subway, tunnel, ferryboat, sidecar*	*rescue, pilot, yacht, sailor, mechanic, shimmering*
Phonemic Awareness	T ↻ /j/ T ↻ /w/	T ↻ /ks/
Phonics	T ↻ /j/ Spelled *Jj* T ↻ /w/ Spelled *Ww* Review /e/ Spelled *Ee*	T ↻ /ks/ Spelled *Xx* Review /j/ Spelled *Jj;* /w/ Spelled *Ww*
High-Frequency Words	T *yellow, blue, green*	T *yellow, blue, green*
Comprehension	T ↻ **Skill** Realism and Fantasy Review Plot	T ↻ **Skill** Cause and Effect Review Sequence
Writing	Caption	Rhyme
Conventions	Questions	Question Marks and Capital Letters
Vocabulary	Transportation Words	Position Words
Speaking/Listening	Ask and Answer Questions	Drama: Respond to Literature

Get Ready to Read

Read and Comprehend

Language Arts

The Big Question

How do people and things get from here to there?

WEEK 3	**WEEK 4**	**WEEK 5**	**WEEK 6**
Trucks Roll! Rhyming Nonfiction pp. 264–277	**The Little Engine That Could** Classic Fantasy pp. 363–381	**On the Move!** Nonfiction pp. 468–479	**This Is the Way We Go to School** Informational Fiction pp. 566–58?
What kinds of transportation help people do their jobs?	What kind of work do trains do?	How do people in different parts of the world travel?	How do children around the world get to school?
trailers, cabs, haul, steering wheel, truckers, headlight	*engine, tracks, passenger, roundhouse, mountain, valley*	*travel, kayak, llama, dogsled, submarine, double-decker bus*	*cable car, trolley, horse-and-buggy, skis, Metro line, vaporetto*
T 🔊 /u/	T 🔊 /u/	T 🔊 /v/ T 🔊 /z/	T 🔊 /y/ T 🔊 /kw/
T 🔊 /u/ Spelled *Uu* **Review** /ks/ Spelled *Xx*	T 🔊 /u/ Spelled *Uu* **Review** Sound-Spellings *Xx, Jj, Ww, Uu*	T 🔊 /v/ Spelled *Vv* T 🔊 /z/ Spelled *Zz* **Review** /u/ Spelled *Uu*	T 🔊 /y/ Spelled *Yy* T 🔊 /kw/ Spelled *Qu* **Review** /v/ Spelled *Vv*; /z/ Spelled *Zz*
T *what, said, was*	T *what, said, was*	T *where, come*	T *where, come*
T 🔊 **Skill** Compare and Contrast **Review** Draw Conclusions	T 🔊 **Skill** Plot **Review** Character	T 🔊 **Skill** Main Idea **Review** Cause and Effect	T 🔊 **Skill** Draw Conclusions **Review** Main Idea
Poem	Formal Letter	Invitation	Writing Process: How-to Report
Prepositions	Nouns	Nouns in Sentences	Verbs
Words for Jobs	Time Words	Compound Words	Action Words
Discuss Literature	Sequence	Oral Presentations: Description	Discuss Literary Elements: Plot

UNIT 5

Monitor Progress
Make Data-Driven Decisions

Data Management
- Assess
- Diagnose
- Prescribe
- Disaggregate

Classroom Management
- Monitor Progress
- Group
- Differentiate Instruction
- Inform Parents

Don't Wait Until Friday!

SUCCESS PREDICTOR	WEEK 1	WEEK 2	WEEK 3	WEEK 4
Phonemic Awareness	T /j/ T /w/	T final /ks/	T /u/	T /u/
Phonics	T /j/ Spelled *Jj* T /w/ Spelled *Ww*	T /ks/ Spelled *Xx*	T /u/ Spelled *Uu*	T /u/ Spelled *Uu*
High-Frequency Words	T yellow T blue T green	T yellow T blue T green	T what T said T was	T what T said T was
Oral Vocabulary/ Concept Development (assessed informally)	plane jetway subway tunnel ferryboat sidecar	rescue pilot yacht sailor mechanic shimmering	trailers cabs haul steering wheel truckers headlight	engine tracks passenger roundhouse mountain valley
Comprehension	T **Skill** Realism and Fantasy **Strategies** Preview and Predict; Retell	T **Skill** Cause and Effect **Strategies** Preview and Predict; Retell	T **Skill** Compare and Contrast **Strategies** Preview and Predict; Retell	T **Skill** Plot **Strategies** Preview and Predict; Retell

Key

T Tested

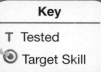 Target Skill

WEEK 5	WEEK 6
T /v/ **T** /z/	**T** /y/ **T** /kw/
T /v/ Spelled *Vv* **T** /z/ Spelled *Zz*	**T** /y/ Spelled *Yy* **T** /kw/ Spelled *Qu*
T where **T** come	**T** where **T** come
travel kayak llama dogsled submarine double-decker bus	cable car trolley horse-and-buggy skis Metro line vaporetto
T **Skill** Main Idea **Strategies** Preview and Predict; Retell	**T** **Skill** Draw Conclusions **Strategies** Preview and Predict; Retell

GO Digital!

See It!

- **Big Question Video**
- **Concept Talk Video**
- **Envision It! Animations**
- **Sing with Me Animations**

Hear It!

- **Sing with Me Animations**
- **eReaders**
- **Grammar Jammer**
- **Leveled Reader Database**

Do It!

- **Story Sort**
- **Letter Tile Drag and Drop**

UNIT 5

Assessment and Grouping
for Data-Driven Instruction

4-Step Plan for Assessment
1 Diagnose and Differentiate
2 Monitor Progress
3 Assess and Regroup
4 Summative Assessment

STEP 1 **Diagnose and Differentiate**

Diagnose

To make initial grouping decisions, use the Baseline Group Test, the Texas Primary Reading Inventory (TPRI), or another initial placement test. Depending on students' ability levels, you may have more than one of each group.

Baseline Group Tests

Differentiate

If... student performance is **SI** **then...** use the regular instruction and the daily **Strategic Intervention** small group lessons.

If... student performance is **OL** **then...** use the regular instruction and the daily **On-Level** small group lessons.

If... student performance is **A** **then...** use the regular instruction and the daily **Advanced** learners small group lessons.

Small Group Time

SI Strategic Intervention

- Daily small group lessons provide more intensive instruction, more scaffolding, more practice, and more opportunities to respond.
- Reteach lessons in *First Stop* provide instruction of target skills.
- Leveled readers, decodable readers, and other weekly texts build background and provide practice for target skills and vocabulary.

OL On-Level

- Explicit instructional routines teach core skills and strategies.
- Daily On-Level lessons provide more practice and more opportunities to respond.
- Independent activities provide practice for core skills.
- Student Readers and Get Set, Roll! Readers provide additional reading and practice for core skills and vocabulary.

A Advanced

- Daily Advanced lessons provide instruction for accelerated learning.
- Independent Leveled Readers provide additional reading tied to lesson concepts and skills.

Additional Differentiated Learning Options

Reading Street Response to Intervention Kit
- Focused intervention lessons on the five critical areas of reading: phonemic awareness, phonics, vocabulary, comprehension, and fluency

My Sidewalks on Reading Street
- Early Reading Intervention

STEP 2 Monitor Progress

Don't Wait Until Friday

Use these tools during lesson teaching to **monitor student progress.**

- **Skill and Strategy** instruction during reading

- **Don't Wait Until Friday** boxes to check letter and sound fluency, word reading, retelling, and oral vocabulary

- **Weekly Assessment** on Day 5 to check phonics, high-frequency words, and comprehension

- **Reader's and Writer's Notebook** pages at point of use

Weekly Phonics and High-Frequency Words Assessment

Weekly Comprehension Assessment

STEP 3 Assess and Regroup

Use these tools during lesson teaching to **assess and regroup.**

- **Weekly Assessments** Record results of weekly assessments for phonics and high-frequency words to track student progress.

- **Unit Benchmark Assessment** Administer this assessment to check progress of unit skills.

- **Regroup** We recommend the first regrouping to be at the end of Unit 2. Use weekly assessment information and Unit Benchmark Assessment performance to inform regrouping decisions. Then regroup at the end of each subsequent unit.

Unit 1 Reading Chart in First Stop

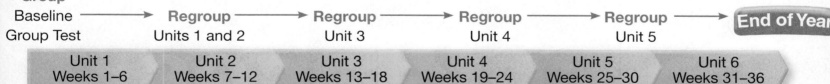

Group					
Baseline Group Test →	Regroup Units 1 and 2 →	Regroup Unit 3 →	Regroup Unit 4 →	Regroup Unit 5 →	End of Year
Unit 1 Weeks 1–6	Unit 2 Weeks 7–12	Unit 3 Weeks 13–18	Unit 4 Weeks 19–24	Unit 5 Weeks 25–30	Unit 6 Weeks 31–36

Outside assessments, such as DRA, TPRI, and DIBELS, may recommend regrouping at other times during the year.

STEP 4 Summative Assessment

Use these tools after lesson teaching to **assess students.**

- **Unit Benchmark Assessments** Use to measure a student's mastery of each unit's skills.

- **End-of-Year Benchmark Assessment** Use to measure a student's mastery of program skills covered in all six units.

Unit and End-of-Year Benchmark Assessments

Understanding By Design

Grant Wiggins, Ed. D.
Reading Street Author

"The big idea connects the dots for the learner by establishing learning priorities. As a teacher friend of ours observed, they serve as 'conceptual Velcro'—they help the facts and skills stick together and stick in our minds!"

Going Places

Reading Street Online

www.ReadingStreet.com

• Big Question Video
• Envision It! Animations
• Story Sort

THE BIG **?**

How do people and things get from here to there?

UNIT 5

Small Group Time
Flexible Pacing Plans

Small Group Time

Sometimes you have holidays, programs, assemblies, or other interruptions to the school week. This plan can help you make Small Group Time decisions if you have less time during the week.

5 Day Plan

DAY 1	• Phonemic Awareness • Phonics • Reading Practice
DAY 2	• Phonemic Awareness • Phonics • Reading Practice
DAY 3	• Phonemic Awareness/ Phonics • Leveled Reader
DAY 4	• Phonemic Awareness • Reading Practice
DAY 5	• Phonics • Reading Practice

4 Day Plan

DAY 1	• Phonemic Awareness • Phonics • Reading Practice
DAY 2	• Phonemic Awareness • Phonics • Reading Practice
DAY 3	• Phonemic Awareness/ Phonics • Leveled Reader
DAY 4	• Phonemic Awareness • Reading Practice

3 Day Plan

DAY 1	• Phonemic Awareness • Phonics • Reading Practice
DAY 2	• Phonemic Awareness/ Phonics • Leveled Reader
DAY 3	• Phonemic Awareness • Reading Practice

ELL

5 Day Plan

DAY 1	• Frontload Concept • Phonemic Awareness/ Phonics • Comprehension
DAY 2	• Comprehension • Vocabulary
DAY 3	• Phonemic Awareness/ Phonics • Conventions
DAY 4	• Phonemic Awareness/ Phonics • Concepts and Oral Language
DAY 5	• Language Workshop • Writing

4 Day Plan

DAY 1	• Frontload Concept • Phonemic Awareness/ Phonics • Comprehension
DAY 2	• Comprehension • Vocabulary
DAY 3	• Phonemic Awareness/ Phonics • Conventions
DAY 4	• Language Workshop • Writing

3 Day Plan

DAY 1	• Frontload Concept • Phonemic Awareness/ Phonics • Comprehension
DAY 2	• Phonemic Awareness/ Phonics • Conventions
DAY 3	• Language Workshop • Writing

My Planning Guide ★★

This Week's ELL Overview

Grade K • Unit 5 • Week 1
Max Takes the Train
7–104
and DI•12–DI•17

ELL Handbook

- Maximize Literacy and Cognitive Engagement
- Research Into Practice
- Full Weekly Support for Every Selection

  ### Max Takes the Train
  - Routines to Support Instruction

- Transfer Activities
- Professional Development

Daily Leveled ELL Notes

ELL notes appear throughout this week's instruction and ELL Support is on the DI pages of your Teacher's Edition. The following is a sample of an ELL note from this week.

English Language Learners

Beginning Build Background After reviewing the Amazing Words, have children draw a picture of each word. Use the pictures on Talk with Me Chart 25A to help children get started.

Intermediate Visual Support Have children draw pictures of things that are *yellow, blue,* or *green.* Then pair children and have them take turns telling about their picture using the color word.

Advanced Physical Response Ask children to choose the character from *On a Jet* whose role they would enjoy the most. Have them act out what the character does.

Advanced High Support Discussion Have children think of different places to go, such as a store, another state, or another country. Then have children think of a form of transportation that can be used to get to that place.

ELL by Strand

The ELL lessons on this week's Support for English Language Learners pages are organized by strand. They offer additional scaffolding for the core curriculum. Leveled support notes on these pages address the different proficiency levels in your class. See pages DI•12–DI•17.

ELL Guy
Dr. Jim Cummins

The Three Pillars of ELL Instruction

ELL Strands	Activate Prior Knowledge	Access Content	Extend Language
Vocabulary p. DI•14	Frontload Vocabulary	Provide Scaffolding	Practice
Reading Comprehension p. DI•14	Provide Scaffolding	Set the Scene	Frontload Vocabulary
Phonics, Spelling, and Word Analysis pp. DI•12, DI•15–DI•16	Frontload Words with /j/	Isolate Initial /w/	Review /e/
Listening Comprehension p. DI•13	Prepare for the Read Aloud	First Listening	Second Listening
Conventions and Writing pp. DI•15, DI•17	Provide Scaffolding/ Introduce and Model	Practice	Leveled Practice Activities/ Leveled Writing Activities
Concept Development p. DI•12	Read the Concept Literacy Reader	Read the Concept Literacy Reader	Develop Oral Language

This Week's Practice Stations Overview

Six Weekly Practice Stations with Leveled Activities can be found at the beginning of each week of instruction. For this week's Practice Stations, see pp. 14–15.

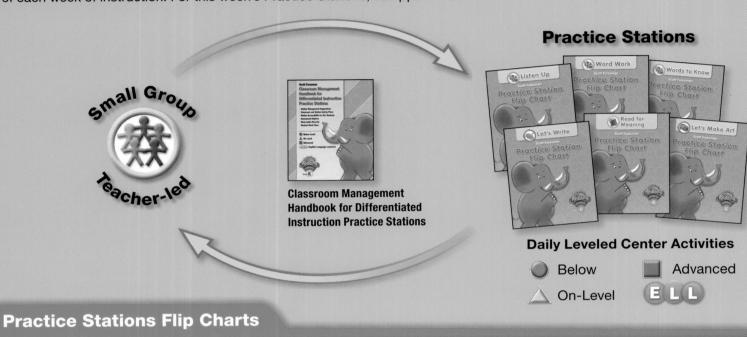

Small Group • Teacher-led

Classroom Management Handbook for Differentiated Instruction Practice Stations

Practice Stations

Daily Leveled Center Activities

⬤ Below   ⬛ Advanced   △ On-Level   Ⓔ Ⓛ Ⓛ

Practice Stations Flip Charts

	Listen Up	Word Work	Words to Know	Let's Write	Read for Meaning	Let's Make Art
Objectives	• Identify words with /e/.	• Identify words with /e/. • Build words with /e/.	• Identify and use words for time: *day, week, month.*	• Write a report about a city.	• Identify story setting.	• Make a picture of a skyline.
Materials	• *Listen Up* Flip Chart Activity 25 • Picture Cards: *egg, bed, jet, desk, hen, ten* • paper, pencils, crayons	• *Word Work* Flip Chart Activity 25 • Alphabet Cards • Picture Cards • Letter Tiles	• *Words to Know* Flip Chart Activity 25 • Teacher-made Word Cards: *day, week, month* • Teacher-made calendar to show *day, week, month* • paper, pencils	• *Let's Write* Flip Chart Activity 25 • Teacher-made Writing Steps Poster 1) Plan 2) Write 3) Revise 4) Edit 5) Share • books about different cities around the world • crayons, paper, pencil	• *Read for Meaning* Flip Chart Activity 25 • Little Book *Max Takes the Train* • pencil, crayons, paper	• *Let's Make Art* Flip Chart Activity 25 • Little Book *Max Takes the Train* • books about cities • construction paper • art tissue • fabric scraps • safety scissors • glue

This Week on Reading Street!

Question of the Week
What are different ways of going places?

Daily Plan

Don't Wait Until Friday

Whole Group
- /j/ Spelled *Jj*
- /w/ Spelled *Ww*
- Realism and Fantasy
- Vocabulary

MONITOR PROGRESS | Success Predictor

Day 1	Day 2	Day 3	Day 4	Day 5
Check Phonemic Awareness	Check Sound-Spelling/ Retelling	Check Word Reading	Check Phonemic Awareness	Check Oral Vocabulary

Small Group

Teacher-Led

- Reading Support
- Skill Support
- Fluency Practice

Practice Stations

Independent Activities

Customize Literacy More support for a Balanced Literacy approach, see pp. CL•1–CL•31

Whole Group
- Writing
- Conventions: Questions
- Listening and Speaking

Assessment
- Day 5 Assessment for Phonics
- Day 5 Assessment for Comprehension

You Are Here!
Unit 5 Week 1

This Week's Reading Selections

Big Book
Genre: **Animal Fantasy**

Decodable Reader 25

Leveled Readers

Get Set Roll!
Reader 25

Resources on Reading Street!

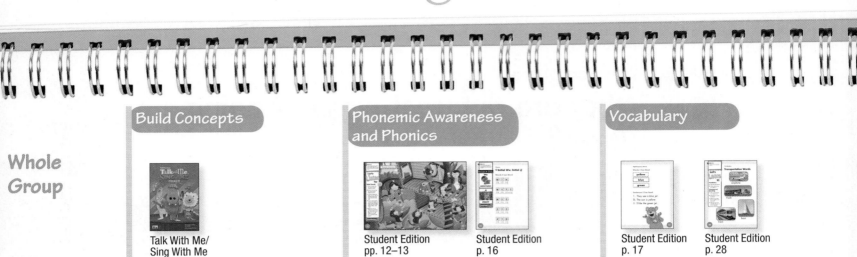

	Build Concepts	Phonemic Awareness and Phonics	Vocabulary
Whole Group	Talk With Me/ Sing With Me	Student Edition pp. 12–13 Student Edition p. 16	Student Edition p. 17 Student Edition p. 28
Go Digital	• Concept Talk Video • Sing with Me Animations	• eReaders	
Small Group and Independent Practice	Practice Station Flip Chart Leveled Readers	Practice Station Flip Chart Decodable Reader 25 Leveled Readers Get Set, Roll! Reader 25	Practice Station Flip Chart Student Edition p. 17
Go Digital	• eReaders	• eReaders • Letter Tile Drag and Drop	
Customize Literacy	• Leveled Readers	• Decodable Reader	• High-Frequency Word Cards
Go Digital	• Concept Talk Video • Big Question Video • eReaders	• eReaders	• Sing with Me Animations

Question of the Week
What are different ways of going places?

Comprehension	Fluency	Conventions and Writing
 Student Edition pp. 14–15 · Big Book	 Decodable Reader 25 · Kdg. Student Reader K.5.1 · Get Set, Roll! Reader 25	Reader's and Writer's Notebook
• Envision It! Animations	• eReaders	• Grammar Jammer
Practice Station Flip Chart · Leveled Readers · Get Set, Roll! Reader 25	Practice Station Flip Chart · Leveled Readers	 Practice Station Flip Chart · Reader's and Writer's Notebook
• Envision It! Animations • eReaders	• eReaders	• Grammar Jammer
• Leveled Readers	• Leveled Readers	• *Reader's and Writer's Notebook*
• Envision It! Animations • eReaders	• eReaders	• Grammar Jammer

You Are Here! Unit 5 Week 1

My 5-Day Planner for Reading Street!

You Are Here! Unit 5 Week 1

Don't Wait Until Friday
MONITOR PROGRESS

	Check Phonemic Awareness **Day 1** pages 16–31	Check Sound-Spelling/Retelling **Day 2** pages 32–49

Get Ready to Read	**Concept Talk,** 16
	Oral Vocabulary, 17
	  plane, jetway, subway, tunnel, ferryboat, sidecar
	Phonemic Awareness, 18–19
	  ◉ Initial /j/
	Phonics, 20–21
	  ◉ /j/ Spelled *Jj*
	Handwriting, 22 Letters *J* and *j*
	High-Frequency Words, 23
	  Introduce *yellow, blue, green*
	READ Decodable Story 25, 24–25
		Concept Talk, 32
		Oral Vocabulary, 33
		  plane, jetway
		Phonemic Awareness, 34–35
		  ◉ Initial /w/
		Phonics, 36–37
		  ◉ /w/ Spelled *Ww*
		Handwriting, 38 Words with *Ww*
		High-Frequency Words, 39 *yellow, blue, green*
		READ Decodable Reader 25, 40–41

Read and Comprehend	**Listening Comprehension,** 26–27
	  ◉ Realism and Fantasy
		Listening Comprehension, 42
		  ◉ Realism and Fantasy
		READ Big Book—First Read, 42
		  Max Takes the Train
		Retell, 43
		Think, Talk, and Write, 44

Language Arts	**Conventions,** 28 Questions **Writing,** 29 Wonderful, Marvelous Me! **Daily Handwriting,** 29 Letters *J* and *j* **Listening and Speaking,** 30 Ask and Answer Questions **Wrap Up Your Day,** 30 **Extend Your Day!,** 31	**Conventions,** 45 Questions **Writing,** 46 Respond to Literature **Daily Handwriting,** 46 Letters *W* and *w* **Vocabulary,** 47 Transportation Words **Wrap Up Your Day,** 48 **Extend Your Day!,** 49

Question of the Week
What are different ways of going places?

Check Word Reading	Check Phonemic Awareness	Check Oral Vocabulary
Day 3 pages 50–77	**Day 4** pages 78–89	**Day 5** pages 90–103
Concept Talk, 50 **Oral Vocabulary,** 51 *subway, tunnel* **Phonemic Awareness,** 52–53 ◎ Initial /j/ and /w/ **Phonics,** 54–55 ◎ /j/ Spelled *Jj*, /w/ Spelled *Ww* **READ Kindergarten Student Reader K.5.1,** 56–57	**Concept Talk,** 78 **Oral Vocabulary,** 79 *ferryboat, sidecar* Review **Phonemic Awareness,** 80 /e/ Review **Phonics,** 81 /e/ Spelled *Ee* **Spelling,** 82 ◎ /j/ Spelled *Jj*, /w/ Spelled *Ww* **READ Get Set, Roll! Reader 25,** 83	**Concept Wrap Up,** 90 **Oral Vocabulary,** 91 *plane, jetway, subway, tunnel, ferryboat, sidecar* Review **Phonemic Awareness,** 92 ◎ /j/ and /w/ Review **Phonics,** 93 ◎ /j/ Spelled *Jj*, /w/ Spelled *Ww* **Assessment,** 94–95 Monitor Progress
Comprehension, 58–59 ◎ Realism and Fantasy **READ Big Book—Second Read,** 60–71 *Max Takes the Train*	**Comprehension,** 84 ◎ Realism and Fantasy Review Plot **READ Big Book—Third Read,** 85 *Max Takes the Train*	**Let's Practice It!,** 96–97 Poem **Assessment,** 98–99 Monitor Progress
Conventions, 72 Pronouns *I* and *me* **Writing,** 73 Genre: Caption **Daily Handwriting,** 73 Letters *J, j, W,* and *w* **Listening and Speaking,** 74–75 Ask and Answer Questions **Wrap Up Your Day,** 76 **Extend Your Day!,** 77	**Conventions,** 86 Questions **Writing,** 87 Extend the Concept **Daily Handwriting,** 87 Letters *J, j, W,* and *w* **Vocabulary,** 88 Transportation Words **Wrap Up Your Day,** 88 **Extend Your Day!,** 89	Review **Conventions,** 100 Questions **Writing,** 101 This Week We… **Daily Handwriting,** 101 Letters *J, j, W,* and *w* **Wrap Up Your Week!,** 102 What are different ways of going places? **Extend Your Day!,** 103

Grouping Options for Differentiated Instruction
Turn the page for the small group time lesson plan.

Planning Small Group Time on Reading Street!

SMALL GROUP TIME RESOURCES

DAY 1

Look for this Small Group Time box each day to help meet the individual needs of all your children. Differentiated instruction lessons appear on the DI pages at the end of each week.

Teacher-Led

SI Strategic Intervention

Teacher-Led
- Phonemic Awareness and Phonics

Reread Decodable Story

OL On-Level

Teacher-Led
- Phonemic Awareness and Phonics

Reread Decodable Story

A Advanced

Teacher-Led
- Phonemic Awareness and Phonics

Reread Decodable Story for Fluency

E L L Place English language learners in the groups that correspond to their reading abilities in English.

Practice Stations
- Listen Up
- Word Work

Independent Activities
- Read Independently
- *Reader's and Writer's Notebook*
- Concept Talk Video

ELL Poster 25

Day 1

SI Strategic Intervention		Phonemic Awareness and Phonics, DI•1 **Reread** Decodable Story 25, DI•1
OL On-Level		Phonemic Awareness and Phonics, DI•6 **Reread** Decodable Story 25, DI•6
A Advanced		Phonemic Awareness and Phonics, DI•9 **Reread** Decodable Story 25 for Fluency, DI•9
E L L English Language Learners		DI•12–DI•13 Frontload Concept Phonemic Awareness and Phonics Comprehension Skill

You Are Here!
Unit 5
Week 1

Question of the Week

What are different ways of going places?

SI Strategic Intervention

Decodable
Reader

Listen to Me Reader

There It Goes!
Concept Literacy Reader

BLUE?
Get Set, Roll! Reader

OL On-Level

Jan and Jem Win!
Kindergarten
Student Reader

BLUE?
Get Set, Roll! Reader

On a Jet
Decodable Reader

A Advanced

The Bus Ride
Independent
Reader

On a Jet
Decodable Reader

Small Group Weekly Plan

Day 2	Day 3	Day 4	Day 5
Phonemic Awareness and Phonics, DI•2 **Reread** Decodable Reader 25, DI•2	**Phonemic Awareness and Phonics,** DI•3 **Read** Concept Literacy Reader K.5.1, DI•3	**Phonemic Awareness and Phonics,** DI•4 **Read** Get Set, Roll! Reader 25, DI•4	**Phonics Review,** DI•5 **Read** Listen to Me Reader K.5.1, DI•5
Phonemic Awareness and Phonics, DI•6 **Reread** Decodable Reader 25, DI•6	**Phonemic Awareness and Phonics,** DI•7 **Read** Kindergarten Student Reader K.5.1, DI•7	**Review Phonics and High-Frequency Words** **Read** Get Set, Roll! Reader 25 DI•8	**Phonics Review,** DI•8 **Reread** Leveled Readers
Phonics and Spelling, DI•9 **Reread** Decodable Reader 25 for Fluency, DI•9	**Read** Independent Reader K.5.1 or Kindergarten Student Reader K.5.1, DI•10	**Read** Get Set, Roll! Reader 25 or **Reread** Kindergarten Student Reader K.5.1, DI•11	**Fluency and Comprehension,** DI•11 **Reread** Independent Reader for Fluency, DI•11
DI•14 Comprehension Skill Frontload Vocabulary	DI•15 Phonemic Awareness and Phonics Conventions	DI•16 Phonemic Awareness and Phonics Concepts and Oral Language	DI•17 Language Workshop Writing

Max Takes the Train

Practice Stations for Everyone on Reading Street!

Listen Up!
Words with /e/

Objectives
• Identify words with /e/.

Materials
Listen Up! Flip Chart Activity 25
Picture Cards: *egg, bed, jet, desk, hen, ten*.
paper, pencils, crayons

Differentiated Activities

● Find the Picture Card for *egg*. Say the sound you hear at the beginning. Find the Picture Card for *hen*. Say the sound you hear in the middle. Draw a picture of something whose name has the sound you hear in the middle of *hen*.

▲ Find the Picture Card for *egg*. Say the sound you hear at the beginning. Find the Picture Card for *hen*. Say the sound you hear in the middle. Find other Picture Cards whose names begin like *egg* or have the middle sound you hear in *hen*.

■ Find the Picture Card for *egg*. Say the sound you hear at the beginning. Find the Picture Card for *hen*. Say the sound you hear in the middle. Look around the room. Find other objects whose names have the sound you hear at the beginning of *egg* and in the middle of *hen*.

Word Work
/e/ Spelled *Ee*

Objectives
• Identify words with /e/.
• Build words with /e/.

Materials
• *Word Work* Flip Chart Activity 25
• Alphabet Cards
• Picture Cards
• Letter Tiles

Differentiated Activities

● Find the Alphabet Card for *Ee*. Say *escalator*. Find a Picture Card that begins with *e* like *escalator* or has *e* in the middle like *bed*.

▲ Find the Alphabet Card for *Ee*. Say *escalator*. Find a Picture Card that begins with *e* like *escalator* or has *e* in the middle like *bed*. Look around the room. Find other objects whose names begin with *e* or have *e* in the middle like *otter* and *bed*.

■ Find the Alphabet Card for *Ee*. Say *escalator*. Find all the Picture Cards that begin with *e* like *escalator* or have *e* in the middle like *bed*. Use Letter Tiles to spell words with the *e* sound you hear in the middle of *bed*.

Technology
• Letter Tile Drag and Drop

Words To Know
Words for time

Objectives
• Identify and use words for time: *day, week, month*.

Materials
• *Words to Know* Flip Chart Activity 25
• Teacher-Made word cards: *day, week, month*.
• Teacher made chart divided into 3 sections; 1) show a calendar month with one *day* highlighted and word *day*; 2) show a calendar month with one full week highlighted and word *week*; show a calendar month all days highlighted and word *month*.
• paper, pencils

Differentiated Activities

● Find the Word Cards for *day, week, month*. Match the Word Cards with the words on the calendar to show *day, week, month*.

▲ Find the Word Cards for *day, week, month*. Match the Word Cards with the words on the calendar to show *day, week, month*. With a partner, use one of the words to tell about something you do.

■ Find the Word Cards for *day, week, month*. Match the Word Cards with the words on the calendar to show *day, week, month*. Work with a partner to think of the names for the days of the week.

You Are Here!
Unit 5
Week 1

Key

- ● Below-Level Activities
- ▲ On-Level Activities
- ■ Advanced Activities

Practice Station Flip Chart

Practice Station Flip Chart

Let's Write!
Write nonfiction.

Objectives
• Write a report about a city.

Materials
• *Let's Write!* Flip Chart Activity 25
• Teacher made writing steps poster 1) Plan 2) Write 3) Revise 4) Edit 5) Share
• books about different cities around the world
• crayons, paper, pencil

Differentiated Activities

Direct all children to look at the Writing Steps poster.

● Look at the books that tell about cities. Draw a picture that shows something you learned. Write a sentence that tells about something you learned.

▲ What do you want to know about a city? Look at the books to find the answer. Think about what you learned. Write three sentences that tell about what you learned.

■ What do you want to know about a city? Look at the books to find the answer. Think about what you learned. Write five sentences that give information about a city.

Technology
• Grammar Jammer

Read For Meaning
Setting

Objectives
• Identify story setting.

Materials
• *Read for Meaning* Flip Chart Activity 25
• Little Book *Max Takes the Train*
• pencil, crayons, paper

Differentiated Activities

The story **setting** is where the story takes place. A good way to understand a story is to think about the setting.

● Read your book. Find a picture that shows where the story takes place. Tell what you see.

▲ Read your book. Draw a picture that shows where the story takes place. Write a sentence to go with your picture.

■ Read your book. Find pictures and words that give information bout the setting. Write a sentence that tells about the setting of the story.

Let's Make Art!

Objectives
• Make a picture of a skyline.

Materials
• *Let's Make Art!* Flip Chart Activity 25
• Little Book *Max Takes the Train*
• books about cities
• construction paper
• art tissue
• fabric scraps
• safety scissors
• glue

Differentiated Activities

● Find pictures that show a city skyline. Look at the shapes and lines of the buildings. Make a city skyline on your paper using art supplies.

▲ Find pictures that show a city skyline. Look at the shapes and lines of the buildings. Notice the different colors. Make a city skyline on your paper using art supplies.

■ Find pictures that show a city skyline. Look at the shapes and lines of the buildings. Notice the different colors. Make a picture that shows a city skyline during the day. Make a picture that shows a city skyline at night.

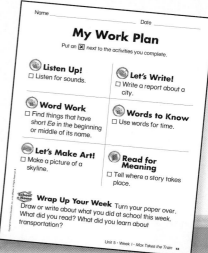

Name _____ Date _____

My Work Plan
Put an ☒ next to the activities you complete.

Listen Up!
☐ Listen for sounds.

Let's Write!
☐ Write a report about a city.

Word Work
☐ Find things that have short *Ee* in the beginning or middle of its name.

Words to Know
☐ Use words for time.

Let's Make Art!
☐ Make a picture of a skyline.

Read for Meaning
☐ Tell where a story takes place.

Wrap Up Your Week Turn your paper over. Draw or write about what you did at school this week. What did you read? What did you learn about transportation?

Unit 5 • Week I • *Max Takes the Train*

My Weekly Work Plan

Objectives
• Share information and ideas about the concept.

Today at a Glance

Oral Vocabulary
plane, jetway, subway, tunnel, ferryboat, sidecar

Phonemic Awareness
Initial /j/

Phonics
/j/ Spelled *Jj*

Handwriting
J and j

High-Frequency Words
yellow, blue, green

Comprehension
Realism and Fantasy

Conventions
Questions

Writing
Wonderful, Marvelous Me!

Listening and Speaking
Compare and Contrast

TRUCKTOWN on Reading Street

Start your engines! Display p. 12 of *Truckery Rhymes*.

• Read aloud "Swing Around with Rosie" and track the print.

• Reread the rhyme and have children chime in as they wish.

• Ask children to identify the rhyming words. (*smashes, bashes*)

Truckery Rhymes

Concept Talk

Question of the Week

 What are different ways of going places?

Introduce the concept

To build concepts and to focus their attention, tell children that this week they will talk, sing, read, and write about **ways to go places**. Write the question of the week and track the print as you read it.

Play the CD that features a story about a ride on a ferryboat. Would you like to travel by boat? Where would you go?

 Background Building Audio

ROUTINE Activate Prior Knowledge Team Talk

1. **Think** Have children think for a minute about what they know about transportation.

2. **Pair** Have pairs of children discuss the question of the week. Remind them to take turns speaking. Have children use complete sentences in their discussions about the different ways to go places.

3. **Share** Call on a few children to share their ideas with the group. Guide discussion and encourage elaboration with prompts such as: How do you get to school?

Anchored Talk

Develop oral language

Display Talk with Me Chart 25A. The pictures show different forms of transportation, or ways we can get from one place to another. This is a picture of an airplane. I like to fly, so that is my favorite form of transportation. What other kinds of transportation do you see here?

We are going to learn six new Amazing Words this week. Listen as I say each word: *plane, jetway, subway, tunnel, ferryboat, sidecar.* Say the Amazing Words with me as I point to each kind of transportation.

Display Sing with Me Chart 25B. Tell children that they are going to sing a song about transportation. Read the title. Have children describe the pictures. Sing the song several times to the tune of "Are You Sleeping?" Listen for the Amazing Words *plane, jetway, subway, tunnel, ferryboat,* and *sidecar.* Have children sing along with you.

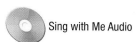 Sing with Me Audio

Talk with Me/Sing with Me Chart 25A

Through the Jetway

Through the jetway, through the jetway,
To the plane, to the plane,
Look at all these things that float,
I can see a ferryboat,
Down below, down below.

Talk with Me/Sing with Me Chart 25B

ELL **Preteach Concepts** Use the Day 1 instruction on ELL Poster 25 to assess and build background knowledge, develop concepts, and build vocabulary.

ELL Poster 25

Amazing Words

plane	jetway
subway	tunnel
ferryboat	sidecar

Differentiated Instruction

SI **Strategic Intervention**
Support Vocabulary To help children better understand the Amazing Words *plane, subway, ferryboat,* and *sidecar,* discuss with children where these forms of transportation travel. For example, a *plane* travels in the air.

ELL

English Language Learners
Build Background After reviewing the Amazing Words, have children draw a picture of each word. Use the pictures on Talk with Me Chart 25A to help children get started.

ELL Support Additional ELL support and modified instruction is provided in the *ELL Handbook* and in the ELL Support Lessons on pp. DI•12–17.

Objectives
Learn initial /j/.
Identify words with initial /j/.
Discriminate words with initial /j/.
Blend words with /j/.

Check Phonemic Awareness
SUCCESS PREDICTOR

My Skills Buddy, pp. 12–13

Phonemic Awareness
Initial /j/

Introduce

Today we are going to learn a new sound. Listen carefully: /j/ /j/ /j/. Say it with me: /j/ /j/ /j/. Display the *jug* Picture Card. *Jug* begins with /j/ /j/, *jug*. What sound does *jug* begin with? Continue the routine with *jam, jet,* and *juice* Picture Cards.

Model

Have children look at the picture on pp. 12–13 of *My Skills Buddy.* Tell them that they will be listening for a new sound—/j/. These monkeys look like they are in the jungle. What sound do you hear at the beginning of *jungle?* I hear /j/ at the beginning of *jungle.* The first sound in *jungle* is /j/. What other things do you see that begin with that sound?

Picture Card

Guide practice

As children name example words from the picture, guide them in stating that /j/ is the beginning sound. Discuss with children some of the bulleted items on p. 12 of *My Skills Buddy.* Save the other bulleted items for discussion on Day 2.

Corrective feedback

If... children have difficulty naming words with /j/,
then... say *jungle* again, stretching the beginning sound—/j/ /j/ /j/, *jungle.*

8 Going Places • Unit 5 • Week 1

Discriminate sounds

I am going to say two words. Listen carefully to the first sound. One word begins with /j/, and the other word does not: *bag, jump. Jump* begins with /j/.

Have children stand in a circle. I am going to say a word. If the word begins with /j/, I want you to jump. If the word does not begin with /j/, stand still. Listen carefully: *jog* (jump), *hide* (stand still), *joke* (jump). Continue with the following words: *jeans, fence, bear, jar, jig, lamb, just, safe, head, joy.*

Corrective feedback

If... children cannot discriminate initial /j/,
then... then have them say /j/ /j/ /j/, *jog.*

When you say the first sound in *jog,* your tongue is pressed against the top of your mouth, and your lips stick out in a square. Say /j/ with me: /j/ /j/ /j/. Did your tongue press the top of your mouth? Did your lips stick out in a square? Say *jog* with me: *jog.* Repeat the activity with *jet, Jim,* and *jam.*

Blend

Review blending sounds. Listen to these sounds: /j/ /e/ /t/. Say the sounds with me: /j/ /e/ /t/. Now blend the sounds to say the word *jet.* Continue the blending practice with *jam, jab,* and *Jen.*

Don't Wait Until Friday

MONITOR PROGRESS ↻ Check Phonemic Awareness   Words with Initial /j/

Display Picture Cards *fox, jam,* and *lake.* These are pictures of *fox, jam,* and *lake.* Which word begins with /j/? Continue with the *jet, kite, bag, frog, jug,* and *kitten* Picture Cards.

If... children cannot discriminate initial /j/,
then... use the small-group Strategic Intervention lesson, p. DI•1, to reteach /j/.

Day 1	Day 2	Day 3	Day 4	Day 5
Check Phonemic Awareness	Check Sound-Spelling/ Retelling	Check Word Reading	Check Phonemic Awareness	Check Oral Vocabulary

Success Predictor

Differentiated Instruction

Ⓐ **Advanced**
Discriminate Initial /j/ After children identify words that begin with /j/, have them jump as they say the word in this sentence: *I jump when I say joke.*

Ⓔ Ⓛ Ⓛ

English Language Learners
Support Pronunciation French, Hmong, and Spanish do not have /j/ that is heard in words like *jam* and *jet.* In Polish, the letter *j* is pronounced like the letter *y* in English. Provide additional practice saying words with /j/.

19

Phonemic Awareness

Succes
Predicto

bjectives

Recognize uppercase *J* and
lowercase *j*.
Associate the sound /j/ with the
spelling *j*.
Blend and read words with /j/.

kills Trace

Consonant /j/ Spelled *Jj*
troduce U52W1D1
ractice U5W1D2; U5W1D3;
eteach/Review U5W1D5;
W2D4; U5W4D4
ssess/Test Benchmark
ssessment U5

EY:
=Unit   W=Week   D=Day

Phonics—Teach/Model
 /j/ Spelled *Jj*

Introduce

Display the *Jj* Alphabet Card. Point to the *jaguar* on the Alphabet Card. *Jaguar* begins with /j/. Say the word with me: *jaguar.* Write *jaguar* on the board and point to the *j. Jaguar* begins with /j/ spelled *j.* Now point to the letters *Jj* on the card. The sound for this letter is /j/. The names of this letter are uppercase *J* and lowercase *j.* What is the sound for this letter? What are the names of this letter?

Alphabet Card

Model

Write "Jill Jones Was a Juggler" on the board. Point to the first *J.* When I see this letter, I think of the sound /j/. The first word is *Jill*—/j/, *Jill.* Point to *Jones.* The next word also begins with *J.* I know that when I see a *J* the sound will be /j/. The second word is /j/, *Jones.* Point to the *J* in *Juggler.* The sound for *J* is /j/. The song we will sing is "Jill Jones Was a Juggler."

Guide practice

Display Phonics Songs and Rhymes Chart 25. Teach children the song "Jill Jones Was a Juggler" sung to the tune of "The Itsy Bitsy Spider." Play the CD and sing the song several times. I hear many words that begin with /j/. When you hear a word that begins with /j/, jump. As you sing the song, point to the words that begin with *j.*

Phonics Songs and Rhymes
Chart 25

Phonics Songs and Rhymes Audio

On their own

Have children find uppercase *J* and lowercase *j* around the classroom. Have them say /j/ when they point to *J* or *j.*

Blend Words

Review

To review sound spellings, use Alphabet Cards *Aa, Bb, Ee, Ll, Mm, Nn, Oo,* and *Tt* and the *ant, bat, egg, leaf, man, nut, otter,* and *ten* Picture Cards. Then use this routine for sound-by-sound blending to have children blend new words.

ROUTINE — Sound-by-Sound Blending

1. **Connect** Write the letter *j*. What is the sound for this letter? The sound is /j/. Say it with me: /j/ /j/ /j/. When you see this letter in a word, what sound will you say?

2. **Model** Write *jet* on the board.

   - Touch under the letter *j:* What is the sound for this letter? Say it with me: /j/ /j/ /j/. Repeat the routine touching under *e* and *t*.

   - Let's blend the sounds together. Listen as I blend the sounds: /j/ /e/ /t/. Say it with me: *jet*. Now say it without me.

   - Listen as I use *jet* in a sentence. *A jet flew across the sky.* Say it with me. Then have children use *jet* in their own sentences.

3. **Guide Practice** Continue the routine established in step 2 with the words below:

   | Jen | job | jam | Jill | Jim | jog |

   Children should successfully read these words before reading Decodable Story 25 on pp. 323–324 of *Reader's and Writer's Notebook.*

   Corrective Feedback If children have trouble reading a word, model blending the sounds to read the word. Then have children say it with you.

Routines Flip Chart

Differentiated Instruction

SI **Strategic Intervention**

Connect Sound-Spelling Have children with initial /j/ names stand up. Have the class say the name of each child chorally. As children say a name, have them say the letter the /j/ names begin with. Write the names on the board. Point to the letter *j*. What is the sound for this letter?

 E L L

English Language Learners

Support Phonemic Awareness Speakers of Hmong, Khmer, Korean, Tagalog, and Vietnamese may have difficulty distinguishing the /j/ sound from /ch/ or /sh/. Spanish or Russian speakers may pronounce the /j/ sound as /ch/. Pronounce word pairs such as *Jill/chill* and *jelly/Shelly*.

bjectives
• Write *J* and *j*.
• Learn high-frequency words.

Handwriting

Introduce

Write *Jj* on the board. Words that begin with /j/ are written with an uppercase *J* or a lowercase *j*. Which letter is uppercase *J*? Which letter is lowercase *j*?

Model uppercase *J*

Write *Jim* on the board. Point to the uppercase *J*. This is an uppercase *J*. We use uppercase letters to begin sentences and for the first letter in a name. Watch as I trace the uppercase *J* with my finger. Follow the stroke instructions pictured below.

Guide practice

Have children write the uppercase *J* in the air. Use your finger to make an uppercase *J* in the air. Now write it on the palm of your hand.

Model lowercase *j*

Write *jam* on the board. Point to the lowercase *j*. This is a lowercase *j*. Watch as I trace a lowercase *j* with my finger. Write another lowercase *j* on the board following the stroke instructions. Again, have children write *j* in the air and on their hands.

Guide practice

Have children use their Write-On Boards to write a row of uppercase *J* and a row of lowercase *j*.

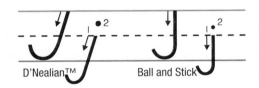

D'Nealian™   Ball and Stick

More practice

Use *Reader's and Writer's Notebook,* pp. 321, 322, for additional practice with initial *j*. Save the practice with initial *w* for Day 2.

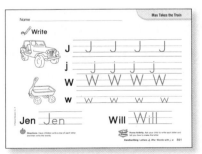

Reader's and Writer's Notebook, p. 321

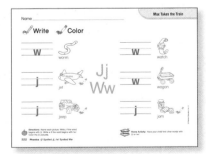

Reader's and Writer's Notebook, p. 322

High-Frequency Words

Introduce   Use the routine below to teach high-frequency words *yellow, blue,* and *green.*

ROUTINE   Nondecodable Words

1. **Say and Spell** Some words we have to learn by remembering the letters rather than saying the sounds. We will say and spell the words to help learn them. Write *yellow* on the board. This is the word *yellow.* It has six letters. The letters in *yellow* are *y, e, l, l, o,* and *w.* Have children say and spell the word, first with you and then without you.

2. **Demonstrate Meaning** I can use the word *yellow* in lots of sentences. Here is one sentence: *The banana is yellow.* Now you use the word in a sentence.

Repeat the routine with the words *blue* and *green.*

Add the words *yellow, blue,* and *green* to the Word Wall.

Routines Flip Chart

Academic Vocabulary

Write the following on the board:

realism	**animal fantasy**
caption	**poem**
question	**rhythm**

Point to the list. This week we are going to learn these important words. They are tools for learning. As we work this week you will hear them many times. Read the words. Preteach the Academic Vocabulary at point-of-use by providing a child-friendly description, explanation, or example that clarifies the meaning of each term. Then ask children to restate the meaning of the Academic Vocabulary in their own words.

Differentiated Instruction

A   **Advanced**

Expand Vocabulary Have children share other color word they know. Have children spell the color words they know, such as *red.* Have children use complete sentences to tell one thing that is the color, such as *A ladybug is red.*

English Language Learners

Visual Support Have children draw pictures of things that are *yellow, blue,* or *green.* Then pair children and have them take turns telling about his or her picture using the color word.

Decodable Story 25
/j/ Spelled *Jj* and High-Frequency Words

Review

Review the following high-frequency words by having children read each word as you point to it on the Word Wall.

| blue | the | is | a | have | like | go | to | they | see | you |

Read Decodable Story 25

Distribute Decodable Story 25. Have children look at the cover of the reader and make inferences based on the cover. Have them tell what they think the story will be about. For example, children should infer that this story will be about two children named Jen and Will. Today we will read a story about two people named Jen and Will. What is the title of the story? Point to the title of the story. The title of the story is *Jen and Will*. What sound do you hear at the beginning of *Jen?* We will read lots of words that begin with /j/ in this story. Have children read Decodable Story 25 on pp. 323–324 in *Reader's and Writer's Notebook*.

Use the routine for reading decodable books to read Decodable Story 25.

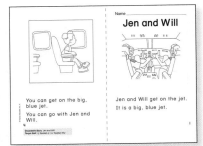

Reader's and Writer's Notebook, pp. 323–324

ROUTINE

Reading Decodable Books

1. **Read Silently** Have children whisper read the story page by page as you listen in.

2. **Model Fluent Reading** Have children finger point as you read a page. Then have children reread the page without you.

3. **Read Chorally** Have children finger point as they chorally read the page. Continue reading page by page, repeating steps 1 and 2.

4. **Read Individually** Have children take turns reading aloud a page.

5. **Reread and Monitor Progress** As you listen to individual children reread, monitor progress and provide support.

6. **Reread with a Partner** Have children reread the story page by page with a partner.

Routines Flip Chart

Small Group Time

DAY 1

Break into small groups after reading the Decodable Story and before the comprehension lesson.

Teacher-Led

SI Strategic Intervention	OL On-Level	A Advanced
Teacher-Led Page DI•1 • Phonemic Awareness and Phonics • **Reread** Decodable Story 25	**Teacher-Led** Page DI•6 • Phonemic Awareness and Phonics • **Reread** Decodable Story 25, DI•6	**Teacher-Led** Page DI•9 • Phonemic Awareness and Phonics • **Reread** Decodable Story 25 for Fluency, DI•9

ELL Place English language learners in the groups that correspond to their reading abilities in English.

Practice Stations
• Visit the Listen Up! Station
• Visit the Word Work Station

Independent Activities
• Read independently
• Concept Talk Video
• *Reader's and Writer's Notebook*

Differentiated Instruction

SI Strategic Intervention

Access Content Before childre read *Jen and Will,* review media /i/ and /e/ words with the following Picture Cards: *bed, hen, net, pig, six, wig*. Then display the *Ii* and *Ee* Alphabet Cards and have children name the sounds and the letter name of each.

English Language Learners

Build Background Before reading *Jen and Will,* explain to children that the people who fly a jet are called pilots. In this story, Jen and Will have jobs on a jet. They are the pilots of the jet. *Jet* is another word for *plane* or *airplane.*

jectives

Identify elements of realism
and fantasy.

ills Trace

Realism and Fantasy

troduce U2W4D1; U2W6D1;
W1D1

actice U2W4D2; U2W4D3;
W4D4; U2W6D2; U2W6D3;
W6D4; U5W1D2; U5W1D3;
W1D4

teach/Review U2W4D5;
W6D5; U3W2D4; U4W6D4;
W1D5; U6W5D4

EY:

Unit   W=Week   D=Day

My Skills Buddy, pp. 14–15

Listening Comprehension
Realism and Fantasy

Introduce In some stories, we read about people, places, and events that can really happen. These stories have **realism**. A **fantasy** tells about people, places, or events that are make-believe.

Envision It! Have children turn to pp. 14–15 in *My Skills Buddy*.

- Does the first picture show realism or fantasy? How? (It shows realism because it shows a real fish swimming in a fishbowl.)

- Does the second picture show realism or fantasy? How? (It shows fantasy because it shows fish doing something they can't really do: go to school.)

Model Tell children that you will read a story about a family going to the airport. Read **"Going to the Moon"** and model how to identify realism and fantasy.

 Think Aloud To decide whether a story is realism or fantasy, I pay attention to the characters, the setting, and the events. I ask myself whether each story part tells about something that could really happen.

In "Going to the Moon," the characters are people. They drive in a car to the airport like people do. When they talk about whether a bike can go to the moon, Katie says bikes cannot go to the moon and that a teddy bear cannot be an astronaut. Since these answers are true, the story is realistic.

Guide practice

Suppose the story told about a bike that goes to the moon and a teddy bear that is an astronaut. Would the story be realism or fantasy? (fantasy) How do you know? (In the real world, bikes cannot go the moon, and teddy bears cannot be astronauts.)

More practice

Display Trade Book *Goldilocks and the Three Bears.* Help children decide whether the story could really happen or if it is make-believe. Tell me about the three bears. Do bears live in houses? Do bears eat porridge? Do bears sleep in bed?

Connect to everyday life

Sometimes when you play, you play make-believe. When you play house, are you really a mom or dad?

Academic Vocabulary

realism a story that is possible

fantasy stories that are not possible

English Language Learners
Oral Comprehension To prepare English learners for the Read Aloud, use the modified Read Aloud in the ELL Support lesson p. DI•13.

Going to the Moon

Katie and Zach were excited. They were going with their dad to pick up their mom at the airport.

"Dad," Katie asked, "can we stop and watch the planes?"

"Sure," Dad answered. "Let's do that."

"Will we see a rocket ship?" Zach asked.

"Well, no," Dad said. "Rocket ships don't take off from the airport."

"Do only rocket ships go to the moon?" Zach asked. "Or could a bike go there?"

Dad and Katie laughed. "Bikes that go to the moon are make-believe, Zach," Katie said. "It's like saying your teddy bear is an astronaut in that rocket ship!"

Zach clutched his bear. "Teddy could drive a rocket ship to the moon," he said.

Objectives

Identify and use questions.
Write or dictate a sentence about something that makes you special.

Conventions
Questions

Teach questions

When we want to know more about someone or something, we ask a question. A question is a sentence that asks something. Questions begin with an uppercase letter and end with a question mark. Write a question mark on the board. This is a question mark.

Model

Write this question on the board: *How did you get to school today?* Point to each word as you read it aloud. This is a question. It asks something. Point to the uppercase letter. It begins with an uppercase letter. Point to the question mark. A question always ends with a question mark.

Guide practice

Write these sentences on the board:

> **what did you do today**
>
> **when did you eat lunch**
>
> **i ran to school**
>
> **what time is it**
>
> **i must leave**

Read each sentence one at a time. Have children identify the questions. What type of punctuation mark do you need at the end of a question? Have children tell you what letters to capitalize and where to add question marks to the questions. Have children practice writing question marks on their Write-On Boards.

Team Talk Pair children and have them take turns asking questions about each other.

Daily Fix-It

Use the Daily Fix-It for more conventions practice.

Writing
Wonderful, Marvelous Me!
I Am Special Because…

Introduce Talk with children about how everyone is special. Everyone in this room is special. What makes us special? Lots of wonderful, marvelous things make each of us special. We are special because of who we are on the inside, what we can do, even how we look. These special things make us unique. Encourage children to share their thoughts and ideas about things that can make each of them special.

Model Today we're going to write about something that makes us special. I'm going to close my eyes and think about my family and me. I am a middle child. I have an older sister and a younger brother. Draw three people on the board. Write your name under the middle person. Write the words *sister* and *brother* under the other two people. My sister has a daughter, so I have a niece. Draw a little girl. Write the word *niece* underneath. That means I am an aunt! I am special because of the great family I have.

Guide practice Encourage children to help you name other things that make you special. Write their ideas and draw pictures when appropriate.

Independent writing Now you're going to share something about you. Close your eyes and think about wonderful, marvelous you. What is something that makes you special? Remember, there are so many things about you that are special, but today pick just one. Have children write or dictate their ideas and then illustrate them.

Daily Handwriting

Write *Jill* and *jet* on the board. Review the correct letter formation of uppercase *J* and lowercase *j*.

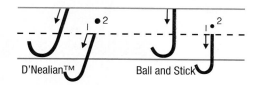

D'Nealian™   Ball and Stick

Have children write *Jill* and *jet* on their Write-On Boards. Remind them to use proper left-to-right and top-to-bottom progression and proper spacing between letters when writing *J* and *j*.

 **Write Guy**
Jeff Anderson

Writers Write!

Student writers succeed in classrooms where they write. Simple, isn't it? Are you trying to meet some mandate or standard with such blinders on that you're forgetting daily writing? Children need to read every day and to write every day.

Academic Vocabulary

question a sentence that asks something and ends with a question mark

Daily Fix-It

Is it monday
Is it Monday?

This week's practice sentences appear on Teacher Resources DVD-ROM.

Writing Routine

Day 1 Wonderful, Marvelous Me!

Day 2 Respond to Literature

Day 3 Genre Writing

Day 4 Extend the Concept

Day 5 This Week We…

Objectives
Practice asking and answering questions.
Speak loudly and clearly.

Listening and Speaking
Ask and Answer Questions

Teach   A sentence that asks something is a question. When we ask someone a question, he or she tells us an answer. When we ask and answer questions, we must remember to speak loudly and clearly.

Model   I am going to ask you a question: *What is your favorite color?* Designate a child to answer the question. Now I am going to answer a question. Have a volunteer ask you a question. Did I speak loudly and clearly when I asked and answered questions?

Guide practice   Have children work with a partner. Have them take turns asking each other about the form of transportation they use to get to school. Then have volunteers share their questions with the class. Refer children to the Rules for Listening and Speaking on pp. 1–2 of *Reader's and Writer's Notebook.* Remind them to speak loudly and clearly when asking and answering questions.

Name _____

🌀 **Listening Rules**
1. Face the person who is speaking.
2. Be quiet while someone is speaking.
3. Pay attention to the speaker.
4. Ask questions if you don't understand.

Reader's and Writer's Notebook, p. 1

Wrap Up Your Day

✔ **Oral Language** Today we talked about transportation. Say the Amazing Words with me: *plane, jetway, subway, tunnel, ferryboat, sidecar.*

✔ **Conventions** Point to a child in the room. How would you ask a question to find out about someone's favorite food?

✔ **Homework Idea** Send home the Family Times Newsletter Let's Practice It! TR DVD•49–50.

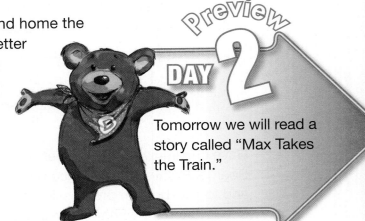

Preview DAY 2

Tomorrow we will read a story called "Max Takes the Train."

ELL

English Language Learners
Informal Language Explain that answering questions with complete sentences is using formal language, and answering with a few words is informal language. Have children answer their partners' questions using both formal and informal language.

Extend Your Day!

Social Studies
Traffic Signals and Signs
Materials: paper, crayons

Discuss Traffic Signals Draw or show examples of the following signs and traffic signals. Ask children if they have ever seen any of these signals or signs. Point to each sign and help children tell what it is. Ask children why it is important for drivers and pedestrians to obey the traffic rules.

Draw and Label a Picture Have children draw a picture of someone obeying a traffic sign. Have them write or dictate labels for their pictures.

Red light says stop!

Comprehension
Realism and Fantasy
Materials: white paper and crayons

Real and Silly Transportation Discuss the following forms of transportation with children: *car, plane, train, ship, walking, bike, bus.* Write them on the board.

Tell children to select one of the forms of transportation from the board and write the word at the top of the paper. Have them draw and color the form of transportation they selected twice, once showing something that could really happen and once showing a make-believe situation.

bus

Phonemic Awareness
J Jars
Materials: counters, small jars

Say /j/ Words Give each child a jar and a small handful of counters. Ask children to say a word that begins with /j/. If they can name a /j/ word, they may place a counter in the jar. If children have difficulty, give clues to the following words: *jacks, joy, jar, jump, just, jaw, jet, job, jug, junk.*

Objectives
• Discuss the concepts to develop oral language.
• Build oral vocabulary.

Today at a Glance

Oral Vocabulary
plane, jetway

Phonemic Awareness
Initial /w/

Phonics
/w/ Spelled *Ww*

Handwriting
Words with *Ww*

Comprehension
Realism and Fantasy

Conventions
Questions

Writing
Respond to Literature

Vocabulary
Transportation Words

TRUCKTOWN on Reading Street

Start your engines! Display p. 12 of *Truckery Rhymes.* Point to "Swing Around with Rosie." Which truck is this rhyme about? Yes, it's about Rosie. Let's read the rhyme together. Have a child point to the rhyming words as the class reads the rhyme again. Give children the opportunity to say the rhyme aloud and track the print.

Truckery Rhymes

Concept Talk

 Question of the Week
What are the different ways of going places?

Build concepts

Write the question of the week and track the print as you read it aloud. Ask children to answer the question in complete sentences. To reinforce the concept and focus children's attention, display Talk with Me/Sing with Me Chart 25B. Tell children that they are going to sing about ways to travel.

🔘 Sing with Me Audio

Listen for Amazing Words

The Amazing Words *plane* and *jetway* are in the song "Through the Jetway." Read the title and ask children to describe the pictures. Sing the song several times to the tune of "Are You Sleeping?" Have children sing with you and clap when they hear *plane* and *jetway.*

ELL Reinforce Vocabulary Use the Day 2 instruction on ELL Poster 25 to reinforce the meanings of high-frequency words.

Through the Jetway

Through the jetway, through the jetway,
To the plane, to the plane,
Look at all these things that float,
I can see a ferryboat,
Down below, down below.

Talk with Me/Sing with Me Chart 25B

 ELL Poster 25

Oral Vocabulary
Amazing Words

Teach Amazing Words

Amazing Words Oral Vocabulary Routine

1. **Introduce the Word** A *plane* is a kind of transportation. A *plane* flies high in the sky. Jet engines make a *plane* go. What is our new Amazing Word for a form of transportation in the sky? Say it with me: *plane.*

2. **Demonstrate** Provide examples to show meaning. *You can take a plane when you have to travel somewhere far away.* What else do you know about *planes?*

    Repeat steps 1 and 2.

    Introduce the Word To get on a plane, you have to walk through a *jetway.* A *jetway* connects the plane to the airport. What is our new Amazing Word for the walkway to a plane? Say it with me: *jetway.*

    Demonstrate *Once people walk through the jetway, they can find their seats on the plane.*

3. **Apply** Encourage children to use *plane* and *jetway* in complete sentences. Have them show you how they would walk through a jetway to get on a plane.

Routines Flip Chart

Use Amazing Words

To reinforce the concept and the Amazing Words, have children supply the appropriate Amazing Word for each sentence.

People walked through the _____ to get into the plane. (jetway)

A big _____ landed at the airport. (plane)

Differentiated Instruction

A Advanced

Discuss Vocabulary Have children share experiences they have had on a plane. Where were you going? How long were you on the plane? What happens on a plane?

English Language Learners
Access Content Ask children to say *plane* in their home languages. In Spanish, plane is called *aeroplano.* There is no translation for *jetway.*

Phonemic Awareness
⟲ Initial /w/

Picture Card

Introduce

Today we are going to learn a new sound. Listen carefully: /w/ /w/ /w/. Say it with me: /w/ /w/ /w/. Display the *wagon* Picture Card. This is a *wagon. Wagon* begins with /w/. What sound does wagon begin with? Continue the routine with the *waffle, web,* and *wolf* Picture Cards.

Model

Have children look at the picture on *My Skills Buddy* pp. 12–13. Tell them they will be listening for a new sound—/w/. I see a monkey wiggle. What sound do you hear at the beginning of *wiggle?* I hear /w/ at the beginning of *wiggle.* The first sound in *wiggle* is /w/. What other things do you see that begin with that sound?

My Skills Buddy, pp. 12–13

Guide practice

As children name example words from the picture, guide them in stating that /w/ is the beginning sound. Discuss with children those bulleted items on p. 12 not discussed on Day 1.

Corrective feedback

If... children have difficulty naming words with /w/,

then... say *wiggle* again, stretching the beginning sound, /w/ /w/ /w/, *wiggle.*

Discriminate sounds

I am going to say two words. Listen carefully to the first sound in each word. One word begins with /w/; the other word does not: *will, tell. Will* begins with /w/. Continue the routine with the following words: *wave, hill; wax, sock; wire, rock; mouse, worm.*

Display Phonics Songs and Rhymes Chart 25, "Jill Jones Was a Juggler." Remind children of the tune: "The Itsy Bitsy Spider." Sing the song several times. When you hear a word that begins with /w/, wave your hands. Children should wave their hands for *was, we'll, wanted, west, went,* and *way.*

Jill Jones Was a Juggler

Jill Jones was a juggler.
We'll say she was the best.
She jumped on a jet.
She wanted to go west.
Will Jones went with her.
He juggled jelly jars.
So the jolly jugglers journeyed
Way west under the stars!

Phonics Songs and Rhymes
Chart 25

Corrective feedback

If... children cannot discriminate initial /w/,
then... then have them enunciate /w/ as they say *will.*

When you say /w/, your lips are round as if you're saying "oo." Say /w/ and feel the shape of your lips. Have children say /w/ words and feel the position of their lips. Repeat the activity with *well* and *web.*

Review

Segmentation Listen to the word *wig.* What sounds do you hear? Say them with me: /w/ /i/ /g/. How many sounds do you hear? There are three sounds in *wig.* Continue with *web, wet, wag,* and *well.*

Differentiated Instruction

SI Strategic Intervention

Discriminate Initial /w/
If children have difficulty discriminating initial /w/, say a /w/ word and identify the initial sound as /w/. Then use that word to compare the initia sound of another initial /w/ wor For example: *Will* begins with /w/. Does the word *win* begin the same as *Will*? Say the word with me: *win, Will.*

ELL

English Language Learners
Support Phonemic Awareness
If English language learners hav difficulty pronouncing words tha begin with *w,* show children how to round their lips to produce the /w/ sound. Provide additional practice with words that begin with *w.*

Phonics—Teach/Model
/w/ Spelled Ww

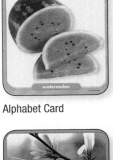

Alphabet Card

Picture Card

Review /w/ Ww

Display the *Ww* Alphabet Card. Point to the *watermelon* on the Alphabet Card. *Watermelon* begins with /w/. Say the word with me: *watermelon*. Write *watermelon* on the board and point to the *w*. *Watermelon* begins with /w/ spelled *w*. Now point to the letters *Ww* on the card. The sound for this letter is /w/. The names of these letters are uppercase *W* and lowercase *w*. What is the sound for this letter? What are the names of these letters?

Model

Display the *web* Picture Card. What is this? Say the sounds in *web* with me: /w/ /e/ /b/, *web*. Where do you hear /w/ in *web*? (at the beginning) Write *web* on the board. Point to each letter as you say the sounds, /w/ /e/ /b/, *web*. Continue the routine with the following words: *Will, wet.*

Guide practice

Envision It!

Have children open *My Skills Buddy* to p. 16. Demonstrate using the blending arrows on *My Skills Buddy*, p. 16, as you model blending the first word. Put your finger on the red arrow below the *w*. Continue with the letters *i* and *n*. Now run your finger along the blue arrow as you blend the letters quickly to read the word *win*. Have children recognize and describe the difference between the letter *w* and the word *win*. Repeat the routine with the word *well*. Remind children that sometimes /l/ is spelled *ll* at the end of a word. Have children work with a partner to blend the rest of the words on the page.

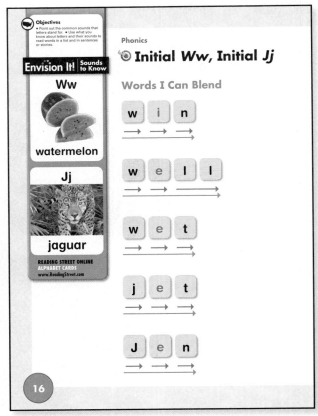

My Skills Buddy, p. 16

Blend

Use the routine to review blending /w/ words.

ROUTINE · Sound-by-Sound Blending

① **Connect** Write the letter *w*. What is the sound for this letter? The sound is /w/. Say it with me: /w/ /w/ /w/. When you see this letter in a word, what sound will you say?

② **Model** Write the word *win* on the board.

- Point to *w* and ask: What is the sound for this letter? Say it with me: /w/ /w/ /w/. Repeat the routine with *i* and *n*.

- Let's blend the sounds together. Listen as I blend the sounds: /w/ /i/ /n/. Say it with me: /w/ /i/ /n/, *win*. Now say it without me.

- Listen as I use *win* in a sentence: *I will win the game.* Say it with me. Have children use *win* in a sentence.

③ **Guide Practice** Continue the routine in step 2 with these words:

Wes	wet	will	job	jet	Jen	big	grin

Have children successfully read all of the words before reading Decodable Reader 25 on pp. 18–25 of *My Skills Buddy*.

Corrective Feedback Model blending the sounds to read the word. Then have children say it with you.

Routines Flip Chart

MONITOR PROGRESS ⟳ Check Sound-Spelling /w/ Spelled *Ww*; /j/ Spelled *Jj*

Have children write *Jj* and *Ww* on separate cards. I am going to say a word. If the word begins with /j/, hold up your *Jj* card. If the word begins with /w/, hold up your *Ww* card. Say: *jump, went, jet, wet, Jan, Jim, Wes, jam, well, jelly, walrus, jaguar.*

If... children cannot discriminate initial /w/ or /j/,

then... use the small-group Strategic Intervention lesson, p. DI•2, to reteach /j/ and /w/.

Continue to monitor children's progress using other instructional opportunities during the week so that children can be successful with the Day 5 Assessment.

Day 1	Day 2	Day 3	Day 4	Day 5
Check Phonemic Awareness	Check Sound-Spelling/ Retelling	Check Word Reading	Check Phonemic Awareness	Check Oral Vocabulary

Success Predictor

Differentiated Instruction

SI **Strategic Intervention**

Connect Sound-Spelling Hav children stand in a circle. Wher I say a /w/ words, I want you to waddle like a duck. Demonstra how to waddle. As you waddle I want you to say what letter spells /w/. Say these words: *waffle, wig, yarn, wagon, egg, wolf.*

Succe Predict

Handwriting

Review

Write *Ww* on the board. Words that begin with /w/ are written with an uppercase *W* or a lowercase *w*. Which letter is uppercase *W*? Which letter is lowercase *w*?

Model uppercase W

Write *Will* on the board. This is the name *Will*. Point to the uppercase W. We use uppercase letters to begin sentences and for the first letter in a name. Watch as I trace the uppercase *W* with my finger. Follow the stroke instructions pictured below.

Guide practice

Have children write uppercase *W* in the air. Use your finger to make an uppercase *W* in the air. Now write it on the palm of your hand.

Model lowercase w

Write *wet* on the board. This is the word *wet*. This is a lowercase *w*. Watch as I trace a lowercase *w* with my finger. Write another lowercase *w* on the board following the stroke instructions. Use your finger to make a lowercase *w* in the air and on your hand.

Guide practice

Have children use their Write-On Boards to make a row of uppercase *W* and a row of lowercase *w*.

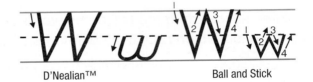

D'Nealian™   Ball and Stick

More practice

Use *Reader's and Writer's Notebook,* p. 322, for additional practice with *w*.

High-Frequency Words

Model reading

Have children turn to p. 17 of *My Skills Buddy.* Read the high-frequency words *yellow, blue,* and *green* together. Then have children point to each word and read it themselves. Read the sentences on *My Skills Buddy* page together to read the new high-frequency words in context.

Team Talk Pair children and have them take turns reading each of the sentences aloud.

High-Frequency Words

Words I Can Read

yellow

blue

green

Sentences I Can Read

1. They see a blue jet.
2. The sun is yellow.
3. I like the green jet.

17

My Skills Buddy, p. 17

On their own

Use *Reader's and Writer's Notebook,* p. 325, for additional practice with this week's high-frequency words.

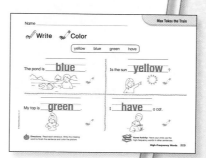

Reader's and Writer's Notebook, p. 325

Differentiated Instruction

 **Strategic Intervention**

Develop Vocabulary Have children identify things in the classroom that are *yellow, blue* or *green.* Have them identify th object in a complete sentence, such as *The pencil is yellow.*

E L L

English Language Learners

High-Frequency Words Explain to children that *yellow, green,* and *blue* are color words. Have them say the high-frequency words in their home languages.

Objectives
Read decodable text.
Read high-frequency words.

Decodable Reader 25
/j/ Spelled *Jj* and /w/ Spelled *Ww*, and High-Frequency Words

Review Review the previously taught high-frequency words. Have children read each word as you point to it on the Word Wall.

a	the	yellow	with	blue	go	green

Have children turn to Decodable Reader 25, *On a Jet,* on p. 18 of *My Skills Buddy.* Point to the title. What is the title of the story? *On a Jet* is the title of the story. Point to the names of the author and the illustrator. The author's name is Mike O'Hern. The illustrator's name is Joan Tortle. What does an illustrator do? Have children make inferences based on the title and illustrations in the story. For example, children should infer that this story will be about people flying on a jet plane.

Use the routine for reading decodable books to read Decodable Reader 25.

My Skills Buddy, pp. 18–25

ROUTINE Reading Decodable Books

1. **Read Silently** Have children whisper read the book page by page as you listen in.

2. **Model Fluent Reading** Have children finger point as you read a page. Then have children reread the book without you.

3. **Read Chorally** Have children finger point as they chorally read the page. Continue reading page by page, repeating steps 1 and 2.

4. **Read Individually** Have children take turns reading aloud a page.

5. **Reread and Monitor Progress** As you listen to individual children reread, monitor progress and provide support.

6. **Reread with a Partner** Have children reread the book page by page with a partner.

Routines Flip Chart

Small Group Time

 DAY 2 Break into small groups after reading the Decodable Reader and before the comprehension lesson.

Teacher-Led

SI Strategic Intervention	OL On-Level	A Advanced
Teacher-Led Page DI•2	Teacher-Led Page DI•6	Teacher-Led Page DI•9
• Phonemic Awareness and Phonics	• Phonemic Awareness and Phonics	• Phonics and Spelling
• **Reread** Decodable Reader 25	• **Reread** Decodable Reader 25	• **Reread** Decodable Reader 25 for Fluency

ELL Place English language learners in the groups that correspond to their reading abilities in English.

Practice Stations
• Visit the Word Work Station
• Visit the Words to Know Station

Independent Activities
• Read independently
• Background Building Audio
• *Reader's and Writer's Notebook*

illustrator the person who draws pictures for a book

Differentiated Instruction

 A Advanced

Expand Vocabulary Explain to children that Wes is a *mechanic* and then a *passenger,* and Jen is a *pilot.* Have children use the pictures and what they know to explain what these words mean

ELL

English Language Learners
Physical Response Ask children to choose the characte from *On a Jet* whose role they would enjoy the most. Have them act out what the character does.

bjectives
Practice realism and fantasy.
Preview and predict.
Retell a story.

Check Retelling
SUCCESS PREDICTOR

Listening Comprehension
Realism and Fantasy

Review
Envision It!

Have children turn to pp. 14–15 of *My Skills Buddy.* Remind children that realistic stories are about real people and things that can really happen. Fantasies cannot happen in real life. Good readers pay attention to whether a story is realistic or a fantasy to help them understand the story.

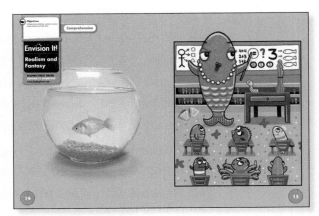

My Skills Buddy, pp. 14–15

First Read—Big Book
Max Takes the Train

Concepts of print

Point to the title of the story. The title of this book is *Max Takes the Train.* The author of this book is Rosemary Wells. What does an author do? (The author writes the book.)

Preview and predict

Think Aloud

Display *Max Takes the Train.* What do you see on the cover? I see a bunny standing by a train. The title of the book is *Max Takes the Train.* What do you think this book will be about?

Use illustrations

Take children on a picture walk through the book. Have children describe the illustrations.

Introduce genre

An animal fantasy is a story about animal characters that think, talk, and act like people. In this story, we will read about animals taking different forms of transportation.

Set purpose

Say the question of the week: *What are different ways of going places?* Listen as I read for the different forms of transportation Max takes.

Model

Read *Max Takes the Train* with expression for enjoyment.

DAY 2
Read for enjoyment

DAY 3
Reread using Develop Vocabulary notes

DAY 4
Reread using Guide Comprehension notes

Retell

Check retelling

Envision It!

Have children turn to p. 26 of *My Skills Buddy.* Walk through the retelling boxes as children retell *Max Takes the Train.* Let's retell what happens in the first box—the beginning of the story. Max wants to get a Whamburger but Zeke's is too far away. Let's retell what happens next. Continue with the rest of the boxes. After children retell the story as a group, have them draw a picture to retell a favorite part of the story. Have them write or dictate a word or sentence to go with their picture.

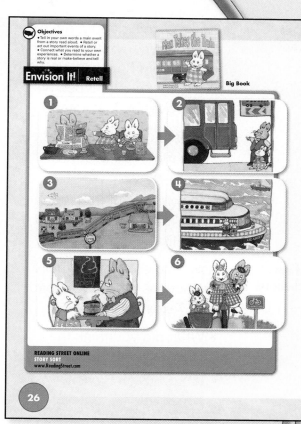

My Skills Buddy, p. 26

Top-Score Response A top-score response describes events in sequence with details.

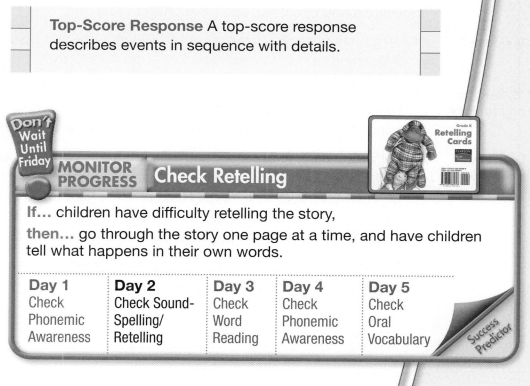

MONITOR PROGRESS **Check Retelling**

If... children have difficulty retelling the story,

then... go through the story one page at a time, and have children tell what happens in their own words.

Day 1	Day 2	Day 3	Day 4	Day 5
Check Phonemic Awareness	Check Sound-Spelling/ Retelling	Check Word Reading	Check Phonemic Awareness	Check Oral Vocabulary

Academic Vocabular

animal fantasy story about animal characters that think, talk, and act like people

Differentiated Instruction

SI Strategic Intervention

Practice Retelling If children have difficulty retelling the stor have them pretend to be Max and retell the story in the first person. For example, *I want a Whamburger so Uncle Bunny and I go to Zeke's. First, we tak a bus.*

Retelling Plan

☑ **This week assess Advanced students.**

☐ **Week 2** Assess On-Level students.

☐ **Week 3** Assess Strategic Intervention students.

☐ **Week 4** Assess Advanced students.

☐ **Week 5** Assess On-Level students.

☐ **Week 6** Assess Strategic Intervention students.

ELL

English Language Learners
Cognates Spanish speakers may recognize that the cognate *tren* means *train.* Have children draw a picture of a train and label it with the word *train.*

Succe Predict

Think, Talk, and Write

Discuss concept

We're learning about different ways to get places. Think about how you would like to ride on the types of transportation Max uses.

- Which form of transportation that Max took would you like best? Why?
- Which form of transportation that Max took would you like least? Why?

Confirm predictions

Ask children to recall their predictions before you read *Max Takes the Train.*

- What did you think the story would be about?
- Was your prediction correct?

Have children turn to p. 27 of *My Skills Buddy.* Read the questions and directives and have children respond.

Think, Talk, and Write

1. Which are ways you have traveled? Text to Self

2. Which story is about real animals? Which is about make-believe animals?

   Realism and Fantasy

3. Look back and write.

My Skills Buddy, p. 27

Text to self

1. Which are ways you have traveled? Where were you going? Did you like traveling that way? Which way would you like to try?

Realism and fantasy

2. Which story is about real animals? (*Little Panda*) Which is about make-believe animals? (*Max Takes the Train*) How do you know? (Max does things like talk and take transportation that real animals do not do.)

Look back and write

3. Let's look back at our story and write about it. We remember that Max and Uncle Bunny travel in a plane. Listen for what Max and Uncle Bunny do once they take their seats. Read p. 13 of *Max Takes the Train.* Now let's write our ideas. Discuss with children what happens once Max and Uncle Bunny get on the plane. Record their responses on chart paper.

Possible responses: *They fastened their seatbelts. They put their tray tables up. They are offered coffee, tea, or milk.*

Conventions
Questions

Review

Remind children that questions are sentences that ask about something. Questions begin with an uppercase letter and end with a question mark.

Guide practice

When we meet a new friend, we want to find out about that person. One question we can ask is *What is your name?* What are other questions we can ask a new friend? Write children's suggestions on the board. As you write each question, ask: How should I write the first letter in the question? What should I put at the end of the question?

Display p. 21 of *Max Takes the Train.* Guide children to identify the question on the page. Prompt them by pointing out the question mark at the end of the question.

On their own

Use *Reader's and Writer's Notebook,* p. 326, for more practice with questions.

Daily Fix-It

Use the Daily Fix-It exercise for more conventions practice.

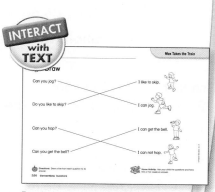

Reader's and Writer's Notebook, p. 326

Differentiated Instruction

 Strategic Intervention

Discuss Concept Before discussing the forms of transportation they like best, have childre generate a list of the forms of transportation Max and Uncle Bunny use in the story.

A **Advanced**

Act It Out Have children act ou how each form of transportatio moves. For example, spreading their arms out could be for a plane flying.

Daily Fix-It

is it wet
Is it wet?

This week's practice sentences appear on Teacher Resources DVD-ROM.

ELL

English Language Learners
Sentence Order Speakers of Asian languages often form questions by adding words to statements, such as *You need a break, no?* Provide extra practice with English questions.

Writing
Respond to Literature

Discuss Display *Max Takes the Train.* Discuss with children the make-believe things Max and Uncle Bunny do in the story.

Model Many things in the story are make-believe. Rabbits don't talk and ride on buses. Can you think of other things from the story that are make-believe? For my sentences, I'm going to write:

> **A rabbit that talks is make-believe.**
>
> **The plane with rabbits is make-believe.**

Guide practice Help children write other sentences about things from the story that are make-believe.

> **Rabbits do not eat ice cream.**
>
> **A rabbit with glasses is make-believe.**

Independent writing Have children write or dictate about a make-believe detail in *Max Takes the Train.* Some children may wish to use the sentence frame:

> **A rabbit _____ is make-believe.**

Then have children illustrate their sentences.

A rabbit in clothes is make-believe.

Daily Handwriting

Write *Wes* and *wig* on the board. Review correct letter formation of uppercase *W* and lowercase *w.*

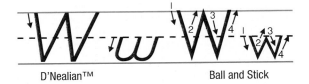

D'Nealian™   Ball and Stick

Have children write *Wes* and *wig* in their Write-On Boards. Remind children to use proper left-to-right and top-to-bottom progression when writing *W* and *w.*

Vocabulary
Transportation Words

Model

Have children turn to p. 28 of *My Skills Buddy.* Use the first Vocabulary bullet on the page to guide the discussion. Direct them to the picture of the truck. This is a *truck.* It travels on the road. Direct children to the picture of an airplane. This is an *airplane.* It travels in the air. Direct children to the picture of a boat. A *boat* travels on water. Direct children to the picture of a train. This is a *train.* What does a *train* travel on?

Guide practice

Write the words *train, truck, airplane,* and *boat* on the board. Point to each word as you read it.

My Skills Buddy, p. 28

| train | truck | airplane | boat |

Let's practice our new words. Write the words on separate sheets of paper. Display the words in different parts of the classroom. I am going to describe a form of transportation that we learned. I want you to draw a picture of it. You can use p. 28 of *My Skills Buddy* to help you. Once you draw the picture, take your drawing and stand by the word on the wall. Listen: This form of transportation is used on the water. Repeat with *truck, train,* and *airplane.*

On their own

Have children think about the type of transportation they have used, want to try, or like the best. Once children choose a word, have them find a partner and take turns telling about the transportation.

Differentiated Instruction

SI Strategic Intervention

Support Writing Before writing, have children make a list of make-believe things the characters do in *Max Takes the Train.* Then have them use the list to write or dictate complete sentences about the story.

ELL

English Language Learners

Access Content Have children name the forms of transportatio in their home languages.

Objectives
- Review skills learned and practiced today.
- Identify words that begin with /w/.

Wrap Up Your Day

✔ **Concept Talk** Today we read about Max and his adventures with boats, trains, and buses in *Max Takes the Train*. What are some other kinds of transportation Max uses?

✔ **Phonemic Awareness** I am going to say a sentence. Clap when you hear words that begin with /w/. *Wes and Will rode a train with big windows to work.*

✔ **Vocabulary Skill** Describe each form of transportation: truck, train, airplane, boat. Have children identify the form you are describing.

✔ **Homework Idea** Have children write or dictate a question they would want to ask Max or Uncle Bunny and draw a line under the question mark.

Preview DAY 3

Tomorrow we will read *Max Takes the Train* again. Where is Max trying to go?

Social Studies
Forms of Transportation

Materials: patterns—train, plane, car, ship (one per child); crayons; scissors; tape; craft sticks (four per child); world map

How Do We Get from Place to Place? Discuss with children when they would use different forms of transportation, such as a plane, train, ship, or car. For example, they wouldn't use a plane to go to the grocery store. They might use a car.

Give each child a set of patterns to color and cut out. Tape craft sticks to the back of each form of transportation. Gather children in a circle and, one by one, name common destinations, such as the library or a faraway city. Have children hold up the picture of the form of transportation that would be used to travel to the destination named and explain why (e.g., a ship or plane would be needed to cross the ocean).

Comprehension
Fantasy

Materials: mural paper, crayons, markers

Act Out a Scene in *Max Takes the Train*
Review the illustrations in *Max Takes the Train*, pointing out the places that Max and Uncle Bunny visit. Have pairs of children pretend to be Max and Uncle Bunny traveling on the bus to the city center, on the Blue Comet in the country, or on the ferryboat across the lake. Encourage children to say a list of the things they would see along the way.

Social Studies
Story Travel

Materials: mural paper, paint, paintbrushes

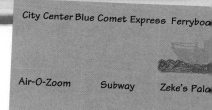

Traveling Place a large sheet of mural paper on the floor. Divide the paper into six sections and write one of these names in each section: *City Center, Blue Comet Express, Ferryboat, Air-O-Zoom, Subway, Zeke's Palace*. Divide the class into six groups and assign a section to each group. Have the groups of children illustrate the sections with each child painting a part. Then have children retell the story, using the mural for the sequence of the travels of Max and Uncle Bunny.

DAY 3 Get Ready to Read

20–25 mins.

jectives

Share information and ideas about the concept.
Build oral vocabulary.

oday at a Glance

al Vocabulary
bway, tunnel

onemic Awareness
Initial /w/ and /j/

onics
/w/ Spelled *Ww*
/j/ Spelled *Jj*

mprehension
Realism and fantasy

nventions
estions

riting
ption

stening and Speaking
k and Answer Questions

TRUCKTOWN on Reading Street

Start your engines! Display p. 12 of *Truckery Rhymes.* Do you know the original "Ring Around the Rosy"? Recite it first, and then have children repeat it with you:

Ring around the rosy,
A pocketful of posies.
Ashes, ashes.
We all fall down!

Truckery Rhymes

Concept Talk

Question of the Week

What are different ways of going places?

Write and read the question of the week as you track the print. Talk with children about different forms of transportation. Have them answer the question in complete sentences. Remind them to speak clearly and to take turns speaking.

Listen for Amazing Words

Let's Sing Display Sing with Me Chart 25B. Remind children that yesterday they sang "Through the Jetway" and listened for the words *plane* and *jetway*. Today we are going to listen for the Amazing Words *subway* and *tunnel*. Sing the song several times to the tune of "Are You Sleeping?" Have children sing with you. Tell them to clap when they hear the words *subway* and *tunnel*.

 Sing with Me Audio

Through the Jetway

Through the jetway, through the jetway,
To the plane, to the plane,
Look at all these things that float,
I can see a ferryboat,
Down below, down below.

Talk with Me/Sing with Me Chart 25B

Oral Vocabulary
Amazing Words

Amazing Words

plane	jetway
subway	tunnel
ferryboat	sidecar

Teach Amazing Words

Amazing Words — Oral Vocabulary Routine

1. **Introduce the Word** A *subway* is a train that travels in an underground tunnel. The *subway* carries people under a city. What is our new Amazing Word for a train that travels underground? Say it with me: *subway*.

2. **Demonstrate** Provide examples to show meaning. *A subway can take people from one part of the city to another*.

   Repeat steps 1 and 2.

   Introduce the Word A long, underground road is called a *tunnel*. Trains and cars may travel through a *tunnel* to go under a mountain or a body of water. What is our new Amazing Word for a long, underground road? Say it with me: *tunnel*.

   Demonstrate *A tunnel underneath a tall building lets cars drive right under the building.*

3. **Apply** Ask children to use *subway* and *tunnel* in complete sentences. Have them draw a picture of a subway going through a tunnel.

Routines Flip Chart

Use Amazing Words

To reinforce the concept and the Amazing Words, have children supply the appropriate Amazing Word for each sentence.

In the city, people can go to work on a _____. (subway)

The car drove through a long _____. (tunnel)

 Expand Vocabulary Use the Day 3 instruction on ELL Poster 25 to help children expand vocabulary.

ELL Poster 25

Differentiated Instruction

A Advanced

Build Vocabulary With children brainstorm additional words with the word part *way*, such as *roadway, pathway, walkway,* and *freeway*. Have children describe how people use each one.

ELL

English Language Learners

Support Discussion Have children think of different places to go, such as a store, another state, or another country. Then have children think of a form of transportation that can be used to get to that place.

Objectives
- Isolate initial /j/ and /w.
- Discriminate sounds.
- Segment sounds in words.
- Substitute phonemes.

Phonemic Awareness
↻ Initial /j/ and /w/

Review

Initial /j/ and /w/ Display the *jam* Picture Card. Listen as I say the word: *jam*. What is the first sound in *jam?* Listen carefully: /j/ /j/ /j/, *jam*. Continue with the following words: *job, jug, jet*. Display the *wig* Picture Card. Listen as I say the word: *wig*. What is the first sound in *wig?* Listen carefully: /w/ /w/ /w/, *wig*. Continue with the following words: *well, will, wet*.

Discriminate sounds

Display the *jet* and *web* Picture Cards. Point to each card as you say the word. Which word has the same first sound as *waffle?* Say the words with me: *jet, waffle, web*. I hear /w/ at the beginning of *waffle* and *web*. Which word has the same beginning sound as *joy?* Say the words with me: *joy, jet, web*. I hear /j/ at the beginning of *jet* and *joy*.

On their own

Have children draw a picture of something that begins with /j/ or /w/.

Picture Card

Picture Card

Segment

How many sounds are in the word *wig?* Hold up a finger for each sound. Listen carefully: /w/ /i/ /g/. How many sounds do you hear? There are three sounds in *wig.* Continue with these words: *well, wet, went, web, jam, jet, jog, Jim.*

Corrective feedback

If... children cannot segment the words into sounds, **then...** provide practice segmenting the words into chunks, such as *wi- /g/* or */j/ -am.*

Substitute final sounds

I am going to say a word: *wet.* Say it with me: /w/ /e/ /t/, *wet.* I can make a new word by changing the first sound. Listen: /b/ /e/ /t/. Say it with me: /b/ /e/ /t/. What is the new word? The new word is *bet.* Continue practice with the following words: *jam, Sam; went, sent; well, tell.*

Differentiated Instruction

 Strategic Intervention

Support Phonemic Awareness Have children whose names begin with /j/ or /w/ stand up. Then point to one child at a time and have that child say his or her name. Have the class repeat the name. Have them identify the initial sound of the name.

E L L

English Language Learners

Transfer Skill Some children may substitute /v/ for /w/ because several languages do not have the sound /w/. Point out that when pronouncing /v/, the top front teeth touch the bottom lip, whereas when pronouncing /w/ they do not. Have children practice producing /w/ and then practice the word pair *vet, wet.*

ELL Support For additional support for language transfer, see Linguistic Contrastive Analysis in the *ELL Handbook.*

jectives

Practice /j/ spelled *Jj*.
Practice /w/ spelled *Ww*.
Read /j/ and /w/ words.
Read high-frequency words.

Check Word Reading
SUCCESS PREDICTOR

Phonics—Teach/Model
 /j/ Spelled *Jj* and /w/ Spelled *Ww*

Review

/j/Jj, /w/Ww Display the *Jj* Alphabet Card and point to the jaguar. What sound do you hear at the beginning of *jaguar?* What letter spells that sound? Point to the letters *Jj*. What is the sound for these letters? What are the names of these letters? Repeat the routine with the *Ww* Alphabet Card.

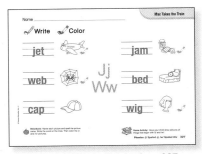

Alphabet Card

Review

Letter Names and Sounds Use Alphabet Cards to review the following letters names and sounds: *Aa, Bb, Ee, Gg, Ii, Ll, Mm, Nn, Oo, Ss, Tt*.

Blend sounds

Write *job* on the board. Point to each letter as you say the sound: /j/ /o/ /b/. When I blend these sounds together, I make the word *job*. Say the sounds with me: /j/ /o/ /b/. Now blend the sounds together: /j/ /o/ /b/, *job*. Repeat the blending routine with *jam, wig, Will, Jen,* and *west*.

Alphabet Card

More practice

Use *Reader's and Writer's Notebook,* p. 327, for additional practice with /w/ and /j/.

Reader's and Writer's Notebook, p. 327

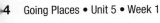

Review   **Sound-Spelling** Display the *Rr* Alphabet Card. What sound do you hear at the beginning of *river*? What letter spells that sound? Yes, the letter *r* spells /r/. Review the following sounds and letters with these Alphabet Cards: *Aa, Cc, Dd, Hh, Mm, Pp, Rr, Ss, Tt*.

Review   **High-Frequency Words** Write *yellow* on the board. This is the word *yellow*. What is this word? Continue this routine with *blue, green, go, here,* and *from*.

Alphabet Card

Differentiated Instruction

SI Strategic Intervention

Practice High-Frequency Words For more practice, review previously taught high-frequency words that are not in Kindergarten Student Reader K.5.1. Remind children that these are words they have to memorize.

Don't Wait Until Friday

MONITOR PROGRESS   Check Word Reading   High-Frequency Words

Write *yellow, green, blue, see, look,* and *they* on the board. Have children take turns reading the words.

Practice reading these words from Kindergarten Student Reader K.5.1, *Jan* and *Jem Win!*

Jem	win	Jan	will	hat	spot
cap	can	red	cat	pig	kit

If... children cannot read the high-frequency words,
then... write the words on cards for them to practice at home.

If... children cannot blend sounds to read the words,
then... provide practice blending the words in chunks, /j/ -em.

If... children can successfully blend sounds to read the words,
then... have them read Kindergarten Student Reader K.5.1, *Jan and Jem Win!*

Day 1	Day 2	Day 3	Day 4	Day 5
Check Phonemic Awareness	Check Sound-Spelling/ Retelling	Check Word Reading	Check Phonemic Awareness	Check Oral Vocabulary

Success Predictor

Word Reading

Succes
Predicto

Objectives
Read /j/ and /w/ words.
Read high-frequency words.

Kindergarten Student Reader K.5.1
↻ /j/ Spelled *Jj*, /w/ Spelled *Ww*, and High-Frequency Words

Review

High-Frequency Words Review the previously taught high-frequency words. Have children read each word as you point to it on the Word Wall.

look	he	see	a
you	with	the	they

Teach rebus words

Write the word *pink* on the board. This is the word *pink.* Name the letters with me: *p, i, n, k; pink.* What is something that is *pink*? Look for the word *pink* in the book we read today. There will be a picture above the word to help you read it.

Read Kindergarten Student Reader K.5.1

Display Kindergarten Student Reader K.5.1. Today we are going to read a new book. Point to the title of the book. The title of the story is *Jan and Jem Win!* The author's name is D.M. Longo. The story was illustrated by Hector Borlasca.

Use the reading decodable books routine to read the Kindergarten Student Reader.

ROUTINE — Reading Decodable Books

Small Group

1. **Read Silently** Have children whisper read the book page by page as you listen in.
2. **Model Fluent Reading** Have children finger point as you read a page. Then have children reread the page without you.
3. **Read Chorally** Have children finger point as they chorally read the page. Continue reading page by page, repeating steps 1 and 2.
4. **Read Individually** Have children take turns reading aloud a page.
5. **Reread and Monitor Progress** As you listen to individual children reread, monitor progress and provide support.
6. **Reread with a Partner** Have children reread the book page by page with a partner.

Routines Flip Chart

Kindergarten Student Reader K.5.1

Look at Jem!
He can see Jan.

2

Jem can see a green hat.
Can you see the green hat?
Jem can win it!

3

Jan can spot a blue cap.
Can Jan hit a blue cap?
Jan can win it!

4

Jem can see a red cat.
Can you see a red cat?
Jem can win it!

5

Jan can spot a pink pig.
Can you spot a pink pig?
Jan can win it!

6

Jem can see a yellow kit!
Will he win it?
Jem can win it!

7

Look at Jem with Jan!
They can win a lot!

8

Differentiated Instruction

SI Strategic Intervention

Practice Decoding As children read *Jan and Jem Win!*, have them copy the words they have difficulty reading on a sheet of paper. When they finish reading the book, have children practice reading the words on the list.

Small Group Time

DAY 3

Break into small groups to read the Kindergarten Student Reader before the comprehension lesson.

Teacher-Led

SI Strategic Intervention	**OL** On-Level	**A** Advanced
Teacher-Led Page DI•3	**Teacher-Led** Page DI•7	**Teacher-Led** Page DI•10
• Phonemic Awareness and Phonics	• Phonemic Awareness and Phonics	• **Read** Independent Reader K.5.1 or Kindergarten Student Reader K.5.1
• **Read** Concept Literacy Reader K.5.1 or Kindergarten Student Reader K.5.1	• **Read** Kindergarten Student Reader K.5.1	

ELL Place English language learners in the groups that correspond to their reading abilities in English.

Practice Stations
• Visit the Words to Know Station
• Visit the Let's Write! Station

Independent Activities
• Read independently
• Audio Text of Big Book
• *Reader's and Writer's Notebook*

ELL

English Language Learners
Retelling Have children retell what happens in *Jan and Jem Win!* Then have them illustrate their summaries and label the illustrations with decodable words from the story.

Objectives
- Recall and retell a story.
- Practice realism and fantasy.
- Develop and use vocabulary.
- Develop and use comprehension skills.

Comprehension

Retell the story

Have children turn to p. 26 of *My Skills Buddy* and use the retelling boxes to retell the story *Max Takes the Train*.

Envision It!

 Think Aloud Direct students to the first retell box. This is when Max says he wants to get a Whamburger. Tell me how he travels to get one.

Continue reviewing the retelling boxes and having children retell the story.

My Skills Buddy, p. 26

Review

Realism and Fantasy Display *Max Takes the Train*. This story has animal characters that do things that real animals cannot do. This is a make-believe story. Let's discuss how real rabbits behave.

- How do bunny rabbits really travel? **(They hop.)**
- What kinds of clothes do real rabbits wear? **(None; their fur keeps them warm.)**
- What do bunny rabbits really eat? **(plants, not ice cream)**

More practice

Use *Reader's and Writer's Notebook*, p. 328, for additional practice with realism and fantasy.

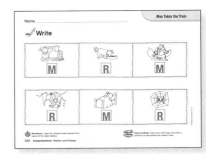

Reader's and Writer's Notebook, p. 328

 Develop vocabulary

Second Read—Big Book
Max Takes the Train

Reread *Max Takes the Train*. Follow the Day 3 arrow beginning on p. 60, and use the Develop Vocabulary notes to prompt conversations about the story.

Have children use the Amazing Words *plane, jetway, subway, tunnel, ferryboat,* and *sidecar* to talk about the story.

DAY 2
Read for enjoyment

DAY 3
Reread using Develop Vocabulary notes

DAY 4
Reread using Guide Comprehension notes

Differentiated Instruction

 **SI** Strategic Intervention

Support Retelling Pair children and have them take turns telling what happens in *Max Takes the Train*.

 **E L L**

English Language Learners
Extend Concept To help understand this week's concept, create a word map on the board. Write *transportation* in the center. Have children think of all the forms of transportation they have read about or already know about. Write those words on the outer circles. Explain to children that this week they learn about how to get places, and these words each tell a different way to do that.

Develop Vocabulary

DAY 3

Distancing

What did Max want from Zeke's Palace of Ice Cream? (a Whamburger)

- What is your favorite food?

Zeke's Palace of Ice Cream ran a special on their double chocolate ice cream Whamburger with coconut curls and red sprinkles.

Max wanted one.
"No, Max," said Max's sister, Ruby.
"Zeke's Palace of Ice Cream is too far away."
But Uncle Bunny said, "Let's go!"

2

3

Big Book, pp. 2–3

Guide Comprehension

DAY 4

Wh- question

Max really wants a chocolate ice cream Whamburger. Why does Ruby say "no"? (Zeke's Palace of Ice Cream is too far away.)

Wh- question

What does Max put on to get ready for the trip? (his Junior Citizen Transport Pass)

- Max puts his Junior Citizen Transport Pass around his neck so he can take different types of transportation. What form of transportation do he and Uncle Bunny take first?

Max put his Junior Citizen Transport Pass around his neck, and they went out and waited for the bus at the bus stop sign.

4

A big red bus came along.
Putt, putt, putt! went the bus.

5

Big Book, pp. 4–5

Inferential

Why do you think Uncle Bunny and Max choose the bus as their first form of transportation to go to Zeke's Palace of Ice Cream? (Buses travel short distances all around a city or town, so chances were good that it would go by the ice cream parlor.)

Develop Vocabulary, continued

DAY 3

Recall

Where do Max and Uncle Bunny get off the bus? (the city center)

- The bus goes into the city center. Does it take Max and Uncle Bunny to Zeke's Palace of Ice Cream?

The bus went into the city center,
but it did not pass Zeke's Palace of Ice Cream.

Max and Uncle Bunny got off the bus.
"Where to?" asked Uncle Bunny. Max saw the sign
for the Blue Comet Express. They went up the
escalator and boarded the Blue Comet.

6

7

Big Book, pp. 6–7

Guide Comprehension, continued

DAY 4

Inferential

Max and Uncle Bunny decide to get on the Blue Comet Express next. Why do they want to do this? (They were still trying to get to Zeke's Palace of Ice Cream.)

Distancing

What is the Blue Comet? (a train)

- Max and Uncle Bunny board a train called the Blue Comet. Have you ever ridden on a train? Tell us about it.

Develop Vocabulary train

Choo, choo, choo! went the Blue Comet.

The train passed houses and farms.
But it did not go to Zeke's Palace of Ice Cream.

8

9

Big Book, pp. 8–9

Inferential

How do the places the Blue Comet goes differ from the places the bus goes? (The bus stays in the city; the train goes into the country near houses and farms.)

Develop Vocabulary, continued

DAY 3

Recall

What do Max and Uncle Bunny ride after they get off the train? (a ferryboat)

- Next, Max and Uncle Bunny ride a ferryboat. Where does the ferryboat take them?

Max and Uncle Bunny hopped off the train. Max spotted a sign for the ferryboat. They boarded the ferryboat.

10

Chugga, chugga, chugga! went the ferryboat. The ferryboat crossed the lake. But it did not go to Zeke's Palace of Ice Cream.

11

Big Book, pp. 10–11

Guide Comprehension, continued

DAY 4

Open-ended

Were you surprised that the ferryboat did not go to Zeke's Palace of Ice Cream? Why or why not? (Children may respond "no" because it goes across the water; the ice cream parlor is not likely to be on the lake.)

Recall

What form of transportation do Max and
Uncle Bunny take next? (a plane)

- One person who works on a plane is
  called a flight attendant. What is the flight
  attendant's job? What does he ask Max and
  Uncle Bunny?

Expand Vocabulary flight attendant

On the other side of the lake was a sign for
Air-O-Zoom. Max and Uncle Bunny followed the
arrows down the jetway.

12

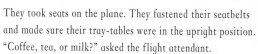

They took seats on the plane. They fastened their seatbelts
and made sure their tray-tables were in the upright position.
"Coffee, tea, or milk?" asked the flight attendant.

13

Big Book, pp. 12–13

Inferential

What do Max and Uncle Bunny do after they
take their seats on the plane? Why do they
do these things? (They fasten their seatbelts
and put their tray-tables in the upright
position for safety.)

Develop Vocabulary, continued

DAY 3

Recall

Does the plane land at Zeke's? (no)

- Where does the plane land?

Max did not want coffee, tea, or milk.
He wanted the chocolate Whamburger.
Zoom, zoom, zoom! went the plane.

14

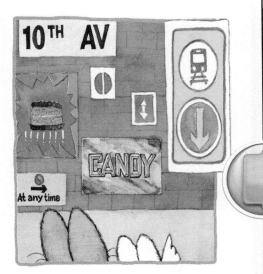

But the plane did not land at Zeke's Palace of
Ice Cream. In the airport there was a sign for the
Metro Subway Liner.

15

Big Book, pp. 14–15

Guide Comprehension, continued

DAY 4

Inferential

What sign is in the airport? Why do you think Max might be interested in this sign? (There was a sign for the Metro Subway Liner. Max still hadn't reached Zeke's and thought the subway might take him there.)

Recall

Where does the subway travel? (underground)

- The subway is like a train that travels underground. What picture do Max and Uncle Bunny see in the subway station?

Max and Uncle Bunny went down, down, down, underground into the subway tunnel. They chose the Yellow line. They minded the gap and the closing doors. Clicka, clicka, clicka! went the Metro Subway Liner.

16

The subway came to its first stop. In the station was a picture of a double chocolate Whamburger with coconut curls and red sprinkles. "Let's go!" said Uncle Bunny.

17

Big Book, pp. 16–17

Open-ended

How do you think Max feels when he sees the picture of the double chocolate Whamburger? (He feels hungry.)

Develop Vocabulary, continued

DAY 3

Recall
What is at the top of the steps?
(Zeke's)

• Max and Uncle Bunny finally arrive
at Zeke's. What do they order?

At the top of the steps was Zeke, large as life.
Max and Uncle Bunny put in their orders.
"Two double Whamburgers with the works!"
yelled Zeke.

18

But two double Whamburgers were too much
for Max and Uncle Bunny to finish.
"We had better call Ruby!" said Uncle Bunny.

19

Big Book, pp. 18–19

Guide Comprehension, continued

DAY 4

Inferential
Who does Uncle Bunny want to
call? Why? (He wants to call Ruby
because they can't finish their
Whamburgers, and he thinks she
can help.)

Distancing

Where does Max find his telephone number?
(on his Junior Citizen Transport card)

- Max knows his phone number is on the
  back of his Junior Citizen Transport Pass.
  Do you know your own phone number?

On the back of Max's Junior Citizen Transport
Pass was his telephone number. Max dialed it.

Ruby answered. "Where are you?" asked Ruby.
"At Zeke's," said Max.

20

21

Big Book, pp. 20–21

Open-ended

How do you think Ruby feels when Max
calls her? (She probably feels excited about
her trip.)

Develop Vocabulary, continued

Wh- question

How does Ruby get to Zeke's? (She rides her bicycle.)

- Ruby rides a bicycle that can fit more than one person. How many people can fit on Ruby's bicycle?

Ruby attached the sidecar to her Bicycle Built for Two. She rode all the way to Zeke's Palace of Ice Cream without stopping.

22

Zeke kept the Whamburger cold for Ruby. But even Ruby couldn't finish it.

23

Big Book, pp. 22–23

Guide Comprehension, continued

Recall

What happens when Ruby gets to Zeke's? (Zeke has kept the Whamburger cold for her; she eats some but can't finish it.)

Distancing

What do you call the type of bicycle that Max, Ruby, and Uncle Bunny were riding? **(a bicycle built for two with a sidecar)**

- Max, Ruby, and Uncle Bunny ride home on the bicycle built for two and the sidecar. Have you ever seen a bicycle built for two?

Continue with **DAY** **3**

Conventions p. 72

They all got on the Bicycle Built for Two with the sidecar and brought the rest of the Whamburger back to Grandma.

24

Big Book, p. 24

Recall

What do Max, Ruby, and Uncle Bunny do with the rest of the Whamburger? **(They bring it back to Grandma.)**

Skip to **DAY** **4**

Conventions p. 86

Objectives
• Review pronouns *I* and *me*.
• Dictate or write a caption.

Conventions
Pronouns *I* and *me*

Review

Write these sentences on the board:

> I like to read books.
>
> My friends share books with me.

Remind children about what they learned about the pronouns *I* and *me*. When I want to tell you something about myself—something I like or do— I use the pronouns *I* or *me.* These words take the place of my name in a sentence. Point to *I* and *me* as you read the sentences with children.

Guide practice

When you tell me things about yourselves, you also use the word *I*. When AlphaBuddy points at you, tell him something you do in the morning before you come to school. Use the words *I* or *me.* Have AlphaBuddy point to each child.

Write these sentence frames on the board:

> _____ have a cap.
>
> The cat can sit by _____.

Read the first sentence frame with children. Which word should we write here, *I* or *me?* Say the sentence with children using both words. Have children decide which word is correct and write it on the line. Repeat with the second sentence.

Team Talk Pair children and have them practice writing the pronouns *I* and *me* on their Write-On Boards. Then have each child say a sentence with the word *I* and then with the word *me*.

On their own

Use *Reader's and Writer's Notebook,* p. 329, for more practice reading, writing, and saying pronouns *I* and *me*.

Daily Fix-It

Use the Daily Fix-It for more conventions practice.

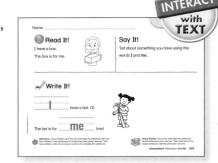

Reader's and Writer's Notebook, p. 329

Writing
Caption

Teach

Display simple pictures you have drawn of a car, a horse, a bicycle, and in-line skates. Pictures tell us what things look like. Point to the car. This car has wheels and a door. Point to the horse. This horse has four legs and a tail. Point to the bicycle. This bicycle has two wheels and handlebars. Point to the in-line skates. These in-line skates look like shoes with wheels.

Model

Draw a picture of the sun. This picture shows me something that is round. It also shows me that it is yellow. How can we tell what this picture shows? This picture needs a caption.

I am going to write a caption for this picture. A *caption* is words next to a picture that tell about the picture. Write the words *yellow sun* under the picture. Read the caption. This caption tells me that this is a picture of the yellow sun.

Guide practice

Have children provide captions for the pictures you drew. Write their captions under the pictures.

Independent writing

Have children turn to p. 330 of *Reader's and Writer's Notebook*. Have children draw a picture of an animal home. Then have them write or dictate a caption for their picture.

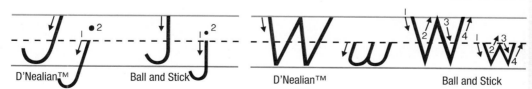

Reader's and Writer's Notebook, p. 330

Daily Handwriting

Write *Jan, Will, jog,* and *win* on the board. Review correct letter formation of uppercase *J* and *W* and lowercase *j* and *w*.

D'Nealian™   Ball and Stick   D'Nealian™   Ball and Stick

Have children write *Jan, Will, jog,* and *win* on their Write-On Boards. Remind children to use proper left-to-right and top-to-bottom progression and proper spacing between letters when writing *W, w, J,* and *j.*

Differentiated Instruction

 Advanced

Extend Writing Have children write their caption in a comple sentence. Remind them to begin their sentence with an uppercase letter and end it wit a period.

Academic Vocabulary

caption words next to a pictur that tell about the picture

Daily Fix-It

I like to go in A car?
I like to go in a car.

This week's practice sentences appear on Teacher Resources DVD-ROM.

E L L

English Language Learners
Support Writing Before childre begin the independent writing activity, have children brainstor animal homes they have previously learned. Write the lis on the board for children to refe to when writing a caption.

DAY 3 Language Arts

Objectives

- Practice asking and answering questions.
- Speak loudly and clearly.

Listening and Speaking
Ask and Answer Questions

Review Remind children that when they ask questions they are trying to find out some information. When they answer questions they are sharing information. Remind children to speak clearly and loudly when asking and answering questions.

Model We are going to practice asking and answering questions. When we ask a question, we often start with the words *who, what, where, when, why,* or *how.* Say: What animal do you like best? Have children practice answering the question. Remind them to answer in a complete sentence.

Guide practice Have children turn to p. 29 of *My Skills Buddy.* Look at the picture of the boys. Read the first Listening and Speaking bullet on p. 28 of *My Skills Buddy.* Who is a friend that lives close to you? How can we answer that question? Have volunteers answer the question. Continue with the other pictures on p. 29 and the rest of the Listening and Speaking bullets on p. 28 of *My Skills Buddy.*

My Skills Buddy, p. 29

Independent practice

Have children come to the front of the class to ask a question that the rest of the children can answer. Remind them that questions sometimes begin with words such as *who, what, when, where,* and *why.* Then have children in the class answer the questions one at a time. Refer children to the Rules for Listening and Speaking on pp. 1–2 of *Reader's and Writer's Notebook.* Tell children to speak loudly and clearly when they ask and answer questions.

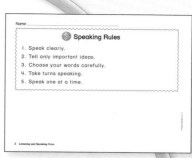

Name _____

😊 Speaking Rules

1. Speak clearly.
2. Tell only important ideas.
3. Choose your words carefully.
4. Take turns speaking.
5. Speak one at a time.

2 Listening and Speaking Rules

Reader's and Writer's Notebook, pp. 1–2

Be a Good Speaker

1. Speak clearly.
2. Tell only important ideas.
3. Choose your words carefully
4. Take turns speaking.
5. Speak one at a time.

Differentiated Instruction

 Strategic Intervention

Access Content Before childre ask the class questions, have them brainstorm topics they can ask questions about, such as *animals, transportation,* or *games.* If children have difficulty generating an appropriate question their classmates can answer, provide one of the topics for children to use to focus their question.

English Language Learners
Conversational English
Conversational fluency "represents the ability to carry on a conversation in face-to-face situations. Most native speakers of English have developed conversational fluency by age 5. English learners generally develop fluency in conversational English within a year or two of intensive exposure to the language in school if in their neighborhood environment."

—Dr. Jim Cummins

Allow children to listen to others ask and answer questions before joining in the activity.

Objectives
- Review skills learned and practiced today.
- Identify an object that begins with /j/ or /w/.

Wrap Up Your Day

✔ **Concept Talk** Today we read about Max and Uncle Bunny riding on a jet. Where can you walk through a jetway?

✔ **Respond to Literature** Today we read about Jem and Jan winning prizes at the fair. Have you ever been to a fair?

✔ **Conventions** Tell me what you like to do after school. Use the pronouns *I* and *me*.

✔ **Homework Idea**
Have children draw a picture of something at home that begins with /j/ or /w/. Then have them write or dictate a label for their picture.

Preview DAY 4

Tomorrow we will read a story about our Trucktown friends.

Social Studies
Exploring Transportation
Materials: chart paper

How Have You Traveled? Ask children to share the forms of transportation they have used. Ask what form of transportation they would like to ride if they could choose. Discuss which forms are faster than others.

What's Your Favorite? Make a chart on the board. Write *plane, car, train,* and *bus* in the chart. Ask children to pick their favorite way to travel from the list in the chart and record their answers with tally marks. When everyone has voted, count the number of tally marks. Ask

which type of transportation has the most votes and which has the least. Ask children to explain the reasons they voted as they did. Have children illustrate the form of transportation with the most points.

plane	⨌ ⨌ II
car	⨌ IIII
train	⨌ ⨌
bus	⨌ III

Comprehension
Real or Make-Believe?

Finding Picture Clues Choose a storybook from the classroom library. Page through the book with children and ask them to categorize the book as something that could really happen or something that is make-believe. Encourage children to find clues in the illustrations that tell them whether the book is real or make-believe. Continue with additional books, including some stories that are realistic and some that are fantasy. Sort the books into two lists, *Real* and *Make-Believe*.

Phonics
Jumping Words
Materials: jump rope, construction paper squares, crayons

Write Words Attach a jump rope to a bulletin board and label the display *Jumping Words.* Have children write words that begin with /j/, such as *jumping,* or /w/, such as *words,* on the squares of construction paper. After children have collected a number of words, ask them to read their words and pin the words by the jump rope.

Objectives
- Discuss the concept to develop oral language.
- Build oral vocabulary.

Today at a Glance

Oral Vocabulary
ferryboat, sidecar

Phonemic Awareness
Initial and Medial /e/

Phonics
/e/ Spelled Ee
Spell Words

Comprehension
Realism and Fantasy

Conventions
Questions

Writing
Extend the Concept

Vocabulary
Transportation Words

TRUCKTOWN on Reading Street

Start your engines!

- Display "Swing Around with Rosie" and lead the group in saying the rhyme a few times.
- Have the group clap the rhythm as they recite the rhyme.
- When children master the rhythm, have them march around the room as they say the rhyme.

Truckery Rhymes

Concept Talk

Question of the Week
What are different ways of going places?

Build concepts

Write the question of the week on the board. Read the question as you track the print. Tell children to respond in complete sentences. Display Sing with Me Chart 25B.

Listen for Amazing Words

We are going to sing this song again. Listen for the Amazing Words *ferryboat* and *sidecar*. Sing the song several times to the tune of "Are You Sleeping?" Have them clap when they hear *ferryboat* and *sidecar*.

Sing with Me Audio

ELL **Produce Oral Language** Use the Day 4 instruction on ELL Poster 25 to extend and enrich language.

Through the Jetway

Through the jetway, through the jetway,
To the plane, to the plane,
Look at all these things that float,
I can see a ferryboat,
Down below, down below.

Talk with Me/Sing with Me Chart 25B

ELL Poster 25

Oral Vocabulary
Amazing Words

Amazing Words

Amazing Words **Oral Vocabulary Routine**

Teach Amazing Words

1 **Introduce the Word** A *ferryboat* is a boat used to carry people, cars, and other things across a river or lake. Cars and trucks drive right into the *ferryboat's* big empty space. People ride the *ferryboat* a floor above the cars. What is our new Amazing Word for a boat that carries people and cars? Say it with me: *ferryboat*.

2 **Demonstrate** *A ferryboat is much larger than a sailboat.* How many cars do you think a *ferryboat* might hold?

Repeat steps 1 and 2.

Introduce the Word A *sidecar* is a small seat that can be added to the side of a motorcycle or bicycle to carry another person. What is our new Amazing Word for a seat added to the side of a motorcycle? Say it with me: *sidecar*.

Demonstrate *A sidecar has one wheel and cannot travel by itself.* Would you like to ride in a *sidecar*?

3 **Apply** Have children act out the Amazing Words *ferryboat* and *sidecar* in questions about an adventure. Have them illustrate the words.

Routines Flip Chart

Use Amazing Words

To reinforce the concept and the Amazing Words, have children supply the appropriate Amazing Word for each sentence.

The man's motorcycle had a _____ on it. (sidecar)

They took the _____ across the lake. (ferryboat)

Amazing Words

plane	jetway
subway	tunnel
ferryboat	sidecar

Differentiated Instruction

 **Strategic Intervention**

Scaffold Meaning Show the pictures of a *ferryboat* and a *sidecar* in *Max Takes the Train* children can connect the word to the pictures.

ELL

English Language Learners
Access Content Ask children i they know how to say *ferryboa* and *sidecar* in their own languages. In Spanish, the wor for *ferryboat* is *el transbordado* or *el ferry*. In Spanish, the word for *sidecar* is *el sidecar*.

Phonemic Awareness
Review /e/

Display the *elbow* Picture Card. This is an *elbow*. *Elbow* begins with /e/. What sound does *elbow* begin with? Continue the routine with the *egg* and *elephant* Picture Cards.

Display the *hen* Picture Card. This is a *hen*. Where do you hear /e/ in the word *hen*? /e/ is in the middle of *hen*. Continue the routine with the *ten, net,* and *bed* Picture Cards.

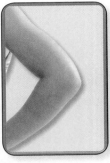

Picture Card

Corrective feedback

If... children cannot discriminate /e/, **then...** have them enunciate /e/ as they say *elbow*.

When you say /e/, your mouth is open and slightly down. Say /e/ and feel where your mouth and tongue are located. Have children say /e/ words and feel the position of their mouth and tongue. Then repeat the discrimination activity.

Picture Card

Phonics
/e/ Spelled *Ee*

Review

Display the *Ee* Alphabet Card. This is an *escalator*. *Escalator* begins with /e/. What letter spells the sound /e/? Yes, the letter *e*.

Write the word *bed* on the board. Help me blend this word. Listen as I say each sound: /b/ /e/ /d/. Now let's blend the sounds together to read the word: /b/ /e/ /d/, *bed*. What is the word? (*bed*) Let's try more. Repeat the routine with *pen* and *red*.

Alphabet Card

Don't Wait Until Friday

MONITOR PROGRESS ⟳ **Check Phonemic Awareness**

Phoneme Segmentation I am going to say a word. Tell me all of the sounds you hear in the word.

| wet | well | jam | Jill | wig | jet | Jack | win |

If... children cannot segment the sounds in each word,

then... use the small-group Strategic Intervention lesson, p. DI•4, to reteach segmentation skills.

Continue to monitor children's progress using other instructional opportunities during the week so that they can be successful with the Day 5 Assessment. See the Skills Trace on p. 20.

Day 1	Day 2	Day 3	Day 4	Day 5
Check Phonemic Awareness	Check Sound-Spelling/ Retelling	Check Word Reading	Check Phonemic Awareness	Check Oral Vocabulary

Success Predictor

Differentiated Instruction

A Advanced

Connect Sound-Spelling Say the names *Jen, Wes, Pam,* an Sam. Have children write the two names that have medial /e

ELL

English Language Learners

Support Phonemic Awareness Remember, some languages do not have any short vowel sound or only approximations. Provide extra practice with /e/ if children have difficulty producing the sound.

bjectives
- Spell words.
- Blend and segment words.
- Read decodable text.
- Read high-frequency words.

Spelling
🎯 /j/ Spelled *Jj*, /w/ Spelled *Ww*

Spell words

ROUTINE **Spell Words**

1) **Review Sound-Spellings** Display the *Jj* Alphabet Card. This is a *jaguar. Jaguar* begins with /j/. What is the letter we learned for /j/? (*j*) Continue the routine with the following Alphabet Cards: *Aa, Bb, Cc, Dd, Ee, Ff, Hh, Ii, Kk, Ll, Mm, Nn, Oo, Pp, Rr, Ss, Tt, Ww.*

2) **Model** Today we are going to spell some words. Listen to the three sounds in *job:* /j/ /o/ /b/.

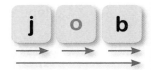

- What is the first sound in *job?* (/j/) What is the letter for /j/? (*j*) Write *j* on the board.
- What is the middle sound you hear? (/o/) What is the letter for /o/? (*o*) Write *o* on the board.
- What is the last sound you hear? (/b/) What is the letter for /b/? (*b*) Write *b* on the board.
- Point to *job.* Help me blend the sound of each letter together to read this word: /j/ /o/ /b/. The word is *job.* Repeat modeling with the word *wet.*

3) **Guide Practice** Now let's spell some words together. Listen to this word: /j/ /a/ /m/. What is the first sound in *jam?* (/j/) What is the letter for /j/? (*j*) Write *j* on the board. Now you write *j* on your paper. What is the middle sound in *jam?* (/a/) What is the letter for /a/? (*a*) Write *a* on the board. Now you write *a* on your paper. What is the last sound in *jam?* (/m/) What is the letter for /m/? (*m*) Write *m* on the board. Now you write *m* on your paper. Now we can blend the sound of each letter together to read the word: /j/ /a/ /m/. What is the word? (*jam*) Continue spell and blend practice with the following words: *jot, Jim, web, went.*

4) **On Your Own** This time I am going to say a word. I want you to write it on your paper. Remember, first say the word slowly in your head and then write the letter for each sound. Listen carefully. Write the word *jet.* Give children time to write the word. How do you spell the word *jet?* Listen to the sounds: /j/ /e/ /t/. The first sound is /j/. What is the letter for /j/? Did you write *j* on your paper? What is the letter for /e/? Did you write *e* on your paper? What is the letter for /t/? Did you write *t* on your paper? Name the letters in *jet. Jet* is spelled *j, e, t.* Continue the activity with the following words: *fan, bit, ten, mop, win.*

Get Set, Roll! Reader 25
↻ Practice /j/ Spelled *Jj* and /w/ Spelled *Ww*

Differentiated Instruction

SI Strategic Intervention

Comprehension Have childre[n] tell whether *Blue?* is a realisti[c] story or a fantasy. Tell childre[n] explain their choice.

Review | Review the high-frequency words *yellow, blue, green, the, with,* and *go.* Have children find each word on the Word Wall.

Teach rebus words | Write the word *light* on the board. This is the word *light.* Name the letters with me: *l, i, g, h, t.* Repeat the procedure with *trucks, street,* and *heard.* Look for the words *light, trucks, street,* and *heard* in the book today. A picture above the word will help you read it.

Read Get Set, Roll! Reader 25 | Display Get Set, Roll! Reader 25. Today we will read a new story called *Blue?* Point to the title of the story. What is the title of this story? We will read words with /j/ and /w/ in this story.

Use the routine for reading decodable books found in the Routines Flip Chart to read Get Set, Roll! Reader 25.

Get Set, Roll! Reader 25

Small Group Time

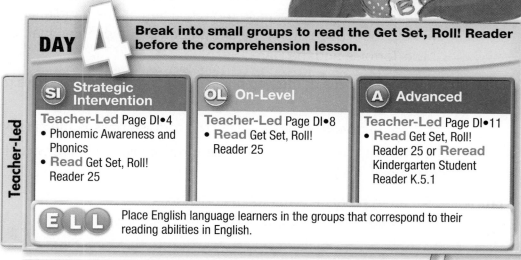

DAY 4 — Break into small groups to read the Get Set, Roll! Reader before the comprehension lesson.

Teacher-Led	**SI Strategic Intervention**	**OL On-Level**	**A Advanced**
	Teacher-Led Page DI•4 • Phonemic Awareness and Phonics • **Read** Get Set, Roll! Reader 25	**Teacher-Led** Page DI•8 • **Read** Get Set, Roll! Reader 25	**Teacher-Led** Page DI•11 • **Read** Get Set, Roll! Reader 25 or **Reread** Kindergarten Student Reader K.5.1

ELL Place English language learners in the groups that correspond to their reading abilities in English.

Practice Stations
• Visit the Let's Write! Station
• Visit the Read for Meaning Station

Independent Activities
• Read independently
• Audio Text of the Big Book
• *Reader's and Writer's Notebook*

Comprehension
↻ Realism and Fantasy

Practice realism and fantasy

Envision It!

Have children turn to the Realism and Fantasy picture on pp. 14–15 of *My Skills Buddy.* As you look at the picture, remind children that things that can really happen are realistic and things that could not happen are called fantasy.

Team Talk Pair children and have them play a pretend game where they fly. Can you really fly? Is that realism or fantasy? Then have children tell about real things they can do.

My Skills Buddy, pp. 14–15

Plot

Review

Direct children to the Literary Elements picture on p. 74–75 of *My Skills Buddy.*

The events in a story happen in a certain order. All stories have a beginning, a middle, and an end. This is called the plot. Good readers pay attention to what happens in the beginning, in the middle, and at the end to help them understand the story. Look at the pictures that tell the story of "The Tortoise and the Hare."

- What happens at the beginning? (The tortoise and the hare get ready to race.)
- What happens in the middle? (The tortoise passes the sleeping hare.)
- What happens at the end? (The tortoise wins the race while the hare tries to catch up.)

More practice

For more practice with plot, use *Reader's and Writer's Notebook,* p. 331.

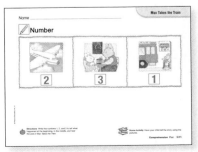
Reader's and Writer's Notebook, p. 331

 Triple Day Read!

Third Read—Big Book
Max Takes the Train

Guide comprehension

Display *Max Takes the Train.* We can retell the story by telling what happens in the beginning, in the middle, and at the end.

- In the beginning of the story, Max wants to go to Zeke's for a Whamburger.

- What happens in the middle of the story? (Max and Uncle Bunny ride on a bus, a train, a ferryboat, a jet, and a subway to get to Zeke's.)

- What happens at the end of the story? (Max, Uncle Bunny, and Ruby eat Whamburgers; they go home on Ruby's bike.)

Reread *Max Takes the Train.* Return to p. 60. Follow the Day 4 arrow and use the Guide Comprehension notes to give children the opportunity to gain a more complete understanding of the story.

Differentiated Instruction

 SI **Strategic Intervention**

Support Comprehension Ha children draw a picture to go along with what happens in the beginning, middle, and en of *Max Takes the Train.* Pair children and have them show their drawings.

DAY **2**
Read for enjoyment

DAY **3**
Reread using Develop Vocabulary notes

DAY **4**
Reread using Guide Comprehension notes

Conventions
Questions

Review Remind children of what they learned about questions. A question asks something. It begins with an uppercase letter and ends with a question mark. Listen to how a telling sentence sounds: *I feel fine.* Now listen to how a question sounds: *How do you feel?*

Guide practice Write these sentences on the board:

> **I feel fine.**
>
> **How do you feel?**

Read each sentence aloud. Which one is a question? How do you know? Encourage children to respond that questions ask something, begin with an uppercase letter, and end with a question mark. A question needs an answer. Who can answer this question?

Now write these questions on the board, omitting initial capitalization and end punctuation.

> **where is the library**
>
> **what is your name**

Read each question aloud. Have children tell you what words to capitalize and what end punctuation to use.

On their own Use *Reader's and Writer's Notebook,* p. 332, for more practice with questions.

Daily Fix-It Use the Daily Fix-It for more conventions practice.

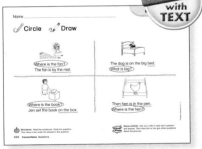

Reader's and Writer's Notebook, p. 332

Writing
Extend the Concept: Text to Self

Discuss transportation

We just read about the different forms of transportation Max uses to get to Zeke's. He uses a *bus, train, ferryboat, plane, subway,* and *bicycle with a sidecar.* Like Max, we use transportation.

Guide practice

Ask children to think about the different kinds of transportation they have used. Talk about a place they were going and what form of transportation they used to get there.

Use children's contributions to the discussion to write sentences.

A car takes me to...	**the store.**
	school.
The subway takes me to...	**my grandma's house.**
	the library.

Independent writing

Have children write or dictate their own sentence about a form of transportation they have used or copy a sentence from the board. Invite children to read their sentence to the class.

Daily Handwriting

Write *Jen, Will, job,* and *wed* on the board. Review correct letter formation of uppercase *J* and *W* and lowercase *j* and *w*.

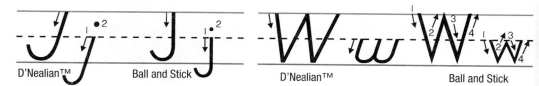

D'Nealian™   Ball and Stick   D'Nealian™   Ball and Stick

Have children write *Jen, Will, job,* and *wed* on their Write-On Boards. Remind them to use proper left-to-right and top-to-bottom progression and proper spacing between letters when writing.

Differentiated Instruction

SI **Strategic Intervention**
Support Discussion Have children draw a picture of the form of transportation they h. used before.

Daily Fix-It

Is max on the bus
Is Max on the bus?

This week's practice sentenc appear on Teacher Resource DVD-ROM.

 ELL

English Language Learners
Support Writing To extend th dialogue, encourage children use connecting words to add additional information to the sentences, such as A bus take me to the store because it is too far to walk. Write their sug gestions on the board. Discus how adding more information can make their writing more interesting.

ectives
ractice using transportation
ords in sentences.

Vocabulary
Transportation Words

Teach

Write the words *train, truck, airplane,* and *boat* on the board. Point to each word as you read it. These are transportation words. Have children turn to p. 28 of *My Skills Buddy.* Incorporate the second Vocabulary bullet on the page in the discussion. Which form of transportation is used in the air? Which is used on water? Which ones are used on land? Have children say the word and point to the picture as they answer the questions.

My Skills Buddy, p. 28

Team Talk Pair children and have them take turns using one of the transportation words to tell an adventure story. Remind them to tell the story in complete sentences.

Wrap Up Your Day

✔ **Oral Language** Ask the person sitting across from you what his or her favorite story is. Listen and answer when that person asks you the same question.

✔ **Phonemic Awareness** I am going to say a word. I want you to say words that rhyme with it: *jet.*

✔ **Homework Idea** Tell children to ask a family member a question and bring the answer back to share with the class.

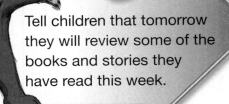

Preview DAY 5

Tell children that tomorrow they will review some of the books and stories they have read this week.

Extend Your Day!

Social Studies
Family Roles
Materials: Big Book *Max Takes the Train*, Trade Book *Abuela*

Who Makes a Family? Display *Max Takes the Train* and *Abuela.* In these books, there are different families. Who are the family members in *Abuela?* Who are the family members in *Max Takes the Train?* Continue identifying family members in the books. Are they parents? What do they do to keep Rosalba and Max safe?

Role Reversal Play a role-playing game. Ask children to act out the characters from the story and show what else the characters could have done.

- Max wants to go to Zeke's Palace. What else could he say to Uncle Bunny?
- Rosalba wants another adventure. Where else can she go and who will go with her?

Science
Mixing Colors
Materials: paper plates, yellow and blue paint, paintbrushes, paper

Yellow + Blue = Green When we mix yellow and blue, we get a new color. Do you think you know what color we will get? I will give you a clue: When we mix yellow and blue, we get the color of grass and leaves in the summertime. Write *yellow + blue = green* with the appropriate colors on the board.

Show children how to mix the paints to get green. Have them paint a picture that shows the colors, such as a yellow sun, a blue sky, and green grass. Display the pictures on a bulletin board.

Art
Make a Bus Pass
Materials: Big Book *Max Takes the Train*, construction paper, crayons or markers

Proper Identification Give each child a sheet of paper. Display p. 4 of *Max Takes the Train.* Max has to show his Junior Citizen Transport Pass before he gets on the bus. Discuss with children why people need a bus pass. Let's make our own bus passes. Have children use the picture in the book as a model. Have them draw a picture of themselves and write their name on the pass. As you pretend to be the bus driver, have children show you their pass before they get on the bus.

Objectives
- Review the concepts.
- Build oral vocabulary.

Day at a Glance

Vocabulary
plane, jetway, subway, tunnel, ferryboat, sidecar

Phonemic Awareness
Initial /w/ and /j/

Phonics
/w/ Spelled *Ww*
/j/ Spelled *Jj*

Comprehension
Realism and Fantasy

Conventions
Questions

Writing
This Week We…

Check Oral Vocabulary

SUCCESS PREDICTOR

TRUCKTOWN on Reading Street

Start your engines!

- Display "Swing Around with Rosie" and lead the group in saying the rhyme a few times.
- Have half the group recite the rhyme while the other half acts it out.
- Then have the groups change roles.

Truckery Rhymes

Concept Wrap Up

Question of the Week
What are different ways of going places?

Listen for Amazing Words

Write the question of the week on the board. Track the print as you read it to children. Have them use the Amazing Words in their responses (*plane, jetway, subway, tunnel, ferryboat, sidecar*). Display Sing with Me Chart 25B. Let's sing "Through the Jetway." I want you to listen for the Amazing Words we learned this week. Remind children that the words *plane, jetway, subway, tunnel, ferryboat,* and *sidecar* are in the song. Sing the song several times to the tune of "Are You Sleeping?" Have children discuss different forms of transportation. Remind children to speak one at a time.

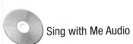 Sing with Me Audio

E L L Check Concepts and Language Use Day 5 instruction on ELL Poster 25 to monitor children's understanding of the lesson concept.

Through the Jetway
Through the jetway, through the jetway,
To the plane, to the plane,
Look at all these things that float,
I can see a ferryboat,
Down below, down below.

Sing with Me Chart 25B

E L L Poster 25

Oral Vocabulary
Amazing Words

plane	jetway
subway	tunnel
ferryboat	sidecar

Review

Let's Talk Display Talk with Me Chart 25A. We learned six new Amazing Words this week. Let's say the Amazing Words as I point to the pictures on the chart. Point to each picture and give children the chance to say the appropriate Amazing Word.

Dad drove the car through a long, dark _____. (tunnel)

We walk down some stairs to ride on the _____. (subway)

Would you like to have a _____ on your bike? (sidecar)

We can fly high above the clouds in a _____. (plane)

We walk to the plane through a _____. (jetway)

The _____ takes cars and people across the water. (ferryboat)

Differentiated Instruction

 Advanced

Produce Sentences Have children choose one Amazing Word and use it in a complete sentence.

Talk with Me/Sing with Me Chart 25A

It's Friday

MONITOR PROGRESS ⟳ **Check Oral Vocabulary**

Demonstrate Word Knowledge Monitor the Amazing Words by asking the following questions. Have children use the Amazing Word in their answer.

• **What do you walk through to get to a plane?** (jetway)

• **What could you use to ride alongside a bike or motorcycle?** (sidecar)

• **What could you ride across a river or lake?** (ferryboat)

• **What is the name for a long underground road?** (tunnel)

• **What flies through the air to take people places?** (plane)

• **What is a train that travels in an underground tunnel?** (subway)

If... children have difficulty using the Amazing Words,

then... reteach unknown words using the Oral Vocabulary Routine on the Routines Flip Chart.

Day 1	Day 2	Day 3	Day 4	Day 5
Check Phonemic Awareness	Check Sound-Spelling/ Retelling	Check Word Reading	Check Phonemic Awareness	**Check Oral Vocabulary**

Success Predictor

ectives

view initial /j/ and /w/.
view /j/ spelled *Jj*.
view /w/ spelled *Ww*.

Phonemic Awareness Review
/j/ and /w/

Isolate initial /j/ and /w/

Display the *jet* Picture Card. What is the first sound in *jet*? Say the word with me: /j/ /j/ /j/, *jet*. The first sound in *jet* is /j/. Review initial /j/ with the *jam* and *jug* Picture Cards.

Display the *web* Picture Card. What is the first sound in *web*? Say the word with me: /w/ /w/ /w/, *web*. The first sound in *web* is /w/. Review initial /w/ with the *waffle* and *wagon* Picture Cards.

Picture Card

Discriminate initial /j/ and /w/

Have children stand up. I am going to read some words. When you hear /j/ in the word, I want you to jump straight up. When you hear /w/ in the word, I want you to wave your hand. Let's try the first one together. Listen carefully: *jet*. Do you hear /j/ or /w/ in *jet*? I hear /j/ in *jet* so I am going to jump straight up. Continue with the following words: *wet, jam, wall, window, jack, wag, joke, jug, wax, win.*

Picture Card

Phonics Review
↻ /j/ Spelled *Jj* and
/w/ Spelled *Ww*

Teach /w/Ww and /j/Jj

High-frequency words

Apply phonics to familiar text

Display the *Jj* Alphabet Card. This is a *jaguar*. What sound do you hear at the beginning of *jaguar*? What letter spells that sound? Repeat with the *Ww* Alphabet Card.

Write the word *yellow* on the board. This is the word *yellow*. What is this word? Repeat the routine with *green* and *blue*.

Let's Reread Have children reread one of the books specific to the target letter sounds. You may wish to review the decodable words, rebus words, and high-frequency words that appear in each book prior to rereading.

Alphabet Card

Alphabet Card

Decodable Reader 25
My Skills Buddy, p. 18

Kindergarten
Student Reader K.5.1

Get Set, Roll!
Reader 25

Small Group Time

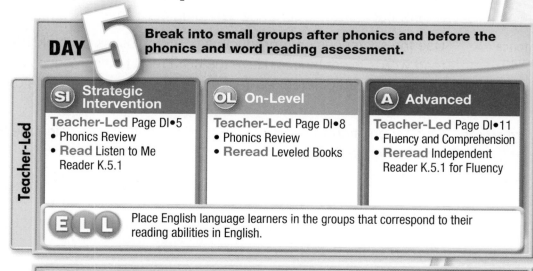

DAY 5 Break into small groups after phonics and before the phonics and word reading assessment.

Teacher-Led

SI Strategic Intervention
Teacher-Led Page DI•5
• Phonics Review
• **Read** Listen to Me Reader K.5.1

OL On-Level
Teacher-Led Page DI•8
• Phonics Review
• **Reread** Leveled Books

A Advanced
Teacher-Led Page DI•11
• Fluency and Comprehension
• **Reread** Independent Reader K.5.1 for Fluency

ELL Place English language learners in the groups that correspond to their reading abilities in English.

Practice Stations
• Visit the Read for Meaning Station
• Visit the Let's Make Art Station

Independent Activities
• Read independently
• Story Sort
• Concept Talk Video

ess
ead words with /w/ and /j/.
ead high-frequency words.
ead sentences.

Assessment
Monitor Progress

/w/ Spelled Ww and /j/ Spelled Jj

Whole Class Have children number a sheet of paper from 1 to 6. Read the list of words below. For each word, have children write *w* or *j* next to the corresponding number to match the initial sound.

1. jet	**2. wet**	**3. jug**
4. was	**5. job**	**6. will**

MONITOR PROGRESS | **Check Word and Sentence Reading**

If... children cannot complete the whole-class assessment,
then... use the Reteach lesson in *First Stop*.

If... you are unsure of a child's grasp of this week's skills,
then... use the assessment below to obtain a clearer evaluation of the child's progress.

/j/ Spelled Jj, /w/ Spelled Ww, and high-frequency words

One-on-One To facilitate individual progress monitoring, assess some children on Day 4 and the rest on Day 5. While individual children are being assessed, the rest of the class can reread this week's books and look for words with /j/ and /w/.

Word reading

Use the word list on reproducible p. 95 to assess each child's ability to read words that begin with /j/ and /w/. We are going to read some words. I'll read the first word, and you read the rest. The first word is *wet*, /w/ /e/ /t/. For each child, record any decoding problems.

Sentence reading

Use the sentences on reproducible p. 95 to assess each child's ability to read words in sentences. Have the child read two sentences aloud. Have each child read different sentences. Start over with sentence one if necessary.

Record scores

Monitor children's accuracy by recording their scores using the Word and Sentence Reading Chart for this unit in *First Stop*.

Name _____

Read the Words

wet ☐	will ☐
jet ☐	Jill ☐
yellow ☐	went ☐
win ☐	blue ☐
job ☐	jig ☐
green ☐	web ☐

Read the Sentences

1. Wes sat in the little blue jet.

2. Did Jeff win the green hat?

3. Jill went to get a yellow bag.

4. The blue jet went fast.

5. Jan will get the green cap.

Note to Teacher: Children read each word. Children read two sentences.

Scoring for Read the Words: Score 1 point for each correct word.

/w/ *Ww* (*wet, win, will, went, web*) _____ / __5__

/j/ *Jj* (*jet, job, jill, jig*) _____ / __4__

High-Frequency Words (*yellow, green, blue*) _____ / __3__

My Skills Buddy, pp. 30–31

Let's Practice It!
Poem

Teach

Today we are going to read a poem by a famous author. A poem is a type of creative writing. **Review the features of a poem with children.**

- A poem can have rhyming words.

- A poem uses words and phrases to help the reader visualize.

- A poem can have rhythm. Rhythm is a strong beat.

Have children turn to pp. 30–31 of *My Skills Buddy*. I am going to read a poem by Robert Louis Stevenson called "The Swing." Look at the pictures as I read. **Read the text of "The Swing." As you read, direct children to look at the appropriate picture.**

Guide practice

Discuss the features of a poem with children and the bulleted text on p. 30 of *My Skills Buddy*.

- A poem can have rhyming words. What are the rhyming words in "The Swing"? (*swing/thing; blue/do; wall/all; wide/countryside; brown/down*)

- A poem uses words and phrases to help the reader visualize. How do you know the child is high in the swing? (**The poem says the child can see so wide and look down on the roof of a house.**) Can you picture what that is like in your mind? Close your eyes and imagine you are that high on a swing. What else can you see?

- A poem can have rhythm. Listen to the rhythm of "The Swing" as I read and clap my hands to the beat. **Reread the poem, clapping to the beat. Emphasize the rhythm with the rhyming words. Then have children clap the rhythm with you.**

The Swing

by Robert Louis Stevenson

How would you like to go up in a swing

Up in the air so blue?

Oh, I do think it the pleasantest thing

Ever a child can do!

Up in the air and over the wall,

Till I can see so wide,

River and trees and cattle and all

Over the countryside—

Till I look down on the garden green,

Down on the roof so brown—

Up in the air I go flying again,

Up in the air and down!

Academic Vocabular

poem an imaginative piece o writing that often has rhythm and rhyme

rhythm a strong beat found i songs and poems

E L L

English Language Learners

Access Content Explain to children that sometimes when poets write, they use words in certain order to make the poe rhyme or fit the rhythm. This poem uses color words after the noun they describe, such a *garden green* and *roof so brov* Remind children that although this isn't wrong in the poem, they need to remember to use adjectives before the noun the describe, such as *green garde* and *brown roof*.

Narrating Have children deve skill in narrating with increasing specificity and detail by writing story about the girl on the swir (pp. 30-31). Have them start b listing specific details in the pic ture—*cows, farm, swing, flow- ers.* Then have them write thre sentences using these details. Finally, work with them to mak their details more precise—for example, *A girl swings* might b rewritten to read, *A girl in a pin dress swings high.*

ectives

eview realism and fantasy.

ess

ecognize a story as realism or
ntasy.

Comprehension Assessment
Monitor Progress

 Review

Realism and Fantasy Some stories are about people who could be real and things that could really happen. What do we call stories with people and events that could be real? (realism) Some stories are make-believe, or could not happen in real life. What do we call stories that are make-believe and could not happen in real life? (fantasy)

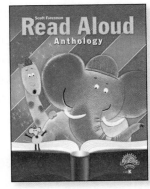

Read Aloud Anthology

Read "The Naughty Shoes"

Tell children that you are going to read them a story about some naughty shoes. Listen carefully. I am going to read you a story, and then we will decide if the story is real or make-believe. Read "The Naughty Shoes" on p. 59 of the *Read Aloud Anthology*.

Check realism and fantasy

After you read the story, ask children to identify whether the story is real or make-believe.

- What did the shoes in the story do one night? (They went walking.)
- What do real shoes do at night? (They stay under beds and chairs.)
- Could this story really happen? Why or why not? (No, shoes are not alive. They can't move around on their own.)

Corrective feedback

If... children cannot differentiate realism and fantasy, then... reteach realism and fantasy using the Reteach lesson in *First Stop*.

Assess realism and fantasy

Use the blackline master found on p. 99. Copy one page for each child. Have children color the picture that is make-believe.

Realism and Fantasy

Color the make-believe picture.

Note to Teacher: Have children color the scene that is make-believe.

Conventions
Questions

Review Remind children of what they learned about questions. Questions are sentences that ask something. When we ask people questions, they give an answer. A question has a naming part and an action part. It begins with an uppercase letter and ends with a question mark.

Model Write this question on the board:

Where does a subway travel?

Read the question aloud, pointing to each word as you say it. This is a question. It asks something. Point to the uppercase letter. It begins with an uppercase letter. Point to the question mark. It ends with a question mark. I know the answer to this question. A subway travels in an underground tunnel.

Guide practice Have children draw a large question mark on one side of a sheet of paper and a large dot on the other side. Ask them to raise the side with the question mark if you ask them a question and raise the side with the period if you say a telling sentence.

1. **Does Max get to Zeke's?**	5. **Have you been on a ferryboat?**
2. **I like the story.**	6. **I've been on a subway.**
3. **Max takes a train ride.**	7. **Does Ruby pick up Max?**
4. **What is a jetway?**	8. **The tunnel is dark.**

On their own Have children write or dictate a question about *Max Takes the Train*. Remind them to begin the question with an uppercase letter and end it with a question mark.

Daily Fix-It Use the Daily Fix-It exercise for more conventions practice.

Writing
This Week We...

Review

Display *Max Takes the Train,* Sing With Me Chart 25B, Phonics Songs and Rhymes Chart 25, Decodable Reader 25 from *My Skills Buddy,* Kindergarten Student Reader K.5.1, and Get Set, Roll! Reader 25. This week we learned about different forms of transportation. We read new books, and we sang new songs. Which book or song was your favorite? Let's share our ideas with each other.

Team Talk Pair children and have them take turns telling which book or song was their favorite and why.

Model

Today we are going to write a short poem about the kinds of transportation Max takes to get to Zeke's. Let's think about the kinds of transportation he used that will finish this poem. Read the poem to children.

> **Max rides in the sky on a _____.** (plane)
>
> **He passes farms on a _____.** (train)
>
> **He rides in a _____ over a lake.** (ferryboat)
>
> **Which kind of ride would you like to take?**

Guide practice

Work with children to complete the poem using forms of transportation. Have children echo read each line when the poem is completed.

On their own

Have children write or dictate their answer to the last question in the poem. Have them illustrate their answer.

Daily Handwriting

Write uppercase *J* and *W* and lowercase *j* and *w* on the board. Review correct letter formation with children.

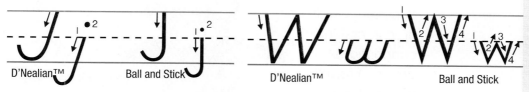

D'Nealian™   Ball and Stick   D'Nealian™   Ball and Stick

Have children write a row of uppercase *J* and *W* and lowercase *j* and *w* on the Write-On Boards. Remind them to use proper left-to-right and top-to-bottom progression.

Differentiated Instruction

SI Strategic Intervention
Support Writing Have childre look through familiar books to find sentences that ask a question. Read the questions to the children and have them answer.

Daily Fix-It

did you eat dinner
Did you eat dinner?

This week's practice sentence appear on Teacher Resources DVD-ROM.

ELL

English Language Learners
Poster Preview Prepare children for next week by using Week 2 ELL Poster number 26 Read the Poster Talk-Through to introduce the concept and vocabulary. Ask children to identify and describe objects and actions they see.

ectives
eview weekly concept.
eview realism and fantasy.

Wrap Up Your Week!

Question of the Week
What are different ways of going places?

Illustrate realism and fantasy

This week we talked about different forms of transportation.

- Make a four-column chart like the one shown or use Graphic Organizer 5. Fill it in with children's responses about whether the forms of transportation are used on land, in the air, or in the water. Then have them say a make-believe place where the forms of transportation can travel.

- Have children fold a sheet of paper in half. Tell them to choose one form of transportation from the chart. Have them draw the real place where it travels on one half and a make-believe place where it can travel on the other.

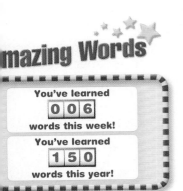

Amazing Words

You've learned
0 0 6
words this week!

You've learned
1 5 0
words this year!

Transportation	Land	Air	Water
plane train subway ferryboat subway car			

Next Week's Question
What kinds of transportation help us in an emergency?

Discuss next week's question. Guide children in making connections between forms of transportation used every day and those used in emergencies.

Preview
NEXT WEEK

Tell children that next week they will read about emergency transportation.

Social Studies
Our Transportation
Materials: paper, drawing tools

Identify Transportation Give children a sheet of paper. Show them how to fold the paper in half twice to make four boxes. Have children number the boxes 1 to 4. Ask the following questions. Have children draw a picture of the type of transportation that answers each question in the corresponding box.

1. What form of transportation would you use to cross the water?

2. What form of transportation would you use to fly somewhere?

3. What form of transportation would you use to get to school?

4. What form of transportation would you use in a tunnel?

Conventions
What Would You Ride?
Materials: pictures of unusual forms of transportation, construction paper, drawing tools

Show pictures and talk about other forms of transportation, such as *escalator, scooter, wheelchair, submarine, unicycle,* and *hot air balloon.* Ask children a question about each of the forms of transportation. Have children choose one unusual form of transportation and draw a picture of someone taking a ride on it. Have them write or dictate a question to go with it, using proper capitalization and punctuation.

Do you have a scooter?

Science
Make-Believe Animals
Materials: construction paper, drawing tools

Comparing Characteristics Distribute construction paper to children and tell them to fold it in half. On one side draw a picture of animals doing something that real animals do. On the other side draw a picture of animals doing something make-believe that real animals could not do.

Weekly Assessment

Use the whole-class assessment on pages 94–95 and 98–99 in this Teacher's Edition to check:

✔ 🎯 **/j/ Spelled** *Jj*

✔ 🎯 **/w/ Spelled** *Ww*

✔ 🎯 **Comprehension Skill** *Realism and Fantasy*

✔ **High-Frequency Words**   *yellow*   *green*   *blue*

Teacher's Edition, Day 5

Managing Assessment

Use the Assessment Handbook for:

✔ **Observation Checklists**

✔ **Record-Keeping Forms**

✔ **Portfolio Assessment**

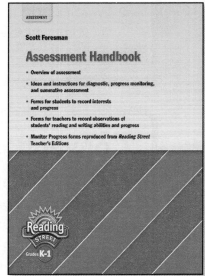

Assessment Handbook

Teacher Notes

acing Small
roup Instruction

5 Day Plan

AY 1
- Phonemic Awareness/ Phonics
- Decodable Story 25

AY 2
- Phonemic Awareness/ Phonics
- Decodable Reader 25

AY 3
- Phonemic Awareness/ Phonics
- Concept Literacy Reader K.5.1 or Kindergarten Student Reader K.5.1

AY 4
- Phonemic Awareness/ Phonics
- Get Set, Roll! Reader 25

AY 5
- Phonics Review
- Listen to Me Reader K.5.1

3 or 4 Day Plan

AY 1
- Phonemic Awareness/ Phonics
- Decodable Story 25

AY 2
- Phonemic Awareness/ Phonics
- Decodable Reader 25

AY 3
- Phonemic Awareness/ Phonics
- Concept Literacy Reader K.5.1 or Kindergarten Student Reader K.5.1

AY 4
- Phonemic Awareness/ Phonics
- Get Set, Roll! Reader 25

y Plan: Eliminate the shaded box.

SI *Strategic Intervention*

DAY 1

Phonemic Awareness•Phonics

■ **Isolate /j/** Display the *juice* Picture Card. This is a glass of *juice. Juice* begins with /j/. Say it with me: /j/ /j/ /j/, *juice.* Repeat with *jam, jet,* and *jug.*

■ **Connect /j/ to** *Jj* I am going to say two words. I want you to tell me which word begins with /j/. I will write the letter *j* on the board. Use the following word pairs: *jeep, keep; car, jar; jug, mug; hump, jump; jet, net; jacks, sacks.*

Decodable Story 25

■ **Review** Review the high-frequency words *the, is, a, have, like, to, go, they, see, you,* and *with.* Write each word on the board and have children read the word with you.

> **If...** children have difficulty reading the words,
> **then...** say a word and have children point to the word.
> Repeat several times, giving assistance as needed.

■ **Read** Have children read the story orally. Then have them reread the story several times individually.

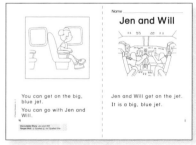

Reader's and Writer's Notebook, pp. 323–324

Objectives
- Isolate the initial sound in spoken one-syllable words.
- Identify the common sounds that letters represent.
- Read at least 25 high-frequency words from a commonly used list.

SI Strategic Intervention   DAY **2**

Phonemic Awareness•Phonics

■ **Discriminate /j/ and /w/** Display Phonics Songs and Rhymes Chart 25. Sing the song "Jill Jones Was a Juggler" to the tune of "The Itsy Bitsy Spider" with children. Ask them to jump when they hear a /j/ word and walk in place when they hear a /w/ word.

■ **Recognize *Jj* and *Ww*** Ask children to name words that begin with /j/ and /w/. List the words on chart paper as they say them. Have children echo read the list of words. Then ask children to take turns circling *j* and *w* in the words on the list.

Decodable Reader 25

■ **Review** Review the high-frequency words by writing *yellow* on the board. This is the word *yellow.* What word is this? Continue with the following words: *a, the, with, blue, go, green.*

> **If...** children have difficulty reading the words,
> **then...** say a word and have children point to the word. Repeat several times, giving assistance as needed.

■ **Read** Display the cover of *On a Jet* on p. 18 of *My Skills Buddy.* Ask a volunteer to read the first page of the story. Have children tell about each person's job. Continue through the story in this manner.

My Skills Buddy

More Reading

Use Leveled Readers or oth text at children's instruction level.

Objectives
- Isolate the initial sound in spoken one-syllable words.
- Identify the common sounds that letters represent.
- Read at least 25 high-frequency words from a commonly used list.
- Retell a main event from a story read aloud.

SI *Strategic Intervention*

DAY **3**

Phonemic Awareness•Phonics

- **Isolate Initial /j/ and /w/** Display the *jet* Picture Card. This is a jet. What is the first sound in *jet*? The first sound is /j/. Continue with *jam* and *jug*. The use the following Picture Cards to isolate initial /w/: *wig, wolf, web.*

- **Connect /j/ to Jj and /w/ to Ww** Write *Jj* on the board. These are the letters *Jj*. When I see *J or j*, I may say /j/. Write the word *jump* on the board and jump once. This is the word *jump. Jump* begins with /j/. Say it with me: /j/ /j/ /j/, *jump.* When you hear a word that begins with /j/, jump once. Use the following words: *jam, run, joy, job, jar, man, sit, July.* Repeat the routine for /w/ and have children wave when they hear a word that begins with /w/ from this list: *work, sleep, wet, will, girl, woman, doll, wait, wall.*

- **Blend Sounds** Write *job* on the board. Have children blend the sound of each letter to read the word. Repeat the routine with the words *will, jet,* and *win.*

- **Review High-Frequency Words** Write *green* on the board. Have volunteers say the word and use it in a sentence. Continue with the word *blue* and *yellow.*

- To practice phonics and high-frequency words, have children read Kindergarten Student Reader K.5.1. Use the instruction on pp. 56–57.

For a complete lesson plan and additional practice, see the **Leveled Reader Teaching Guide**.

Concept Literacy Reader K.5.1

- **Preview and Predict** Display the cover of the Concept Literacy Reader K.5.1. Point to the title of the book. The title of the book is *There It Goes!* What do you think the book is about? Have children tell about the picture and what they think the book might be about.

- **Set a Purpose** We talked about the title of the book. Let's read the book to learn about types of transportation. Have children read the Concept Literacy Reader.

- **Read** Provide corrective feedback as children read the book orally. During reading, ask them if they are able to confirm any of the predictions they made prior to reading.

If... children have difficulty reading the book individually,
then... read a sentence aloud as children point to each word. Then have the group reread the sentences as they continue pointing to the words.

- **Retell** Have children retell the content as you page through the book. Help them identify what the book is about. Also call attention to the how people get in or on these forms of transportation.

Concept Literacy Reader K.5.1

Objectives
- Identify the common sounds that letters represent.
- Predict what might happen next based on the title.
- Predict what might happen next based on the cover.
- Retell important facts in a text, heard or read.

 Strategic Intervention

DAY 4

Phonemic Awareness•Phonics

■ **Segmenting** Demonstrate segmenting *job,* /j/ /o/ /b/. Then lead children in segmenting these words: *won, wag, jot, jam.*

■ **Sing a Song** Write the following song on the board. Sing it to the tune of "Here We Go 'Round the Mulberry Bush." Have children sing it with you several times. Then have them trace a *w* in the air when they hear a /w/ word. Repeat the rhyme using the phrase "jog and jump." Children can trace a *j* in the air when they hear a /j/ word.

> This is the way we wash our windows
> Wash our windows, wash our windows.
> This is the way we wash our windows
> So early Wednesday morning.

Get Set, Roll! Reader 25

■ **Review** Review the following high-frequency words with children prior to reading the story: *yellow, blue, green, the, with,* and *go.*

■ **Teach Rebus Words** Write the word *street* on the board. This is the word *street.* Cars drive on a *street.* What else can drive on a street? Repeat the routine with the words *light, trucks,* and *heard.* These words are in the story we will read today. A picture above the word will help us read it.

Get Set, Roll! Reader 25

■ **Read** Display Get Set, Roll! Reader 25. Today we will read a new story. The title of the story is *Blue?* Where is the title on the story? Point to the title of the story. Look at the picture and think about the title. What do you think this story will be about?

> **If...** children have difficulty reading the story individually,
> **then...** read a sentence aloud as children point to each word. Then have the group reread the sentences as they continue pointing to the words.

■ **Reread** Use echo reading of *Blue?* to model fluent reading. Model where to pause, when to change pitch, and which words to stress. Then have children reread orally three to four times, or until they can read with few or no mistakes.

Objectives
• Identify the common sounds that letters represent.
• Read at least 25 high-frequency words from a commonly used list.
• Predict what might happen next based on the cover.

More Reading
Use Leveled Readers or oth▪ text at children's instruction▪ level.

SI *Strategic Intervention*

ore Reading

e Leveled Readers or other
t at children's instructional
el.

Phonics Review

■ **Recognize /j/ and /w/** Tell children you will tell them a story and they should listen for /j/ and /w/. When you say a word that begins with /j/, the children should do a jumping jack and repeat the word. When you say a word that begins with /w/, the children should wiggle around and repeat the word. Tell a simple story, emphasizing the initial /j/ and /w/ words and pausing to give children a chance to do a jumping jack or wiggle and repeat the word. *Jesse* is a *jazzy* dresser. He *wears wild jumpsuits* and a belt around his *waist* with *wacky words* on it. *Jesse jumps* and *wiggles* in his *wild* and *wacky jumpsuits!* Write *Jj* on the board. /j/ is spelled *J* or *j*. Write *Ww* on the board. /w/ is spelled *W* or *w*.

Listen to Me Reader K.5.1

■ **Preview and Predict** Display the cover of the book. The title of this story is *The Jet.* It is written by Grace Winslow. It is illustrated by Yoshiko Z. Jaeggi. Where can a jet take you? Who do you think is taking a trip on the jet? Tell me your ideas.

Listen to Me Reader K.5.1

■ **Set a Purpose** Review children's ideas. Point out that after they read, they will know more about riding a jet. Tell children that you will read the story with them. Follow along with your finger as I read. Then we will take turns reading this page. Repeat this routine through all of the pages. Guide children to decode words.

■ **Reread for Fluency** Use echo reading of Listen to Me Reader K.5.1 to model reading fluently. Use your oral reading to model for children when to pause, when to change pitch, and which words to stress. Then have children reread orally three to four times, or until they can read with few or no mistakes.

Objectives
• Identify the common sounds that letters represent.
• Predict what might happen next based on the cover.

OL On-Level — DAY 1

Phonemic Awareness•Phonics

- **Discriminate /j/** Display the *jet* Picture Card. This is a *jet*. *Jet* begins with /j/. Say it with me: /j/ /j/ /j/, *jet*. Then say the following words and have children tell which words begin with /j/: *jump, joy, run, junk, top, jolly, jeep.*

- **Blend Sounds** Write *Jim* on the board. Help me blend the sounds in this word to read it: /j/ /i/ /m/. The word is *Jim*. Repeat the routine with the words *job* and *jab*.

Objectives
- Blend spoken phonemes to form one-syllable words.
- Identify the common sounds that letters represent.

OL On-Level — DAY 2

Phonemic Awareness•Phonics

- **Discriminate /w/** Wave your hand. What am I doing? I am waving. The word *wave* has /w/ at the beginning. Write *Ww* on the board. /w/ is spelled *W* or *w*. Say it with me: /w/ /w/ /w/, *wave*. When I say a word that starts with /w/, I want you to wave. Use the following words: *worry, happy, want, wish, hope, wallet, purse, hat, wig.*

- **High-Frequency Words** Display the following word cards: *yellow, blue, green, from, go, here.* Say the word *yellow* and select a child to point to the word. Have children say the word and use it in a sentence. Continue with the other words.

Objectives
- Isolate the initial sound in spoken one-syllable words.
- Read at least 25 high-frequency words from a commonly used list.

Pacing Small Group Instruction

5 Day Plan

DAY 1	• Phonemic Awarenes: Phonics • Decodable Story 25
DAY 2	• Phonemic Awarene: Phonics • High-Frequency Wo • Decodable Reader 2
DAY 3	• Phonemic Awareness Phonics • Kindergarten Studer Reader K.5.1
DAY 4	• Get Set, Roll! Reader 25
DAY 5	• Phonics Review • Reread Leveled Boo

3 or 4 Day Plan

DAY 1	• Phonemic Awarenes: Phonics • Decodable Story 25
DAY 2	• Phonemic Awarenes Phonics • High-Frequency Wor • Decodable Reader 2
DAY 3	• Phonemic Awarenes Phonics • Kindergarten Studen Reader K.5.1
DAY 4	• Get Set, Roll! Reader 25

3 Day Plan: Eliminate the shaded box.

More Practice

For additional practice with this week's phonics skills, have children reread the Decodable Story (Day 1) and the Decodable Reader (Day :

OL On-Level

DAY 3

Phonemic Awareness•Phonics

■ **Discriminate /j/ and /w/** Draw four jugs and four glasses of water on the board. Gather about twelve Picture Cards, including the following *j* and *w* cards: *jam, jet, jug, juice, web, wig, wolf, woman.* Mix the cards and display them one at a time. Have a child name the picture. If the name has initial /j/, have the child write a lowercase *j* in one of the jars. If the name has initial /w/, have the child write a lowercase *w* in one of the glasses of water.

Kindergarten Student Reader K.5.1

■ **Preview and Predict** Display the cover of the book. The title of this story is *Jan and Jem Win!* Look at the cover. What kind of game are they playing? What does it mean to *win?* Tell me what you think will happen in this story.

■ **Introduce Rebus Word** Write the word *pink* on the board. This is the word *pink.* Name the letters with me: *p, i, n, k, pink. Pink* is a color. What is something in the classroom that is *pink?* Look for this word in our story. There will be a picture above it to help us read the word.

Kindergarten Student Reader K.5.1

■ **Set a Purpose** Review the list of things children think might happen in the story. Remind children they will read to find out what Jan and Jem win.

■ **Read** Have children follow along as they read the story with you. After reading p. 3, ask children to tell what kind of game Jem is playing. Continue with each page. Ask the following questions:

  • What are they trying to win?

  • How do you play the game?

■ **Summarize** Have children retell the story to a partner and tell what Jan and Jem win at the end.

■ **Text to Self** Help children make personal connections to the story as they tell about a game they like to play.

Objectives
• Identify the common sounds that letters represent.
• Predict what might happen next based on the cover.
• Make connections to own experiences.

More Reading

Use Leveled Readers or o...
text at children's instructio...
level to develop fluency.

OL On-Level — DAY 4

Get Set, Roll! Reader 25

■ **Review** Review the words *go, the, with, yellow, green,* and *blue* by writing each word on the board and saying the word with children. Then give clues to a word and have children tell which word it is.

■ **Review Rebus Words** Write *light* on the board and read the word with children. This is the word *light.* Point to the lights in the classroom. These are the lights in our classroom. When the lights are on, we can see what we are doing. Where are there lights when we are driving? Repeat the routine with the words *heard, street,* and *trucks.* Remember, there will be a picture above these words to help us read them.

■ **Read** Display Get Set, Roll! Reader 25, *Blue?* Point to the title of the story. What is the title of the story? *Blue?* is the title of the story. We will read /j/ and /w/ words in this story. Let's read the story together.

Objectives
• Read at least 25 high-frequency words from a commonly used list.

OL On-Level — DAY 5

Phonics Review

■ **Jump for *Jj*** Write uppercase and lowercase letters on index cards, including the uppercase *J* and lowercase *j*. Mix the cards. I am going to show you some letters one at a time. When you see a letter you know, I want you to say the name of the letter. But if you see a *J* or *j*, don't name the letter—say the /j/ sound for the letter, and jump! Show the letters one at a time, giving children a chance to jump if they see *j* and to name the other letters. Repeat the activity with "Walk for *Ww.*"

Objectives
• Identify upper-case letters.
• Identify lower-case letters.
• Identify the common sounds that letters represent.

cing Small up Instruction

Day Plan

1
- Phonemic Awareness/ Phonics
- Decodable Story 25

2
- Phonics
- Spelling
- Decodable Reader 25

3
- Independent Reader K.5.1 or Kindergarten Student Reader K.5.1

4
- Get Set, Roll! Reader 25 or Kindergarten Student Reader K.5.1

5
- Fluency/Comprehension
- Independent Reader K.5.1

or 4 Day Plan

1
- Phonemic Awareness/ Phonics
- Decodable Story 25

2
- Phonics
- Spelling
- Decodable Reader 25

3
- Independent Reader K.5.1 or Kindergarten Student Reader K.5.1

4
- Get Set, Roll! Reader 25 or Kindergarten Student Reader K.5.1

Plan: Eliminate the shaded box.

re Practice

additional practice with week's phonics skills and evelop fluency, have chil- reread the Decodable ry (Day 1) and the codable Reader (Day 2).

A Advanced — DAY 1

Phonemic Awareness•Phonics

■ **Connect /j/ to Jj** Give each child a blank card to write the letters *Jj*. I am going to say some words. If the word begins with /j/, raise your *Jj* card. Listen carefully: *joyful Jesse.* Did you raise your *Jj* card for *joyful*? Did you raise your *Jj* card for *Jesse*? Let's try some more. Use the following words: *big jungle, jump rope; jug of juice; warm jacket.*

Objectives
- Isolate the initial sound in spoken one-syllable words.

A Advanced — DAY 2

Phonics•Spelling

■ **Connect /j/ to Jj and /w/ to Ww** Display the *Jj* Alphabet Card. What sound does *jaguar* begin with? What letter spells that sound? Repeat the routine with the *Ww* Alphabet Card.

■ **Spell Sounds** Give each child the following letter tiles: *e, g, i, j, m, n, o, t, w.* Listen to the sounds in the word *wet:* /w/ /e/ /t/, *wet.* What is the letter for /w/? It is *w.* Place your *w* tile in front of you. Continue with the remaining sounds.

Let's blend the sounds to read the word: /w/ /e/ /t/, *wet.* Have children use the word *wet* in a complete sentence. Then repeat the routine with the words *win, Jem, jog,* and *wig.*

Objectives
- Identify the common sounds that letters represent.
- Use letter-sound correspondences to spell consonant-vowel-consonant (CVC) words.

A **Advanced** DAY **3**

For a complete lesson plan and additional practice, see the **Leveled Reader Teaching Guide**.

Independent Reader K.5.1

■ **Practice High-Frequency Words** Write *blue* on the board. Have volunteers say the word and use it in a sentence. Continue with the word *green.*

■ **Activate Prior Knowledge** Remind children that there are many ways to travel from place to place. The children in the book ride a bus to get to the zoo. Encourage children to share their experiences riding a bus or using another form of transportation. Have you ever ridden a bus to the zoo?

■ **Realism and Fantasy** Display the cover of *The Bus Ride.* Have children discuss whether the story could really happen.

Independent Reader K.5.1

■ **Reread for Fluency** After rereading with children, model reading fluently for them. I am going to read this book aloud. I will read the words with no mistakes. I want you to read it aloud with me. Try to read the words just as I do.

Use echo reading of Independent Reader K.5.1 to model reading fluently. Use your oral reading to model for children where to pause, when to change pitch, and which words to stress. Then have children reread orally three to four times, or until they can read with few or no mistakes.

■ For more practice with phonics and high-frequency words and to develop fluency, have children read Kindergarten Student Reader K.5.1. Use the instruction on pp. 56–57.

More Reading
Use Leveled Readers or o text at children's instructi level.

Objectives
• Read at least 25 high-frequency words from a commonly used list.
• Identify content as realism or fantasy.

e Reading

eveled Readers or other
children's instructional

A *Advanced*   DAY **4**

Kindergarten Student Reader K.5.1

■ **Revisit Rebus Words** Write *pink* on the board. This is the word *pink*. What is something in our classroom that is pink?

■ **Reread** Use Kindergarten Student Reader K.5.1 to practice fluent reading.

■ **Text to Self** Ask children to think about something they have won. Jan and Jem win the games they play. They win prizes. I bet they are happy to win. How do you feel when you win something?

■ Have children read Get Set, Roll! Reader 25, *Blue?* Use the instruction on p. 83.

Kindergarten Student
Reader K.5.1

Objectives
• Read at least 25 high-frequency words from a commonly used list.
• Make connections to own experiences.

A *Advanced*   DAY **5**

Fluency•Comprehension

■ **Reread for Fluency** Use the Independent Reader K.5.1 to model reading fluently for children. I am going to read this selection aloud. I will read the words with no mistakes. I want you to read it aloud with me. Try to read the words just as I do.

■ **Comprehension** After children have finished reading, have them retell what happens in the selection. Then have children write or draw a picture of a real way to get to the zoo and make-believe way to get to the zoo.

Independent Reader K.5.1

Objectives
• Read at least 25 high-frequency words from a commonly used list.
• Identify content as realism or fantasy.

DAY 1

Concept Development

■ **Read the Concept Literacy Reader** To build background and vocabulary, read *There It Goes!*, pausing to discuss each page. Model sentence patterns and vocabulary that describe modes of transportation. These people are riding in a car. There are four people riding in the car. On a second reading, invite children to talk about the mode of transportation on each page.

■ **Develop Oral Language** Revisit *There It Goes!*, pointing out the different modes of transportation people use. Then have children sing the following song with you to the tune of "Frère Jacques":

> Rolling buses, rolling buses,
> Flying planes, flying planes,
> Any place that you know,
> Little cars and boats go,
> Row, row, row. Row, row, row.

Phonemic Awareness/Phonics

■ **Frontload Words with /j/** Have children look at the picture on pp. 12–13 of *My Skills Buddy*. This picture shows monkeys playing in the jungle. What do you know about the jungle? Listen to the word *jungle*. What sound does *jungle* begin with? *Jungle* begins with /j/; /j/, *jungle*. Then sing the following song to the tune of "Baa, Baa, Black Sheep" to introduce picture words beginning with /j/: *Monkey, monkey in the tree—do you have some juice for me?* What other words start with /j/? Have children point to the juice in the picture. *Juice* begins with /j/ /j/ /j/. What sound does juice begin with? Let's see what else the monkeys have. Repeat the activity with other words in the picture that begin with /j/.

■ **Connect /j/ to Jj** Use letter tiles to display the word *jet* or write it on the board. This word is *jet*: /j/ /e/ /t/, *jet*. Say the word with me. Have children write the word *jet* and circle the letter that makes /j/. Write and read aloud the following sentence: *Juicy fruits make jam, jelly, and juice.* Point to the *j* in *juicy* and ask: What letter is this? Yes, this is *j*. Repeat for *jam, jelly,* and *juice*.

Content Objective
• Develop content knowle related to transportation

Language Objectives
• Understand and use grade-level content area vocabulary.

• Recognize the sounds o English.

Concept Literacy Reader K.5.1

Daily Planner

DAY 1	• Concept Developm • Phonemic Awarene Phonics • Listening Comprehension
DAY 2	• Comprehension • Vocabulary
DAY 3	• Phonemic Awarene Phonics • Conventions
DAY 4	• Phonemic Awarene Phonics • Concepts and Oral Language
DAY 5	• Language Worksho • Writing

 tent Objective

derstand realism and
tasy.

guage Objective

arn and use academic
cabulary.

ls Buddy, pp. 14–15

Learning Strategies

iew Have children study
llustrations on pp. 14–15
y Skills Buddy to preview
stic and fantasy details.
er the right half of the
e. What do you see? (a
What color is the fish?
d) What does the fish live
a fishbowl) What is the
doing? (swimming) Now
er the left half of the page.
t do you see here? (a
sroom underwater) Who
e teacher? (a fish)

Listening Comprehension: Realism and Fantasy

■ **Provide Scaffolding** Discuss the illustrations on pp. 14–15 in *My Skills Buddy* to frontload vocabulary. Point to the illustration on p. 14. This illustration shows realism, or something that could really happen. A fish can really swim in a fishbowl. Then point to the illustration on p. 15. This illustration shows fantasy, or something that could not really happen. A fish cannot really teach a class. Compare the fish in the underwater school to a real fish and to a real classroom in your school.

■ **Prepare for the Read Aloud** The modified Read Aloud below prepares children for listening to the oral reading "Going to the Moon" on p. 27.

Read Aloud

Going to the Moon

    Katie and Zach are going to the airport. They are going with their dad. Their mom is at the airport.

    "Dad," Katie asks, "can we stop and watch the planes?"

    "Sure," Dad says. "Let's do that."

    "Will we see a rocket ship?" Zach asks.

    Dad says rockets don't take off from the airport.

    "Do only rockets go to the moon?" Zach asks. "Can a bike go there?"

    Dad and Katie laugh. "Bikes that go to the moon are make-believe." Katie says. "It's like saying your teddy bear is an astronaut!"

    Zach clutches his bear. "Teddy could fly to the moon," he says.

■ **First Listening** Write the title of the Read Aloud on the board. This is about Katie and Zach. They go to the airport. Listen to find out what they learn about rocket ships. After reading: Who goes to the airport? Why do they go there? Why can't a bike go to the moon?

■ **Second Listening** Write the words *rocket ship* and *bike* on the board. As you listen to the story, think about what can go to the moon. After reading, ask children to tell what a rocket can do. Repeat the routine for *bike*. Then have children tell what a bike cannot do.

Objectives

• Read linguistically accommodated content area material with a decreasing need for linguistic accommodations as more English is learned. • Use visual and contextual support to enhance and confirm understanding needed to comprehend increasingly challenging language.

 **DAY 2**

Comprehension

■ **Provide Scaffolding** Display *Max Takes the Train*. Lead a detailed picture walk through the story, naming what you see in the illustrations and describing what is happening. Use gestures and facial expressions to convey meaning. Focus on the following:

• **Set the Scene** Use the cover of the Big Book to help children understand that part of this story takes place on a train. A train rides on rails. It has many cars that are hooked together. People ride in the train cars. They take the train to places they want to go.

• **Frontload Vocabulary** Use the illustrations to introduce unfamiliar words and phrases in the text. The bunny has a pass. Look at this picture on page 4. He has a bus pass. When have you used a pass? Include other words such as *jetway* (p. 12) and *airport* (p. 15). Also point out expressions that are specific to going places, such as *Where to?* (p. 7) and *Let's go!* (p. 17). Read and discuss words *Whamburger* (p. 2) and *Air-O-Zoom* (p. 12). Explain that these are made-up for this story.

Vocabulary: Transportation Words

■ **Frontload Vocabulary** Have children turn to p. 28 of *My Skills Buddy*. Talk about what is happening in each picture, using the transportation words *train, truck, airplane,* and *boat*. This is an airplane. The airplane has wings. People fly in the airplane. Then invite children to talk about the pictures using the transportation words.

■ **Provide Scaffolding** Write the words *train, truck, airplane,* and *boat* on the board. Read the words aloud. These words tell us about ways people travel. Point to the word *airplane*. Who can tell something about an airplane? Invite children to tell one thing they know about airplanes. Repeat with the other transportation words.

■ **Practice** Have children work in pairs. Assign one of the transportation words (*train, truck, airplane,* or *boat*) to each pair. One child should act out one of the transportation words. The partner should say a sentence about what the first child is doing: *Jonah is driving a truck*.

Content Objective
• Develop background knowledge.

Language Objective
• Learn and use transporta[tion] words.

Use Learning Strategi[es]
Remind children that if they have trouble relating sound[s,] objects, and motions to transportation words, they [can] ask their partners for help. [For] further understanding, have partners share prior experiences with transportation. [For] example: Tell about a time when you rode on a train o[r] an airplane.

Big Book

Objectives
• Use prior knowledge to understand meanings in English. • Learn new expressions heard during classroom instruction and interactions. • Use support from peers and teachers to enhance and confirm understanding needed to comprehend increasingly challenging language.

tent Objective

se learning strategies.

guage Objectives

nnect /j/ with *Jj* and
/ with *Ww*.

se questions.

Transfer Skills

nouncing /j/ Explain that
er languages use sounds
lar to /j/, including /sh/,
and /ch/. Point out that
n children say /h/, they
uld hear their voice, but
sounds like /sh/ and
, speakers do not use their
ce. Pronounce word pairs
h as *jam/sham* and *Jill/*
, and have children repeat
r you.

Learning Strategies

children understand that
stions often begin with
h- word. For example,
ere is the bus? Other *wh-*
rds are *who, what, when,*
why. When students see
of these words at the
inning of a sentence, they
be sure the sentence is
ing a question.

ELL *English Language Learners*

DAY 3

Phonemic Awareness/Phonics

■ **Isolate Initial /w/** Help children hear /w/ in words by saying words that contain the sound: *well, will, wet.* Emphasize the /w/ in each word. Next, segment and blend each word: /w/ /e/ /l/, *well.*

■ **/j/ Spelled *Jj* and /w/ Spelled *Ww*** Use letter tiles to spell the words *jet* and *job.* Call on children to read the words. What sound does the *j* make in these words? Read each word aloud and confirm that *j* makes /j/. Then use the tiles to spell *wet* and *win.* Have children read the words. What sound does *w* make in these words? Confirm that it makes /w/.

Conventions: Questions

■ **Provide Scaffolding** Point to the image on p. 7 of *Max Takes the Train.* There are signs in this picture. One sign shows a train. Where are the bunnies going? They are going on a train. The word *where* asks a question. Invite children to think of a question that begins with *where.* Remind them that questions often begin with *wh-* words. What are some other *wh-* words?

■ **Practice** What questions might the bunnies ask? Lead a picture walk through the Big Book and have children think of questions that relate to each picture. Encourage children to begin their questions with *wh-* words. Point out *Where to?* (p. 7) and *Where are you?* (p. 21).

Beginning/Intermediate Point to the illustration on pp. 2–3. On the board write *Wh___ is he reading?* Read aloud the question and have a child choose a *wh-* word to complete the sentence. (*What*) Repeat the activity using other pictures in the story.

Advanced/Advanced-High Have children look at the illustrations and ask *Wh-* questions about the different modes of transportation. Remind children to ask for help if they have trouble thinking of content-related questions.

Objectives
• Internalize new academic language by using and reusing it in meaningful ways in speaking activities that build concept and language attainment. • Develop repertoire of learning strategies commensurate with grade-level learning expectations. • Decode (sound out) words using a combination of skills.

 ELL English Language Learners

DAY 4

Phonemic Awareness/Phonics

■ **Review /e/** To review /e/, ask a question with words that contain initial and medial /e/: When did Ed get the egg from the nest? Then remind children that some words have /e/ in the middle, and others have /e/ at the beginning. Repeat the question a few words at a time, and have children chorally repeat after you. Listen to these words: *when, Ed, get, egg, nest.* Which words start with /e/? Which words have /e/ in the middle?

■ **/e/ Spelled Ee** Show the words *end, jet, elk,* and *best* with letter tiles or by writing on the board. Model reading the words, isolating /e/ and pointing out *Ee.* Show all the sound-letter correspondences (for example, /e/ /n/ /d/ = *end*).

Concepts and Oral Language

■ **Revisit Talk with Me Chart 25A** Display the chart. Have students describe the images in the photos. Help them by asking *wh-* questions about ways the different objects move and how the settings in each picture are different.

■ **Develop Oral Language** Introduce language patterns that help describe the types of transportation on Talk with Me Chart 25A. Write this sentence frame on the board: *The _____ flies in the sky.* What flies in the sky? (plane) Where does the plane fly? (in the sky) Use *wh-* questions to discuss the pictures in the chart. What do passengers use to get on a plane? (the jetway) Then add this sentence frame: *I ride _____ the _____.* Now let's use this sentence pattern to talk about the pictures. *I ride in the sidecar.* Would you ride *on* the sidecar? (no) Have children suggest other sentences using the sentence frames. Then change the verb. In place of *ride,* repeat the exercise using the verbs *fly* and *sit.* Then play a game with students in which you ask a question about the pictures. Which picture shows a train in the subway? Have children point to the correct picture and then answer your question with a sentence, such as *This picture shows a train in the subway.*

 Leveled Support

Beginning Have children repeat the question you ask. Let them take a turn pointing to a picture on the chart.

Intermediate Ask *wh-* questions to help children notice more details about the pictures, such as Who is riding in the sidecar?

Advanced/Advanced-High Encourage children to use their prior knowledge about transportation to think of other words that describe the pictures, such as *engine, ticket,* or *helmet.*

Content Objectives
- Develop oral language.
- Use learning strategies.

Language Objectives
- Connect /e/ with *Ee.*
- Learn English language patterns.

Use Learning Strategie
Work with children to create a concept map titled *How D Different Machines Move?* Include these categories: *F Float, Roll.*

Talk with Me Chart 25A

DAY 5

Language Workshop: Talk About the Story

- **Introduce and Model** Display pp. 2–3 of *Max Takes the Train*. Look at this picture. What is happening? (Max is pointing.) Max sees a Whamburger in the paper. How does he feel? (excited) What does Max want to do? (get a Whamburger) Explain to children that the events in a story happen in order, or in a sequence. Tell them that it is often helpful to use the words *first, next,* and *last* when retelling the events of a story. First, Max sees the Whamburger. Then Max and Uncle Bunny go to the bus stop.

- **Practice** On the board, create a flowchart detailing the events of *Max Takes the Train,* beginning with the bunnies at the bus stop. *Where do they go?* (the city) Add each successive event to the flowchart to illustrate sequence. Look at the picture on pages 8–9. Where are the bunnies? (on the train) Look at the picture on page 11. Where are the bunnies now? (on the boat) Look at the picture on page 12. Where do you think the bunnies go next? (on a plane) Turn to the picture on pages 16–17. What are the bunnies doing? (riding the subway) What happens next? (They get ice cream.) Turn to page 22. What is happening? (Ruby rides her bike.) What happens last? (They all go home.)

Writing: Write About *Max Takes the Train*

- **Prepare for Writing** We have talked about ways people travel. Now let's write about it. Have each child fold a piece of paper in half, creating a four-page book.

- **Create Sentences About Transportation** Have children draw a boat on the first page of their book. Write the word *boat* and have children copy the word under their drawing. Have them copy the sentence frame *Boats go _____.* Have children write or dictate a motion, place, or sound to complete the sentence frame. Continue the activity with other forms of transportation, using the remaining three pages. Have children share their sentences and drawings.

Beginning Write the sentence frames for children and have them write or dictate words to complete the sentences.

Intermediate Guide children in copying the sentence frames and writing words to complete the sentences.

Advanced/Advanced-High Encourage children to write sentences on their own. Have children help less-proficient partners complete their sentences.

Content Objectives
- Understand *Max Takes the Train.*
- Practice sequence of events.

Language Objectives
- Retell story events through speaking and writing.
- Write using grade-level vocabulary.

Monitor and Self-Correct
- Remind children that if they don't know how to write the words, they can see if the words on the class chart will help them.

Home Language Support
- Invite children to share ideas in their home languages before creating their sentences.

Objectives
- Monitor written language production and employ self-corrective techniques or other resources.
- Expand and internalize initial English vocabulary by retelling simple stories and basic information represented or supported by pictures. • Narrate with increasing specificity and detail as more English is acquired.

My Planning Guide

This Week's ELL Overview

Grade K • Unit 5 • Week 2
Mayday! Mayday!
105–210
and DI•29–DI•34

ELL Handbook

- Maximize Literacy and Cognitive Engagement
- Research Into Practice
- Full Weekly Support for Every Selection

   Mayday! Mayday!
   - Routines to Support Instruction

- Transfer Activities
- Professional Development

Daily Leveled ELL Notes

ELL notes appear throughout this week's instruction and ELL Support is on the DI pages of your Teacher's Edition. The following is a sample of an ELL note from this week.

English Language Learners

Beginning Build Background Use the pictures on Talk with Me/ Sing with Me Chart 26A to help children understand words such as *yacht* and *shimmering.*

Intermediate Vocabulary Development Walk children through *Fox Can Fix It!* Have them identify Pig, Fox, Cat, and Ox in the story. Display a word card for each of these characters and have a child match each card with an appropriate picture.

Advanced Support High-Frequency Words Have children copy the high-frequency words *yellow, blue,* and *green* with a crayon of the matching color. Matching the words with their visual representations will help English learners remember them.

Advanced High Access Content Encourage children to act out a selection event (effect) and tell why it happens (cause). If they have difficulty coming up with English words, supply the word and have them repeat it in their sentence.

ELL by Strand

The ELL lessons on this week's Support for English Language Learners pages are organized by strand. They offer additional scaffolding for the core curriculum. Leveled support notes on these pages address the different proficiency levels in your class. See pages DI•29–DI•34.

ELL Guy
Dr. Jim Cummins

The Three Pillars of ELL Instruction

ELL Strands	Activate Prior Knowledge	Access Content	Extend Language
Vocabulary p. DI•31	Frontload Vocabulary	Provide Scaffolding	Practice
Reading Comprehension p. DI•31	Provide Scaffolding	Set the Scene	Frontload Vocabulary
Phonics, Spelling, and Word Analysis pp. DI•29, DI•32–DI•33	Frontload Words with /ks/	Isolate Final /ks/	Review /j/ and /w/
Listening Comprehension p. DI•30	Prepare for the Read Aloud	First Listening	Second Listening
Conventions and Writing pp. DI•32, DI•34	Provide Scaffolding/ Introduce and Model	Practice	Leveled Practice Activities/ Leveled Writing Activities
Concept Development p. DI•29	Read the Concept Literacy Reader	Read the Concept Literacy Reader	Develop Oral Language

This Week's Practice Stations Overview

Six Weekly Practice Stations with Leveled Activities can be found at the beginning of each week of instruction. For this week's Practice Stations, see pp. 112–113.

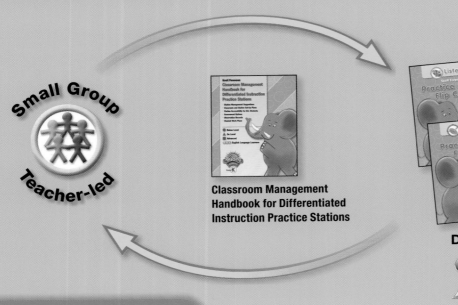

Small Group — Teacher-led

Classroom Management Handbook for Differentiated Instruction Practice Stations

Practice Stations

Daily Leveled Center Activities

○ Below   ▢ Advanced

△ On-Level   Ⓔ Ⓛ Ⓛ

Practice Stations Flip Charts

	Listen Up	Word Work	Words to Know	Let's Write	Read for Meaning	Let's Make Art
Objectives	• Identify words with /w/.	• Identify words with /w/. • Build words with /w/.	• Identify and use words for transportation.	• Write a caption for a picture.	• Tell what is real and what is make-believe in a story.	• Draw types of transportation.
Materials	• *Listen Up* Flip Chart Activity 26 • Picture Cards: *waffle, wagon, web, wig, wolf* • paper, pencil, crayons	• *Word Work* Flip Chart Activity 26 • Alphabet Cards • Picture Cards • Letter Tiles	• *Words to Know* Flip Chart Activity 26 • Picture Cards: *train, truck, bus, boat, jet* • Teacher-made Word Cards: *train, truck, jet, boat, bus* • paper, pencils	• *Let's Write* Flip Chart Activity 26 • Picture Cards: *boat, bus, jet, taxi, train, truck, van* • paper, pencil	• *Read for Meaning* Flip Chart Activity 26 • Little Book *Max Takes the Train* • Trade Book *Mayday! Mayday!*	• *Let's Make Art* Flip Chart Activity 26 • Leveled Readers • Picture Cards • colored pencils • crayons • paper

This Week on Reading Street!

 Question of the Week

What kinds of transportation help us in an emergency?

Going Places

Daily Plan

Don't Wait Until Friday

Whole Group

◉ /ks/ Spelled *Xx*
◉ Cause and Effect
• Vocabulary

MONITOR PROGRESS | **Success Predictor**

Day 1	Day 2	Day 3	Day 4	Day 5
Check Phonemic Awareness	Check Sound-Spelling/ Retelling	Check Word Reading	Check Phonemic Awareness	Check Oral Vocabulary

Small Group

 Teacher-Led

• Reading Support
• Skill Support
• Fluency Practice

Practice Stations

Independent Activities

Customize Literacy More support for a Balanced Literacy approach, see pp. CL•1–CL•31.

Whole Group

• Writing
• Conventions: Question Marks and Uppercase Letters
• Listening and Speaking

Assessment

• Day 5 Assessment for Phonics
• Day 5 Assessment for Comprehension

You Are Here! Unit 5 Week 2

This Week's Reading Selections

Trade Book
Genre: **Nonfiction**

Decodable Reader 26

Leveled Readers

Get Set Roll! Reader 26

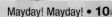

Resources on Reading Street!

	Build Concepts	Phonemic Awareness and Phonics	Vocabulary
Whole Group	Talk With Me/ Sing With Me	Student Edition pp. 32–33 Student Edition p. 36	Student Edition p. 37 Student Edition p. 48
Go Digital	• Concept Talk Video • Sing with Me Animations	• eReaders	
Small Group and Independent Practice	Practice Station Flip Chart Leveled Readers	Practice Station Flip Chart Decodable Reader 26 Leveled Readers Get Set, Roll! Reader 26	Practice Station Flip Chart Student Edition p. 37
 **Go Digital**	• eReaders	• eReaders • Letter Tile Drag and Drop	
Customize Literacy	• Leveled Readers	• Decodable Reader	• High-Frequency Word Cards
Go Digital	• Concept Talk Video • Big Question Video • eReaders	• eReaders	• Sing with Me Animations

Comprehension

Student Edition
pp. 34–35

Trade Book

- Envision It! Animations

Practice Station
Flip Chart

Leveled Readers

Get Set, Roll!
Reader 26

- Envision It! Animations
- eReaders

- Leveled Readers

- Envision It! Animations
- eReaders

Fluency

Decodable
Reader 26

Kdg. Student
Reader K.5.2

Get Set, Roll!
Reader 26

- eReaders

Practice Station
Flip Chart

Leveled Readers

- eReaders

- Leveled Readers

- eReaders

Conventions and Writing

Reader's and
Writer's Notebook

- Grammar Jammer

Practice Station
Flip Chart

Reader's and
Writer's Notebook

- Grammar Jammer

- *Reader's and Writer's Notebook*

- Grammar Jammer

You Are Here!
Unit 5
Week 2

My 5-Day Planner for Reading Street!

Don't Wait Until Friday
MONITOR PROGRESS

Check Phonemic Awareness

Day 1 pages 114–129

Check Sound-Spelling/Retelling

Day 2 pages 130–147

Get Ready to Read

Concept Talk, 114
Oral Vocabulary, 115
rescue, pilot, yacht, sailor, mechanic, shimmering
Phonemic Awareness, 116–117
◉ Final /ks/
Phonics, 118–119
◉ /ks/ Spelled Xx
Handwriting, 120 Letters X and x
High-Frequency Words, 121 Introduce
yellow, blue, green
READ Decodable Story 26, 122–123

Concept Talk, 130
Oral Vocabulary, 131 rescue, pilot
Phonemic Awareness, 132–133
◉ Final /ks/
Phonics, 134–135
◉ /ks/ Spelled Xx
Handwriting, 136 Words with Xx
High-Frequency Words, 137 yellow, blue, green
READ Decodable Reader 26, 138–139

Read and Comprehend

Listening Comprehension, 124–125
◉ Cause and Effect

Listening Comprehension, 140
◉ Cause and Effect
READ Trade Book—First Read, 140
Mayday! Mayday!
Retell, 141
Think, Talk, and Write, 142

Language Arts

Conventions, 126 Question Marks and Capital Letters
Writing, 127 Wonderful, Marvelous Me!
Daily Handwriting, 127 Letters X and x
Listening and Speaking, 128
Drama—Respond to Literature
Wrap Up Your Day, 128
Extend Your Day!, 129

Conventions, 143 Question Marks and Capital Letters
Writing, 144 Respond to Literature
Daily Handwriting, 144 Letters X and x
Vocabulary, 145 Position Words
Wrap Up Your Day, 146
Extend Your Day!, 147

You Are Here!
Unit 5
Week 2

Check Word Reading	Check Phonemic Awareness	Check Oral Vocabulary
Day 3 pages 148–183	**Day 4** pages 184–195	**Day 5** pages 196–209
Concept Talk, 148 **Oral Vocabulary,** 149 *yacht, sailor* **Phonemic Awareness,** 150–151 ◉ Final /ks/ **Phonics,** 152–153 ◉ /ks/ Spelled *Xx* **READ Kindergarten Student Reader K.5.2,** 154–155	**Concept Talk,** 184 **Oral Vocabulary,** 185 *mechanic, shimmering* Review **Phonemic Awareness,** 186 /j/ and /w/ Review **Phonics,** 187 /j/ Spelled *Jj*, /w/ Spelled *Ww* **Spelling,** 188 ◉ /ks/ Spelled *Xx* **READ Get Set, Roll! Reader 26,** 189	**Concept Wrap Up,** 196 **Oral Vocabulary,** 197 *rescue, pilot, yacht, sailor, mechanic, shimmering* Review **Phonemic Awareness,** 198 ◉ /ks/ Review **Phonics,** 199 ◉ /ks/ Spelled *Xx* **Assessment,** 200–201 Monitor Progress
Comprehension, 156–157 ◉ Cause and Effect **READ Trade Book—Second Read,** 158–177 *Mayday! Mayday!*	**Comprehension,** 190 ◉ Cause and Effect Review Sequence **READ Trade Book—Third Read,** 191 *Mayday! Mayday!*	**Let's Practice It!,** 202–203 Fable **Assessment,** 204–205 Monitor Progress
Conventions, 178 Questions **Writing,** 179 Genre: Rhyme **Daily Handwriting,** 179 Letters *X* and *x* **Listening and Speaking,** 180–181 Drama—Respond to Literature **Wrap Up Your Day,** 182 **Extend Your Day!,** 183	**Conventions,** 192 Question Marks and Capital Letters **Writing,** 193 Extend the Concept **Daily Handwriting,** 193 Letters *X* and *x* **Vocabulary,** 194 Position Words **Wrap Up Your Day,** 194 **Extend Your Day!,** 195	Review **Conventions,** 206 Question Marks and Capital Letters **Writing,** 207 This Week We… **Daily Handwriting,** 207 Letters *X* and *x* **Wrap Up Your Week!,** 208 What kinds of transportation help us in an emergency? **Extend Your Day!,** 209

Grouping Options for Differentiated Instruction
Turn the page for the small group time lesson plan.

Planning Small Group Time on Reading Street!

SMALL GROUP TIME RESOURCES

DAY 1

Look for this Small Group Time box each day to help meet the individual needs of all your children. Differentiated instruction lessons appear on the DI pages at the end of each week.

Teacher-Led

SI Strategic Intervention	OL On-Level	A Advanced
Teacher-Led	**Teacher-Led**	**Teacher-Led**
• Phonemic Awareness and Phonics	• Phonemic Awareness and Phonics	• Phonemic Awareness and Phonics
Reread Decodable Story	**Reread** Decodable Story	**Reread** Decodable Story for Fluency

ELL Place English language learners in the groups that correspond to their reading abilities in English.

Practice Stations
- Listen Up
- Word Work

Independent Activities
- Read Independently
- *Reader's and Writer's Notebook*
- Concept Talk Video

ELL

ELL Poster 26

Day 1

SI Strategic Intervention	**Phonemic Awareness and Phonics,** DI•18 **Reread** Decodable Story 26, DI•18
OL On-Level	**Phonemic Awareness and Phonics,** DI•23 **Reread** Decodable Story 26, DI•23
A Advanced	**Phonemic Awareness and Phonics,** DI•26 **Reread** Decodable Story 26 for Fluency, DI•26
ELL English Language Learners	DI•29–DI•30 Frontload Concept Phonemic Awareness and Phonics Comprehension Skill

Reading Street Response
to Intervention Kit

Reading Street Leveled
Practice Stations Kit

Question of the Week
What kinds of transportation help us in an emergency?

SI Strategic Intervention

Listen to Me Reader

Decodable
Reader

We Help
Concept Literacy Reader

Get Set, Roll! Reader

OL On-Level

Our Boat

Kindergarten
Student Reader

Get Set, Roll! Reader

Decodable Reader

A Advanced

The Boat Ride

Independent
Reader

Decodable Reader

Small Group Weekly Plan

Day 2	Day 3	Day 4	Day 5
Phonemic Awareness and Phonics, DI•19 Reread Decodable Reader 26, DI•19	**Phonemic Awareness and Phonics,** DI•20 Read Concept Literacy Reader K.5.2, DI•20	**Phonemic Awareness and Phonics,** DI•21 Read Get Set, Roll! Reader 26, DI•21	**Phonics Review,** DI•22 Read Listen to Me Reader K.5.2, DI•22
Phonemic Awareness and Phonics, DI•23 Reread Decodable Reader 26, DI•23	**Phonemic Awareness and Phonics,** DI•24 Read Kindergarten Student Reader K.5.2, DI•24	**Review Phonics and High-Frequency Words** Read Get Set, Roll! Reader 26, DI•25	**Phonics Review,** DI•25 Reread Leveled Books, DI•25
Phonics and Spelling, DI•26 Reread Decodable Reader 26 for Fluency, DI•28	Read Independent Reader K.5.2 or Kindergarten Student Reader K.5.2, DI•27	Read Get Set, Roll! Reader 26 or Reread Kindergarten Student Reader K.5.2, DI•28	**Fluency and Comprehension,** DI•28 Reread Independent Reader K.5.2 for Fluency, DI•28
DI•31 Comprehension Skill Frontload Vocabulary	DI•32 Review Phonemic Awareness and Phonics Scaffold Conventions	DI•33 Review Phonemic Awareness and Phonics Concept and Oral Language	DI•34 Language Workshop Writing

Mayday! Mayday! •

Practice Stations for Everyone on Reading Street!

Listen Up!

Objectives
- Identify words with /w/.

Materials
Listen Up! Flip Chart Activity 26

Picture Cards: waffle, wagon, web, wig, wolf, boat, lemon, otter, taxi, and zebra

paper, pencil, crayons

Differentiated Activities

🔵 Find the Picture Card for *wig*. Say the sound you hear at the beginning of *wig*. Find another Picture Card that begins with the same sound as *wig*.

🔺 Find the Picture Card for *wig*. Say the sound you hear at the beginning of *wig*. Find all the Picture Cards that begin with the same sound as *wig*.

🟥 Find the Picture Card for *wig*. Say the sound you hear at the beginning. Find other Picture Cards that begin like *wig*. Draw pictures of other things that begin like *wig*.

Technology
- Letter Tile Drag and Drop

Word Work
/w/ Spelled *Ww*

Objectives
- Identify words with /w/
- Build words with /w/

Materials
- *Word Work* Flip Chart Activity 26
- Alphabet Cards
- Picture Cards
- Letter Tiles

Differentiated Activities

🔵 Find the *Ww* Alphabet Card. Say the picture name: *watermelon*. Look for Picture Cards that begin like *watermelon*.

🔺 Find the *Ww* Alphabet Card. Say the picture name: *watermelon*. Find Picture Cards that begin like *watermelon*. Then look around the room for other objects that begin the same.

🟥 Find the *Ww* Alphabet Card. Say the picture name: *watermelon*. Find Picture Cards that begin like *watermelon*. Then look around the room for other objects that begin the same. Use Letter Tiles to spell others words that begin with /w/.

Technology
- Letter Tile Drag and Drop

Words To Know
Words for transportation

Objectives
- Identify and use words for transportation.

Materials
- *Words to Know* Flip Chart Activity 26
- Picture Cards: train, truck, bus, boat, jet and several picture cards that DO NOT show means of transportation
- Teacher-made word cards: *train, truck, jet, boat, bus*
- paper, pencils

Differentiated Activities

🔵 Choose the Picture Cards that show ways people go places. Say the name for each picture.

🔺 Choose the Picture Cards that show ways people go places. Match the Picture Cards with the Word Cards.

🟥 Match the Picture Cards and Word Cards that show how people go places. Write a sentence that tells about each Picture Card.

You Are Here! Unit 5 Week 2

Use this week's materials from the Reading Street Leveled Practice Stations Kit to organize this week's stations.

Key

● Below-Level Activities

▲ On-Level Activities

■ Advanced Activities

Practice Station Flip Chart

Let's Write!
Write a caption.

Objectives
• Write a caption for a picture.

Materials
• *Let's Write!* Flip Chart Activity 26
• Picture Cards: *boat, bus, jet, taxi, train, truck, van*
• paper, pencil

Differentiated Activities

● Choose a Picture Card. Tell what you see in the picture. Write about what you see.

▲ Choose a Picture Card. Tell what you see in the picture. Write a caption that tells the most important thing about the picture.

■ Choose three Picture Cards. Write a caption for each picture. Make sure the caption tells the important thing about each picture.

Read For Meaning
Realism and Fantasy.

Objectives
• Tell what is real and what is fantasy in a story.

Materials
• *Read for Meaning* Flip Chart Activity 26
• Little Book *Max Takes the Train*
• Trade Book *Mayday! Mayday!*

Differentiated Activities

A real story tells about something that can really happen. A fantasy story tells about something that cannot really happen.

● Look through *Max Takes the Train* with a partner. Discuss why this is a fantasy. Choose one of the pictures from the book and tell what you'd change so that the story could be real.

▲ Look at the pictures in *Mayday! Mayday!* Tell why you think this is probably a realistic story.

■ Think of other stories you have read. Were they fantasies like *Max Takes the Train* or realistic stories like *Mayday! Mayday!?* Tell how you know.

Let's Make Art!

Objectives
• Draw types of transportation

Materials
• *Let's Make Art!* Flip Chart Activity 26
• Leveled Readers
• Picture Cards [that show different kinds of transportation]
• colored pencils
• crayons
• paper

Differentiated Activities

● Look at the pictures in your book. Look at the Picture Cards. Think about the shapes and lines that artists use to draw pictures of transportation. Draw a picture of your favorite way to go places.

▲ Look at the pictures in your book. Look at the Picture Cards. How do artists use shapes, lines, and color when they draw pictures? Choose your favorite transportation. Draw a picture to show how it goes.

■ Look at the pictures in your book. Look at the Picture Cards. How do artists use shapes, lines, and color when they draw pictures? Draw a picture to show your favorite type of transportation. Use details to make your drawing better

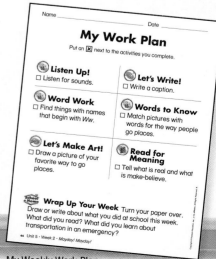

Name _____ Date _____

My Work Plan
Put an ☒ next to the activities you complete.

Listen Up!
☐ Listen for sounds.

Let's Write!
☐ Write a caption.

Word Work
☐ Find things with names that begin with *Ww*.

Words to Know
☐ Match pictures with words for the way people go places.

Let's Make Art!
☐ Draw a picture of your favorite way to go places.

Read for Meaning
☐ Tell what is real and what is make-believe.

Wrap Up Your Week Turn your paper over. Draw or write about what you did at school this week. What did you read? What did you learn about transportation in an emergency?

Unit 5 • Week 2 • *Mayday! Mayday!*

My Weekly Work Plan

bjectives
• Share information and ideas about the concept.

oday at a Glance

ral Vocabulary
scue, pilot, yacht, sailor, echanic, shimmering

nonemic Awareness
Final /ks/

nonics
/ks/ Spelled Xx

andwriting
and x

igh-Frequency Words
ellow, blue, green

omprehension
Cause and Effect

onventions
uestion Marks and Uppercase etters

Vriting
onderful, Marvelous Me!

stening and Speaking
espond to Literature: Drama

TRUCKTOWN on Reading Street

Start your engines! Display p. 13 of *Truckery Rhymes*.

• Read aloud "It's Raining, It's Pouring" and track the print.

• Reread the rhyme and have children say it with you.

• Ask children to identify the rhyming words. (*pouring, roaring; slid, lid*)

Truckery Rhymes

Concept Talk

Question of the Week

What kinds of transportation help us in an emergency?

Introduce the concept

To build concepts and to focus their attention, tell children that this week they will talk, sing, read, and write about **emergency transportation**. Write the question of the week and track the print as you read it.

Play the CD that features more information about Coast Guard rescues. What form of transportation is used? In what situations do people need help?

🔘 Background Building Audio

ROUTINE   Activate Prior Knowledge   Team Talk

1 **Think** Have children think for a minute about what they know about transportation that can help in an emergency.

2 **Pair** Have pairs of children discuss the question of the week. Tell children to take turns speaking. Have children share ideas by speaking clearly using the conventions of language, such as complete sentences in their discussions about emergency transportation.

3 **Share** Call on a few children to share their ideas with the group. Guide discussion and encourage elaboration with prompts such as: What sounds or sights let you know they are going to an emergency?

Anchored Talk

Develop oral language

Display Talk with Me Chart 26A. The pictures show types of transportation and people who can help us in an emergency. Look at this helicopter. What is it doing? What else do you see in the pictures? Tell children to respond in complete sentences and to speak loudly and clearly when sharing their ideas.

This week we will talk about how people use different types of transportation to help during emergencies. We are going to learn six new words. Listen as I say each word: *rescue, pilot, yacht, sailor, mechanic, shimmering.* Have children say each word as you point to the picture.

Display Sing with Me Chart 26B. Tell children that they are going to sing a song about the Coast Guard making a rescue. Read the title and describe the pictures. Sing the song several times to the tune of "Pop! Goes the Weasel." Listen for the Amazing Words: *rescue, pilot, yacht, sailor, mechanic, shimmering.* Tell children to sing along with you.

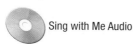 Sing with Me Audio

Talk with Me/Sing with Me Chart 26A

The Coast Guard to the Rescue

The yacht called "Mayday!" from the sea,
To pilot and to crew;
The mechanic stowed the swimmer's gear,
The Coast Guard to the rescue!

Talk with Me/Sing with Me Chart 26B

ELL **Preteach Concepts** Use the Day 1 instruction on ELL Poster 26 to assess and build background knowledge, develop concepts, and build oral vocabulary.

ELL Poster 26

Amazing Words

rescue	pilot
yacht	sailor
mechanic	shimmering

Differentiated Instruction

SI **Strategic Intervention**
Build Background To help children understand words such as *pilot* and *sailor,* use the pictures on Talk with Me/Sing with Me Chart 26A. Talk with children about what these jobs entail.

ELL

English Language Learners
Build Background Use the pictures on Talk with Me/Sing with Me Chart 26A to help children understand words such as *yacht* and *shimmering.*

ELL Support Additional ELL support and modified instruction is provided in the *ELL Handbook* and in the ELL Support lessons on pp. DI•29–34.

Objectives

Learn final /ks/.

Identify words with final /ks/.

Discriminate words with final /ks/.

Substitute other sounds in words that end with /ks/.

Check Phonemic Awareness
SUCCESS PREDICTOR

My Skills Buddy, pp. 32–33

Phonemic Awareness
Final /ks/

Introduce	Today we will learn a new sound. Listen as I say the sound: /ks/ /ks/ /ks/. Say it with me: /ks/ /ks/ /ks/. Display the *box* Picture Card. *Box* ends with /ks/ /ks/ /ks/, *box.* What sound does *box* end with? Continue the routine with the words *wax, mix,* and *Rex.*

Picture Card

Model	Have children look at the picture on pp. 32–33 of *My Skills Buddy.* Tell them that they will be listening for words that end with /ks/. I see someone is working to fix a door in the picture. What sound do you hear at the end of the word *fix*? I hear /ks/ at the end of *fix.* The ending sound in *fix* is /ks/. What other things do you see that end with /ks/?
Guide practice	As children name example words from the picture, guide them in stating that /ks/ is the final sound. Discuss some of the bulleted items on p. 32 of *My Skills Buddy.* Save the other bulleted items for Day 2.
Corrective feedback	**If...** children have difficulty naming words that end with /ks/, **then...** say *fix* again, segment the word into individual phonemes before blending the sounds to say the whole word.

Discriminate sounds

I am going to say two words, and one of those words will end with /ks/. I want you to tell me which word ends with /ks/. Listen carefully. I will do the first one: *six, soon.* Which word ends with /ks/? I hear /ks/ at the end of *six.* Do you? Now you try. Use the following word pairs: *fog, fox; box, bog; fit, fix; tax, tan.*

Have children stand in a circle. I am going to say a word and if it ends with /ks/, I want you to sit down. If it does not end with /ks/, I want you to put your hands up. Let's practice one together. Display the *fox* Picture Card. What is this? What sound is at the end of *fox?* Say the ending sound with me: /ks/ /ks/ /ks/, *fox.* It ends with /ks/. Do you sit down or put your hands up? That's right. You sit down. Continue the routine with the following words: *tax* (sit down), *tan* (hands up), *lax* (sit down), *land* (hands up), *dime* (hands up), *fix* (sit down), *mix* (sit down).

Corrective feedback

If... children cannot discriminate final /ks/,
then... have them enunciate /ks/ as they say *box.*

When you say /ks/, your tongue starts at the very back of your mouth to make /k/ and quickly slides forward to make /s/. Have children say /ks/ words and feel the position of their mouth and tongue. Then repeat the discrimination activity.

Sound substitution

Listen to this word: *six.* Say the sounds in *six* with me: /s/ /i/ /ks/, *six.* We can make a new word by changing the last sound in *six* to /p/. Say the sounds with me: /s/ /i/ /p/. The new word is *sip.* Continue substituting with the following pairs of words: *fit, fix; wax, wag; at, ax; tap, tax.*

> **Don't Wait Until Friday**
> **MONITOR PROGRESS** ↺ **Check Phonemic Awareness** **Final /ks/**
>
> Say *ox* and *map.* Have children identify the word that ends with /ks/. Continue using the following word pairs: *box, bag; five, six; wax, runs; fox, top.*
>
> **If...** children cannot discriminate final /ks/,
> **then...** use the small-group Strategic Intervention lesson, p. DI•18, to reteach /ks/.
>
> | Day 1 | Day 2 | Day 3 | Day 4 | Day 5 |
> |---|---|---|---|---|
> | Check Phonemic Awareness | Check Sound-Spelling/ Retelling | Check Word Reading | Check Phonemic Awareness | Check Oral Vocabulary |
>
> *Success Predictor*

Differentiated Instruction

 Advanced

Support Phonemic Awarenes Have children tell silly sentenc using multiple words that end with /ks/, such as *The fox can fix the box.* Have them identify any rhyming words in their sentences.

Teacher Tip

Children who speak some dialects of English pronounce words such as *ask* as if they en in /ks/ instead of /sk/. Help the learn to hear the difference by having them watch your mouth as you say several words such as *ask* and *ax.*

E L L

English Language Learners

Support Phonemic Awarenes Point to images in the picture on pp. 32–33 of *My Skills Budd* as you say the corresponding words. To clarifying understand ing, have children point to the images as you say the words.

Phonemic Awareness

jectives

Recognize uppercase *X* and owercase *x*.

Associate the sound /ks/ with he spelling *x*.

Blend and read words with /ks/.

ills Trace

ks/ Spelled *Xx*
roduce U5W2D1
actice U5W2D2; U5W2D3
each/Review U5W2D5;
V3D4; U5W4D4; U6W1D4
sess/Test Benchmark
essment U5 Assessment U2

Y:
Unit   W=Week   D=Day

Phonics—Teach/Model
/ks/ Spelled Xx

Introduce Display the *box* Picture Card. This is a *box*. The last sound in *box* is /ks/. Say it with me: *box, /ks/.* Write *box* on the board and point to the *x*. *Box* ends with /ks/ spelled *x*. There are not very many words that begin with *x*. Most of the *x* words we read have *x* at the end. Write *Xx* on the board. The sound for this letter is /ks/. The name of this letter is uppercase *X* and lowercase *x*. What is the sound for this letter? What is the name of this letter?

Picture Card

Model Write *Mr. Max Mox, What's in the Box?* on the board. Point to the *x* in *Max*. When I see this letter, I think of the sound /ks/. The first word is the name *Max*—/m/ /a/ /ks/, *Max.* Point to *Mox*. This word has *x* too. The word is /m/ /o/ /ks/, *Mox.* It's a name. This man's name is Mr. Max Mox. Continue with *box*. The song we will sing is "Mr. Max Mox, What's in the Box?"

Guide practice Display Phonics Songs and Rhymes Chart 26. Teach children the song "Mr. Max Mox, What's in the Box?" sung to the tune of "Are You Sleeping?" Play the CD and sing the song several times. When children are familiar with the song, have them clap when they hear /ks/ words. Choose individuals to come up and point to words that end with /ks/. I will try the first one. I see an *x* here: /ks/ /ks/ /ks/, *Max. Max* ends with *x*.

Phonics Songs and Rhymes Audio

Mr. Max Mox, What's in the Box?

What's in the box? What's in the box?
Mr. Max Mox, Mr. Max Mox.
Could it be an ox or a little fox?
Mr. Max Mox, Mr. Max Mox.

What's in the box? What's in the box?
Mr. Max Mox, Mr. Max Mox.
Open it by six o'clock, open it by six o'clock.
Mr. Max Mox, Mr. Max Mox.

Phonics Songs and Rhymes Chart 26

On their own Display *My Lucky Day* and *Max Takes the Train*. Tell children to identify characters on their covers whose names end in /ks/. (fox, Max)

Blend Words

Review

To review sound spellings, use Alphabet Cards *Dd, Ee, Ii, Oo,* and the *dog, egg, inch,* and *otter* Picture Cards. Then use this routine for sound-by-sound blending to have children blend new words.

ROUTINE   Sound-by-Sound Blending

① **Connect** Write the letter *x* on the board. What is the sound we learned for this letter? The sound is /ks/. Say it with me: /ks/ /ks/ /ks/. When you see this letter in a word, what sound will you say?

② **Model** Write *Max* on the board.

- Touch under the letter *M:* What is the sound for this letter? Say it with me: /m/ /m/ /m/. Repeat the routine for *a* and *x*.

- Let's blend the sounds together. Listen as I blend the sounds: /m/ /a/ /ks/. Say it with me: /m/ /a/ /ks/. Now say it without me.

- Listen as I use *Max* in a sentence: *I eat lunch with my friend Max.* Say the sentence with me. Then have children use *Max* in their own sentences.

③ **Guide Practice** Continue the routine established in step 2 with the words below:

six	hid	box	fox	mix
ox	pal	Rex	red	

Children should successfully read these words before reading Decodable Story 26 on pp. 335–336 of *Reader's and Writer's Notebook.*

Corrective Feedback If children have trouble reading a word, model blending the sounds to read the word. Then have children say it with you.

Routines Flip Chart

Differentiated Instruction

SI Strategic Intervention

Support Print Awareness Wh blending the letters in *Max,* remind children that names an the first word of sentences beç with uppercase letters.

Teacher Tip

Support Print Awareness Poi out that the sound /ks/ can als be produced with the letter combination *-cks.* Let children know that usually words endin in *-cks* mean more than one of something, such as *socks* or *jacks.*

Objectives
Write *X* and *x*.
Learn high-frequency words.

Handwriting

Introduce	Write *Xx* on the board. Words that end with /ks/ are written with lowercase *x*. Which letter is lowercase *x*? Very few words or names begin with *Xx* because it is hard to say as a beginning sound of a word. Which letter is uppercase *X*?
Model uppercase X	Write an uppercase *X* on the board. Watch as I trace the uppercase *X* with my finger. Follow the stroke instructions pictured below.
Guide practice	Have children write the uppercase *X* in the air. Use your finger to make an uppercase *X* in the air. Now write it on the palm of your hand.
Model lowercase x	Write *mix* on the board and point to lowercase *x*. This is the word *mix.* It has a lowercase *x* at the end. See how I make a lowercase *x*. Watch as I trace a lowercase *x* with my finger. Write another *x* on the board following the stroke instructions below. Again, have children write *x* in the air and on their hands.
Guide practice	Have children use their Write-On Boards to write a row of uppercase *X* and a row of lowercase *x*.

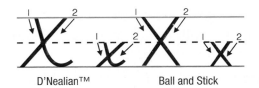

D'Nealian™   Ball and Stick

More practice	Use *Reader's and Writer's Notebook,* p. 333, 334, for additional practice with final *x*.

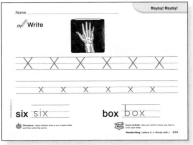   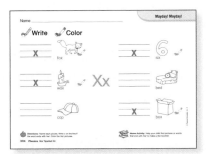

Reader's and Writer's Notebook, p. 333   Reader's and Writer's Notebook, p. 334

High-Frequency Words

Introduce

Use the routine below to teach high-frequency words *yellow, blue,* and *green.*

ROUTINE **Nondecodable Words**

1. **Say and Spell** Some words we have to learn by remembering the letters rather than saying the sounds. We will say and spell the words to help learn them. Write *yellow* on the board. This is the word *yellow.* It has six letters. The letters are *y, e, l, l, o,* and *w.* Have children say and spell the word, first with you and then without you.
2. **Demonstrate Meaning** I can use the word *yellow* in lots of sentences. Here is one sentence: *My favorite sweater is yellow.* Now you use the word in a sentence.

Repeat the routine with the words *blue* and *green.*

Routines Flip Chart

Academic Vocabulary

Write the following words on the board:

cause	**effect**
question mark	**sequence**
fable	

Point to the list. This week we are going to learn these important words. They are tools for learning. As we work this week you will hear them many times. Read the words. Preteach the Academic Vocabulary at point-of-use by providing a child-friendly description, explanation, or example that clarifies the meaning of each term. Then ask children to restate the meaning of the Academic Vocabulary in their own words.

Differentiated Instruction

SI Strategic Intervention

Support High-Frequency Words To help children who are having difficulty reading th high-frequency words, have them practice naming each le in the words and then reading the words.

ELL

English Language Learners

Support High-Frequency Words Have children copy the high-frequency words *yellow, blue,* and *green* with a crayon of the matching color. Matchin the words with their visual representations will help Englis learners remember them.

jectives
Read high-frequency words.
Decode and read words in context and isolation.

Decodable Story 26
/ks/ Spelled Xx and High-Frequency Words

Review

Review the following high-frequency words by having children read each word as you point to it on the Word Wall.

is	he	a	from	look	like
four	blue	green	see	yellow	and

Read Decodable Story 26

Display Decodable Story 26, *Max.* Today we will read a story about some fun a boy named Max has. Point to the title of the story. The title of the story is the boy's name, *Max.* What is the title of the story? We will read lots of /ks/ words in this story. Have children read Decodable Story 26 on pp. 335–336 in *Reader's and Writer's Notebook.*

Use the routine for reading decodable books to read Decodable Story 26.

Reader's and Writer's Notebook, pp. 335–336

ROUTINE Reading Decodable Books

1. **Read Silently** Have children whisper read the story page by page as you listen in.

2. **Model Fluent Reading** Have children finger point as you read a page. Then have children reread the page without you.

3. **Read Chorally** Have children finger point as they chorally read the page. Continue reading page by page, repeating steps 1 and 2.

4. **Read Individually** Have children take turns reading aloud a page.

5. **Reread and Monitor Progress** As you listen to individual children reread, monitor progress and provide support.

6. **Reread with a Partner** Have children reread the story page by page with a partner.

Routines Flip Chart

Differentiated Instruction

SI Strategic Intervention

Support Reading Before reading *Max,* remind children that the letter *s* can be added t the end of a word to mean mor than one. Write the word *legs* on the board and explain that i means more than one leg.

Small Group Time

DAY 1 Break into small groups after reading the Decodable Story and before the comprehension lesson.

Teacher-Led

SI Strategic Intervention	**OL** On-Level	**A** Advanced
Teacher-Led Page DI•18	Teacher-Led Page DI•23	Teacher-Led Page DI•26
• Phonemic Awareness and Phonics	• Phonemic Awareness and Phonics	• Phonemic Awareness and Phonics
• **Reread** Decodable Story 26	• **Reread** Decodable Story 26	• **Reread** Decodable Story 26 for Fluency

E L L Place English language learners in the groups that correspond to their reading abilities in English.

Practice Stations
• Visit the Listen Up! Station
• Visit the Word Work Station

Independent Activities
• Read independently
• Concept Talk Video
• *Reader's and Writer's Notebook*

ills Trace

Cause and Effect

roduce U3W3D1; U4W2D1;
V2D1

actice U3W3D2; U3W3D3;
V3D4; U4W2D2; U4W2D3;
V2D4; U5W2D2; U5W2D3;
V2D4

teach/Review U3W3D5;
V2D5; U5W2D5; U5W5D4;
V3D4

EY:
Unit W=Week D=Day

My Skills Buddy, pp. 34–35

Listening Comprehension
Cause and Effect

Introduce   Many times we see or read about something that happened and we wonder why it happened. This is called **cause and effect**. A cause is why something happens. An effect is what happens.

Envision It!   Have children turn to pp. 34–35 in *My Skills Buddy* and look at the two pictures. These pictures tell a story about a girl who likes to paint.

- What happens in the second picture? (The paint spills.)

- Why does it happen? (The dog pushes on the table.)

What happens—the paint spilling—is the effect. *Why* it happens—the dog pushing on the table—is the cause. The paint spills *because* the dog pushes on the table.

Model   Tell children that you will read a story about some children visiting a fire station. Read **"Firefighting"** and model how to identify cause and effect.

 Think Aloud   When I read, I pay attention to causes and effects to help me understand what happens and why it happens. In this story, the firefighter explains some causes and effects to the children. He says that the firefighters turn on the sirens because they want the cars to know they are coming. The word *because* is a clue word that helps me find a cause and effect.

Guide practice

After reading, have children identify examples of cause and effect.

- Why do firefighters drive fast on their way to a fire? (so they can put the fire out faster and save the people and buildings)
- Why do firefighters need an ax? (to chop the roof or windows to let the smoke out)

More practice

Display *Goldilocks and the Three Bears.* Have children briefly retell the story. Recall with them that when Goldilocks sits in the baby bear's chair, it breaks. What is the cause of the chair breaking? What is the effect of Goldilocks sitting in the chair?

Connect to everyday life

If you say something nice to other people, how does it make them feel? They feel good because you said something nice. Feeling good is what happens and hearing someone say something nice is why it happens.

Read Aloud

Firefighting

Mrs. Parker's class was visiting a fire station. A firefighter was showing the kids the fire engines.

"When someone calls 911 and says there is a fire," he told them, "we take the fire engines there as fast as we can. We turn on the sirens because we want the cars to know we are coming and they must get out of our way."

"Why do you go so fast?" Jenny asked.

"Because the faster we get to the fire, the faster we can put it out and save people and buildings," the firefighter answered. Then he showed the class the firefighters' tools.

"Why do you have an ax?" Dan asked.

"Because sometimes we need to chop the roof or windows to let the smoke out," the firefighter answered.

"Pretty cool," Juan said.

"No, pretty hot!" the firefighter smiled.

Differentiated Instruction

 Strategic Intervention

Support Cause and Effect If children struggle to recognize cause-and-effect relationships, supply sentences with the word *because* and have them identify the cause and effect. For example, say: *I shared Roxi's lunch* because *I forgot mine.* What is the cause? (I forgot my lunch.) What is the effect? (I shared Roxi's lunch.)

Academic Vocabulary

cause a person, thing, or event that makes something else happen

effect thing brought about by a action; a result

E L L

English Language Learners
Oral Comprehension To prepare English learners for the Read Aloud, use the modified Read Aloud in the ELL Support lesson p. DI•30.

bjectives
- Introduce question marks and capital letters.
- Write or dictate a sentence about feelings.

Conventions
Question Marks and Uppercase Letters

Teach question marks Write a question mark on the board. This is a question mark. A question mark is used at the end of a sentence that asks a question. *How did you get to school today?* is a question. If a sentence asks a question, you write a question mark at the end of it instead of a period. Questions start with a capital, or uppercase, letter like all other sentences.

Model Write the question *How did you get to school today?* on the board. As you do so, point out to children that you are writing the first word of the question with an uppercase letter and adding a question mark at the end.

Guide practice Write these questions on the board: *what can I do, how old are you, what time is it, where is my pencil,* and *why is it cold.* Read each question aloud and have children change the first letter of the first word to an uppercase letter and add the question mark at the end.

Team Talk Pair children and have them take turns asking each other questions. Have them tell where the uppercase letter and question mark would go.

Daily Fix-It Use the Daily Fix-It for more conventions practice.

Writing
Wonderful, Marvelous Me!
Today I Feel...

Teach

Talk with children about feelings. Think about all the ways we can feel. We may feel *happy* when we are with our friends. We may feel *curious* when we are about to learn something new. We may feel *tired* when we have had a long day. Display the following list of emotion words and review it with children.

silly	tired	afraid	lonely	sad	proud
happy	surprised	angry	scared	shy	nervous

All of our feelings are important. Why is it important to share our feelings with others? Encourage children to share their thoughts and ideas.

Model

Today we are going to share how we feel. I'm going to close my eyes and look inside at my feelings. I know that we are going to learn about emergency transportation this week. I don't know a lot about emergency transportation but I would like to know more. Today I feel *curious* to learn more about emergency transportation.

Guide practice

Encourage children to tell other things that make people feel curious. Have them complete the sentence *I feel curious when _____*. Write their ideas and draw pictures when appropriate.

Independent writing

Now you're going to share how you feel today. Close your eyes and look inside at your wonderful, marvelous feelings. How do you feel? Review the list of emotions with children. Why do you feel that way? Have children write or dictate their ideas in complete sentences. Then have them illustrate the sentences.

Daily Handwriting

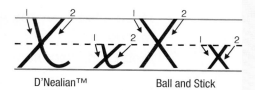
D'Nealian™   Ball and Stick

Write *X* and *ox* on the board. Review correct letter formation of uppercase *X* and lowercase *x*.

Have children write the letter *X* and the word *ox* on their Write-On Boards. Remind them to use proper left-to-right and top-to-bottom progression and proper spacing between letters when writing *X* and *x*.

Write Guy
Jeff Anderson

Let Me Check My List

Encourage children to keep a list of words they come across that are exciting or interesting. They can use their lists to increase their vocabulary and incorporate them in their own writing. This is a great way to improve vocabulary and word choice.

Academic Vocabulary

question mark an ending punctuation mark used at the end of a question

Daily Fix-It

did you see a blue fox
<u>D</u>id you see a blue fox<u>?</u>

This week's practice sentences appear on Teacher Resources DVD-ROM.

Writing Routine

Day 1 Wonderful, Marvelous Me!

Day 2 Respond to Literature

Day 3 Genre Writing

Day 4 Extend the Concept

Day 5 This Week We...

Listening and Speaking
Respond to Literature: Drama

Teach
Today we are going to act like the characters we read about in *Goldilocks and the Three Bears*. By acting out the things that happen, we can better understand the story. Picture walk through *Goldilocks and the Three Bears*. Have children describe the events on each page.

Model
Demonstrate how you might act like Goldilocks. Arrange children into small groups. Instruct children to work in their group and act out the events in the story *Goldilocks and the Three Bears*.

Guide practice
Direct groups to take turns acting out different parts of *Goldilocks and the Three Bears*. For example, groups can pretend to try the porridge, the chairs, or the beds. They can pretend to be the bears discovering Goldilocks asleep or be Goldilocks startled awake by three bears. Refer children to the Rules for Speaking on p. 2 of the *Reader's and Writer's Notebook*. Remind them to speak loudly and clearly when they are acting out scenes from the story.

Name _____
Speaking Rules
1. Speak clearly.
2. Tell only important ideas.
3. Choose your words carefully.
4. Take turns speaking.
5. Speak one at a time.

2   Listening and Speaking Rules

Reader's and Writer's Notebook, p. 2

Wrap Up Your Day

✔ **Concept Talk** This week we will be talking about emergency transportation. Today we read about firefighting. Tell me about what firefighters do.

✔ **Oral Language** Today we sang about the Coast Guard making a rescue. Let's say the Amazing Words: *rescue, pilot, yacht, sailor, mechanic, shimmering.*

✔ **Homework Idea** Send home the Family Times Newsletter, Let's Practice It! TR DVD•51–52.

Preview DAY 2

Tomorrow we will read about the Coast Guard in the selection *Mayday! Mayday!*

Extend Your Day!

Science
Weather

Materials: books about weather, chart paper, construction paper, drawing tools

Weather Wonders Have children look through some books about weather and then brainstorm a list of different types of weather. Write children's responses on the chart paper. Some examples may be:

sunny	snowy	windy
rainy	stormy	cloudy

Ask questions about the weather, such as: During which season—fall, winter, spring, or summer—will these types of weather typically occur? Is the weather the same every day? How does the weather help you choose what clothes you will wear or what activities you will do?

Draw and Label a Picture Review with children that there are many kinds of storms, such as thunderstorms, snowstorms, hurricanes, and tornadoes. Have children draw and label a weather picture.

thunderstorm

Social Studies
Economics

Materials: paper, drawing tools

Just My Job Have children draw a picture of one of their parents or another adult at work doing his or her job. Have children share their pictures with the class and have them explain the job that is shown. Discuss different jobs people do and why each job is important.

Math
Counting Wheels

Materials: Big Books *The Little School Bus, Dig Dig Digging,* and *Max Takes the Train;* paper, writing tools

Mechanical Math Display Big Books that include various forms of transportation, such as *The Little School Bus, Dig Dig Digging,* and *Max Takes the Train.* Have children count the number of wheels they can find in a book. Record the number with tally marks on the board. Continue picture walking through other books, using tally marks to record the number of wheels. Then have children compare the numbers to find the book with the most wheels.

jectives

- Discuss the concepts to develop oral language.
- Build oral vocabulary.

oday at a Glance

al Vocabulary
cue, pilot

onemic Awareness
Final /ks/

onics
/ks/ Spelled *Xx*

ndwriting
rds with *Xx*

mprehension
Cause and Effect

nventions
estion Marks and Uppercase
tters

riting
spond to Literature

ocabulary
sition Words

TRUCKTOWN on Reading *Street*

Start your engines! Display p. 13 of *Truckery Rhymes.* Point to "It's Raining, It's Pouring." Who remembers which truck this rhyme is about? Yes, this rhyme is about Monster Max. Let's read the rhyme together. Have a child point to the rhyming words as the class reads the rhyme again. Give additional children the opportunity to point to the rhyming words as you repeat the rhyme.

Truckery Rhymes

Concept Talk

Question of the Week

 What kinds of transportation help us in an emergency?

Build concepts

Write the question of the week on the board and track the print as you read it aloud. Have children answer the question in complete sentences. Remind them to speak loudly and clearly when sharing their ideas. Display Sing with Me Chart 26B. Tell children that they are going to sing about the Coast Guard.

💿 Sing with Me Audio

Listen for Amazing Words

Read the title and ask children to describe the picture. The Amazing Words *rescue* and *pilot* are in the song. Tell children to listen for those two Amazing Words as you sing the song to the tune of "Pop! Goes the Weasel." Sing the song several times and have children sing with you. Have children clap their hands when they hear the Amazing Words *rescue* and *pilot*.

Talk with Me/Sing
with Me Chart 26B

E L L **Reinforce Vocabulary** Use the Day 2 instruction on ELL Poster 26 to reinforce the meanings of high-frequency words.

E L L Poster 26

Oral Vocabulary
Amazing Words

Amazing Words

rescue	pilot
yacht	sailor
mechanic	shimmering

Teach Amazing Words

 **Amazing Words** **Oral Vocabulary Routine**

1. **Introduce the Word** *Rescue* means to help people get out of danger. When people are in danger, the Coast Guard can *rescue* them. What's our new Amazing Word for helping people get out of danger? Say it with me: *rescue.*

2. **Demonstrate** Provide examples to show meaning. *Firefighters can rescue people in danger.*

   Repeat steps 1 and 2.

   Introduce the Word A *pilot* is a person who flies an airplane or a helicopter. What's our new Amazing Word for a person who flies an airplane or a helicopter? Say it with me: *pilot.*

   Demonstrate *Pilots in the Coast Guard fly helicopters.*

3. **Apply** Have children use *rescue* and *pilot* in complete sentences.

Routines Flip Chart

Use Amazing Words

To reinforce the concept and the Amazing Words, have children supply the appropriate Amazing Word for each sentence.

The person who flies an airplane is the _____. (pilot)

The firefighter will _____ the kitten in the tree. (rescue)

Differentiated Instruction

 Strategic Intervention

Vocabulary For children whose background knowledge and experience do not include rescues or pilots, provide magazine or newspaper picture of airplanes and local rescues. Explain that pilots are the peop who "drive" the airplanes. Discuss what happened during the pictured rescue.

English Language Learners

Access Content Have children tell what words in their home languages are used for *rescue* and *pilot.*

Objectives
Practice final /ks/.
Substitute initial sounds.

Phonemic Awareness
🔄 Final /ks/

Picture Card

Isolate /ks/
Display the *box* Picture Card. This is a box. *Box* ends with /ks/. What is this picture? What sound does it end with?

Model
Remember that /ks/ most often comes at the end of words because it's too hard to say /ks/ at the beginning of words. **Display the *fox* Picture Card.** This is a *fox.* Listen carefully to the sounds: /f/ /o/ /ks/. I hear /ks/ at the end of *fox.* What is the ending sound you hear in *fox?* Say it with me: *fox,* /ks/ /ks/ /ks/.

Continue the routine with the *ox* and *six* Picture Cards.

Picture Card

Guide practice
Have children look at the picture on *My Skills Buddy,* pp. 32–33. Remember that we saw someone trying to fix a door. *Fix* ends with /ks/. What other things that end with /ks/ did we find in the picture? Name other things that end like *fix.* **Discuss with children those bulleted items on p. 32 not discussed on Day 1.**

My Skills Buddy, pp. 32–33

Corrective feedback
If... children cannot discriminate final /ks/,
then... have them enunciate /ks/ as they segment final /ks/ words.

Listen as I segment a word: /p/ /o/ /ks/. Say it with me: /p/ /o/ /ks/, *pox.* What sound do you hear at the end? I hear /ks/ at the end. **Continue with the following words:** *mix, Rex, ox.*

On their own Display Phonics Songs and Rhymes Chart 26. Remind children of the song "Mr. Max Mox, What's in the Box?" sung to the tune of "Are You Sleeping?" Play the CD or sing the song several times. Raise your hand when you hear a word that ends with /ks/. Identify words in the song that end with /ks/: *box, Max, Mox, ox, fox, six.*

Review **Sound Substitution** Listen to this word: *ax.* Say the sounds in *ax* with me: /a/ /ks/. We can make a new word by adding a new sound to the beginning of the word. We can add /w/ to the beginning of *ax.* Say the sounds with me: /w/ /a/ /ks/. The new word is *wax.* Let's make another word. We can change the first sound of the word *wax* to /t/. Say the sounds with me: /t/ /a/ /ks/. The new word is *tax.* Continue substituting sounds with the following sets of words: *box, pox, fox; fox, fax, fix; fix, fin, fit.*

Phonics Songs and Rhymes Chart 26

Differentiated Instruction

SI **Strategic Intervention**

Support Phonemic Awareness
If children struggle to find words with final /ks/, point to an object in the picture. Have children name the object and ask if ends with /ks/. For example, point to a fox. After children name it, as Does *fox* end with /ks/?

Teacher Tip

Make sure children can hear and repeat the ending sounds of words.

ELL

English Language Learners
Support Phonemic Awareness
Speakers of Cantonese, Vietnamese, and Hmong may not be familiar with /ks/ in words such as *box, Max, Mox, ox, fox,* and *six.* Spanish uses this sound in words such as *taxi* and *extra,* but it is not common for Spanish words to end with /ks/. Provide extra practice with words that end in *x.*

bjectives
- Practice /ks/ spelled *Xx*.
- Blend /ks/ words.

Check Sound-Spelling
SUCCESS PREDICTOR

Phonics—Teach/Model
/ks/ Spelled *Xx*

Picture Card

Teach /ks/Xx

Display the *fox* Picture Card. This is a *fox.* The last sound in *fox* is /ks/. Say it with me: *fox,* /ks/. Write *fox* on the board and point to the *x. Fox* ends with /ks/ spelled *x.* There are not very many words that begin with *x.* Most of the *x* words we read have *x* at the end. Write *Xx* on the board. The sound for this letter is /ks/. The name of this letter is uppercase *X* and lowercase *x.* What is the sound for this letter? What is the name of this letter?

Model

Display the *box* Picture Card. What is this? Say the sounds in *box* with me: /b/ /o/ /ks/, *box.* Where do you hear /ks/ in *box?* I hear /ks/ at the end.

Write *Rex* on the board. Point to each letter as you say the sounds, /r/ /e/ /ks/, *Rex.* Continue the routine with the names *Lex* and *Max.*

Picture Card

Guide practice

Envision It!

Have children open *My Skills Buddy* to p. 36. Demonstrate using the blending arrows on *My Skills Buddy,* p. 36, as you model blending the first word. Put your finger on the red arrow below the *s.* Say the sound that *s* stands for: /s/. Continue with the letters *i* and *x.* Now I run my finger along the blue arrow as I blend the letters quickly to read *six.* Repeat with the word *ox.* Have children work with a partner to blend the rest of the words on the page. Explain that the words for *fox* and *box* are created when adding *f* and *b* to *ox.*

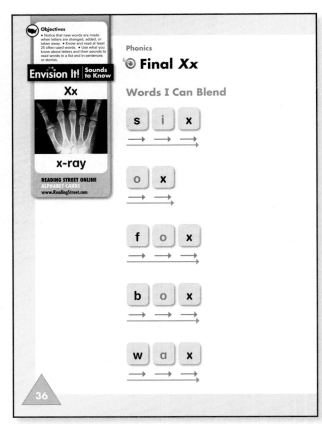

My Skills Buddy, p. 36

Blend Use the following routine to review blending *x* words.

ROUTINE Sound-by-Sound Blending

① **Connect** Write the letter *x*. What is the sound we learned for this letter? The sound is /ks/. Say it with me: /ks/ /ks/ /ks/. When you see this letter in a word, what sound will you say?

② **Model** Write the word *fix* on the board.

- Point to *f*. What is the sound for this letter? Say it with me: /f/ /f/ /f/. Repeat the routine for *i* and *x*.

- Let's blend the sounds together. Listen as I blend the sounds: /f/ /i/ /ks/. Say it with me: /f/ /i/ /ks/. Now say it without me.

- Listen as I use *fix* in a sentence: *Dan can fix the broken swing.* Say it with me. Have children use *fix* in a sentence.

③ **Guide Practice** Continue the routine established in step 2 with these words:

pig	cap	rip	fox	cat	box	top	ox

Have children successfully read all of the words before reading Decodable Reader 26 on pp. 38–45 of *My Skills Buddy*.

Corrective Feedback If children have difficulty blending words, model blending the sounds to read the word. Then have children say it with you.

Routines Flip Chart

MONITOR PROGRESS ↻ Check Sound-Spelling /ks/ Spelled *Xx*

Have children write the letters *Xx* on a card. I am going to read some words. When you hear a /ks/ word, hold up your *Xx* card. Say: *box, Bob, fix, mix, fit, ox, ten, six.*

If... children cannot discriminate /ks/,

then... use the small-group Strategic Intervention lesson, p. DI•19, to reteach /ks/.

Continue to monitor children's progress using other instructional opportunities during the week so that children can be successful with the Day 5 Assessment.

Day 1	Day 2	Day 3	Day 4	Day 5
Check Phonemic Awareness	Check Sound-Spelling/ Retelling	Check Word Reading	Check Phonemic Awareness	Check Oral Vocabulary

Success Predictor

Sound-Spelling

Succes
Predicto

jectives
Write *X* and *x*.
Read high-frequency words.

Handwriting
Write Words with *Xx*

Model

Write *Xx* on the board. Remember that very few words or names begin with *Xx* because it is hard to say /ks/ as a beginning sound of a word. /ks/ usually comes at the end of a word. Watch me make an uppercase *X*. Write an uppercase *X* on the board using the instructional strokes indicated in the model.

Write *fox* on the board. What word is this? This is the word *fox*. I use a lowercase *x* at the end of *fox*. See how I make a lowercase *x*. Write another *x* on the board following the stroke instructions below.

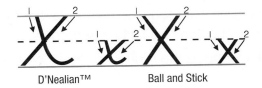

D'Nealian™   Ball and Stick

Guide practice

Have children use their Write-On Boards to make a row of uppercase *X* and a row of lowercase *x*. Circulate around the room, assisting children as necessary. Then have children write the following words: *mix, wax, Lex.*

High-Frequency Words

Model reading

Have children turn to p. 37 of *My Skills Buddy.* Read the high-frequency words *yellow, blue,* and *green* together. Then have children point to each word and read it themselves. Read the sentences on *My Skills Buddy* page together to read the new high-frequency words in context.

[Team Talk] Pair children and have them take turns reading each sentence aloud.

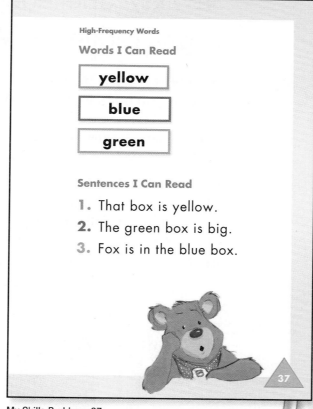

High-Frequency Words

Words I Can Read

| yellow |
| blue |
| green |

Sentences I Can Read

1. That box is yellow.
2. The green box is big.
3. Fox is in the blue box.

37

My Skills Buddy, p. 37

On their own

Use *Reader's and Writer's Notebook,* p. 337, for additional practice with this week's high-frequency words.

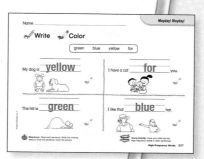

Reader's and Writer's Notebook, p. 337

Differentiated Instruction

SI Strategic Intervention

Support Handwriting Point ou to children that although *X* doe not come at the beginning of many words, it does come at th beginning of some words that they will learn later. Therefore, it is important to learn how to make a capital *X,* even if it will not be used as often as lower-case *x.*

Objectives
Read decodable text.
Read high-frequency words.

Decodable Reader 26

/ks/ Spelled *Xx* and High-Frequency Words

Review Review previously taught high-frequency words. Have children read each word as you point to it on the Word Wall.

a	blue	yellow	to	green	have	is	the

Have children turn to Decodable Reader 26, *Fox Can Fix It!* on page 38 of *My Skills Buddy.* Today we will read a book about a fox who can fix almost anything. Point to the title of the book. What is the title of the book? *Fox Can Fix It!* is the title of the book. It was written by Roger Bines. It was illustrated by Chris Lemon. What does an illustrator do?

Use the routine for reading decodable books to read Decodable Reader 26.

My Skills Buddy, pp. 38–45

Differentiated Instruction

A Advanced

Support Reading Let capable readers read the text on their own; then continue with steps and 6.

ROUTINE **Reading Decodable Books**

1) **Read Silently** Have children whisper read the book page by page as you listen in.

2) **Model Fluent Reading** Have children finger point as you read a page. Then have children reread the book without you.

3) **Read Chorally** Have children finger point as they chorally read the page. Continue reading page by page, repeating steps 1 and 2.

4) **Read Individually** Have children take turns reading aloud a page.

5) **Reread and Monitor Progress** As you listen to individual children reread, monitor progress and provide support.

6) **Reread with a Partner** Have children reread the book page by page with a partner.

Routines Flip Chart

Small Group Time

DAY 2 **Break into small groups after reading the Decodable Reader and before the comprehension lesson.**

Teacher-Led

SI Strategic Intervention	**OL** On-Level	**A** Advanced
Teacher-Led Page DI•19 • Phonemic Awareness and Phonics • **Reread** Decodable Reader 26	**Teacher-Led** Page DI•23 • Phonemic Awareness and Phonics • **Reread** Decodable Reader 26	**Teacher-Led** Page DI•26 • Phonics and Spelling • **Reread** Decodable Reader 26 for Fluency, DI•26

 Place English language learners in the groups that correspond to their reading abilities in English.

Practice Stations
• Visit the Word Work Station
• Visit the Words to Know Station

Independent Activities
• Read independently
• Background Building Audio
• *Reader's and Writer's Notebook*

English Language Learners
Vocabulary Development
Walk children through *Fox Can Fix It!* Have them identify Pig, Fox, Cat, and Ox in the story. Display a word card for each of these characters and have a child match each card with an appropriate picture.

jectives

Practice cause and effect.
Preview and predict.
Retell a selection.

Check Retelling
SUCCESS PREDICTOR

Listening Comprehension
Cause and Effect

Review

Envision It!

Have children turn to p. 34 of *My Skills Buddy*. Remind children that things usually happen because other things made them happen. Good readers ask *why* things happen because it helps them understand the story.

My Skills Buddy, pp. 34–35

First Read— Trade Book
Mayday! Mayday!

Concepts of print

Display p. 3 of *Mayday! Mayday!* Look at this picture. It's called a *diagram*. It shows the parts of a special swimmer's suit. These words are called *labels*. Lines point to where the labeled parts are pictured. The title of the diagram is on the bottom of the page.

Preview and predict

Display *Mayday! Mayday!* Look at the cover and tell me what you see. I see a helicopter trying to rescue some people in the water. What do you think this book will be about? Let's read to find out.

Use illustrations

Take children on a picture walk through the book. Have children describe the pictures and tell what they think is happening.

Introduce genre

Informational text gives information about an object, an idea, or a theme. It tells facts and often uses graphics or diagrams. In this selection, we will learn about the Coast Guard.

Set purpose

Remind children of the question of the week: *What kinds of transportation help us in an emergency?* Have children listen as you read to see how the Coast Guard uses transportation to help in an emergency.

Model

Read *Mayday! Mayday!* with expression for enjoyment.

Read for enjoyment

Reread using Develop Vocabulary notes

Reread using Guide Comprehension notes

Retell

Check retelling

Envision It!

Have children turn to p. 46 of *My Skills Buddy*. Walk through the retelling boxes as children retell *Mayday! Mayday!* Let's retell what happens in the first box— the beginning of the selection. The sailors on the yacht call the Coast Guard for help because they are stuck in a storm. Let's retell what happens in the next box. Continue with the rest of the boxes. After children retell the selection as a group, have them draw pictures to retell a favorite part of the selection. Have them write or dictate a word or sentence to go with their picture.

My Skills Buddy, p. 46

Top-Score Response A top-score response identifies the topic and details.

Don't Wait Until Friday

MONITOR PROGRESS | **Check Retelling**

If... children have difficulty retelling the selection,

then... go through the selection one page at a time, and ask children to tell what happens in their own words.

Day 1	Day 2	Day 3	Day 4	Day 5
Check Phonemic Awareness	Check Sound-Spelling/ Retelling	Check Word Reading	Check Phonemic Awareness	Check Oral Vocabulary

Success Predictor

Differentiated Instruction

SI Strategic Intervention

Build Background Help build background by clarifying a few words that children will encounter in the selection. Tell them that *mayday* is a call for help, a H-60 Jayhawk is a helicopter, and *mech* is short for *mechanic*

Retelling Plan

☑ **Week 1** Assess Advanced students.

☑ **This week assess On-Level students.**

☐ **Week 3** Assess Strategic Intervention students.

☐ **Week 4** Assess Advanced students.

☐ **Week 5** Assess On-Level students.

☐ **Week 6** Assess Strategic Intervention students.

ELL

English Language Learners

Access Content Encourage children to act out a selection event (effect) and tell why it happens (cause). If they have difficulty coming up with English words, supply the word and have them repeat it in their sentence.

Succe Predict

Retelling

jectives

Practice cause and effect.
Confirm predictions.
Practice question marks and uppercase letters.

Think, Talk, and Write

Discuss concept

Imagine what it would be like to be on that boat caught in the storm!

- Would you feel scared? Why or why not?
- How would you feel when you heard the helicopter and saw its lights?
- How did the pictures help you understand what was happening?

Confirm predictions

Have children recall their predictions before you read *Mayday! Mayday!*

- What did you think the selection would be about?
- Was your prediction correct?

Have children turn to p. 47 of *My Skills Buddy*. Read the questions and directives and have children respond.

Text to world

1. How can a helicopter help in an emergency? Which would be more helpful if a boat has an emergency: a helicopter or a police car? Is a helicopter most helpful when the emergency is nearby or far away?

Cause and effect

2. What does the Coast Guard do in *Mayday! Mayday!* (rescues the sailors) What caused the sailors to need help? (the storm)

Look back and write

3. Let's look back at our selection and write about it. What does the crew of the Jayhawk have to do before the helicopter can take off? Listen for the steps they must take. Read pp. 6–9 of *Mayday! Mayday!* Now let's write our ideas. Discuss with children the steps the crew took to get the helicopter ready and record their responses on chart paper.

Possible responses: *The crew waits for a call that help is needed. They put fuel in the helicopter. They make sure the gear is put away. They fasten their safety belts. The pilot reads a checklist. The pilot starts the rotors.*

Think, Talk, and Write

1. How can a helicopter help in an emergency? Text to World

2. In *Mayday! Mayday!* the Coast Guard rescues sailors. What happened that made the sailors need help?

Cause and Effect

3. Look back and write.

47

My Skills Buddy, p. 47

Conventions
Question Marks and Uppercase Letters

Review   Remind children that all sentences begin with a capital, or uppercase, letter and end with an ending punctuation mark. The ending punctuation mark for questions is called a question mark.

Guide practice   Display pp. 4–5 of *Mayday! Mayday!* Guide children to ask a number of questions about the illustration. Write the questions on the board without capital letters or question marks. Have children tell you where to add the capital letter and question mark in each question.

On their own   Use the *Reader's and Writer's Notebook*, p. 338, for more practice with question marks and capital letters.

Daily Fix-It   Use the Daily Fix-It exercise for more conventions practice.

INTERACT with TEXT

✏ Write ✎ Draw

can I get a pet

Can I get a pet?

Reader's and Writer's Notebook, p. 338

bjectives
- Write questions about *Mayday! Mayday!*
- Identify and use words that name position.
- Write *X* and *x*.

Writing
Respond to Literature

Discuss Display *Mayday! Mayday!* Discuss with children the things the Coast Guard does that help save the sailors in the selection.

Model The sailors are in trouble because of a storm. By the end of the selection, the sailors are safe. What questions could we ask the sailors about their rescue?

> **Were you scared?**
> **Was it hard to get into the raft?**

Guide practice Have children think of questions they could ask the rescuers. Help them write their questions, using a capital letter for the first word and adding a question mark at the end.

Independent writing Have children write or dictate questions about *Mayday! Mayday!* or copy one of the questions the class wrote together. Have them illustrate answers to their questions.

Daily Handwriting

Write *X* and *box* on the board. Review correct letter formation of uppercase *X* and lowercase *x*.

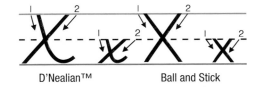

D'Nealian™   Ball and Stick

Have children write the letter *X* and the word *box* on their Write-On Boards. Remind them to use proper left-to-right and top-to-bottom progression and proper spacing between letters when writing *X* and *x*.

Vocabulary
Position Words

Model

Have children turn to p. 48 of *My Skills Buddy* and use the first Vocabulary bullet to guide the discussion. Direct children to the label pointing to the top of the stack of books. This book is in the highest place of all the books, so it is on the *top* of the stack of books. Direct children to the label pointing to the bottom of the stack of books. This book is in the lowest place of all the books, so it is on the *bottom* of the stack of books. Display the front cover of *Mayday! Mayday!* This part of the book is the first part you see, so it is the *front* of the book. Turn the book over and point to the back cover. This part of the book is the last part you see, so it is the *back* of the book.

My Skills Buddy, p. 48

Guide practice

Write the words *top, bottom, front*, and *back* on the board. Point to each word as you read it.

top	bottom	front	back

Let's practice our new words. Put your hands on the *top* of your desk. Now put your hands on the *bottom* of your desk. Put your hands on the *front* of your legs. Now put your hands on the *back* of your legs. *Top, bottom, front,* and *back* are words that show position, or where something is.

On their own

Have children take turns acting out one of the positions words, such as patting the *top* of their heads, opening the *bottom* drawer in a desk, marching to the *front* of the room, and walking backward in the *back* of the room. Have them tell you what they are doing, using the position word in their explanation.

Differentiated Instruction

SI **Strategic Intervention**

Access Content Explain to children that one of the jobs of the Coast Guard is to protect people on the water. This includes the coastlines of oceans as well as the Great Lakes and other waterways. Point out these areas on a map.

English Language Learners

Access Content Have children tell what words in their home languages are used for *top, bottom, front,* and *back*.

Objectives
- Review skills learned and practiced today.

Wrap Up Your Day

- **Concept Talk** Today we read about a fox who fixes everything to help people in emergencies. What does Fox do?
- **Phonemic Awareness** I'm going to say some sentences. Make a big *X* with your fingers when you hear /ks/ words*. The fox jumped over the box. Ben is six. Dad will fix my bike.*
- **Conventions** Write on the board *did they rescue the swimmer* and have children rewrite it correctly with a capital letter and a question mark.
- **Homework Idea** Have children write questions about the position of objects in the room, using the words *top, bottom, front,* or *back*.

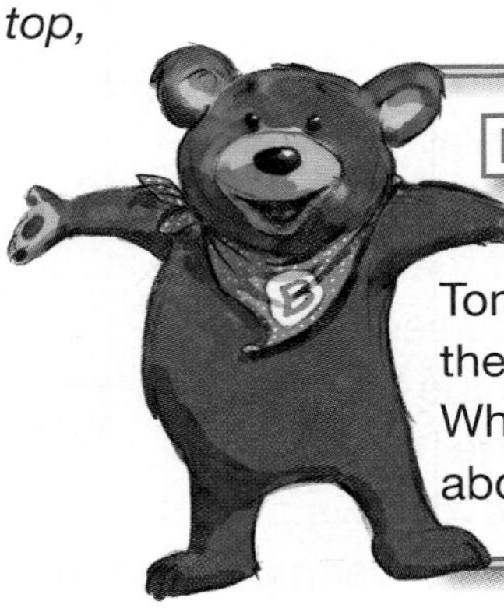

Preview DAY 3

Tomorrow we will read about the Coast Guard again. What do you remember about the Coast Guard?

Extend Your Day!

Social Studies
Jobs
Materials: cards with nine squares, counters, crayons

Identify Jobs People Do Remind children that there are many different jobs that people can do that help one another. *Let's name some jobs people do that help others.* As children name the jobs, make a list on the board. Possible jobs include doctor, nurse, police officer, firefighter, paramedic, postal worker, construction worker, and teacher.

What Job? Give children cards with nine squares. In each square, have children draw a picture or write the name of a job. Distribute counters.

Play "What Job?" by describing a job to the children. If they have a job that fits the description, they put a counter on that square on their card. Continue with other job descriptions until someone covers three squares in a row on his or her card.

Comprehension
Cause and Effect
Materials: paper, crayons

Emergency Transportation Explain to children that there are many transportation vehicles that help in an emergency. Discuss examples, such as police cars, fire trucks, ambulances, and helicopters.

Have children draw a picture of a situation in which an emergency vehicle might be needed. Then have them turn the paper over and draw the vehicle that would help in that emergency. Have children take turns showing their emergency situation. Ask volunteers to tell which emergency vehicle would help and to explain how the emergency vehicle would help.

Phonics
Consonant Xx
Materials: magazines, newspapers, large cardboard X, scissors, glue

X Marks the Spot Have children look in newspapers and magazines for the letter Xx. Tell them to cut out or copy the words on paper. Then have them glue the words on the large cardboard X. Display the X on a bulletin board in the room with the title *X Marks the Spot.*

jectives
Share information and ideas
about the concept.
Build oral vocabulary.

day at a Glance

al Vocabulary
ht, sailor

onemic Awareness
Final /ks/

onics
ks/ Spelled *Xx*

mprehension
Cause and Effect

nventions
estion Marks and Uppercase
ters

riting
yme

tening and Speaking
spond to Literature: Drama

TRUCKTOWN on Reading Street

Start your engines! Display p. 13 of *Truckery Rhymes.* Read "It's Raining, It's Pouring" to children. Do you know the original "It's Raining, It's Pouring"? Recite it first, and then have children repeat it with you:

It's raining, it's pouring, The old man is snoring; He went to bed and bumped his head, And couldn't get up in the morning.

Truckery Rhymes

Concept Talk

Question of the Week

 What kinds of transportation help us in an emergency?

Write the question of the week on the board. Read the question as you track the print. Have children answer the question in complete sentences and remind them to take turns speaking.

Listen for Amazing Words

Let's Sing Display Sing with Me Chart 26B. Remind children that yesterday they sang "The Coast Guard to the Rescue." Today we are going to listen for the Amazing Words *yacht* and *sailor.* Sing the song several times. Have children join in. Tell children to clap when they hear the Amazing Words *yacht* and *sailor* in the song.

Sing with Me Audio

The Coast Guard to the Rescue

The yacht called "Mayday!" from the sea,
To pilot and to crew,
The mechanic stowed the swimmer's gear,
The Coast Guard to the rescue!

Talk with Me/Sing with Me Chart 26B

Oral Vocabulary
Amazing Words

Amazing Words

rescue	pilot
yacht	sailor
mechanic	shimmering

Teach Amazing Words

Amazing Words Oral Vocabulary Routine

1 **Introduce the Word** A boat that is big enough to go in the ocean is called a *yacht*. A *yacht* has an upstairs and one or two rooms downstairs. What's our new Amazing Word for a boat big enough to go in the ocean? Say it with me: *yacht*.

2 **Demonstrate** Provide examples to show meaning. *In* Mayday! Mayday! *there were several sailors on the yacht.*

Repeat steps 1 and 2.

Introduce the Word A man or woman who is in the U.S. Navy or Coast Guard is called a *sailor*. A *sailor* is someone who works on a boat. What's our new Amazing Word for someone who works on a boat? Say it with me: *sailor*.

Demonstrate *Sailors wear special hats and uniforms.*

3 **Apply** Tell children to use *yacht* and *sailor* in complete sentences.

Routines Flip Chart

Use Amazing Words

To reinforce the concept and the Amazing Words, have children supply the appropriate Amazing Word for each sentence.

That big boat is called a _____. (yacht)

We saw a _____ in a white uniform. (sailor)

ELL **Expand Vocabulary** Use the Day 3 instruction on ELL Poster 26 to help children expand vocabulary.

ELL Poster 26

Differentiated Instruction

SI Strategic Intervention

Sentence Production Use the Talk with Me Chart to help children complete the Amazing Word sentences.

ELL

English Language Learners

Access Content Ask children what words in their home languages are used for *yacht* and *sailor*.

Phonemic Awareness
🔊 Final /ks/

Review

Final /ks/ Display the *box* Picture Card. What is the last sound in *box*? Say it with me: *box. Box* ends with /ks/. Continue with the *fox* and *ox* Picture Cards.

Picture Card

Discriminate sounds

I'm going to say some words. One of the words ends in /ks/, but the other does not. Raise your hand when you hear the word that ends in /ks/. Display the *cat* and *fox* Picture Cards. Which word ends in /ks/: *cat* or *fox*? Right, *fox* ends in /ks/. Continue the routine with the following word pairs: *run, six; pox, pal; tug, Tex.*

Teach children the song "Rex's Box," sung to the tune of "Mary Had a Little Lamb."

Rex had a big red fox,
Big red fox, big red fox.
Rex had a big red fox,
He kept in his green box.

Rex had a big blue ox,
Big blue ox, big blue ox.
Rex had a big blue ox,
He kept in his yellow box.

Sing the song several times. Have children clap when they hear /ks/ words.

On their own

Display the *ant, fox, ox,* and *robin* Picture Cards. Have children choose one of the pictures to draw. Have them circle the animal they drew on their paper if the word ends with /ks/.

Picture Card

Segment

Listen to the sounds in *mix:* /m/ /i/ /ks/. Say them with me: /m/ /i/ /ks/. How many sounds do you hear? There are three sounds in *mix.* Let's try some more words. **Continue the routine with** *wax, Rex,* and *pox.*

Corrective feedback

If... children cannot segment words into sounds, **then...** provide practice segmenting the words into chunks, such as /f/-*ox,* /p/-*ox.*

Substitute phonemes

Listen to the word I am going to say: *fan.* Say it with me: /f/ /a/ /n/, *fan.* I can make a new word by changing the last sound. Listen: /f/ /a/ /ks/. Say it with me: /f/ /a/ /ks/. What is the new word? The new word is *fax.* Let's try some more. **Continue practice with the following pairs of words:** *fix, fin; sit, six.*

Differentiated Instruction

 Advanced

Support Phonemic Awareness
Work with children to make up another verse for "Rex's Box" using a word with /ks/ and a color word. Have them teach their new verse to the class.

ELL

English Language Learners
Support Phonemic Awareness
Two sounds, /k/ and /s/, are blended together to make the sound for *x.* In Spanish, words cannot end in consonant blend. As a result, Spanish speakers may delete or substitute consonant sounds when producing English words with final consonant blends (such as *har* for *hard* or *as* for *ask*). Point out these differences in English and Spanish. Help English learners practice spelling and pronouncing English words with final consonant blends.

jectives
Practice /ks/ spelled *Xx.*
Substitute phonemes.
Read /ks/ words.
Read high-frequency words.

Check Word Reading
SUCCESS PREDICTOR

Phonics—Teach/Model
/ks/ Spelled *Xx*

Review **/ks/*Xx*** Display the *six* Picture Card. This is the number word *six.* What sound do you hear at the end of *six.* What letter spells that sound? Write *six* on the board and point to the *x. Six* ends with /ks/ spelled *x.* There are not very many words that begin with *x.* Most of the *x* words we read have *x* at the end. Write *Xx* on the board. The sound for this letter is /ks/. The name of this letter is uppercase *X* and lowercase *x.* What is the sound for this letter? What are the names of these letters?

Picture Card

Review **Letter Names and Sounds** Use Alphabet Cards to review the following letter names and sounds: *Aa, Bb, Dd, Ee, Ff, Gg, Hh, Ii, Jj, Ll, Mm, Nn, Oo, Pp, Rr, Ss.*

Blend sounds Write *mix* on the board. Point to each letter as you say the sound: /m/ /i/ /ks/. When I blend these sounds together, I make the word *mix.* Say the sounds with me: /m/ /i/ /ks/. Now blend the sounds together: /m/ /i/ /ks/, *mix.* Repeat the blending routine with *wax, Rex, fix,* and *pox.*

More practice Use *Reader's and Writer's Notebook,* p. 339, for additional practice with /ks/.

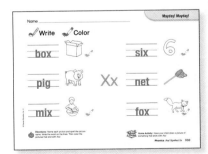

Reader's and Writer's Notebook, p. 339

Review **Sound-Spelling** Display the *Tt* Alphabet Card. What sound do you hear at the beginning of *turtle?* What letter spells that sound? Yes, the letter *t* spells /t/. Review the following sounds and letters with Alphabet Cards: *Aa, Bb, Gg, Ii, Jj, Oo, Pp, Rr, Ss.*

Review **High-Frequency Words** Write *blue* on the board. This is the word *blue.* What is this word? Continue the routine with *yellow, green, they, we,* and *have.*

Tt

Alphabet Card

MONITOR PROGRESS   ↻ Check Word Reading   High-Frequency Words

Write *blue, yellow, green, they, we,* and *have* on the board. Have children take turns reading the words.

Practice reading these words from Kindergarten Student Reader K.5.2, *Our Boat.*

Jem	Rex	Jan	Ox	box	mat	spot
tip	dip	rip	land	Dad	help	fix

If... children cannot read the high-frequency words,
then... write the words on cards for them to practice at home.

If... children cannot blend sounds to read the words,
then... provide practice blending the words in chunks, /j/ -em.

If... children can successfully blend sounds to read the words,
then... have them read Kindergarten Student Reader K.5.2, *Our Boat.*

Day 1	**Day 2**	**Day 3**	**Day 4**	**Day 5**
Check Phonemic Awareness	Check Sound-Spelling/ Retelling	Check Word Reading	Check Phonemic Awareness	Check Oral Vocabulary

Success Predictor

Differentiated Instruction

SI Strategic Intervention

High-Frequency Words Ask children to name each letter in *green.* Then have them write each of these lowercase letters on their Write-On Boards.

ELL

English Language Learners
Access Content Have children tell what words in their home languages are used for *yellow, blue,* and *green.*

Word Reading

Succe Predict

Kindergarten Student Reader K.5.2
/ks/ Spelled *Xx* and High-Frequency Words

Review

Review the previously taught high-frequency words. Have children read each word as you point to it on the Word Wall.

they	have	a	yellow	blue
green	the	we	for	to

Read Kindergarten Student Reader K.5.2

Display Kindergarten Student Reader K.5.2, *Our Boat.* Today we are going to read a new book about a big yellow box. Point to the title of the book. The title of the book is *Our Boat.* The author's name is Maura Albrecht. The book was illustrated by Hector Borlasca.

Use the reading decodable books routine to read the Kindergarten Student Reader.

ROUTINE **Reading Decodable Books**   *Small Group*

1. **Read Silently** Have children whisper read the book page by page as you listen in.
2. **Model Fluent Reading** Have children finger point as you read a page. Then have children reread the page without you.
3. **Read Chorally** Have children finger point as they chorally read the page. Continue reading page by page, repeating steps 1 and 2.
4. **Read Individually** Have children take turns reading aloud a page.
5. **Reread and Monitor Progress** As you listen to individual children reread, monitor progress and provide support.
6. **Reread with a Partner** Have children reread the book page by page with a partner.

Routines Flip Chart

Jem and Rex get Jan and Ox.
They have a big yellow box.

2

Jem, Rex, and Jan have
a big yellow box.
They will get a blue mat.

3

Jan got a big green spot.
Jan got the mat on the spot.
Rex and Jem get the box on the mat.

4

Kindergarten Student Reader K.5.2

Get in, Rex! Get in, Jan!
We fit in the yellow box.
We have a spot for Ox.

5

We tip, tip, tip.
We dip, dip, dip.
We rip, rip, rip.

6

We rip the yellow box.
Get to land, Jem!
Dad, Dad, help!

7

Rex, Jem, and Jan get Dad!
Dad will fix the big yellow box.

8

Differentiated Instruction

 Strategic Intervention

Support High-Frequency Words Have children use the high-frequency words in sentences to help them becom[e] more familiar with the words.

Small Group Time

DAY 3 Break into small groups to read the Kindergarten Student Reader before the comprehension lesson.

Teacher-Led

SI Strategic Intervention	**OL On-Level**	**A Advanced**
Teacher-Led Page DI•20 • Phonemic Awareness and Phonics • **Read** Concept Literacy Reader K.5.2 or Kindergarten Student Reader K.5.2	**Teacher-Led** Page DI•24 • Phonemic Awareness and Phonics • **Read** Kindergarten Student Reader K.5.2	**Teacher-Led** Page DI•27 • **Read** Independent Reader K.5.2 or Kindergarten Student Reader K.5.2

 Place English language learners in the groups that correspond to their reading abilities in English.

Practice Stations
• Visit the Words to Know Station
• Visit the Let's Write! Station

Independent Activities
• Read independently
• Audio Text of Trade Book
• *Reader's and Writer's Notebook*

English Language Learners

Access Content Ask children t[o] point out naming words in *Our Boat,* such as *mat, land, box,* and *spot.* Have children act out the action words *fix, tip, dip,* and *rip.*

Mayday! Mayday! • 15[7]

Comprehension

Retell the selection

Have children turn to p. 46 of *My Skills Buddy* and use the retelling boxes to retell the selection *Mayday! Mayday!*

 **Envision It!**

Think Aloud Direct children to the first retell box. This is when the sailors get in trouble from the storm. They call for help from the Coast Guard. Tell me what the Coast Guard does to help the sailors.

Continue reviewing the retelling boxes and having children tell about the selection.

My Skills Buddy, p. 46

Review **Cause and Effect** Display illustrations in *Mayday! Mayday!* Let's review cause and effect, or what happens and why it happens, in the selection.

• The sailors call for help. Why? (because they get caught in a storm)

• The Coast Guard gets the helicopter ready. Why? (because they got a mayday call from the sailors)

• The Coast Guard and the Jayhawk helicopter are back at the base. Why? (because they have finished rescuing the sailors)

More Practice

Use *Reader's and Writer's Notebook,* p. 340, for additional practice with cause and effect.

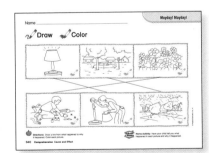

Reader's and Writer's Notebook, p. 340

Develop vocabulary

Second Read—Trade Book
Mayday! Mayday!

Reread *Mayday! Mayday!* Follow the Day 3 arrow beginning on p. 158, and use the Develop Vocabulary Notes to prompt conversations about the selection.

Have children use the Amazing Words *rescue, pilot, yacht, sailor, mechanic,* and *shimmering* to talk about the selection.

DAY **2**
Read for enjoyment

DAY **3**
Reread using Develop Vocabulary notes

DAY **4**
Reread using Guide Comprehension notes

Differentiated Instruction

SI **Strategic Intervention**

Activate Prior Knowledge
Ask children to tell you about a time they witnessed a terrible storm. Ask them if they have ever witnessed a storm near th ocean.

English Language Learners

Access Content Ask children to describe what the sky looks like after a storm. If they strugg to come up with English words supply the word and have them repeat it.

Develop Vocabulary

DAY 3

Open-ended

What does this picture show?
(a rescue swimmer)

• This is a rescue swimmer with all of the equipment he or she has to wear. **Point to and name each item.** How would the rescue swimmer use this?

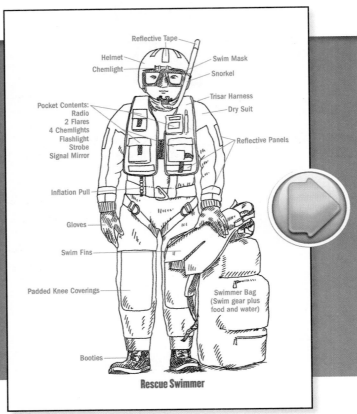

Reflective Tape

Helmet
Chemlight

Swim Mask
Snorkel

Trisar Harness
Dry Suit

Pocket Contents:
Radio
2 Flares
4 Chemlights
Flashlight
Strobe
Signal Mirror

Reflective Panels

Inflation Pull

Gloves

Swim Fins

Padded Knee Coverings

Swimmer Bag
(Swim gear plus food and water)

Booties

Rescue Swimmer

Trade Book, p. 3

Guide Comprehension

DAY 4

Cause and Effect

Why do you think a rescue swimmer needs to have all this equipment?
(because the rescue swimmer never knows what will be needed when he or she gets to the rescue)

Open-ended

What is happening to this boat? (Water is coming into it.)

• Water is pouring into it. What will happen if the sailors on the boat do not get help soon?

A thirty-foot yacht, adrift well out to sea, sends, "MAYDAY! MAYDAY! Please respond to our plea!"

Trade Book, pp. 4–5

Monitor and Fix Up

Do you ever want to make sure you understand something in a book? You can raise your hand and ask a question. On this page you may want to ask: *What is the man on the boat holding?* What other questions might you ask?

Develop Vocabulary, continued

DAY 3

Wh- question

What type of vehicle will the Coast Guard use for the rescue mission? (a helicopter)

- The helicopter they are going to use is called an H-60 Jayhawk. How many rescuers are going on the helicopter?

Expand Vocabulary fueled

The call is received at the Coast Guard air base. An H-60 'hawk has been fueled for the chase.

Trade Book, pp. 6–7

Guide Comprehension, continued

DAY 4

Compare and Contrast

Look at the illustration. How is the helicopter different from the airplane in the sky? (The helicopter has a propeller above it; the plane does not.) How is it the same? (Both can fly.)

Distancing

How do the flight mech and swimmer prepare? (They stow their gear and fasten their seat belts.)

• The rescuers put their gear in its place and fasten their seat belts. How is this like what you do before a trip?

Develop Vocabulary swimmer

The flight "mech" and swimmer stow gear and belt in. The pilots' checklist done, the rotors now spin.

Trade Book, pp. 8–9

Compare and Contrast

Do you have a checklist before you leave home in the morning the way the pilots do? How is it different from the pilots'? How is it the same? (The lists are the same because they tell what needs to be done; they are different because the tasks they list are different.)

Develop Vocabulary, continued

DAY 3

Open-ended
Where is the helicopter now? (over the water)

- The helicopter is flying over the ocean water. Tell me about the ocean and the sky in this picture.

Develop Vocabulary taxi

Expand Vocabulary turbines

In minutes, twin turbines drown out any sound.
A short taxi and then wheels lift off the ground.

Trade Book, pp. 10–11

Guide Comprehension, continued

DAY 4

Activate Prior Knowledge
Have you ever seen a bad storm? What was it like? Have you ever seen a storm over the ocean? Tell us about it. (Answers will vary.)

Wh- question

What happens to the yacht? (It gets knocked
on its side by the storm.)

- The yacht is getting pushed around by the
  wind and waves. What do you think will
  happen now?

The yacht, with sails reefed, gets knocked on its side.
Then righted, it battles a frightening ride.

Trade Book, pp. 12–13

Open-ended

How do you think the people in the yacht are
feeling right now? What makes you think so?
(They are probably scared and worried.)

DAYS 3 & 4 Read and Comprehend

Develop Vocabulary, continued

DAY 3

Open-ended
Where are the pilots? (in the cockpit of the helicopter)

- There are many buttons, lights, and pieces of equipment in the helicopter. What do you think the pilot uses them for?

Expand Vocabulary radar

On radar, the small boat appears dead ahead.

Trade Book, pp. 14–15

Guide Comprehension, continued

DAY 4

Draw Conclusions
What do you think the instrument called *radar* does? (It helps the pilots see in the dark.)

Wh- question

What is the red streak in the sky? (a flare)

- A flare lights the sky red. Where did the flare come from?

Then a flare lights the sky a shimmering red.

Trade Book, pp. 16–17

Cause and Effect

Why do you think the people in the boat send up the flare? (so the people in the helicopter can see where they are)

Develop Vocabulary, continued

Open-ended

What is the swimmer doing?
(jumping into the water)

- The swimmer is jumping into the water. What do you think he will do next?

With winds steadily whipping into a gale, a lowered winch line could entangle the sail.

So the swimmer is tapped. He knows his job well. Thumbs-up from the mech; he drops into the swell.

U.S. COAST GUARD

Trade Book, pp. 18–19

Guide Comprehension, continued

Inferential

How will the swimmer find the boat?
(The helicopter is shining a spotlight on it.)

Open-ended

What is the swimmer wearing on his face?
(a face mask)

- The swimmer is wearing a face mask. Why
  do you think he needs one?

A perfect drop aids the rescue swimmer's task.
His chemlight glows brightly atop his face mask.

Trade Book, pp. 20–21

Predicting

Where is the swimmer going? What will happen next? (He is going toward the boat where
he will help the sailors.)

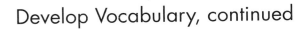
Develop Vocabulary, continued

DAY 3

Open-ended

What is the rescue swimmer doing in this picture? (He is helping the sailors onto a raft.)

- The rescue swimmer is helping the sailors onto a raft. Why do they need a raft?

Battling waves, the swimmer reaches the craft, then guides the weary sailors into their raft.

Trade Book, pp. 22–23

Guide Comprehension, continued

DAY 4

Open-ended

Where do you think the raft came from? Why? (It might have been dropped by the helicopter, because if the sailors had it earlier, they would have used it.)

Wh- question

What is the flight mechanic doing here?
(letting down a big basket)

The flight mechanic is lowering a basket into
the water. What is the basket for?

Next the flight mechanic calls, "Basket away,"
then guides the pilot through the swirling salt spray.

Trade Book, pp. 24–25

Draw Conclusions

Is the helicopter over the yacht? How can you
tell? (Yes, because the basket is being lowered so that it is close to the yacht.)

Develop Vocabulary, continued

Wh- question

Where is one sailor now? (in the basket)

DAY 3

- One sailor is safely in the basket. What will the rescue swimmer do next?

From the raft a sailor drops into the sea and is guided into the basket safely.

Trade Book, pp. 26–27

Guide Comprehension, continued

DAY 4

Sequence

What will the pilot and the rescuer in the helicopter do after a sailor is in the basket? (They will pull the basket up so the sailor can get into the helicopter. Then they will lower the basket again to get the next sailor.)

Wh- question

What is the mech doing at the doorway of the
helicopter? (watching the basket)

- The mech is watching the basket. Why
  does he need to watch?

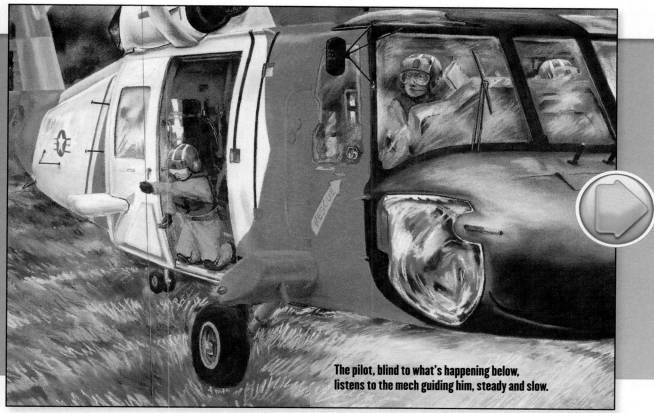

The pilot, blind to what's happening below,
listens to the mech guiding him, steady and slow.

Trade Book, pp. 28–29

Cause and Effect

Why can't the pilots see what is happening
below? (They are too busy flying the
helicopter to watch.)

Develop Vocabulary, continued

DAY 3

Open-ended
Who is being lifted into the helicopter? (the sailors)

- The sailors are being lifted into the helicopter. How are they being hoisted up?

Expand Vocabulary hoisted

One by one, the sailors are hoisted aboard.
Then a last drop before the basket is stored.

Trade Book, pp. 30–31

Guide Comprehension, continued

DAY 4

Draw Conclusions
The letters on the bottom of the helicopter stand for *United States Coast Guard.* Why do you think the letters are on the bottom? (The letters are on the bottom so people below know that the helicopter is from the Coast Guard.)

Wh- question

How are the sailors feeling as they are strapped into seats on the helicopter?
(tired and cold)

• The sailors are tired and cold. Why are they cold?

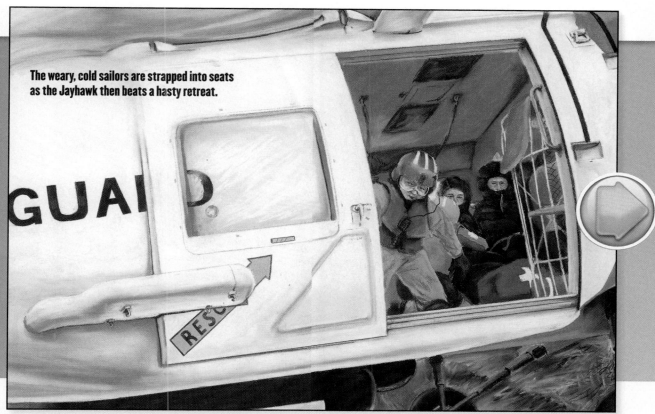

The weary, cold sailors are strapped into seats as the Jayhawk then beats a hasty retreat.

Trade Book, pp. 32–33

Drawing Conclusions

Where is the helicopter going with the sailors?
(back to base, where they will all be safe)

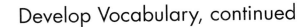
Develop Vocabulary, continued

DAY 3

Open-ended

Where is the Jayhawk now? (at the base)

• The Jayhawk is parked at the base. What do the helicopter and workers do when they aren't on a rescue?

Now back at the base, parked just off the runway, the refueled Jayhawk awaits the next "MAYDAY!"

Trade Book, pp. 34–35

Guide Comprehension, continued

DAY 4

Wh- question

Look at the picture. Is the storm almost over? How can you tell? What does the sky look like now? (The storm is almost over because the clouds are leaving.)

Recall

What does this diagram show? (a helicopter)

• This diagram shows the type of helicopter used to save the sailors in the selection. **Point to the rescue hoist.** We saw this used for the rescue in the selection. Do you remember what this is for?

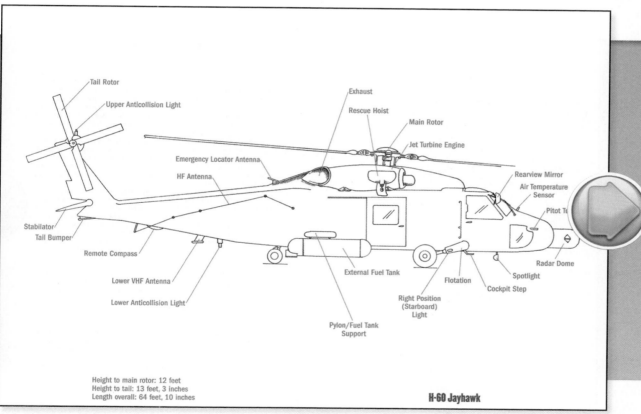

Tail Rotor
Upper Anticollision Light
Exhaust
Rescue Hoist
Main Rotor
Jet Turbine Engine
Emergency Locator Antenna
HF Antenna
Rearview Mirror
Air Temperature Sensor
Pitot T
Stabilator
Tail Bumper
Remote Compass
Lower VHF Antenna
Lower Anticollision Light
External Fuel Tank
Pylon/Fuel Tank Support
Right Position (Starboard) Light
Flotation
Cockpit Step
Spotlight
Radar Dome

Height to main rotor: 12 feet
Height to tail: 13 feet, 3 inches
Length overall: 64 feet, 10 inches

H-60 Jayhawk

Trade Book, pp. 36–37

Graphics

Who can point to the door where the basket comes out? Where does the pilot sit? (The door is under the main rotor. The pilot sits at the front.)

Develop Vocabulary, continued

DAY 3

Wh- question

What does this diagram show?
(a member of a flight crew)

- This diagram shows a Coast Guard helicopter pilot. He has a pad of paper and a pen on his knee. How do you think he uses them?

Night-Vision Goggle Attachment

Flight Helmet

Visor Adjustment (Visor in full "up" position)

Microphone

Life Vest Inflation Bladder

Pocket (Penholder)

Inflation Pull

Pocket Contents: Signal Mirror Radio Pencil Flares

Survival Vest

Dry Suit

Closure

Gloves

Knee Board with Pen (Pilots; holds flight information)

Knee Pads (Flight mechanic)

Pocket

Closure

Leather Flight Boots

Flight Crew

AUTHOR'S NOTE

The U.S. Coast Guard is the country's oldest maritime agency. In the late 1700s light-houses and other navigational aids were first built by the Coast Guard to help ships safely reach one of the growing number of coastal ports. Although originally developed for the purpose of public safety on the water, the Coast Guard also took on law enforcement and later aided the U.S. Navy in war efforts. Today, with nine total districts, as far southeast as Miami, Florida, and as far northwest as Juneau, Alaska, the U.S. Coast Guard covers almost 100,000 miles of coastline, including the Great Lakes and inland waterways.

After World War II much of the focus of the Coast Guard turned back toward safety on the water. With the development of the helicopter, Search and Rescue (SAR) took a significant leap forward. People in danger could now be reached much faster than by ship, and unlike airplanes, helicopters could remove people from sinking or disabled vessels. This meant more lives were saved. The word "mayday" comes from the French term *m'aidez*, which means "Help me." "Mayday" is the accepted international call of distress.

In 1992 the H-60 Jayhawk replaced the aging HH-3F Pelican, which had been in service since the early sixties. The Jayhawk is a medium-range rotary-wing aircraft that can cover three hundred nautical miles without stopping, remain on scene for forty-five minutes, and return to shore with a total of six rescuees. If a mayday call comes far from the base, the Coast Guard will launch their faster HU-25 Falcon jet to locate the stricken craft, be it a ship or downed aircraft. They can drop supplies such as an inflatable raft, food, and water and remain on scene until the Jayhawk arrives.

A crew of four operates the Jayhawk: a pilot, copilot, flight mechanic, and rescue swimmer. Unlike in airplanes, where the pilot sits on the left, in rescue helicopters the pilot sits on the right—the same side as the hoist and rescue basket. This enables the pilot to have more visual contact with the vessel below.

When the Jayhawk arrives on scene, the flight mechanic takes over responsibilities for direct-ing the rescue operation. Since the flight mechanic operates the hoist, which is located over the side door eight feet behind the pilot, the flight mechanic becomes the pilot's eyes in guiding the Jayhawk. To ready the rescue basket, the hoist cable is attached to the top of the basket by a large steel clip. The cable runs on a winch system, which allows the basket to be lowered and raised mechanically.

While lowering the rescue basket to the awaiting deck, the flight mechanic keeps the pilot informed of the basket's location in relation to the ship, by giving height and directional com-mands. In addition to concentrating on where the basket is in the air, the flight mechanic and pilot have to pay attention to the rising and falling of the vessel on rough seas to avoid any contact between the two craft.

If the seas are impossibly rough, the risk of entangling the basket in the ship's antennae or masts is greatly increased. To avoid this, a 150-foot guide rope is lowered to the ship by the cable

Trade Book, pp. 38–39

Guide Comprehension, continued

DAY 4

Cause and Effect

The pilot wears what is called a "wet suit." Why does a member of the Coast Guard wear a wet suit?
(to keep him or her dry both in and out of the water)

Distancing

What do you think this picture shows? (Coast Guard members)

- These are just a few members of the Coast Guard. The names of these people are in the caption under the photograph. Would you like to be a member of the Coast Guard when you are grown up?

Continue with DAY 3

Conventions p. 178

before the rescue basket is dropped. Once the weighted end of this rope is lowered onto the deck, the helicopter backs away from the boat. The other end of the rope is attached to the top of the rescue basket, and the basket can now be lowered at a safer angle and guided onboard by the ship's crew.

The rescue swimmer, trained as an emergency medical technician (EMT), gives immediate attention on scene, when needed, before sending the patient aloft. Once a maximum of six victims and the rescue swimmer are aboard the Jayhawk and secured, the flight mechanic gives the pilot a verbal OK. The helicopter flies to the closest medical facility.

The Jayhawk is equipped with the latest navigational technology. Global Positioning Systems (GPS) give the flight crew their exact location. The flight crew is also equipped with night-vision capabilities in both goggles and Forward Looking Infrared Radar (FLIR) to enable a night rescue operation to take place more safely. There are many other automated systems that provide for approaches, hovers, and emergency departures. If a collision with a vessel or a rogue wave threatens to knock the helicopter out of the sky, a button pushed will immediately propel the craft 150 feet upward and out of harm's way.

As with all aspects of the Coast Guard, success comes down to personnel training. Years of experience go into making a team work as one. It's a dedication to saving lives that is the backbone of the U.S. Coast Guard. Those orange and white colors are there to remind the public of their motto: "Always ready."

—C. L. D.

From left to right: Emma D. Dryden, VP & Editorial Director of McElderry Books; Jim McGinley, AMT 3 Flight Mechanic; Brian Laubenstein, AST 1 Rescue Swimmer; Lt. Comdr. Mark Morin, Pilot; Lt. John Mixon, Pilot; and Chris L. Demarest, author/artist, in front of H-60 Jayhawk, U.S. Coast Guard Air Station Cape Cod

Trade Book, p. 40

Judgment

Could this really happen? What makes you think so? (Yes, it could really happen because there really are Coast Guard helicopters whose crews rescue people at sea.)

Skip to DAY 4

Conventions p. 192

Conventions
Questions

Review

Sentences that ask something are called questions. Some questions begin with the words *who, what, when, where, why,* or *how.*

Here are some questions for you about *Mayday! Mayday!*

• Who do the sailors call?
• Who helps the sailors after they get stuck in the storm?

Guide practice

Let's write some questions about the Coast Guard on the board.

• why do Coast Guard members have different jobs
• what kind of transportation does the Coast Guard use in the selection
• where do the Coast Guard members take the sailors at the end of the selection

What do we need at the beginning of each question? What do we need at the end? **Have children add a capital letter and question mark to each question on the board.**

Team Talk Pair children and have them take turns asking each other questions about *Mayday! Mayday!*

On their own

Use *Reader's and Writer's Notebook,* p. 341, for more practice with questions.

Daily Fix-It

Use the Daily Fix-It exercise for more conventions practice.

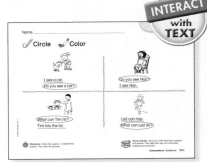

Reader's and Writer's Notebook, p. 341

Writing
Rhyme

Teach

A rhyme is like a short poem. It is a few words or a sentence that sounds like a song. The words at the ends of the lines rhyme, or have the same middle and ending sounds. Like a poem, a rhyme has rhythm, like clapping to a beat.

Model

Display the *box* and *fox* Picture Cards. Write the following rhyme sentence frame on the board:

> **The sly tan _____** (fox)
>
> **hid in the _____.** (box)

Have children help you complete the rhyme using the words *box* and *fox*. Have volunteers write the words to fill in the blanks. Then read the rhyme together, clapping the rhythm as you say the rhyme. Have children identify the rhyming words *fox* and *box*.

Guide practice

Now let's write a rhyme about *Mayday! Mayday!* The sailors have to be saved when their yacht gets stuck in big waves from a storm. Let's write a rhyme using the rhyming words *save* and *wave*. Write the following rhyme on the board and read it aloud with children.

> **On a wave**
> **Time to save!**

Independent writing

Have children turn to p. 342 of *Reader's and Writer's Notebook*. Have them copy the class rhyme and draw a picture to go with it.

Reader's and Writer's Notebook, p. 342

Daily Handwriting

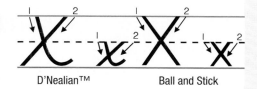

D'Nealian™   Ball and Stick

Write *X* and *wax* on the board. Review correct letter formation of uppercase *X* and lowercase *x*.

Have children write the letter *X* and the word *wax* on their Write-On Boards. Remind them to use proper left-to-right and top-to-bottom progression and proper spacing between letters when writing *X* and *x*.

Differentiated Instruction

 Strategic Intervention

Support Directions Remind children that a period is used at the end of most sentences. If the sentence is a question, a question mark is placed at the end instead.

Teacher Tip

Although questions are commonly described as being pronounced with a raised voice at the end, that is frequently not the case. Therefore, do not stress this with children as one way of identifying questions.

Daily Fix-It

jan ran to see the fox
Jan ran to see the fox.

This week's practice sentences appear on Teacher Resources DVD-ROM.

ELL

English Language Learners

Support Conventions Ask children to identify their favorite part of *Mayday! Mayday!* Then ask children if there is anything in the selection they would like to know more about. Help children frame this in the form of a question.

Objectives
- Practice responding to literature through drama.
- Speak loudly and clearly when sharing ideas.
- Take turns and speak one at a time.

Listening and Speaking
Respond to Literature: Drama

Review

Remind children that when they speak to the class, they need to speak loudly and clearly to make sure everyone can hear and understand them. When they listen, they should face the speaker and raise their hand if they have a question.

Model

Let's watch AlphaBuddy pretend he is in the boat in *Mayday! Mayday!* Put AlphaBuddy in a box. Pretend a storm approaches and AlphaBuddy falls out of his boat. Call on a child to "swim" to AlphaBuddy's rescue and bring him back to shore.

Pretending can help us understand what happens in a book and why it happens. When you read about a rescue mission, you learn what other people do. Have children turn to p. 49 of *My Skills Buddy.* Tell children to share how they think the sailors must have felt when they were rescued.

My Skills Buddy, p. 49

Independent practice

Use the Listening and Speaking bullets on p. 48 of *My Skills Buddy* to guide discussion. Divide the class into small groups. Have groups take turns acting out different parts of *Mayday! Mayday!* Refer children to the Rules for Listening from p. 1 of *Reader's and Writer's Notebook*. Remind children that good speakers take turns and speak one at a time.

Name _____

Listening Rules

1. Face the person who is speaking.
2. Be quiet while someone is speaking.
3. Pay attention to the speaker.
4. Ask questions if you don't understand.

Listening and Speaking Rules 1

Reader's and Writer's Notebook, p. 1

Be a Good Listener

1. Face the speaker.
2. Raise your hand if you have a question.
3. Be quiet when others are speaking.
4. Take turns speaking and listening.

Differentiated Instruction

 Strategic Intervention

Access Content Dramatizing a story or selection is a valuable way for struggling readers to understand the selection. You may want to have children act out other simple rescue missions for additional practice.

Teacher Tip

Watch for children's tendency to repeat too much detail and to include their own opinions and reactions.

English Language Learners
Access Content Allow English language learners to join in the dramatization when they are ready. Use pantomime to illustrate your own narration and encourage English language learners to mimic your motions.

Objectives

- Review skills learned and practiced today.

Wrap Up Your Day

✔ **Concept Talk** Today we read about the Coast Guard helping in an emergency. What did the Coast Guard members do?

✔ **Respond to Literature** Today we read about Jan, Jem, and Rex's boat ride. Dad had to save them. Did you ever need help when you were playing?

✔ **Conventions** Point to a child and have him or her ask a question beginning with *who, what, where, when, why,* or *how*.

✔ **Homework Idea** Have children draw and label a picture of a word that ends in *x*.

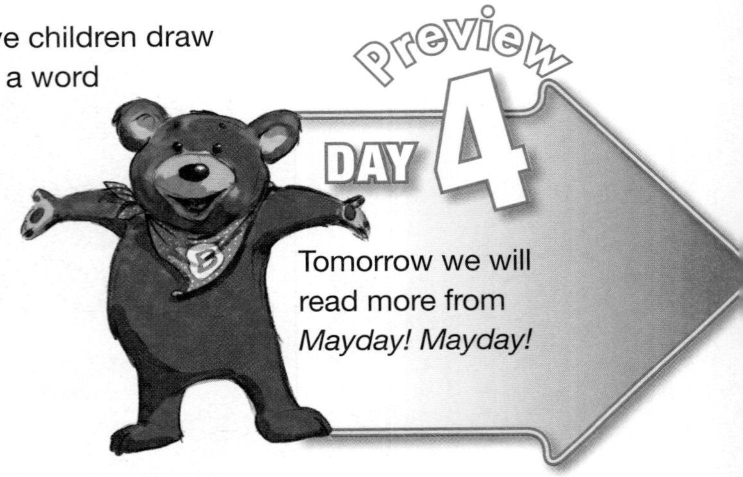

Preview
DAY 4
Tomorrow we will read more from *Mayday! Mayday!*

Extend Your Day!

Social Studies
Geographical Direction
Materials: compass, U.S. map

Points of the Compass Show children the map and point to your state. Point out the compass rose on the map and review the words *north, south, east,* and *west.*

- When we want to travel somewhere, we need to know which direction to go in order to get there.
- A compass is a tool that helps people travel in the right direction.
- The arrow on this compass is pointing north.

Show the compass pointing north and have children face north. Then have them turn to face east, west, and south. Have children say the following as they turn:

Face north. To the right is east, to the left is west, and behind is south.

Practice naming the direction words and having children repeat the words. Then say a direction and have children tell where it is.

Science
Weather Changes
Materials: Graphic Organizer 30

Sun, Wind, and Rain Discuss the different ways the sky can look and how wind changes the weather. Does the wind make it colder or warmer? Where do clouds come from?

The Cycle of Weather Draw a cycle chart or display Graphic Organizer 30. We're going to use the chart to show how the sky changes when a storm comes and goes. How does the sky look on a normal day? Write children's responses, in the top box. Then have children describe what the sky looks like as the storm approaches, during the storm, and as the storm passes by. Record children's ideas.

Conventions
Question Fun

The Asking Game Explain the rules of "The Asking Game." Designate one child to start. Have the first child ask a question of the next child. The second player must answer and then ask a new question about the same subject to the third child. For example, the first player might ask, "What did you do last night?" and the second player might say, "I read a book." Then he or she would say to the third child, "Did you read last night?"

Provide help to players who repeat the question or have difficulty thinking of a new question. Continue until many questions are asked.

bjectives
Discuss the concept to develop oral language.
Build oral vocabulary.

oday at a Glance

ral Vocabulary
echanic, shimmering

honemic Awareness
view /j/ and /w/

honics
Spelled *Jj*
/ Spelled *Ww*
ell Words

omprehension
Cause and Effect

onventions
uestion Marks and Uppercase
etters

riting
xtend the Concept

ocabulary
osition Words

TRUCKTOWN on Reading Street

Start your engines!

- Display p. 13 of *Truckery Rhymes*. Lead the group in saying the rhyme a few times.
- Next, have the group clap the rhythm as they recite the rhyme.
- When children master the rhythm, have them march around the room as they say the rhyme.

Truckery Rhymes

Concept Talk

Question of the Week

What kinds of transportation help us in emergencies?

Build concepts

Write the question of the week on the board. Read the question as you track the print. Have children answer the question in complete sentences. Display Sing with Me Chart 26B.

Listen for Amazing Words

Recall with children that yesterday they sang "The Coast Guard to the Rescue." Today we will sing the song again. I want you to listen for the Amazing Words *mechanic* and *shimmering*. When you hear those Amazing Words, I want you to clap your hands. Sing the song several times to the tune of "Ring Around the Rosie."

💿 Sing with Me Audio

ELL Produce Oral Language Use the Day 4 instruction on ELL Poster 26 to extend and enrich language.

The Coast Guard to the Rescue

The yacht called "Mayday!" from the sea,
To pilot and to crew,
The mechanic stowed the swimmer's gear,
The Coast Guard to the rescue!

Talk with Me/Sing with Me Chart 26B

ELL Poster 26

Oral Vocabulary
Amazing Words

Amazing Words

rescue	pilot
yacht	sailor
mechanic	shimmering

Teach Amazing Words

Amazing Words **Oral Vocabulary Routine**

1 Introduce the Word The Coast Guard helicopter has a *mechanic.* A *mechanic* is a worker who knows how to fix machines and engines. What's our new Amazing Word for a worker who fixes things? Say it with me: *mechanic.*

2 Demonstrate *In* Mayday! Mayday! *the mechanic lowers the rescue basket for the sailors in the water below.*

Repeat steps 1 and 2.

Introduce *Shimmering* is a word that describes something that sparkles in the light. What's our new Amazing Word for something that sparkles in the light? Say it with me: *shimmering.*

Demonstrate *In* Mayday! Mayday! *the flare makes the sky a shimmering red.*

3 Apply Have children use *mechanic* and *shimmering* in complete sentences that describe the rescue in *Mayday! Mayday!*

Routines Flip Chart

Use Amazing Words

To reinforce the concept and the Amazing Words, have children supply the appropriate Amazing Word for each sentence.

We know a _____ who fixes airplane engines. (mechanic)

The light of the moon is _____ on the lake. (shimmering)

Differentiated Instruction

A Advanced

Amazing Words Move a piece of aluminum foil or other shiny material in the light to show children something that is *shimmering*. Then have children make their own shimmering artwork b gluing foil, glitter, or other classroom materials to construction paper.

ELL

English Language Learners
Access Content Have children share how they say *mechanic* and *shimmering* in their home languages.

DAY 4 — Get Ready to Read

Objectives
Review /j/ spelled *Jj*.
Review /w/ spelled *Ww*.

Check Phonemic Awareness
SUCCESS PREDICTOR

Phonemic Awareness
Review /j/ and /w/

Review

Display the *jam* Picture Card. This is *jam*. *Jam* begins with /j/. What sound does *jam* begin with? Say it with me: /j/ /j/ /j/, *jam*. Repeat the routine with the *jet* and *juice* Picture Cards. Display the *waffle* Picture Card. This is a *waffle*. *Waffle* begins with /w/. What sound does *waffle* begin with? Repeat the routine with the *wagon* and *web* Picture Cards.

I am going to say a word. When you hear /j/ at the beginning, I want you to jump. When you hear /w/ at the beginning, I want you to walk like a duck. Let's try one together: *jet*. Did you jump? Good. Continue the routine with the following words: *wet* (duck walk), *jolly* (jump), *jog* (jump), *water* (duck walk), *wagon* (duck walk), *juice* (jump), *woman* (duck walk).

Corrective feedback

If... children cannot discriminate /j/ or /w/,
then... have them say each sound several times.

Have children watch you closely as you say /j/ and /w/. Explain that as you say /j/, your lips do not touch; and when you say /w/, your lips touch. Have children practice saying /j/ and /w/, and then repeat the discrimination activity.

Picture Card

Picture Card

Phonics
/j/ Spelled *Jj* and /w/ Spelled *Ww*

Review Display the *Jj* Alphabet Card. This is a *jaguar. Jaguar* begins with /j/. What letter spells /j/? Yes, the letter *Jj* spells /j/. Repeat the routine with the *Ww* Alphabet Card.

Let's blend sounds to read some names. Write the name *Jim* on the board. Help me blend this name. Listen as I say each sound: /j/ /i/ /m/. Now blend the sounds together to read the name: /j/ /i/ /m/, *Jim*. What is the name? (*Jim*) Let's try more. Continue the routine with the names *Jan, Jill, Wes,* and *Will.*

Alphabet Card

Alphabet Card

Differentiated Instruction

SI Strategic Intervention

Sound Game Pair children and have them each draw somethin that begins with /j/ or /w/. Ther have each child show the draw ing to his or her partner to gues the word. If the partner can't guess, tell the illustrator to pro vide clues. Then have partners switch roles and repeat.

Don't Wait Until Friday

MONITOR PROGRESS   **Check Phonemic Awareness**

Phoneme Segmentation I am going to say a word. Tell me all of the sounds you hear in each word.

| jet | box | will | ox | Rex | jam | mix | wig | fox |

If... children cannot segment the sounds,

then... use the small-group Strategic Intervention lesson, p. DI•21, to reteach segmentation skills.

Continue to monitor children's progress using other instructional opportunities during the week so that they can be successful with the Day 5 Assessment. See the Skills Trace on p. 124.

Day 1	Day 2	Day 3	**Day 4**	Day 5
Check Phonemic Awareness	Check Sound-Spelling/ Retelling	Check Word Reading	Check Phonemic Awareness	Check Oral Vocabulary

Success Predictor

ELL

English Language Learners
Support Phonemic Awareness Speakers of Hmong, Khmer, Korean, Tagalog, and Vietnames may have difficulty distinguishing the voiced /j/ from the unvoiced /ch/ or /sh/. Spanish or Russian speakers may pronounce /j/ as /ch/. Provide additional practice with /j/ words.

Phonemic Awareness

Succes Predicto

Spelling

/ks/ Spelled Xx

Spell words

ROUTINE **Spell Words**

1 **Review Sound-Spellings** Display the *box* Picture Card. This is a *box. Box* ends with /ks/. What is the letter for /ks/? (*x*) Continue the routine with the following letters: *Aa, Ff, Mm, Tt.*

2 **Model** Today we are going to spell some words. Listen to the three sounds in *fox:* /f/ /o/ /ks/.

f   o   x

- What is the first sound in *fox*? (/f/) What is the letter for /f/? (*f*) Write *f* on the board.
- What is the middle sound you hear? (/o/) What is the letter for /o/? (*o*) Write *o* on the board.
- What is the last sound you hear? (/ks/) What is the letter for /ks/? (*x*) Write *x* on the board.
- Point to *fox.* Help me blend the sound of each letter together to read this word: /f/ /o/ /ks/. The word is *fox.* Repeat with the word *six.*

3 **Guide Practice** Now let's spell some words together. Listen to this word: /t/ /a/ /ks/. What is the first sound in *tax*? (/t/) What is the letter for /t/? (*t*) Write *t* on the board. Now you write *t* on your paper. What is the middle sound in *tax*? (/a/) What is the letter for /a/? (*a*) Write *a* on the board. Now you write *a* on your paper. What is the last sound in *tax*? (/ks/) What is the letter for /ks/? (*x*) Write *x* on the board. Now you write *x* on your paper. Now we can blend the sound of each letter together to read the word: /t/ /a/ /ks/. What is the word? (*tax*) Continue spell and blend practice with the following words: *Max, fix, wax, pox.*

4 **On Your Own** This time I am going to say a word. I want you to write it on your paper. Remember, first, say the word slowly in your head and then write the letter for each sound. Listen carefully. Write the word *mix.* Give children time to write the word. How do you spell the word *mix*? Listen to the sounds: /m/ /i/ /ks/. The first sound is /m/. What is the letter for /m/? Did you write *m* on your paper? What is the letter for /i/? Did you write *i* on your paper? What is the letter for /ks/? Did you write *x* on your paper? Name the letters in *mix. Mix* is spelled *m, i, x.* Continue the activity with the following words: *ax, lax, Tex, Rex, fax, ox.*

Routines Flip Chart

Get Set, Roll! Reader 26
Practice /ks/ Spelled *Xx*

Review

Read Get Set, Roll! Reader 26

Review the high-frequency words *the, I, to, a, is, my, he, for, she, you, yellow, green,* and *blue.* Have children read each word as you point to it on the Word Wall.

Today we will read a book about Jack Truck delivering boxes. Point to the title of the book. What is the title of the book? *The Yellow Box* is the title of the book. We will read lots of words with *x* in this book.

Use the routine for reading decodable books found in the Routines Flip Chart to read Get Set, Roll! Reader 26.

Get Set, Roll! Reader 26

Small Group Time

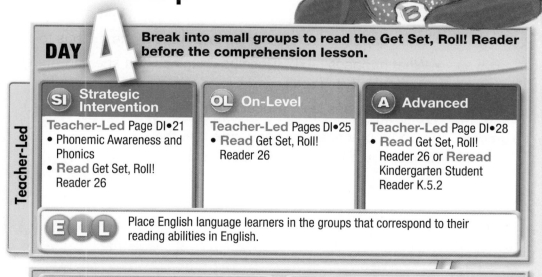

DAY 4 Break into small groups to read the Get Set, Roll! Reader before the comprehension lesson.

Teacher-Led

SI Strategic Intervention	OL On-Level	A Advanced
Teacher-Led Page DI•21	Teacher-Led Pages DI•25	Teacher-Led Page DI•28
• Phonemic Awareness and Phonics	• **Read** Get Set, Roll! Reader 26	• **Read** Get Set, Roll! Reader 26 or **Reread** Kindergarten Student Reader K.5.2
• **Read** Get Set, Roll! Reader 26		

ELL Place English language learners in the groups that correspond to their reading abilities in English.

Practice Stations
• Visit the Let's Write! Station
• Visit the Read for Meaning Station

Independent Activities
• Read independently
• Audio Text of the Trade Book
• *Reader's and Writer's Notebook*

Differentiated Instruction

SI Strategic Intervention

Build Background Take a picture walk through *Truckery Rhymes* with children before reading Get Set, Roll! Reader 2 Remind children that there are many different kinds of trucks. Explain that a character in the story they are about to read is a truck named Jack. Discuss with children what they know about trucks.

ELL

English Language Learners

Frontload Reader Take a picture walk with children to preview the reader before starting the routine.

Objectives
Practice cause and effect.
Review and practice sequence.

Comprehension
Cause and Effect

Practice cause and effect

Envision It!

Have children turn to the Cause and Effect picture on pp. 34–35 of *My Skills Buddy.* As you look at the pictures, remind children that they should look for cause and effect, or what happens and why it happens.

Team Talk Pair children. Have the first child tell something that happens in

My Skills Buddy, pp. 34–35

Mayday! Mayday! Have the second child tell why it happens. Then have children switch roles and repeat the activity.

Sequence

Review

Remember that things happen in a certain order: first, next, and last. This is the sequence of the story. Good readers think about the order of things that happen in stories.

Display Trade Book *Abuela* and take a picture walk through the story. Do you remember what happened in the story *Abuela?* Let's tell what happens first, next, and last in the story. Use the pictures to guide children's answers.

- What happens first? (Rosalba and Abuela ride the bus to the park.)
- What happens next? (Rosalba imagines that she and Abuela are flying over the city.)
- What happens last? (Rosalba and Abuela take a boat ride.)

More practice

For more practice with sequence, use the *Reader's and Writer's Notebook,* p. 343.

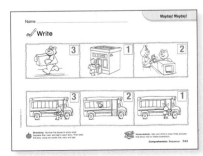

Reader's and Writer's Notebook, p. 343

Third Read—Trade Book
Mayday! Mayday!

Guide comprehension

Display *Mayday! Mayday!* Let's tell the sequence, or what happens first, next, and last in *Mayday! Mayday!*

- What happens first? (There is a storm, and the sailors on a yacht call for help.)

- When they get the mayday signal, what does the Coast Guard do next? (They pack their gear, get into the helicopter, and take off for the rescue mission.)

- After the swimmer reaches the sailors, what happens next? (He guides them to the raft.)

- What happens last? (The sailors get pulled up into the helicopter and they all fly back to the base.)

Reread *Mayday! Mayday!* Return to p. 158. Follow the Day 4 arrow and use the Guide Comprehension Notes to give children the opportunity to gain a more complete understanding of the selection.

DAY **2**

Read for enjoyment

DAY **3**

Reread using Develop Vocabulary notes

DAY **4**

Reread using Guide Comprehension notes

Differentiated Instruction

 Advanced

Support Comprehension Have children retell the events in a story or selection with which they are familiar. Have them tell what happens first, next, and last.

Academic Vocabulary

sequence the order of events

ELL

English Language Learners
Access Content Have English learners join the activity after first observing how the other children are participating.

Objectives

Identify question marks and uppercase letters.
Practice question marks and uppercase letters.

Conventions
Question Marks and Uppercase Letters

Review

Write these questions on the board: *What day is it? Where are we? When is lunch? How are you?* Remind children that every question begins with a capital, or uppercase, letter and ends with a question mark.

Guide practice

What is the name of the special mark that goes at the end of a question? Right, a question mark. Let's draw a question mark in the air.

Play a game in which you recite the written questions from above and children march around the room in time with the words. When you read the first word of the sentence, have children jump in the air to signify the uppercase letter. When the sentence ends, have them stop and draw question marks in the air with their fingers.

On their own

Use *Reader's and Writer's Notebook,* p. 344, for more practice with question marks and uppercase letters.

Daily Fix-It

Use the Daily Fix-It exercise for more conventions practice.

Reader's and Writer's Notebook, p. 344

Writing
Extend the Concept: Text to World

Discuss emergency rescue

In *Mayday! Mayday!* the sailors have an emergency on the water when they get caught in a storm. The Coast Guard uses a helicopter to help them in the emergency. Other people use transportation to help people in emergencies, too.

What kind of transportation do firefighters use to rescue people? What do paramedics use to help people in emergencies? What other kinds of transportation are used to rescue people or animals? List children's responses on the board.

Guide practice

Use children's contributions to the discussion to write sentences.

> **Firefighters use a fire truck.**
>
> **Paramedics use an ambulance.**
>
> **Police officers use a police car.**

Independent writing

Have children write or dictate a sentence about a kind of transportation used in an emergency, or they may copy a sentence from the board. Have them illustrate their sentences.

Daily Handwriting

Write *X* and *Rex* on the board. Review correct letter formation of uppercase *X* and lowercase *x*.

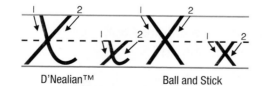

D'Nealian™   Ball and Stick

Have children write the letter *X* and the word *Rex* on their Write-On Boards. Remind them to use proper left-to-right and top-to-bottom progression and proper spacing between letters when writing *X* and *x*.

Vocabulary
Position Words

Teach

Write the words *top, bottom, front,* and *back* on the board. Point to each word as you read it. These words show the position of something, or where it is. Have children turn to p. 48 of *My Skills Buddy.* Direct them to the stack of books. Where is the *top* of the stack of books? Where is the *bottom* of the stack of books? Then direct them to the pictures of the girl. Where is the *front* of the girl? Where is the *back* of the girl? Use the last four Vocabulary bullets on the page to discuss the position of objects in the classroom.

My Skills Buddy, p. 48

Team Talk Pair children and have them take turns using the position words *top, bottom, front,* and *back* in sentences.

Wrap Up Your Day

✔ **Oral Language** Let's sing "Mr. Max Mox, What's in the Box?" again. Clap when you hear an Amazing Word—*rescue, pilot, yacht, sailor, mechanic, shimmering.*

✔ **Phonemic Awareness** I'm going to read some sentences. Jump when you hear a word with /ks/. *The fox jumped over the box. Dad will fix the ax. Are you six?*

✔ **Homework Idea** Have children ask their families a few questions and draw the question mark in the air after each one.

Preview

DAY 5

Tell children that tomorrow they will review some of the books and stories they have read this week.

Science
What Will Float?

Materials: clear plastic tub, small plastic boat, water, ice cubes, small classroom objects, Trade Book *Mayday! Mayday!*, Big Book *If You Could Go to Antarctica*

Float or Sink? Fill the tub with water. Raise your hand if you think this toy boat will float in this tub of water. If the boat doesn't float, what will it do? Display *Mayday! Mayday!* Do you think the yacht might sink in the storm? What would make a boat sink?

Pass objects around the classroom and have children predict what will float and what will sink. Use a three-column chart to keep track of the results as you place the objects one by one in the tub. When putting ice cubes in the water, turn to page 9 of *If You Could Go to Antarctica* and connect the behavior of the ice cubes with that of icebergs in the selection.

Object	Float	Sink
boat	X	
penny		X
ice cubes	X	
car		X

High-Frequency Words
What Color?

Materials: colored markers, writing paper, pencils, crayons

Yellow, Blue, or Green? Write the questions below on mural paper. Write children's answers with colored markers in complete sentences, such as *The sky is _____.*

• What color is the sky when the sun is shining?
• What color is grass in spring?
• What color are bananas?

Tell children to identify questions and telling sentences. Have children copy the sentences, writing the color words with yellow, blue, and green crayons.

Phonics
Sound Patterns

What Comes Next? Write the following letters on the board: j w j w _

Let's say the sounds these letters make, one at a time: /j/ /w/ /j/ /w/. What sound do you think comes next? Extend the pattern until each letter repeats three times. Write the following letters on the board:

j w a j w a j w _

Recite the sounds and have children predict what comes next in the pattern. Then have children suggest sounds for the patterns.

Objectives
- Review the concepts.
- Build oral vocabulary.

Today at a Glance

Oral Vocabulary
rescue, pilot, yacht, sailor, mechanic, shimmering

Phonemic Awareness
Final /ks/

Phonics
/ks/ Spelled Xx

Comprehension
Cause and Effect

Conventions
Question Marks and Uppercase Letters

Writing
This Week We…

Check Oral Vocabulary
SUCCESS PREDICTOR

TRUCKTOWN on Reading Street

Start your engines!

- Display p. 13 of *Truckery Rhymes,* the rhyme "It's Raining, It's Pouring" and lead the group in saying the rhyme a few times.
- Have half the group recite the rhyme while the other half acts it out.
- Then have the groups change roles.

Truckery Rhymes

Concept Wrap Up

Question of the Week

 What kinds of transportation help us in an emergency?

Listen for Amazing Words

Write the question of the week on the board. Track the print as you read it to children. Have them take turns and answer the question in complete sentences. Remind them that this week they talked about a helicopter used in an emergency. Display Sing with Me Chart 26B. Remind children that the Amazing Words *rescue, pilot, yacht, sailor, mechanic,* and *shimmering* are in the song. Sing the song with children. Have them act out the Amazing Words as they sing.

Sing with Me Audio

The Coast Guard to the Rescue

The yacht called "Mayday!" from the sea,
To pilot and to crew.
The mechanic stowed the swimmer's gear,
The Coast Guard to the rescue!

Sing with Me Chart 26B

ELL **Check Concepts and Language** Use the Day 5 instruction on ELL Poster 26 to monitor children's understanding of the lesson concept.

ELL Poster 26

Oral Vocabulary
Amazing Words

rescue	pilot
yacht	sailor
mechanic	shimmering

 Review

Let's Talk We learned six new Amazing Words this week. Let's say the Amazing Words as I point to the pictures on the chart. Point to each picture and give children the chance to say the appropriate Amazing Word before offering it.

Have children supply the appropriate Amazing Word to complete each sentence.

The _____ flies the helicopter. (pilot)

A _____ is a kind of boat. (yacht)

The Coast Guard will _____ the sailors in the water. (rescue)

A person who works on a boat is a _____. (sailor)

The light of the flare is _____ on the water. (shimmering)

A _____ is a person who knows how to fix machines. (mechanic)

Talk with Me/Sing with Me Chart 26A

Differentiated Instruction

 Advanced

Amazing Words Have children write or dictate their own sentence using one of this week's Amazing Words.

It's Friday

MONITOR PROGRESS Check Oral Vocabulary

Demonstrate Word Knowledge Monitor the Amazing Words by asking the following questions. Have children use an Amazing Word in their answer.

- **What did the Coast Guard do for the sailors?** (rescue)
- **Who is the person who flies the helicopter?** (pilot)
- **What kind of boat were the sailors in?** (yacht)
- **Who are the people who work on a boat?** (sailors)
- **What kind of person knows how to fix machines?** (mechanic)
- **How do you describe something that sparkles in the light?** (shimmering)

If... children have difficulty using the Amazing Words,

then... reteach the words using the Oral Vocabulary Routine on the Routines Flip Chart.

Day 1	Day 2	Day 3	Day 4	Day 5
Check Phonemic Awareness	Check Sound-Spelling/ Retelling	Check Word Reading	Check Phonemic Awareness	Check Oral Vocabulary

Success Predictor

Oral Vocabulary

Succes Predicto

bjectives
Review final /ks/.
Review /ks/ spelled *Xx.*

Phonemic Awareness Review
 /ks/

Isolate final /ks/	Display the *box* Picture Card. What is the last sound in *box?* Say the word with me: *box.* The last sound is /ks/. *Box* ends with /ks/. Continue reviewing final /ks/ with the *six* Picture Card and the words *Rex* and *mix.*
Discriminate final sounds	I am going to say some words. When you hear /ks/ at the end of a word, I want you to put your hands on the top of your head. Use the following words: *tax, mom, run, six, fix, plan, land, box, ox, fox, kite, lox.*

Picture Card

Picture Card

Phonics Review

/ks/ Spelled Xx

Teach /ks/Xx

Display the *ox* Picture Card. This is an *ox*. What sound do you hear at the end of *ox*? What letter spells that sound?

High-frequency words

Write the word *yellow* on the board. This is the word *yellow*. What is this word? Repeat the routine with *green* and *blue*.

Apply phonics in familiar text

Let's Reread Have children reread one of the books specific to the target letter sound. You may wish to review the decodable words and high-frequency words that appear in each book prior to rereading.

Picture Card

Decodable Reader 26
My Skills Buddy, p. 38

Kindergarten Student
Reader K.5.2

Get Set, Roll!
Reader 26

Small Group Time

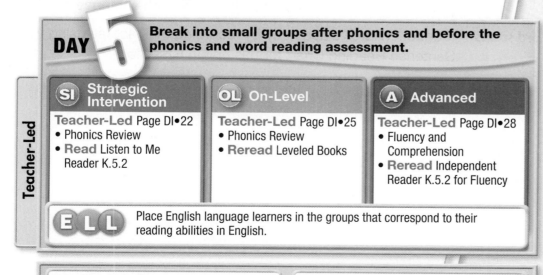

DAY 5 Break into small groups after phonics and before the phonics and word reading assessment.

Teacher-Led

(SI) Strategic Intervention	**(OL) On-Level**	**(A) Advanced**
Teacher-Led Page DI•22 • Phonics Review • **Read** Listen to Me Reader K.5.2	**Teacher-Led** Page DI•25 • Phonics Review • **Reread** Leveled Books	**Teacher-Led** Page DI•28 • Fluency and Comprehension • **Reread** Independent Reader K.5.2 for Fluency

ELL Place English language learners in the groups that correspond to their reading abilities in English.

Practice Stations
• Visit the Read for Meaning Station
• Visit the Let's Make Art Station

Independent Activities
• Read independently
• Story Sort
• Concept Talk Video

ELL

English Language Learners

Support Phonics To help children learn the relationships between sounds and letters, have them spell several words from Decodable Reader 26 on their Write-On Boards. Use the words *Fox, fix,* and *box*.

ssess
- Read /ks/ spelled *Xx*.
- Read high-frequency words.
- Read sentences.

Assessment
Monitor Progress

/ks/ Spelled Xx

Whole Class Tell children you will say some words. If the word ends in *x*, they should make an *x* on their chests by crossing their arms. Use the following words: *ox, box, fit, mix, fox, will, six, pan, wax*.

MONITOR PROGRESS	Check Word and Sentence Reading

If... children cannot complete the whole-class assessment,
then... use the Reteach lesson in *First Stop*.

If... you are unsure of a child's grasp of this week's skills,
then... use the assessment below to obtain a clearer evaluation of the child's progress.

/ks/ Spelled Xx and high-frequency words

One-on-One To facilitate individual progress monitoring, assess some children on Day 4 and the rest on Day 5. While individual children are being assessed, the rest of the class can read this week's books and look for words with /ks/.

Word reading

Use the word lists on reproducible p. 201 to assess each child's ability to read words with /ks/ and high-frequency words. We're going to read some words. I'll read the first word, and you read the rest. The first word is *fox*, /f/ /o/ /ks/. For each child, record any decoding problems.

Sentence reading

Use the sentences on reproducible p. 201 to assess a child's ability to read words in sentences. Have each child read two sentences aloud. Have each child read different sentences. Start over with sentence one if necessary.

Record scores

Monitor children's accuracy by recording their scores using the Word and Sentence Reading Chart for this unit in *First Stop*.

Name _____

Read the Words

fox ☐   green ☐

wax ☐   box ☐

blue ☐   Max ☐

fix ☐   yellow ☐

Rex ☐   tax ☐

mix ☐   six ☐

Read the Sentences

1. I have six green pens.

2. Jan can wax the yellow bin.

3. They will go next on the blue jet.

4. Rex and I look in the little green cup.

5. Will the blue hat fit Max?

Note to Teacher: Children read each word. Children read two sentences.

Scoring for Read the Words: Score 1 point for each correct word.

/ks/Xx (fox, wax, fix, Rex, mix, box, Max, tax, six) _____ /__9__
High-Frequency Words (blue, green, yellow) _____ /__3__

MONITOR PROGRESS
• /ks/Spelled Xx
• High-frequency words

bjectives
• Recognize a fable.
• Identify the moral or lesson in a fable.

My Skills Buddy, pp. 50–51

Let's Practice It!
Fable

Teach

Tell children that today they will listen to a well-known fable. A fable is a type of story that has been told for a long time. Review the features of a fable with children.

- A fable usually has animal characters or characters from nature.
- A fable teaches a moral, or lesson.
- A fable could not really happen.

Have children turn to pp. 50–51 of *My Skills Buddy*. I am going to read a fable called "The Wind and the Sun." Look at the pictures as I read. Read the text of "The Wind and the Sun." As you read, direct children to look at the appropriate picture.

Guide practice

Discuss the features of the fable with children and the bulleted text on *My Skills Buddy* p. 50.

- A fable usually has animal characters or characters from nature. Who are the characters from nature in this fable? (the wind and the sun) Can the wind and the sun talk in real life? (no)

- A fable teaches a moral, or lesson. The moral, or big idea, of this fable is "gentleness often works better than force." What do you think that means? (It is better to ask nicely for something than to just take what you want.)

- A fable could not really happen. Do you think this fable could really happen? Why or why not? (No, because the wind and the sun cannot really talk to each other.)

Academic Vocabulary

fable a story, usually with anim characters, that is written to teach a moral, or lesson

E L L

English Language Learners

Access Content Have children tell what words in their home languages are used for *wind* and *sun*. Remind children that the same sun shines on every part of Earth, regardless of wha people in that area call it.

The Wind and the Sun

The Wind and the Sun were arguing about which one was stronger.

"I am stronger than you," said the Wind.

"No, I am stronger than you," said the Sun.

They would have gone on like this forever, but then they saw a man walking down the road.

The Sun said, "I know how we can settle our argument. Whoever can take off this man's coat is stronger. You go first."

The Sun hid behind a cloud, and the Wind began to blow on the man. It blew as hard as it could, trying to blow the man's coat off.

"Brrr, it is windy and cold today," said the man, and he pulled his coat tightly around himself.

Then the Sun came out and shined down on the man.

"Whew, it is very warm today," said the man, and he took off his coat.

The Sun had won.

Moral: *Gentleness often works better than force.*

Comprehension Assessment
Monitor Progress

Review

⊙ **Cause and Effect** Remember that many things happen in stories and other things make them happen. A cause is what makes something happen. An effect is what happens. Good readers listen for causes and effects to help them understand a story better.

Read "The Mysteries of Flight"

Tell children that you are going to read them a story about a little girl who wants to fly. Tell them to listen carefully to the story. I am going to read you a story and then we will decide what happens in the story and why it happens. We will talk about the causes and effects. Read "The Mysteries of Flight" on p. 63 of the *Read Aloud Anthology.*

Read Aloud Anthology

Check cause and effect

After you read the story, have children identify what happens in the story and why it happens.

- Why does Maria think she can fly? (because she flies in a dream)

- Why do you think no one believes her? (because she can't really fly)

- After she figures out she cannot fly in the daytime or when someone is looking, what does Maria do? (She tries to fly at night when no one is looking.)

Corrective feedback

If... children cannot identify causes and effects,
then... reteach cause and effect using the Reteach lesson in *First Stop.*

Assess cause and effect

Use the blackline master on p. 205. Make one copy for each child. Review the story and have children color the picture of what happens in the story. Then have them color the picture showing why it happens.

Cause and Effect

Color the picture that shows what happens in "The Mysteries of Flight." Then color the picture that shows why it happens.

What happened?

Why did it happen?

Note to Teacher: Have children color the large picture of what happens in the story. Then have them choose and color the picture showing why it happens.

Objectives
• Review question marks and uppercase letters.
• Write questions about a favorite book or song.

Conventions
Question Marks and Uppercase Letters

Review   This week we talked about question marks and capital letters. When you write the beginning of a sentence or a person's name, you use a capital, or uppercase, letter. When you write a sentence that asks a question, you put a question mark at the end.

Model   Watch as I write a sentence on the board. Read it with me. Write the following on the board:

> **can you see the fox**

What kind of sentence is this? What does it need at the beginning? What does it need at the end? Guide children to add a capital letter at the beginning and a question mark at the end.

Guide practice   Write the following sentences on the board. Read the sentences with children. Tell children to add the capital letters and question marks.

> **did you go on the bus**
> **what did you say**
> **am i little**
> **do you have the lid**

On their own   Have children write or dictate their own question and illustrate it. Alternatively, they may choose one of the sentences on the board to copy and illustrate.

Daily Fix-It   Use the Daily Fix-It exercise for more conventions practice.

Writing
This Week We...

Review

Display *Mayday! Mayday!,* Sing With Me Chart 26B, Phonics Songs and Rhymes Chart 26, Decodable Reader 26 from *My Skills Buddy,* Kindergarten Student Reader K.5.2, and Get Set, Roll! Reader 26. This week we learned about transportation that helps us in an emergency. We read new books, and we sang new songs. Which book or song was your favorite? Let's share our ideas with each other.

Team Talk Pair children and have them take turns telling which book or song was their favorite and why.

Model writing a question

Let's write questions about our favorite book or song. Have a child tell which book or song he or she liked. Help the child ask a question about the text and write it on the board next to the child's name.

Questions	
Ms. Chang	What does a helicopter sound like?
Eva	How does Fox learn to fix things?
Rob	How can I be in the Coast Guard?

Guide practice

Continue with all children. Then have children read the questions with you.

On their own

Have each child copy and illustrate the question he or she dictated. Allow time for sharing everyone's completed pages.

Daily Handwriting

Write *X* and *fix* on the board. Review correct letter formation of uppercase *X* and lowercase *x*.

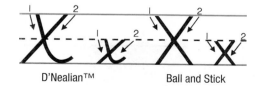

D'Nealian™   Ball and Stick

Have children write the letter *X* and the word *fix* on their Write-On Boards. Remind them to use proper left-to-right and top-to-bottom progression and proper spacing between letters when writing *X* and *x*.

Differentiated Instruction

 SI Strategic Intervention

Support Writing Have children look through this week's books to find questions. Read the sentences they find and have children decide whether they are questions or telling sentences. Have them point out capital letters and question marks.

Daily Fix-It

did you see my red fox
Did you see my red fox?

This week's practice sentences appear on Teacher Resources DVD-ROM.

ELL

English Language Learners
Poster Preview Prepare children for next week by using Week 3 ELL Poster number 27. Read the Poster Talk-Through to introduce the concept and vocabulary. Ask children to identify and describe objects and actions they see.

bjectives
• Review weekly concept.
• Review cause and effect.

Wrap Up Your Week!

Question of the Week
What kinds of transportation help us in an emergency?

This week we talked about emergencies and the kinds of transportation that can help us.

- Make a Cause and Effect Chart like the one shown or use Graphic Organizer 29.
- Have children suggest events that happen in *Mayday! Mayday!* Write their responses under *What happened?*
- Then have children identify what caused each event to happen and write their responses under *Why did it happen?*
- Have them draw their favorite part of the selection listed in the chart.
- Have children write or dictate a phrase or sentence about their picture.

Amazing Words

You've learned
0 0 6
words this week!
You've learned
1 5 6
words this year!

Illustrate cause and effect

```
        ( What happened? )
                |
                v
        ( Why did it happen? )
```

Next Week's Question
What kinds of transportation help people do their jobs?

Discuss next week's question. Guide children in making connections between transportation used in an emergency and for a job.

Preview
NEXT WEEK

Next week we will read a book called *Trucks Roll!* What do you think the book will be about?

Extend Your Day!

Social Studies
Map Work

Materials: globe, U.S. map, outline maps of the United States (one for each child), crayons

Find Our State Show the globe to children. Point out the land areas and the blue water areas. Have children tell whether they see more land or more water areas. Help them identify oceans, lakes, and rivers.

Display a map of the United States. Help children locate the state where your school is located. Have children tell about the location. Is it near water? Is it by an ocean, lake, or river? Show children the location on the globe and have them compare the map and the globe.

Point out that the globe shows the entire Earth while the map of the United States shows only one part of Earth.

Give children an outline map of the United States and have them locate their state and color it.

Social Studies
Preventive Measures

Materials: drawing paper, crayons

Project Safety Sometimes we can keep an emergency from happening by planning to be safe. What are some ways we can be safe in what we do? Prompt children if necessary with questions such as *What do you wear when riding your bike?* Have children illustrate safety measures and write or dictate a slogan for their pictures.

Be safe!

Drama
Jobs

Materials: Big Book *Miss Bindergarten Takes a Field Trip*, Trade Books *Abuela* and *Mayday! Mayday!*, classroom objects for props

Helping Drama Take a picture walk through *Miss Bindergarten Takes a Field Trip*, *Abuela*, and *Mayday! Mayday!* Have children identify people and the different jobs they perform. Use props from the room to put together a skit of someone whose job is helping someone else.

Weekly Assessment

Use the whole-class assessment on pages 200–201 and 204–205 in this Teacher's Edition to check:

✔ ◉ **/ks/ Spelled** *Xx*

✔ ◉ **Comprehension Skill** *Cause and Effect*

✔ **High-Frequency Words**   *yellow   green   blue*

Teacher's Edition, Day 5

Managing Assessment

Use the Assessment Handbook for:

✔ **Observation Checklists**

✔ **Record-Keeping Forms**

✔ **Portfolio Assessment**

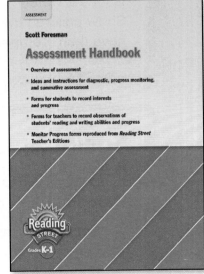

Assessment Handbook

Teacher Notes

5 Day Plan

AY 1
- Phonemic Awareness/ Phonics
- Decodable Story 26

AY 2
- Phonemic Awareness/ Phonics
- Decodable Reader 26

AY 3
- Phonemic Awareness/ Phonics
- Concept Literacy Reader K.5.2 or Kindergarten Student Reader K.5.2

AY 4
- Phonemic Awareness/ Phonics
- Get Set, Roll! Reader 26

AY 5
- Phonics Review
- Listen to Me Reader K.5.2

3 or 4 Day Plan

AY 1
- Phonemic Awareness/ Phonics
- Decodable Story 26

AY 2
- Phonemic Awareness/ Phonics
- Decodable Reader 26

AY 3
- Phonemic Awareness/ Phonics
- Concept Literacy Reader K.5.2 or Kindergarten Student Reader K.5.2

AY 4
- Phonemic Awareness/ Phonics
- Get Set, Roll! Reader 26

Day Plan: Eliminate the shaded box.

SI *Strategic Intervention*

DAY 1

Phonemic Awareness•Phonics

■ **Isolate /ks/** Display the *box* Picture Card. This is a *box. Box* ends with /ks/. Say it with me: *box,* /ks/ /ks/ /ks/. Repeat with *fox* and *ox.*

■ **Connect /ks/ to *Xx*** I am going to say three words. I want you to tell me which word ends with /ks/. Listen carefully: *Max, Mike, Molly.* Say the words with me: *Max, Mike, Molly.* Which word ends with /ks/? *Max* ends with /ks/. *Mike* and *Molly* do not end with /ks/. Write the letters *Xx* on the board. The letter *x* can stand for /ks/ in words. Continue with the following sets of words: *taco, tax, talk; milk, mix, water; Rover, Rex, Buddy.*

Decodable Story 26

■ **Review** Review the previously taught high-frequency words by writing each of these words and having children say the words with you.

is	a	from	look	like	blue	green

If... children have difficulty reading the words,
then... say a word and have children point to the word. Repeat several times, giving assistance as needed.

■ **Read** Have children read *Max* orally. Then have them reread the story several times individually.

Reader's and Writer's Notebook, pp. 335–336

Objectives
- Identify the common sounds that letters represent.
- Read at least 25 high-frequency words from a commonly used list.

SI *Strategic Intervention*

DAY **2**

More Reading

Use Leveled Readers or othe text at children's instructiona level.

Phonemic Awareness•Phonics

■ **Discriminate /ks/** Display Phonics Songs and Rhymes Chart 26. Sing "Mr. Max Mox, What's in the Box?" to the tune of "Are You Sleeping?" several times with children. Ask them to make an *X* in the air when they hear a word that ends with /ks/.

■ **Connect /ks/ to Xx** Ask children to name words in "Mr. Max Mox, What's in the Box?" that end with /ks/*Xx.* List the words as they say them. Have children echo read the list of words. Then ask children to take turns circling the *x* in the words on the list.

Decodable Reader 26

■ **Review** Review the high-frequency words by writing *blue* on the board. *This is the word blue. What word is this?* Continue with the following words: *a, yellow, to, green, have, is, the.*

> **If…** children have difficulty reading the words,
> **then…** say a word and have children point to the word. Repeat several times, giving assistance as needed.

■ **Read** Display the cover of *Fox Can Fix It!* on p. 38 of *My Skills Buddy.* Ask a volunteer to read the first page of the story. Have children tell what Fox can fix. Continue through the story in this manner.

My Skills Buddy

Phonemic Awareness•Phonics

■ **Isolate /ks/** Display the *six* Picture Card. This is *six. Six* is a number. Let's count to *six:* one, two, three, four, five, six. *Six* ends with /ks/. Say it with me: /s/ /i/ /ks/, *six.* Repeat with the *box* and *fox* Picture Cards.

■ **Connect /ks/ to Xx** Write *Xx* on the board. These are the letters *Xx.* The letter *x* can stand for /ks/ in words. Write the word *mix* on the board. This is the word *mix. Mix* ends with /ks/. Say it with me: *mix,* /ks/ /ks/. When you hear a word that ends with /ks/, pretend to mix something in a bowl. Use the following words: *fox, box, bill, open, ox.*

■ **Blend Sounds** Write *Max* on the board. Have children blend the sound of each letter to read the word. Repeat the routine with the words *mix, box,* and *Rex.*

■ **Review High-Frequency Words** Write *green* on the board. Have volunteers say the word and use it in a sentence. Continue with the word *blue, yellow, from, here,* and *go.*

■ To practice phonics and high-frequency words, have children read Kindergarten Student Reader K.5.2. Use the instruction on pp. 154–155.

For a complete lesson plan and additional practice, see the **Leveled Reader Teaching Guide**.

Concept Literacy Reader K.5.2

■ **Preview and Predict** Display the cover of the Concept Literacy Reader K.5.2. What form of transportation is this? Point to the title. The title of the book is *We Help.* How can a fire truck help? Have children tell about the picture and what they think the book might be about.

■ **Set a Purpose** We talked about the title of the book. Let's read the book to learn about how different forms of transportation can help. Have children read the Concept Literacy Reader.

■ **Read** Provide corrective feedback as children read the book orally. During reading, ask them if they are able to confirm any of the predictions they made prior to reading.

If... children have difficulty reading the book individually,
then... read a sentence aloud as children point to each word. Then have the group reread the sentences as they continue pointing to the words.

■ **Retell** Have children retell the content as you page through the book. Help them identify what the book is about. Also call attention to the people that use the different forms of transportation that help.

Concept Literacy Reader K.5.2

Objectives
• Identify the common sounds that letters represent. • Predict what might happen next based on the cover.
• Predict what might happen next based on the title. • Retell important facts in a text, heard or read.

SI *Strategic Intervention*

DAY **4**

Phonemic Awareness•Phonics

■ **Segment** Listen to the name *Tex.* I will separate the name into its separate sounds: /t/ /e/ /ks/. Do it with me. **Have children continue to segment:** *wax, fix, Rex, fox, six.*

■ **Decorate a Box!** Give each child a box. Have children decorate the box by writing words that end with *x* with colorful markers or crayons. Have them draw pictures for the words to complete the decorations. Allow time for children to share their boxes with the group.

Get Set, Roll! Reader 26

■ **Review** Review the following high-frequency words with children prior to reading the story: *the, I, to, a, is, my, he, for, she, you, yellow, green,* and *blue.*

Get Set, Roll! Reader 26

■ **Read** Display Get Set, Roll! Reader 26. Today we will read a story about Jack Truck delivering boxes. The title of the story is *The Yellow Box.* Look at the picture and think about the title. What do you think this story will be about?

> **If...** children have difficulty reading the story individually, **then...** read a sentence aloud as children point to each word. Then have the group reread the sentences as they continue pointing to the words.

■ **Reread** Use echo reading of Get Set, Roll! Reader 26 to model fluent reading. Use your oral reading to model for children where to pause, when to change pitch, and which words to stress. Then have children reread orally three to four times, or until they can read with few or no mistakes.

More Reading

Use Leveled Readers or other text at children's instructional level.

Objectives
- Identify the common sounds that letters represent.
- Read at least 25 high-frequency words from a commonly used list.
- Predict what might happen next based on the cover.

SI *Strategic Intervention*

DAY 5

ore Reading

se Leveled Readers or other
xt at children's instructional
vel.

Phonics Review

■ **Make an Xx** Write *Xx* on the board. *Xx spells /ks/.* Tell children you will tell them a story and they should listen for /ks/. When you say a word that has a /ks/, the children should make an *x* with their arms and repeat the word. Tell a simple story, emphasizing /ks/ words and pausing to give children a chance to make an *x* and repeat the word. *Rex is six. Rex has the chicken pox! The pox made Rex sad. So his dad played the sax and took out Rex's two favorite animals, fox and ox, from his box.*

Listen to Me Reader K.5.2

■ **Preview and Predict** Display the cover of the book. *The title of this story is A Box for Rex. It is written by Mary Pat Doyle. It is illustrated by Elizabeth Butler. What do you think Rex will do with the box? Tell me your ideas.*

Listen to Me Reader K.5.2

■ **Set a Purpose** Review children's ideas. Point out that after they read, they will know more about Rex and his box. Tell children that you will read the story with them. *Follow along with your finger as I read. Then we will take turns reading this page.* Repeat this routine through all of the pages. Guide children to decode words.

■ **Reread for Fluency** Use echo reading of Listen to Me Reader K.5.2 to model reading fluently. Use your oral reading to model for children when to pause, when to change pitch, and which words to stress. Then have children reread orally three to four times, or until they can read with few or no mistakes.

Objectives
- Identify the common sounds that letters represent.
- Predict what might happen next based on the cover.

 OL On-Level **DAY 1**

Phonemic Awareness•Phonics

■ **Discriminate /ks/** Display the *fox* Picture Card. This is a *fox*. *Fox* has /ks/ at the end. Say it with me: /f/ /o/ /ks/, *fox*. Does *mat* end with the same sound as *fox*? No, *mat* does not end with /ks/. Repeat the routine with the following words: *ox, snake, drum, box, starfish, six*.

■ **Connect /ks/ to *Xx*** Place a box on the table. Give each child an index card. Have children write the letter *x* on the card. Ask them to think of a word that ends with /ks/ spelled *Xx*. Have children say their word and place the *x* card in the box.

Objectives
• Identify the common sounds that letters represent.

⏱ 20-30 min

Pacing Small Group Instruction

5 Day Plan

DAY 1	• Phonemic Awareness, Phonics • Decodable Story 26
DAY 2	• Phonemic Awareness, Phonics • High-Frequency Words • Decodable Reader 26
DAY 3	• Phonemic Awareness, Phonics • Kindergarten Student Reader K.5.2
DAY 4	• Get Set, Roll! Reader 26
DAY 5	• Phonics Review • Reread Leveled Books

 OL On-Level **DAY 2**

Phonemic Awareness•Phonics

■ **Discriminate /ks/** Draw five boxes on the board. Gather about ten Picture Cards, including the following *Xx* cards: *box, fox, ox, six*. Mix the cards and display them one at a time. Have a child name the picture. If the name has /ks/, have the child write a lowercase *x* in one of the boxes.

■ **High-Frequency Words** Display the following word cards: *green, blue, yellow, from, go, here*. Say the word *green* and select a child to point to the word. Have children say the word and use it in a sentence. Continue with the other words.

Objectives
• Read at least 25 high-frequency words from a commonly used list.

3 or 4 Day Plan

DAY 1	• Phonemic Awareness/ Phonics • Decodable Story 26
DAY 2	• Phonemic Awareness/ Phonics • High-Frequency Words • Decodable Reader 26
DAY 3	• Phonemic Awareness/ Phonics • Kindergarten Student Reader K.5.2
DAY 4	• Get Set, Roll! Reader 26

3 Day Plan: Eliminate the shaded box.

More Practice

For additional practice with this week's phonics skills, have children reread the Decodable Story (Day 1) and the Decodable Reader (Day 2).

OL On-Level

DAY 3

Phonemic Awareness•Phonics

■ **Look in the Box** Put various Picture Cards in a small box, including the following *Xx*/ks/ Picture Cards: *box, fox, ox, six.* Have a child choose one card from the box. If the picture name ends with /ks/, have children say, *"This is a(n) (Picture Card) in a box."* Continue until children can identify /ks/*Xx* words.

■ **Connect /ks/ to *Xx*** Display the *fox* Picture Card. What is this? Write *fox* on the board. Say the letters with me: *f, o, x.* What is the sound we learned for the letter *x*? Yes, it is /ks/. Repeat with the Picture Cards for *box* and *six.*

Kindergarten Student Reader K.5.2

■ **Preview and Predict** Display the cover of the book. The title of this story is *Our Boat.* Look at the cover. What do the children use to make their boat? What do you think they will do in their boat? Tell me what you think will happen in this story.

Kindergarten Student Reader K.5.2

■ **Set a Purpose** Review the list of things children think might happen in the story. Remind children they will read to find out what the children do in the boat.

■ **Read** Have children follow along as they read the story with you. After reading p. 2, ask children to tell what the color of the box. Continue with each page. Ask the following questions:

• What do Jem, Rex, and Jan use the blue mat for?

• What do they do once they get in the box?

• Who helps fix the box?

■ **Summarize** Have children retell the story to a partner and tell how Dad helps to fix the box.

■ **Text to Self** Help children make personal connections to the story as they tell how they play make-believe.

Objectives
• Identify the common sounds that letters represent.
• Predict what might happen next based on the cover.
• Make connections to own experiences.

 DAY **4**

Get Set, Roll! Reader 26

■ **Review** Review previously taught high-frequency words by writing each word on the board and saying the word with children.

blue   green   yellow   you   she   for   he   my   is   a   to   I

■ **Read** Display Get Set, Roll! Reader 26, *The Yellow Box.* Point to the title of the story. What is the title of the story? *The Yellow Box* is the title of the story. Look at the picture. What do you think will happen in this story? We will read some words that end with /ks/ in this story. Let's read the story together.

Objectives
• Read at least 25 high-frequency words from a commonly used list.
• Predict what might happen next based on the cover.

More Reading
Use Leveled Readers or other text at children's instructional level to develop fluency.

 DAY **5**

Phonics Review

■ **Rhyme in Rhythm** Have children sit in a circle. Explain that rhyming words are words that have the same ending sounds. Demonstrate a set of rhyming words, such as *fix, mix,* and *six.* Then illustrate a simple rhythm pattern involving clapping hands and patting legs, such as *clap, clap, pat, pat.* Have the children practice the rhythm with you. When the rhythm is established, tell children you will all clap and pat the rhythm twice, and then you will say a word. Then the class will go through two more patterns and the child next to you will have to say a word that rhymes with your word. Continue around the circle until children can no longer come up with a word that rhymes. Write the rhyming words on the board. Have children identify the sounds for each letter. Repeat the game with other word families.

Objectives
• Orally generate rhymes in response to spoken words.
• Identify the common sounds that letters represent.

acing Small
roup Instruction

20-30 mins.

5 Day Plan

AY 1	• Phonemic Awareness/ Phonics • Decodable Story 26
AY 2	• Phonics • Spelling • Decodable Reader 26
AY 3	• Independent Reader K.5.2 or Kindergarten Student Reader K.5.2
AY 4	• Get Set, Roll! Reader 26 or Kindergarten Student Reader K.5.2
AY 5	• Fluency/ Comprehension • Independent Reader K.5.2

3 or 4 Day Plan

AY 1	• Phonemic Awareness/ Phonics • Decodable Story 26
AY 2	• Phonics • Spelling • Decodable Reader 26
AY 3	• Independent Reader K.5.2 or Kindergarten Student Reader K.5.2
AY 4	• Get Set, Roll! Reader 26 or Kindergarten Student Reader K.5.2

Day Plan: Eliminate the shaded box.

More Practice

or additional practice with his week's phonics skills and o develop fluency, have children reread the Decodable tory (Day 1) and the ecodable Reader (Day 2).

A — Advanced — DAY **1**

Phonemic Awareness•Phonics

■ **X Words** Write the following words on word cards: *fix, mix, six, ax, tax, wax, box, fox, ox.* Place the cards in a pocket chart. Give a clue to one of the words and have a volunteer take the word card and say the word. Use clues such as the following: *You do this to make something shiny. This number comes after five. You see this animal in the woods.* After children identify the word, have them tell what sound they hear at the end of the word and what letter stands for that sound.

Objectives
• Identify the common sounds that letters represent.

A — Advanced — DAY **2**

Phonics•Spelling

■ **Connect /ks/ to Xx** Display the *six* Picture Card. What is this word? Name the letters with me: *s, i, x, six.* What is the sound we learned for the letter *x*? Yes, it is /ks/.

■ **Spell Sounds** Give each child the following letter tiles: *e, f, g, i, j, m, n, o, t, w, x.* Listen to the sounds in the word *fox*: /f/ /o/ /ks/, *fox.* What is the letter for /f/? It is *f*. Place your *f* tile in front of you. Continue with the remaining sounds. Now let's make a new word by changing the first letter. Have children put a *b* tile in place of the *f* tile. What is this word? Say the sound for each letter and blend them together. The new word is /b/ /o/ /ks/, *box.* Then have children take away the *b* letter tile to make the word *ox.*

f o x

Objectives
• Identify the common sounds that letters represent.
• Recognize that new words are created when letters are changed.
• Use letter-sound correspondences to spell consonant-vowel-consonant (CVC) words.

For a complete lesson plan and additional practice, see the **Leveled Reader Teaching Guide**.

Independent Reader K.5.2

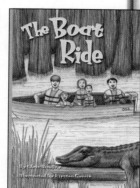

Independent
Reader K.5.2

■ **Practice High-Frequency Words** Write *blue* on the board. Have volunteers say the word and use it in a sentence. Continue with the words *yellow* and *green.*

■ **Activate Prior Knowledge** Remind children that people can travel on water using boats and ships. Picture walk through *The Boat Ride* and discuss what the family sees on their trip. Why must the family keep still when they see the alligator?

■ **Cause and Effect** After children read *The Boat Ride,* display p. 3. The family is going to put on yellow vests. Why do they put on the vests? Have children tell you if the family putting on vests is the cause or the effect.

■ **Reread for Fluency** After rereading with children, model reading fluently for them. I am going to read this book aloud. I will read the words with no mistakes. I want you to read it aloud with me. Try to read the words just as I do.

Use echo reading of Independent Reader K.5.2 to model reading fluently. Use your oral reading to model for children where to pause, when to change pitch, and which words to stress. Then have children reread orally three to four times, or until they can read with few or no mistakes.

■ For more practice with phonics and high-frequency words and to develop fluency, have children read the Kindergarten Student Reader K.5.2. Use the instruction on pp. 154–155.

More Reading
Use Leveled Readers or other text at children's instructional level.

Objectives
• Read at least 25 high-frequency words from a commonly used list.
• Identify what happens in a text and why it happens.

lore Reading

se Leveled Readers or other
xt at children's instructional
vel.

A Advanced

DAY **4**

Kindergarten Student Reader K.5.2

Kindergarten Student
Reader K.5.2

- **Revisit** Open to p. 4 of Kindergarten Student Reader K.5.2. Look at the box the children use for their boat. What do you think the blue mat is for?

- **Reread** Use Kindergarten Student Reader K.5.2 to practice reading fluently.

- **Text to Self** Ask children to think about what they would do with a big yellow box. Encourage them to be creative. Then have them draw a picture of them with the box.

- **Read** Have children read Get Set, Roll! Reader 26, *The Yellow Box*. Use instruction on p. 189.

Objectives
- Read at least 25 high-frequency words from a commonly used list.
- Predict what might happen next based on the illustrations.
- Make connections to own experiences.

A Advanced

DAY **5**

Fluency•Comprehension

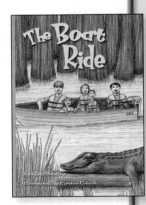

Independent
Reader K.5.2

- **Reread for Fluency** Use the Independent Reader K.5.2 to model reading fluently for children. I am going to read this selection aloud. I will read the words with no mistakes. I want you to read it aloud with me. Try to read the words just as I do.

- **Comprehension** After children have finished reading, have them retell what happens in the selection. Then have children write or draw a picture that shows what causes the family to yell at the end.

Objectives
- Read at least 25 high-frequency words from a commonly used list.
- Identify what happens in a text and why it happens.

 **DAY 1**

Concept Development

■ **Read the Concept Literacy Reader** Read *We Help* with children. Begin by reading the title and author's name. Have children describe what they see on the cover. Then have children look at the pictures in the book. What do you see? What are the automobiles doing? (They are helping.) Read the book aloud, pausing to discuss each page. Model sentence patterns and vocabulary that describe how automobiles and machines help. This is a police car. It has flashing lights. The police help people. On a second reading, invite children to talk about the mode of transportation on each page.

■ **Develop Oral Language** Revisit *We Help,* review the different modes of transportation used to help people. Then have children sing the following song with you to the tune of "Pop! Goes the Weasel":

> Someone called the firehouse,
> Someone called for rescue,
> Someone called emergency,
> They're on their way to help you!

Phonemic Awareness/Phonics

■ **Frontload Words with /ks/** Have children look at the picture on pp. 32–33 of *My Skills Buddy*. This picture shows foxes. Some foxes need help. Other foxes are helping. Listen to the word *fox.* What sound does *fox* end with? *Fox* ends with /ks/; *fox,* /ks/. Then use this chant to introduce picture words ending with /ks/:

> Fox, fox, what words end like *fox?*
> *Mix, mix, mix* ends like *fox.* Who can find someone mixing?

Repeat the chant with other words in the picture that end with /ks/, including *sax, ax, six, fix, wax,* and *box.*

■ **Connect /ks/ to *Xx*** Use letter tiles to display the word *fox* or write it on the board. This word is *fox:* /f/ /o/ /ks/, *fox.* Say the word with me. Have children write the word *fox* and circle the letter that makes /ks/. Write and read aloud the following sentence: *Max put his sax in a box at six.* Point to the *x* in *Max* and ask: What letter is this? Yes, this is *x.* Repeat for the *x* in *sax, box,* and *six.*

Objectives
• Understand the general meaning of spoken language ranging from situations in which topics are familiar to unfamiliar.
• Learn relationships between sounds and letters of the English language.

Content Objective
• Develop content knowledge related to machines that help.

Language Objectives
• Understand and use grade-level content area vocabulary.

• Recognize the sounds of English.

Concept Literacy Reader K.5.2

Daily Planner	
DAY 1	• Concept Development • Phonemic Awareness/Phonics • Listening Comprehension
DAY 2	• Comprehension • Vocabulary
DAY 3	• Phonemic Awareness/Phonics • Conventions
DAY 4	• Phonemic Awareness/Phonics • Concepts and Oral Language
DAY 5	• Language Workshop • Writing

Content Objective

Understand cause and effect.

Language Objective

Learn and use academic vocabulary.

Use Learning Strategies

Preview and Predict Have children preview the illustrations on pp. 34–35 of *My Skills Buddy*. Cover the picture on p. 35 and point to the picture on p. 34. What do you see? (a girl painting) What is the dog doing? (leaning on the table) What is on the table? (a can of paint) What do you think might happen? (Answers will vary.) Show the picture on p. 35. What happened? (The dog knocked over the table. The paint fell on him.)

Skills Buddy, pp. 34–35

Listening Comprehension: Cause and Effect

- **Provide Scaffolding** Discuss the illustrations on pp. 34–35 in *My Skills Buddy* to frontload vocabulary. Point to the illustration on p. 34. This shows a can of paint on a table and a dog leaning on the table. Then point to the illustration on p. 35. This shows the dog covered in paint after he knocked over the table. Explain that the first illustration shows the cause, or reason, why something happens. The second illustration shows the effect, or event that happens. The event happens because of the cause. The dog knocking the table over is the effect of the dog leaning on the table.

- **Prepare for the Read Aloud** The modified Read Aloud below prepares children for listening to the oral reading "Firefighting" on p. 124.

Putting Out Fires

Mrs. Parker is a teacher. Her class goes to a fire station. A firefighter shows them fire trucks.

He says, "People call 911 when there is a fire. We get there fast."

Jenny asks, "Why do you go fast?"

The firefighter says, "We have to save people and buildings."

Dan asks, "Why do you have an ax?"

"We chop to let smoke out," he says.

Juan says, "Pretty cool."

"No," the firefighter says. "Pretty hot!"

- **First Listening** Write the title of the Read Aloud on the board. This is about a class trip. They go to the fire station. Listen to find out what they learn. After reading, ask children to recall the names of the characters and the events. Who goes to the fire station? Why do they go there? Why do firefighters go fast? Why does the firefighter have an ax?

- **Second Listening** Write the words *cause, effect,* and *because* on the board. Point to *because* and explain to children that this word is a clue word. Clarify that *because* helps a reader find cause and effect. Think about what happens in the story. Think about why things happen. After reading, point to *cause* and *effect* on the board and help children examine and discuss two causes and two effects that happen in the story.

Objectives

• Read linguistically accommodated content area material with a decreasing need for linguistic accommodations as more English is learned. • Use visual and contextual support to enhance and confirm understanding needed to comprehend increasingly challenging language.

Comprehension

■ **Provide Scaffolding** Display *Mayday! Mayday!* Lead a detailed picture walk through the story, naming what you see and describing what is happening. Use gestures and facial expressions to convey meaning. Focus on the following:

• **Set the Scene** Use the cover of the Trade Book to help children understand that this story takes place at sea. A sea is a huge body of water. Oceans are often called seas. The water is very deep. Sharks and waves are dangers at sea. What do you know about the sea? Allow children to use their prior knowledge to discuss the setting of the story.

• **Frontload Vocabulary** Use the illustrations to introduce unfamiliar words and phrases in the text. A boat is stuck at sea. The boater calls for help. Look at the picture on pages 6–7. What would it be like if you were called to help the boater? Include other words, such as *taxi* (p. 10); *radar* (p. 14); *raft* (p. 22); *basket* (p. 24); *pilot* (p. 29).

Vocabulary: Position Words

■ **Frontload Vocabulary** Have children turn to p. 48 of *My Skills Buddy.* Talk about each picture, using the position words *top, bottom, front,* and *back.* Look at the books. They are stacked. Point to the top book. This book is on *top.* It is the *top* book. *Top* is a position word. It tells where the book is. Then invite children to talk about the pictures using the position words.

■ **Provide Scaffolding** Write the words *top, bottom, front,* and *back* on the board. Read the words aloud. These words tell us about where things are. Point to the word *front.* Who can show me something that is in *front?* Invite children to point out one thing that is in front. Then say a sentence about the object and have children repeat it: (Object) is in *front.* Repeat with the other position words.

■ **Practice** Have children work in pairs. Assign one of the position words (*top, bottom, front,* or *back*) to each pair. One child should demonstrate one of the position words, such as by pointing to the top block in a stack. The partner should say a sentence about what the first child is doing: *Kayla is pointing to the top block.*

Content Objective
• Develop background knowledge.

Language Objective
• Learn and use position words.

Use Learning Strategies
Remind children that if they have trouble using position words, they can ask their partners for help.

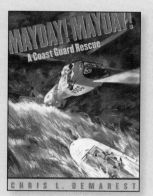
Trade Book

Phonemic Awareness/Phonics

■ **Isolate Final /ks/** Have children read the words *mix* and *wax* as you point to each sound in each word. Then write other words that end in *x*, and have children point out the *x* and read the words: *ox, box, fox, Rex, six, fix, Max, sax.* Check each child's progress in reading. Monitor pronunciation for clarity but not for perfection.

■ **/ks/ Spelled Xx** Say and write the following sentence on the board: *Did you fix the box, Rex?* Underline the words that have /ks/. Repeat the sentence, emphasizing /ks/ as you read the words aloud. Point to the letter *x* in *fix* and ask: What letter is this? Yes, this is *x*. Repeat for the *x* in *box* and *Rex*.

Conventions: Question Marks and Capital Letters

■ **Provide Scaffolding** Point to the image on pp. 6–7 of *Mayday! Mayday!* Read aloud the first sentence. Point to the first word. The first word in this sentence is *The*. The first word in a sentence starts with a capital letter. *The* starts with capital *T*. Repeat with the next sentence, or write simple sentences on the board to help illustrate capital letters. Then point out the term *Coast Guard*. Names also use capital letters. *Coast Guard* is the name of something. We use capital *C* and capital *G*. Continue to distinguish capital letters using other sentences from the story or writing names on the board.

■ **Practice** What are some other capital letters in this story? Page through the Trade Book and have children name different capitals they see. Then ask questions about the story. Write your questions on the board, illustrating the placement of capital letters and question marks.

Leveled LS Support

Beginning/Intermediate For each capital letter, have a child write the capital and matching lowercase letter on the board. While the child is writing the letters, have her state which letter she is writing: capital or lowercase.

Advanced/Advanced-High Write simple statements and questions on the board, intentionally misusing capital and lowercase letters and question marks. Have children examine the sentences and identify the errors.

Content Objective
Use learning strategies.

Language Objectives
Connect /ks/ with *Xx*.

Use question marks and capital letters.

Transfer Skills
Pronouncing /ks/ Some languages use voice in consonants that follow vowels. Children who speak these languages may tend to pronounce /ks/ as /gs/ in words like *mix* or *box*. If children experience this difficulty, have them practice with word pairs like *bogs, box* and *sags, sax.*

Use Learning Strategies
Help children discover that questions always begin with a capital letter. On the board, write *Where is the bus?* Point out the capital *W* that begins the sentence. Then explain that questions end with a question mark. Using basic sentences, show how a question mark is different from a period.

 **ELL** *English Language Learners*   **DAY 4**

Phonemic Awareness/Phonics

■ **Review /j/ and /w/** To review /j/ and /w/ in words, ask questions, such as: Does she have a job on a jet? Will the water get you wet? As children answer, have them pronounce words that begin with /j/ and /w/ (*job, jet, will, water, and wet*). Ask children to say the sounds at the beginning of the words. Have children repeat the questions in pairs. Restate the questions if children need assistance.

■ **/j/ Spelled *Jj* and /w/ Spelled *Ww*** To review /j/ and /w/, hold up the *j* and *w* tiles. Which letter makes /j/? Yes, *j* makes /j/. Repeat with /w/ and *w*. Use the tiles to form the following words: *job, jot, well, will.* Model reading the words, isolating and pointing out /j/ and /w/. Track the letters with your finger to show all the sound-letter correspondence (for example, /j/ /o/ /b/ = *job*).

Concepts and Oral Language

■ **Revisit Talk with Me Chart 26A** Display the chart. Have children describe each image on the page. Help them by describing the jobs of the *pilot, sailor,* and *mechanic.* Use each Amazing Word in a sentence.

■ **Develop Oral Language** Introduce language patterns that help describe the pictures on Talk with Me Chart 26A. Write this sentence frame on the board: *The pilot _____.* What does the pilot do? (flies the helicopter) *The pilot flies the helicopter.* Use new sentence frames and Amazing Words to talk about the other pictures in the chart. Then play a game. Point to one of the pictures on the chart. Ask a volunteer to make up a sentence that describes the picture. Then the volunteer can point to another picture on the chart and pick someone to make up a sentence. Encourage children to come up with a new sentence each time a picture is chosen.

 Leveled LS Support

Beginning Have children repeat the sentences that other children make up. Let them take a turn pointing to a picture on the chart.

Intermediate Ask questions to help children notice more details about the people and things in the pictures, such as: What would it feel like to fly a helicopter?

Advanced/Advanced-High After children say their sentence, have them identify the letter that begins the sentence and write it on the board.

Content Objectives
- Develop oral language.
- Use learning strategies.

Language Objectives
- Connect /j/ with *Jj* and /w/ with *Ww.*
- Learn English language patterns.

Use Learning Strategies
Work with children to create a 2-column chart. In the first column, list the words *rescue, pilot, yacht, sailor, mechanic,* and *shimmering.* In the second column, help students list related words by asking questions, such as *Who fixes the helicopter? What does the Coast Guard do?*

Talk with Me Chart 26A

Support for English Language Learners

Content Objectives

Understand *Mayday! Mayday!*

Take notes.

Language Objectives

Discuss jobs through speaking and writing.

Write using grade-level vocabulary.

Monitor and Self-Correct

Remind children that if they don't know how to write the words, they can see if the notes on the class chart will help them.

Home Language Support

Invite children to share ideas in their home languages before creating their books.

Language Workshop: Talk About Jobs

■ **Introduce and Model** Turn to pp. 4–5 of *Mayday! Mayday!* Look at this picture. What is happening? (A boat is sinking.) How do you think the person feels? (scared) Turn to pp. 6–7. What are the men doing? (going to help) Explain to children that the person on the boat has called the Coast Guard for help. The Coast Guard has a job. Their job is to help people in or near the water. Turn to pp. 8–9. Who flies the helicopter? (pilot) The pilot flies the helicopter. His job is flying the helicopter. Turn to pp. 18–19. What is happening? (The swimmer jumps into the water.) The swimmer has a job. His job is to swim to the boat. The swimmer helps people. Turn to pp. 24–25. What is the mechanic doing? (lowering a basket) Help children see that there are many different jobs in the Coast Guard.

■ **Practice** Draw a T-chart on the board or on chart paper, with the headings *Who* and *What.* Let's fill in the chart as we talk about different jobs. Help children brainstorm a list of jobs that help people. Begin with *swimmer, pilot,* and *Coast Guard.* Your list may also include *police, doctor, firefighter, nurse,* or *plumber.* Record this list in the *Who* column in the chart. What do these people do? How do they help others? Include modes of transportation used to help people, such as *helicopter, police car,* and *fire engine.* List these ideas in the *What* column in the chart. Ask children what type of job they would like to have. Encourage children to think about why they would like to help people.

Writing: Write About Jobs

■ **Prepare for Writing** We have talked about ways people and machines can help. Now let's write about them. Have each child fold a piece of paper in half, creating a four-page book.

■ **Create Books About Jobs** Have children copy this sentence frame at the bottom of each page of their four-page book: _____ *can help.* Then have them draw a person, activity, or situation on each page of the book. At the bottom of each page, they will complete the sentence frame by naming the person or mode of transportation that helps. Have children refer to the chart of jobs that was created for the Language Workshop. Have children share with the class.

Beginning/Intermediate Provide the sentence frame on each page of the book, and have children dictate or write words to complete the sentences.

Advanced/Advanced-High Encourage children to write sentences on their own. Have children help less-proficient partners complete their sentences.

Objectives
• Internalize new academic language by using and reusing it in meaningful ways in writing activities that build concept and language attainment.
• Write using content-based vocabulary.

This Week's ELL Overview

My Planning Guide

Grade K • Unit 5 • Week 3
Trucks Roll!
211–310
and DI•46–DI•51

ELL Handbook

- Maximize Literacy and Cognitive Engagement
- Research Into Practice
- Full Weekly Support for Every Selection

  Trucks Roll!
  - Routines to Support Instruction

- Transfer Activities
- Professional Development

Daily Leveled ELL Notes

ELL notes appear throughout this week's instruction and ELL Support is on the DI pages of your Teacher's Edition. The following is a sample of an ELL note from this week.

English Language Learners

Beginning Build Background Use the pictures on Talk with Me Chart 27A to help children understand words such as *steering wheel* and *headlight.*

Intermediate High-Frequency Words Explain to children that *what* is a question word, or *wh-* word. They can use it to get more information. Ask children to name other *wh-* words (*who, when, where,* and *why*).

Advanced Frontload Decodable Reader Before children read *Fun for Jud,* review /u/ and /a/ words with the following Picture Cards: *can, man, jam, bus, mug, truck.*

Advanced High Amazing Words Explain to children that the word *cabs* can also be used for taxi cabs. Tell children that sometimes words can mean more than one thing. They will need to pay attention to the context to know which meaning is being used.

ELL by Strand

The ELL lessons on this week's Support for English Language Learners pages are organized by strand. They offer additional scaffolding for the core curriculum. Leveled support notes on these pages address the different proficiency levels in your class. See pages DI•46–DI•51.

ELL Guy
Dr. Jim Cummins

The Three Pillars of ELL Instruction

ELL Strands	Activate Prior Knowledge	Access Content	Extend Language
Vocabulary p. DI•48	Frontload Vocabulary	Provide Scaffolding	Practice
Reading Comprehension p. DI•48	Provide Scaffolding	Set the Scene	Frontload Vocabulary
Phonics, Spelling, and Word Analysis pp. DI•46, DI•49–DI•50	Frontload Words with /u/	Isolate Initial and Medial /u/	Review Final /ks/
Listening Comprehension p. DI•47	Prepare for the Read Aloud	First Listening	Second Listening
Conventions and Writing pp. DI•49, DI•51	Provide Scaffolding/ Introduce and Model	Practice	Leveled Practice Activities/ Leveled Writing Activities
Concept Development p. DI•46	Read the Concept Literacy Reader	Read the Concept Literacy Reader	Develop Oral Language

This Week's Practice Stations Overview

Six Weekly Practice Stations with Leveled Activities can be found at the beginning of each week of instruction. For this week's Practice Stations, see pp. 218–219.

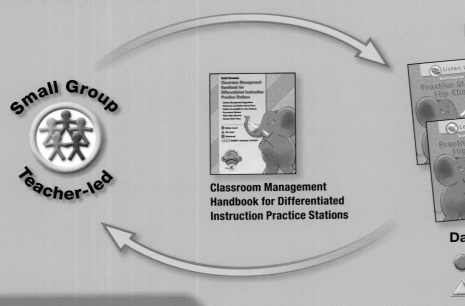

Small Group Teacher-led

Classroom Management Handbook for Differentiated Instruction Practice Stations

Practice Stations

Daily Leveled Center Activities

● Below   ■ Advanced

△ On-Level   **E L L**

Practice Stations Flip Charts

	Listen Up	Word Work	Words to Know	Let's Write	Read for Meaning	Let's Make Art
Objectives	• Identify words with /ks/.	• Identify words with /ks/. • Build words with /ks/.	• Identify and use position words: *top, bottom, front, back.*	• Write a rhyme.	• Identify cause and effect in a story.	• Draw a picture to show ways that transportation can help us in an emergency.
Materials	• *Listen Up* Flip Chart Activity 27 • Picture Cards: *box, fox, ox, six,* and 4 random cards • paper, pencil, crayons	• *Word Work* Flip Chart Activity 27 • Alphabet Cards • Picture Cards • Letter Tiles	• *Words to Know* Flip Chart Activity 27 • Picture Cards: *rabbit, wagon* • Teacher-made Word Cards: *top, bottom, front, back* • paper, pencils, crayons	• *Let's Write* Flip Chart Activity 27 • Picture Cards: *bat, cat, hat; hen, pen, ten; jug, mug, rug; can, fan, man, pan, van* • crayons, paper, pencil	• *Read for Meaning* Flip Chart Activity 27 • Trade Book *Mayday! Mayday!* • pencil, crayons, paper	• *Let's Make Art* Flip Chart Activity 27 • art paper • crayons

This Week on Reading Street!

 Question of the Week
What kinds of transportation help people do their jobs?

Going Places

Daily Plan

 Don't Wait Until Friday

Whole Group
- ◉ /u/ Spelled *Uu*
- ◉ Compare and Contrast
- • Vocabulary

MONITOR PROGRESS | **Success Predictor**

Day 1	Day 2	Day 3	Day 4	Day 5
Check Phonemic Awareness	Check Sound Spelling/ Retelling	Check Word Reading	Check Phonemic Awareness	Check Oral Vocabulary

Small Group

 Teacher-Led

- • Reading Support
- • Skill Support
- • Fluency Practice

Practice Stations

Independent Activities

Customize Literacy More support for a Balanced Literacy approach, see pp. CL•1–CL•31.

Whole Group
- • Writing
- • Conventions: Prepositions
- • Listening and Speaking

Assessment
- • Day 5 Assessment for Phonics
- • Day 5 Assessment for Comprehension

 You Are Here! Unit 5 Week 3

This Week's Reading Selections

Big Book
Genre: **Rhyming Nonfiction**

Decodable Reader 27

Leveled Readers

Get Set Roll! Reader 27

Resources on Reading Street!

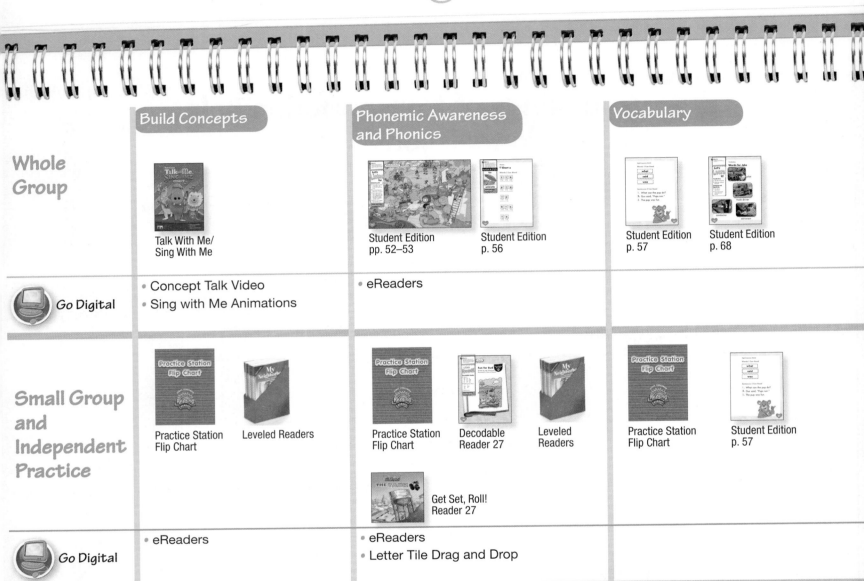

	Build Concepts	Phonemic Awareness and Phonics	Vocabulary
Whole Group	Talk With Me/ Sing With Me	Student Edition pp. 52–53 — Student Edition p. 56	Student Edition p. 57 — Student Edition p. 68
Go Digital	• Concept Talk Video • Sing with Me Animations	• eReaders	
Small Group and Independent Practice	Practice Station Flip Chart — Leveled Readers	Practice Station Flip Chart — Decodable Reader 27 — Leveled Readers Get Set, Roll! Reader 27	Practice Station Flip Chart — Student Edition p. 57
Go Digital	• eReaders	• eReaders • Letter Tile Drag and Drop	
Customize Literacy	• Leveled Readers	• Decodable Reader	• High-Frequency Word Cards
Go Digital	• Concept Talk Video • Big Question Video • eReaders	• eReaders	• Sing with Me Animations

Question of the Week
What kinds of transportation help people do their jobs?

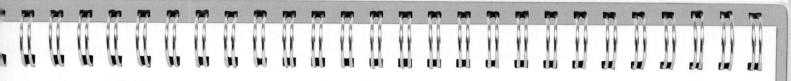

Comprehension	Fluency	Conventions and Writing

Student Edition pp. 54–55	Big Book	Decodable Reader 27	Kdg. Student Reader K.5.3	Get Set, Roll! Reader 27	Reader's and Writer's Notebook

• Envision It! Animations	• eReaders	• Grammar Jammer

Practice Station Flip Chart	Leveled Readers	Get Set, Roll! Reader 27	Practice Station Flip Chart	Leveled Readers	Practice Station Flip Chart	Reader's and Writer's Notebook

• Envision It! Animations • eReaders	• eReaders	• Grammar Jammer

• Leveled Readers	• Leveled Readers	• *Reader's and Writer's Notebook*

• Envision It! Animations • eReaders	• eReaders	• Grammar Jammer

You Are Here!
Unit 5
Week 3

My 5-Day Planner for Reading Street!

Don't Wait Until Friday
MONITOR PROGRESS

Check Phonemic Awareness

Day 1 pages 220–235

Check Sound-Spelling
Check Retelling

Day 2 pages 236–253

Get Ready to Read

Concept Talk, 220
Oral Vocabulary, 221 *trailers, cabs, haul, steering wheel, truckers, headlight*
Phonemic Awareness, 222–223
  ◉ Initial and Medial /u/
Phonics, 224–225
  ◉ /u/ Spelled *Uu*
Handwriting, 226 Letters *U* and *u*
High-Frequency Words, 227
  Introduce *what, said, was*
READ Decodable Story 27, 228–229

Concept Talk, 236
Oral Vocabulary, 237 *trailers, cabs*
Phonemic Awareness, 238–239
  ◉ Initial and Medial /u/
Phonics, 240–241
  ◉ /u/ Spelled *Uu*
Handwriting, 242 Words with *Uu*
High-Frequency Words, 243 *what, said, was*
READ Decodable Reader 27, 244–245

Read and Comprehend

Listening Comprehension, 230–231
  ◉ Compare and Contrast

Listening Comprehension, 246
  ◉ Compare and Contrast
READ Big Book—First Read, 246
  Trucks Roll!
Retell, 247
Think, Talk, and Write, 248

Language Arts

Conventions, 232 Prepositions
Writing, 233 Wonderful, Marvelous Me!
Daily Handwriting, 233 Letters *U* and *u*
Listening and Speaking, 234 Discuss Literature
Wrap Up Your Day, 234
Extend Your Day!, 235

Conventions, 249 Prepositions
Writing, 250 Respond to Literature
Daily Handwriting, 250 Letters *U* and *u*
Vocabulary, 251 Words for Jobs
Wrap Up Your Day, 252
Extend Your Day!, 253

You Are Here!
Unit 5 Week 3

Check Word Reading	**Check Phonemic Awareness**	**Check Oral Vocabulary**
Day 3 pages 254–283	**Day 4** pages 284–295	**Day 5** pages 296–309
Concept Talk, 254 **Oral Vocabulary**, 255 *haul, steering wheel* **Phonemic Awareness**, 256–257 ◉ Initial and Medial /u/ **Phonics**, 258–259 ◉ /u/ Spelled *Uu* **READ Kindergarten Student Reader K.5.3**, 260–261	**Concept Talk**, 284 **Oral Vocabulary**, 285 *truckers, headlight* Review **Phonemic Awareness**, 286 /ks/ Review **Phonics**, 287 /ks/ Spelled *Xx* **Spelling**, 288 ◉ /u/ Spelled *Uu* **READ Get Set, Roll! Reader 27**, 289	**Concept Wrap Up**, 296 **Oral Vocabulary**, 297 *trailers, cabs, haul, steering wheel, truckers, headlight* Review **Phonemic Awareness**, 298 ◉ /u/ Review **Phonics**, 299 ◉ /u/ Spelled *Uu* **Assessment**, 300–301 Monitor Progress
Comprehension, 262–263 ◉ Compare and Contrast **READ Big Book—Second Read**, 264–277 *Trucks Roll!*	**Comprehension**, 290 ◉ Compare and Contrast Review Draw Conclusions **READ Big Book—Third Read**, 291 *Trucks Roll!*	**Let's Practice It!**, 302–303 Signs **Assessment**, 304–305 Monitor Progress
Conventions, 278 Question Marks and Capital Letters **Writing**, 279 Genre: Poem **Daily Handwriting**, 279 Letters *U* and *u* **Listening and Speaking**, 280–281 Discuss Literature **Wrap Up Your Day**, 282 **Extend Your Day!**, 283	**Conventions**, 292 Prepositions **Writing**, 293 Extend the Concept **Daily Handwriting**, 293 Letters *U* and *u* **Vocabulary**, 294 Words for Jobs **Wrap Up Your Day**, 294 **Extend Your Day!**, 295	Review **Conventions**, 306 Prepositions **Writing**, 307 This Week We… **Daily Handwriting**, 307 Letters *U* and *u* **Wrap Up Your Week!**, 308 ❓ What kinds of transportation help people do their jobs? **Extend Your Day!**, 309

Grouping Options for Differentiated Instruction
Turn the page for the small group time lesson plan.

Planning Small Group Time on Reading Street!

SMALL GROUP TIME RESOURCES

DAY 1

Look for this Small Group Time box each day to help meet the individual needs of all your children. Differentiated instruction lessons appear on the DI pages at the end of each week.

Teacher-Led

(SI) Strategic Intervention

Teacher-Led
• Phonemic Awareness and Phonics
Reread Decodable Story

(OL) On-Level

Teacher-Led
• Phonemic Awareness and Phonics
Reread Decodable Story

(A) Advanced

Teacher-Led
• Phonemic Awareness and Phonics
Reread Decodable Story for Fluency

(ELL) Place English language learners in the groups that correspond to their reading abilities in English.

Practice Stations
• Listen Up
• Word Work

Independent Activities
• Read Independently
• *Reader's and Writer's Notebook*
• Concept Talk Video

ELL Poster 27

Day 1

 **SI** Strategic Intervention	**Phonemic Awareness and Phonics,** DI•35	
	Reread Decodable Story 27, DI•35	
 **OL** On-Level	**Phonemic Awareness and Phonics,** DI•40	
	Reread Decodable Story 27, DI•40	
 **A** Advanced	**Phonemic Awareness and Phonics,** DI•43	
	Reread Decodable Story 27 for Fluency, DI•43	
 **ELL** English Language Learners	DI•46–DI•47 Frontload Concept Phonemic Awareness and Phonics Comprehension Skill	

You Are Here! Unit 5 Week 3

Reading Street Response to Intervention Kit

Reading Street Leveled Practice Stations Kit

What kinds of transportation help people do their jobs?

SI Strategic Intervention

Decodable Reader

Listen to Me Reader

Concept Literacy Reader

Get Set, Roll! Reader

OL On-Level

THE TANK

Get Set, Roll! Reader

Kindergarten Student Reader

Decodable Reader

A Advanced

Ming on the Job

Independent Reader

Decodable Reader

Small Group Weekly Plan

Day 2	Day 3	Day 4	Day 5
Phonemic Awareness and Phonics, DI•36 **Reread** Decodable Reader 27, DI•36	**Phonemic Awareness and Phonics**, DI•37 **Read** Concept Literacy Reader K.5.3, DI•37	**Phonemic Awareness and Phonics**, DI•38 **Read** Get Set, Roll! Reader 27, DI•38	**Phonics Review**, DI•39 **Read** Listen to Me Reader K.5.3, DI•39
Phonemic Awareness and Phonics, DI•40 **Reread** Decodable Reader 27, DI•40	**Phonemic Awareness and Phonics**, DI•41 **Read** Kindergarten Student Reader K.5.3, DI•41	**Review Phonics and High-Frequency Words** **Read** Get Set, Roll! Reader 27, DI•42	**Phonics Review**, DI•42 **Reread** Leveled Books, DI•42
Phonics and Spelling, DI•43 **Reread** Decodable Reader 27 for Fluency, DI•43	**Read** Independent Reader K.5.3 or Kindergarten Student Reader K.5.3, DI•44	**Read** Get Set, Roll! Reader 27 or **Reread** Kindergarten Student Reader K.5.3, DI•45	**Fluency and Comprehension**, DI•45 **Reread** Independent Reader for Fluency, DI•45
DI•48 Comprehension Skill Frontload Vocabulary	DI•49 Review Phonemic Awareness and Phonics Scaffold Conventions	DI•50 Review Phonemic Awareness and Phonics Revisit Concept and Oral Language	DI•51 Language Workshop Writing

Practice Stations for Everyone on  Reading Street!

Listen Up!
Words with /ks/

Objectives
• Identify words with /ks/.

Materials
• *Listen Up!* Flip Chart Activity 27
• Picture Cards: *box, fox, ox, six,* and 4 random cards
• paper, pencil, crayons

Differentiated Activities

● Find the Picture Card for *box*. Say the sound you hear at the end. Find other Picture Cards that have /ks/ at the end. Find a Picture Card that shows something that rhymes with *box*.

▲ Find the Picture Card for *box*. Say the sound you hear at the end. Find other Picture Cards that have /ks/ at the end. Draw a picture of something else that rhymes with *box*.

■ Find the Picture Card for *box*. Say the sound you hear at the end. Find all the Picture Cards that have /ks/ at the end. Write a short poem and use in /ks/ rhyming words ending.

Word Work
/ks/ spelled *x*

Objectives
• Identify words with /ks/.
• Build words with /ks/.

Materials
• *Word Work* Flip Chart Activity 27
• Alphabet Cards
• Picture Cards
• Letter Tiles

Differentiated Activities

● Find the Alphabet Card for the letter *Xx*. Look for Picture Cards with the ending sound /ks/.

▲ Find the Alphabet Card for the letter *Xs*. Find Picture Cards with the ending sound of /ks/. Look around the room. Find other objects that have /ks/ at the end.

■ Find the Alphabet Card for the letter *Xx*. Find Picture Cards with ending /ks/. Use the Letter Tiles to spell other words that end with the sound /ks/.

Technology
• Letter Tile Drag and Drop

Words To Know
Position words

Objectives
• Identify and use position words: top, bottom, front, back.

Materials
• *Words to Know* Flip Chart Activity 27
• Picture Cards: *rabbit, wagon*
• Teacher-made word cards: *top, bottom, front, back*
• paper, pencils, crayons

Differentiated Activities

● Work with a partner to point out the *top, bottom, front,* and *back* of a rabbit and the wagon using the Picture Cards.

▲ Choose a Picture Card and place the word cards for *top, bottom, front,* and *back* as labels on the rabbit or wagon.

■ Draw a picture of a car and label the *top, bottom, front,* and *back* using the word cards as a spelling guide.

You Are Here! Unit 5 Week 3

Use this week's materials from the Reading Street Leveled Practice Stations Kit to organize this week's stations.

Key
● Below-Level Activities
▲ On-Level Activities
■ Advanced Activities

Practice Station
Flip Chart

Let's Write!
Rhyme

Objectives
• Write a rhyme.

Materials
• *Let's Write!* Flip Chart Activity 27
• Picture Cards: *bat, cat, hat, hen, pen, ten; jug, mug, rug; can, fan, man, pan, van.*
• crayons, paper, pencil

Differentiated Activities

● Look at the Picture Cards. Say the word for each card. Find the Picture Cards that rhyme. Draw a picture that tells about the rhyming words.

▲ Look at the Picture Cards. Say the word for each card. Find the Picture Cards that rhyme. Write a two-line poem that uses some of the rhyming words.

■ Look at the Picture Cards. Say the word for each card. Find the Picture Cards that rhyme. Write a four-line poem that uses some of the rhyming words.

Read For Meaning
Cause and Effect

Objectives
• Identify cause and effect in a story.

Materials
• *Read for Meaning* Flip Chart Activity 27
• Trade book *Mayday! Mayday!*
• pencil, crayons, paper

Differentiated Activities

The **cause and effect** in a story is when one thing causes another thing to happen.

● Read your book. Think about something that happened. Point to pictures and words that tell why it happened.

▲ Read your book. Point to something that happened in the story. Draw a picture or write a sentence that tells the cause.

■ Read your book. Think about something that happened in the story. Think about the cause. Write a sentence that tells the cause and effect of what happened.

Let's Make Art!

Objectives
• Draw a picture to show ways that transportation can help us in an emergency.

Materials
• *Let's Make Art!* Flip Chart Activity 27
• art paper
• crayons

Differentiated Activities

● What kind of transportation helps someone when there's a fire? Draw a picture to show how a fire truck helps out.

▲ What kind of transportation helps someone who is sick or has been hurt? Draw a picture to show how an ambulance helps out.

■ What kind of transportation helps a boat out on the sea? Draw a picture to show how a rescue boat helps out.

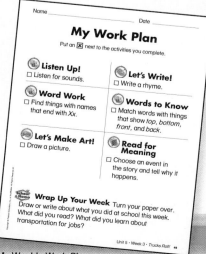

My Weekly Work Plan

a z

Objectives
- Share information and ideas about the concept.

Today at a Glance

Oral Vocabulary
trailers, cabs, haul, steering wheel, truckers, headlight

Phonemic Awareness
◊ Initial and Medial /u/

Phonics
◊ /u/ Spelled Uu

Handwriting
U and u

High-Frequency Words
what, said, was

Comprehension
◊ Compare and Contrast

Conventions
Prepositions

Writing
Wonderful, Marvelous Me!

Listening and Speaking
Discuss Literature

TRUCKTOWN on Reading Street

Start your engines!
Display p. 24 of *Truckery Rhymes*.

- Read aloud "That's What Trucks Are Made Of" and track the print.
- Reread the rhyme and have children chime in as they wish.
- Ask children to identify the rhyming words. (*stuff, tough; ton, fun*)

Truckery Rhymes

Concept Talk

Question of the Week
What kinds of transportation help people do their jobs?

Introduce the concept

To build concepts and to focus their attention, tell children that this week they will talk, sing, read, and write about **transportation that people use while working.** Track each word as you read the question of the week.

Play the CD that features workers talking about how transportation helps them do their jobs. What kind of transportation does a truck driver use?

🔘 Background Building Audio

ROUTINE   Activate Prior Knowledge   Team Talk

1. **Think** Have children think for a minute about what they know about transportation used to help people do their jobs.

2. **Pair** Have pairs of children discuss the question of the week. Tell children to follow agreed-upon rules for discussion, such as taking turns when speaking. Have children share ideas by speaking clearly using complete sentences in their discussions about transportation.

3. **Share** Call on a few children to share their ideas with the group. Guide discussion and encourage elaboration with prompts such as: What kinds of transportation help people do their jobs?

Anchored Talk

Develop oral language

Display Talk with Me Chart 27A. What do you see in the pictures? Point to the first picture. What is this man's job? He is a truck driver. Truck drivers are also called *truckers.* Point to the front of the truck below him. The parts of trucks where truckers ride are called *cabs.* Point to the back of the truck. The backs of trucks where they carry things are called *trailers.* How do you think the truck helps this man do his job?

We are going to learn six new Amazing Words this week. Listen as I say each word: *trailers, cabs, haul, steering wheel, truckers, headlight.* Have children say each word as you point to the picture.

Display Sing with Me Chart 27B. Tell children that they are going to sing a song about truckers. Read the title. Have children describe the illustration. Sing the song several times to the tune of "Frère Jacques." Listen for the Amazing Words: *trailers, cabs, haul, steering wheel, truckers, headlight.* Have children stand up and sing with you.

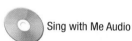 Sing with Me Audio

Talk with Me/Sing with Me Chart 27A

Trucks Are Rolling

Trucks are rolling.
Trucks are rolling.
What do you see?
What do you see?
Truckers' horns
a-blowing,
Early in the morning,
On their way,
on their way.

Talk with Me/Sing with Me Chart 27B

E L L **Preteach Concepts** Use the Day 1 instruction on ELL Poster 27 to assess and build background knowledge, develop concepts, and build oral vocabulary.

E L L Poster 27

Amazing Words

trailers	cabs
haul	steering wheel
truckers	headlight

Differentiated Instruction

SI **Strategic Intervention**

Build Background Display *Truckery Rhymes* and discuss with children the different kinds of trucks they have learned about. Page through the book and help children recall what each kind of truck does.

E L L

English Language Learners
Build Background Use the pictures on Talk with Me Chart 27A to help children understand words such as *steering wheel* and *headlight.*

ELL Support Additional ELL support and modified instruction is provided in the *ELL Handbook* and in the ELL Support lessons on pp. DI•46–51.

Objectives

• Learn initial and medial /u/.

• Identify words with initial and medial /u/.

• Discriminate words with initial and medial /u/.

• Replace medial phonemes.

Check Phonemic Awareness

SUCCESS PREDICTOR

My Skills Buddy, pp. 52–53

Phonemic Awareness
Initial and Medial /u/

Introduce Today we are going to learn a new sound. Listen carefully: /u/ /u/ /u/. Say it with me: /u/ /u/ /u/. Display the *umbrella* Picture Card. *Umbrella* begins with /u/; /u/, *umbrella*. What sound does *umbrella* begin with? Display the *duck* Picture Card. This is a *duck*. The middle sound in *duck* is /u/. What is the middle sound in *duck*? Repeat the routine with the *up* and *truck* Picture Cards.

Picture Card

Model Have children look at the picture on pp. 52–53 of *My Skills Buddy*. Let's listen for words that begin like *umbrella*. I see a little girl who is *upset*. I hear /u/ at the beginning of *upset*. The first sound of *upset* is /u/. What other things do you see that begin with that sound?

Guide practice As children name example words from the picture, guide them in stating that /u/ is the beginning sound. Discuss some of the bulleted items on p. 52 of *My Skills Buddy*. Save the other bulleted items for Day 2.

Corrective feedback If… children have difficulty naming words that begin with /u/, then… say *upset* again, stretching the beginning sound—/u/ /u/ /u/, *upset*.

Discriminate sounds

I am going to say two words; one word will begin with /u/. I want you to tell me which word begins with /u/. Listen carefully. I will do the first one: *under, over.* Which word begins with /u/? *Under* begins with /u/. Repeat with *up* and *down.* Continue the routine for medial /u/ with *cup, cap; bag, bug; fun, fan; rib, rub; not, nut; tub, tab; mad, mud.*

I will say a word. I want you to say each sound in the word. Let's do the first one together: *mud, /m/ /u/ /d/.* This time it's your turn. What are the sounds in *bun?* Continue with *mug, tub, hut, jump, truck, bug,* and *drum.*

Corrective feedback

If... children cannot blend words with /u/,

then... have them enunciate each sound individually, say the word in chunks, and then blend the sounds together: /m/ /u/ /d/, /m/ -*ud, mud.*

When you say /u/, the middle of your tongue is in the middle of your mouth and your mouth and cheeks are relaxed. Have children say /u/ words and feel the position of their mouth and tongue. Then repeat the discrimination activity.

Replace medial phonemes

I will say a word and then ask you to replace the middle sound with a new sound. Listen carefully: the word is *mud, /m/ /u/ /d/.* Change the middle sound to /a/. What is the new word? /m/ /a/ /d/, *mad.* The new word is *mad.* Now you try. Continue the routine by changing *nut* to *net* and *not, bad* to *bed* and *bud, hum* to *him* and *ham,* and *bag* to *big* and *bug.*

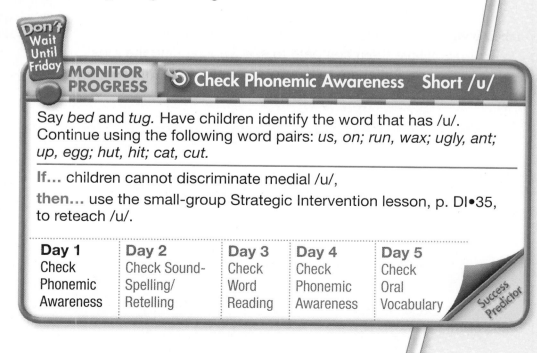

Don't Wait Until Friday

MONITOR PROGRESS ⟳ **Check Phonemic Awareness   Short /u/**

Say *bed* and *tug.* Have children identify the word that has /u/. Continue using the following word pairs: *us, on; run, wax; ugly, ant; up, egg; hut, hit; cat, cut.*

If... children cannot discriminate medial /u/,

then... use the small-group Strategic Intervention lesson, p. DI•35, to reteach /u/.

Day 1	Day 2	Day 3	Day 4	Day 5
Check Phonemic Awareness	Check Sound-Spelling/ Retelling	Check Word Reading	Check Phonemic Awareness	Check Oral Vocabulary

Success Predictor

Differentiated Instruction

 Advanced

Support Phonemic Awareness After studying the picture on pp. 52–53 of *My Skills Buddy,* have children draw their own picture. Ask them to include objects that begin with /u/.

Teacher Tip

If children have difficulty switching medial phonemes, begin by having them first replace initial phonemes and then final phonemes.

ELL

English Language Learners

Language Transfer Speakers of Spanish, Tagalog, and some Asian languages may have a hard time distinguishing the short vowel sounds in words such as *mud* and *mad,* or *pop* and *pup.* Have children practice pronouncing word pairs such as the following: *hut, hat; cup, cap; luck, lock;* and *rub, rob.*

ELL Support For additional support for language transfer, see Linguistic Contrastive Analysis in the *ELL Handbook.*

223   *Phonemic Awareness*

Succes Predicto

Objectives

Recognize uppercase *U* and lowercase *u*.

Associate the sound /u/ with the spelling *u*.

Blend and read words with /u/.

Skills Trace

Short *u* Spelled *Uu*

Introduce U5W3D1; U5W4D1; U6W4D1

Practice U5W3D2; U5W3D3; U5W4D2; U5W4D3; U6W4D2; U6W4D3

Reteach/Review U5W3D5; U5W4D4; U5W4D5; U5W5D4; U6W4D5

Assess/Test Benchmark Assessment U5; U6

KEY:

U=Unit   W=Week   D=Day

Phonics—Teach/Model
 /u/ Spelled *Uu*

Alphabet Card

Introduce　Display the *Uu* Alphabet Card. Point to the *umbrella* on the Alphabet Card. *Umbrella* begins with /u/. Say the word with me: *umbrella.* Write the word *umbrella* on the board and point to the *u. Umbrella* begins with /u/ spelled *u.* Now point to the *Uu* on the card. The sound for this letter is /u/. The names for these letters are uppercase *U* and lowercase *u.* What is the sound for these letters? What are the names of these letters?

Model　Write *What Luck! Here Comes the Bus!* on the board. Point to the *u* in *Luck.* When I see this letter, I think of the sound /u/. This word is *luck.* Where do you hear /u/ in *luck?* Yes, /u/ is in the middle of *luck.* Point to *Bus.* This word has /u/, too. When I see a *u,* I will try the sound /u/. This word is *bus.* Where do you hear /u/ in *bus?*

Guide practice　Display Phonics Songs and Rhymes Chart 27. Teach children the song, "What Luck! Here Comes the Bus!" sung to the tune "Here We Go Looby Loo." Play the CD and sing the song several times. When children are familiar with the song, ask them to cup their hand to their ear when they hear /u/ words. As you sing the song, point to words that have *u.*

🔘 Phonics Songs and Rhymes Audio

Phonics Songs and Rhymes Chart 27

On their own　Give each child a newspaper page or food label. Have them compete to see who can find the most *u*'s. Ask them to highlight uppercase *U* with red and lowercase *u* with blue.

Blend Words

Review

To review sound-spellings, use Alphabet Cards *Aa, Ll, Nn, Pp,* and *Ss* and the *apple, lamp, net, pan,* and *seal* Picture Cards to practice previously taught letters. Then use this routine for sound-by-sound blending to have children blend new words.

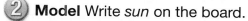

ROUTINE **Sound-by-Sound Blending**

① **Connect** Write the letter *s.* What is the sound we learned for this letter? The sound is /s/. Say it with me: /s/ /s/ /s/. When you see this letter in a word, what sound will you say?

② **Model** Write *sun* on the board.

- Touch under the letter *s:* What is the sound for this letter? Say it with me: /s/ /s/ /s/. Repeat the routine for *u* and *n.*

- Let's blend the sounds together. Listen as I blend the sounds: /s/ /u/ /n/. Say it with me: /s/ /u/ /n/, *sun.* Now say it without me.

- Listen as I use *sun* in a sentence: *The sun is high in the sky.* Say it with me. Then have children use *sun* in their own sentences.

③ **Guide Practice** Continue the routine established in step 2 with the words below:

| Jud | up | plan | fun | will | pals | us |

Children should successfully read these words before reading Decodable Story 27 on pp. 347–348 of *Reader's and Writer's Notebook.*

Corrective Feedback If children have trouble reading a word, model blending the sounds to read the word. Then have children say it with you.

Routines Flip Chart

Differentiated Instruction

 Strategic Intervention
Support Phonics If children identify words with long *u* rather than short *u,* praise them for recognizing the letter. Then ask them to listen as you demonstrate the difference in the vowel sounds. Say *mutt* and *mute* and have students note that only *mutt* has /u/.

Teacher Tip

If children have difficulty distinguishing uppercase *U* from lowercase *u,* have them note which letter is two times taller.

ELL

English Language Learners
Support Phonics Spanish speakers may pronounce the letter *u* like the *ue* in *due.* Give children extra practice pronouncing words with /u/, such as *nut, hut,* and *rut.*

bjectives
Write *U* and *u*.
Learn high-frequency words.

Handwriting

Introduce	Write *Uu* on the board. Words that begin with /u/ are written with an uppercase *U* or a lowercase *u*. Which letter is uppercase *U*? Which letter is lowercase *u*?
Model uppercase U	Write the name *Ursula* on the board. Point to the uppercase *U*. This is the uppercase *U*. We use uppercase letters to begin sentences and for the first letter in a person's name. Watch as I trace the uppercase *U* with my finger. Follow the stroke instructions pictured below.
Guide practice	Have children write the uppercase *U* in the air. Use your finger to make an uppercase *U* in the air. Now write it on the palm of your hand.
Model lowercase u	Point to the lowercase *u* in *Ursula*. This is a lowercase *u*. Watch as I trace a lowercase *u* with my finger. Write another lowercase *u* on the board following the stroke instructions. Again, have children write *u* in the air and on their hands.
Guide practice	Have children use their Write-On Boards to write a row each of uppercase *U* and lowercase *u*.

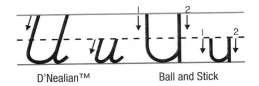

D'Nealian™   Ball and Stick

More practice   Use *Reader's and Writer's Notebook,* pp. 345, 346, for additional practice with initial *u*.

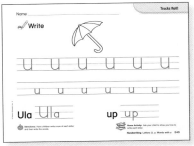

Reader's and Writer's Notebook, p. 345

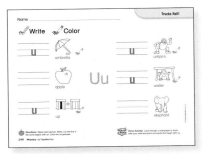

Reader's and Writer's Notebook, p. 346

High-Frequency Words

Introduce Use the routine below to teach high-frequency words *what, said,* and *was.*

Routines Flip Chart

Academic Vocabulary

Write the following on the board:

compare	contrast
preposition	poem
literature	draw conclusions

Point to the list. This week we are going to learn these important words. They are tools for learning. As we work this week you will hear them many times. Read the words. Preteach the Academic Vocabulary at point-of-use by providing a child-friendly description, explanation, or example that clarifies the meaning of each term. Then ask children to restate the meaning of the Academic Vocabulary in their own words.

Differentiated Instruction

 Strategic Intervention

High-Frequency Words Write this week's high-frequency words on cards for children to tape to the tops of their desks. As they read this week's stories remind them to look at the high-frequency words and practice saying them.

English Language Learners
High-Frequency Words
Explain to children that *what* is a question word, or *wh-* word. They can use it to get more information. Ask children to name other *wh-* words (*who, when, where,* and *why*).

Decodable Story 27
/u/ Spelled *Uu* and High-Frequency Words

Review

Review the previously taught high-frequency words by having children read each word as you point to it on the Word Wall.

the	was	from	to	have	what	he
do	for	see	they	said	go	we

Read Decodable Story 27

Display Decodable Story 27. Today we will read a story about a boy named Jud. What is the title of the story? Point to the title of the story. The title of the story is *Fun for Jud*. What sound do you hear in the middle of *fun*? We will read lots of words that have /u/ in this story. Have children read Decodable Story 27 on pp. 347–348 in *Reader's and Writer's Notebook*.

Reader's and Writer's Notebook, pp. 347–348

Use the routine for reading decodable books to read Decodable Story 27.

Routine — Reading Decodable Books

1. **Read Silently** Have children whisper read the story page by page as you listen in.

2. **Model Fluent Reading** Have children finger point as you read a page. Then have children reread the page without you.

3. **Read Chorally** Have children finger point as they chorally read the page. Continue reading page by page, repeating steps 1 and 2.

4. **Read Individually** Have children take turns reading aloud a page.

5. **Reread and Monitor Progress** As you listen to individual children reread, monitor progress and provide support.

6. **Reread with a Partner** Have children reread the story page by page with a partner.

Routines Flip Chart

Differentiated Instruction

 Strategic Intervention

Build Background Before children read *Fun for Jud*, display the *Uu* Alphabet Card. Have children name the sound and then the letter names. Repeat the routine with the *Aa* and *Oo* Alphabet Cards.

Small Group Time

DAY 1

Break into small groups after reading the Decodable Story and before the comprehension lesson.

Teacher-Led

SI Strategic Intervention	**OL** On-Level	**A** Advanced
Teacher-Led Page DI•35	**Teacher-Led** Page DI•40	**Teacher-Led** Page DI•43
• Phonemic Awareness and Phonics	• Phonemic Awareness and Phonics	• Phonemic Awareness and Phonics
• **Reread** Decodable Story 27	• **Reread** Decodable Story 27, DI•40	• **Reread** Decodable Story 27 for Fluency, DI•43

ELL Place English Language learners in the groups that correspond to their reading abilities in English.

Practice Stations
• Visit the Listen Up! Station
• Visit the Word Work Station

Independent Activities
• Read independently
• Concept Talk Video
• *Reader's and Writer's Notebook*

English Language Learners

Frontload Decodable Story
Before children read *Fun for Jud*, review /u/ and /a/ words with the following Picture Cards: *can*, *man*, *jam*, *bus*, *mug*, *truck*.

Skills Trace

Compare and Contrast

Introduce U2W1D1; U3W1D1; U3W3D1; U6W1D1

Practice U2W1D2; U2W1D3; U3W1D4; U3W1D2; U3W3D3; U3W1D4; U5W3D2; U5W3D3; U6W3D4; U6W1D2; U6W1D3; U6W1D4

Reteach/Review U2W1D5; U3W3D4; U3W1D5; U3W3D4; U3W5D4; U4W1D4; U5W3D5; U6W1D5; U6W6D4

KEY:

U=Unit W=Week D=Day

My Skills Buddy, pp. 54–55

Listening Comprehension
 Compare and Contrast

Introduce

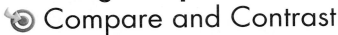
Envision It!

When we tell what is alike and what is different about things in a story, it is called comparing and contrasting. We **compare** when we find things that are alike. We **contrast** when we find things that are different. Good readers compare and contrast characters, places, and events in a story to help them understand what happens and why.

Have children turn to pp. 54–55 in *My Skills Buddy* and look at the pictures. Help me describe the bikes in this picture. Guide children as they describe the pictures.

- How are the bikes alike? (They have the same size, shape, and purpose.)

- How are they different? (One has training wheels; the other does not.)

- How do you think the boy will decide which bike to ride? (Answers will vary. Possible answer: He might want the training wheels because he cannot yet ride the other bike.)

Model

Today I will read aloud a story about vans used for work. Read **"Two Vans"** and model how to compare and contrast two objects.

Think Aloud When a writer describes two things together, I look at how they are alike and different. I think about their parts, size, shape, and uses. In "Two Vans," the moving van and the carpenter's van are alike in some ways. They are both used to haul things. Most of their space is used for cargo. They are also different. The carpenter's van is small and the moving van is large.

Guide practice

After you read aloud "Two Vans" to children, ask them to respond to these questions about the text.

- Are the vans alike or different in what they carry? (different)
- What is found in the moving van? (a family's belongings)
- What is found in the carpenter's van? (tools and wood)

More practice

Display *Max Takes the Train.* Recall with children that Max uses several kinds of transportation. Show pictures of a subway and a ferryboat. How are the subway and the ferryboat alike? (Both are ways of moving a lot of people.) How are they different? (A subway goes underground very fast; a ferryboat goes slowly on water.)

Connect to everyday life

A bus and a bike are two different ways to get to school. Buses ride down roads and streets. How is riding on a bike different?

Differentiated Instruction

 Advanced

Support Comprehension
Display the covers of *Goldilocks and the Three Bears* and *If You Could Go to Antarctica.* Have children use the cover illustrations to tell you how the stories are alike and different.

Academic Vocabulary

compare to note similarities between two objects, people, animals, or ideas

contrast to note differences between two objects, people, animals, or ideas

ELL

English Language Learners
Oral Comprehension To prepare English learners for the Read Aloud, use the modified Read Aloud in the ELL Support lesson p. DI•47.

 Read Aloud

Two Vans

Amy's dad helps people move from one house to another. He and his crew pack people's things into boxes. Then they put the boxes into a big moving van. They carry the people's furniture out and put it all into the van. They pack everything carefully so it will all fit in the van. Then they drive to the people's new house, take everything out of the van, and put it into the new house.

Josh's dad drives a van for his job too. He is a carpenter. His van is much smaller than the big moving van. It is full of tools. Sometimes he carries boards in it to use when he is building a new kitchen or garage.

Many people use vans to do their jobs. Their jobs are different, and so are their vans!

bjectives
Identify and use prepositions.
Write or dictate something you
wonder about trucks.

Conventions
Prepositions

Teach prepositions Tell children that you are going to teach them about a new kind of word in a sentence. A preposition is a word that tells us more about a noun in a sentence. It tells how the noun is related to the other parts of the sentence.

Model Write the words *on, in, over,* and *under* on the board. These words are prepositions. Then write the following sentence:

> **The book is on the shelf.**

Point to *on* as you read the sentence. The word *on* is the preposition in this sentence. It tells us where to find the book: *on the shelf.* Underline the word *on*.

Guide practice Set AlphaBuddy on a chair. Where is AlphaBuddy sitting? (on a chair) AlphaBuddy sits on the chair. *On* is a preposition. It tells us about where AlphaBuddy sits. Put a crayon in AlphaBuddy's hand. Where is the crayon? (in AlphaBuddy's hand) The crayon is in AlphaBuddy's hand. *In* is a preposition. It tells us about where the crayon is. Repeat the routine by holding a hat *over* AlphaBuddy's head and then *under* AlphaBuddy's chair. Then have students write the words *on, in, over,* and *under* on their Write-On Boards.

[**Team Talk**] Pair children and have them take turns using the words *on, in, over,* and *under* to tell about the position of things in the classroom. Have their partner identify the preposition in the sentence.

Daily Fix-It Use the Daily Fix-It exercise for more conventions practice.

Writing
Wonderful, Marvelous Me!
I Wonder About...

Introduce
Talk with children about learning. What do you like to learn about most? What do you wish you could learn more about? Encourage children to share their thoughts and ideas, and make a list on the board.

Model
Today we're going to share what we wish we could learn more about. I'm going to close my eyes and think of something I have always wanted to learn about. Show a picture of the outside of a semitruck and trailer. I know that some people who drive trucks a long way stay in their trucks overnight. I wonder about how they sleep in their trucks.

Guide practice
Encourage children to help you describe how long-distance truck drivers may spend the night in their trucks. Write their ideas on the board and draw pictures when appropriate. Then show a picture of the inside of the sleeper cab of a truck. Point out the bed behind the driver's seat. (Many long-distance truck drivers sleep in the bed behind their seat. Some sleep during the day and drive at night when there are fewer cars on the road. Sometimes they get hotel rooms and park their trucks outside.)

Independent writing
Now you are going to share something you wonder about trucks. Close your eyes and use your wonderful, marvelous wish to learn. What do you wish to learn about trucks? What question could you ask to learn more about them? Have children write or dictate their ideas and then illustrate them.

Daily Handwriting

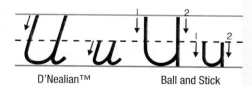

D'Nealian™   Ball and Stick

Write *Uma* and *rug* on the board. Review correct letter formation of uppercase *U* and lowercase *u*.

Have children write *Uma* and *rug* on their Write-On Boards. Remind them to use proper left-to-right and top-to-bottom progression and proper spacing between letters when writing *U* and *u*.

Write Guy
Jeff Anderson

Writers Write!

Child writers succeed in classrooms where they write. Simple, isn't it? Are you trying to meet some mandate or standard with such blinders on that you're forgetting daily writing? Children need to read every day and to write every day. Teachers do not need to read and assess everything that children write.

Academic Vocabulary

preposition a word that shows the relationship of a noun or pronoun to another word; the first word in a prepositional phrase

Daily Fix-It

bud was sad
<u>B</u>ud was sad<u>.</u>

This week's practice sentences appear on Teacher Resources DVD-ROM.

Writing Routine

Day 1 Wonderful, Marvelous Me!

Day 2 Respond to Literature

Day 3 Genre Writing

Day 4 Extend the Concept

Day 5 This Week We...

bjectives

- Practice discussing literature.
- Face the speaker when listening.
- Speak loudly and clearly.
- Take turns when speaking.

Listening and Speaking
Discuss Literature

Teach

After we read a story, we talk about it. Discussing what happened in a story and how we feel about it helps good readers understand why the story is important.

Model

Take a picture walk through *My Lucky Day*. Have children look at the pictures on each page. Then read the book to children with expression. *I really enjoy My Lucky Day. I think it is funny that the piglet gets Mr. Fox to cook dinner for him. What do you like about the book?* Ask several children for responses. Continue with questions such as:

- Why does Mr. Fox think it is his lucky day?
- Have you ever had a lucky day? Why was it lucky?
- Why does Mr. Fox get tired? Have you ever worked until you were tired?
- Why do you think the piglet knocks on Mr. Fox's door?

Guide practice

Divide the class into groups. Have children discuss *My Lucky Day*. Have each group select their favorite part of the story and retell it for the class. Refer children to the Rules for Listening and Speaking on pp. 1–2 of the *Reader's and Writer's Notebook*. Remind them to face the speaker when listening and to take turns and speak one at a time.

Name _____

Listening Rules

1. Face the person who is speaking.
2. Be quiet while someone is speaking.
3. Pay attention to the speaker.
4. Ask questions if you don't understand.

Reader's and Writer's Notebook, p. 1

Wrap Up Your Day

✔ **Oral Language** Today we talked about the job of a truck driver. Say the Amazing Words with me: *trailers, cabs, haul, steering wheel, truckers, headlight.*

✔ **Homework Idea** Send home the Family Times Newsletter Let's Practice It! TR DVD•53–54.

Preview DAY 2

Tomorrow we will read about the job of a truck driver.

Social Studies
What Workers Do
Materials: chart paper or Graphic Organizer 4, marker, watercolor paints and brushes

Types of Jobs Tell children there are many different types of jobs. Some jobs do something for other people, such as doctors, nurses, and police officers. Other jobs make a product to sell, such as farmers, toy makers, car makers, and food makers. Brainstorm a list of jobs and record them on a T-chart. Talk about how each worker helps people or what the worker makes.

Helping People	Making Things
doctor	farmer
nurse	toy maker
police officer	car maker
firefighter	baker

Have children choose a job and write the title on a card. Have them pantomime doing the job. As each "worker" acts out the job, have children guess the title. When a correct guess is made, have the actor show his or her card.

Social Studies
When I Grow Up
Materials: scissors, glue, mural paper, markers, crayons

Career Collage Talk with children about types of jobs and write their ideas on the board. Have children tell what they think a worker does in each job. Then have children choose a job they would like to do and draw a picture to show their choice. Let children tell the class about their jobs. Help them label their drawings with the job name.

Math
How Many Ways?
Materials: books about transportation, paper, writing tools

Transportation Count Display books that have various forms of transportation. Have children look through the books to identify different ways people move themselves from place to place. List these forms of transportation on the board.

Read each form of transportation listed, asking children to raise their hands if they have ever ridden on that form.

Make a tally mark for each response. Have children count the marks.

bjectives
Discuss the concepts to develop oral language.
Build oral vocabulary.

Today at a Glance

ral Vocabulary
ailers, cabs

honemic Awareness
Initial and Medial /u/

honics
/u/ Spelled *Uu*

andwriting
ords with *Uu*

omprehension
Compare and Contrast

onventions
repositions

Vriting
espond to Literature

ocabulary
'ords for Jobs

TRUCKTOWN on Reading Street

Start your engines! Display p. 24 of *Truckery Rhymes*. Point to "That's What Trucks Are Made Of." Who remembers which trucks are in this rhyme? Yes, all the trucks! Let's read the rhyme together. Now have a child point to the rhyming words as the class reads the rhyme again.

Truckery Rhymes

Concept Talk

Question of the Week

What kinds of transportation help people do their jobs?

Build concepts

Write the question of the week and track the print as you read it aloud. Have children answer the question in complete sentences and speak loudly and clearly. To reinforce the concept and focus children's attention, display Talk with Me/Sing with Me Chart 27B. Tell children that they are going to sing about trucks.

Sing with Me Audio

Listen for Amazing Words

The Amazing Words *trailers* and *cabs* are in the song "Trucks Are Rolling." Have children describe the people, animals, and trucks in the picture. Sing the song several times to the tune of "Frère Jacques." Ask children to sing along with you. Have them wave when they hear *trailers* and *cabs*.

ELL Reinforce Vocabulary Use the Day 2 instruction on ELL Poster 27 to reinforce the meanings of high-frequency words.

Trucks Are Rolling
Trucks are rolling.
Trucks are rolling.
What do you see?
What do you see?
Truckers' horns
a-blowing,
Early in the morning,
On their way,
on their way.

Talk with Me/Sing with Me Chart 27B

ELL Poster 27

Oral Vocabulary
Amazing Words

Amazing Words

trailers	cabs
haul	steering wheel
truckers	headlight

Teach Amazing Words

Amazing Words — Oral Vocabulary Routine

① **Introduce the Word** *Trailers* are the back parts of trucks where things are carried. What's our new Amazing Word for the back parts of trucks? Say it with me: *trailers*.

② **Demonstrate** Provide examples to show meaning. *Truck drivers carry goods in their trailers.*

Repeat steps 1 and 2.

Introduce the Word *Cabs* are the front parts of trucks where drivers sit. What's our new Amazing Word for the front parts of trucks? Say it with me: *cabs*.

Demonstrate *Truck drivers sleep in their cabs.*

③ **Apply** Tell children to use *trailers* and *cabs* in complete sentences. Have them draw a picture of a truck with a trailer and cab.

Routines Flip Chart

Use Amazing Words

To reinforce the concept and the Amazing Words, have children supply the appropriate Amazing Word for each sentence.

> **The truck drivers sit in the _____ to drive.** (cabs)
>
> **Then they unload wood from their _____.** (trailers)

Differentiated Instruction

SI **Strategic Intervention**

Sentence Production If children have difficulty completing the sentences, say a sentence using each Amazing Word and ask children to choose the one that makes sense. Say the sentence together.

English Language Learners
Amazing Words Explain to children that the word *cabs* can also be used for taxi cabs. Tell children that sometimes words can mean more than one thing. They will need to pay attention to the context to know which meaning is being used.

Objectives
- Practice initial and medial /u/.
- Substitute medial phonemes.

Phonemic Awareness
↻ Initial and Medial /u/

Picture Card

Isolate /u/

Display the *up* Picture Card. This sign says "up." *Up* begins with /u/. What is this? What sound does it begin with?

Display the *tub* Picture Card. This is a *tub*. *Tub* has /u/ in the middle. What is this? What sound does it have in the middle?

Picture Card

Model

Display the *sun* Picture Card. This is the *sun*. Listen as I say the sounds: /s/ /u/ /n/, *sun*. I hear /u/ in the middle of *sun*. What is the middle sound you hear in *sun*? Say it with me: /s/ /u/ /n/; /u/ is in the middle. Let's try some more. Continue with the following words: *cup, bun, fun, sum, luck, puff, bug, hug, tuck.*

Picture Card

Guide practice

Have children look at the picture on *My Skills Buddy*, pp. 52–53. Remember we saw a girl who is upset in the picture. *Upset* begins with /u/. Now let's look for things in the picture that have /u/ in the middle. Discuss with children those bulleted items on p. 52 not discussed on Day 1.

My Skills Buddy, pp. 52–53

Corrective feedback

If... children cannot discriminate initial and medial /u/, then... have them enunciate /u/ as they segment short *u* words.

Listen as I segment a word: /s/ /u/ /m/. What sound do you hear in the middle of *sum*? I hear /u/ in the middle of *sum*. Continue with the following words: *tub, mug, fuzz, cub.*

On their own   Display Phonics Songs and Rhymes Chart 27, "What Luck! Here Comes the Bus!" Remind children of the tune, "Here We Go Looby Loo." Have them sing the song with you several times. This time I want you to jump up when you hear a word with /u/.

Review

Sound Substitution Listen to the sounds in the word *fun:* /f/ /u/ /n/. Say them with me: /f/ /u/ /n/, *fun.* Now change the middle sound to /a/: /f/ /a/ /n/. What new word did we make? The new word is *fan.* Continue the activity, changing *fan* to *fin.* Then repeat the routine with the following sets of words: *big, bug, bag, beg; bud, bed, bad, bid.*

Phonics Songs and Rhymes
Chart 27

Differentiated Instruction

 Strategic Intervention

Support Phonemic Awareness Say /u/ and have children find something in the classroom that has that sound in the middle. If they can't find anything, have them say a word they know that has that sound.

ELL

English Language Learners
Phonemic Awareness Point to images in the picture on pp. 52–53 of *My Skills Buddy* as you say the corresponding words. To clarify understanding, have children point to the images as you say the words. Then have children say the words.

Objectives
- Practice /u/ spelled *Uu*.
- Blend /u/ words.

Check Sound-Spelling
SUCCESS PREDICTOR

Phonics—Teach/Model
/u/ Spelled *Uu*

Alphabet Card

Teach /u/Uu

/u/Uu Point to the *umbrella* on the *Uu* Alphabet Card. What is this? What sound does *umbrella* begin with? *Umbrella* begins with /u/. Write *umbrella* on the board and point to the letter *u*. The letter for /u/ is *u*. What letter does *umbrella* begin with?

Model

Display the *jug* Picture Card. What is this? Say the sounds in *jug* with me: /j/ /u/ /g/, *jug*. Where do you hear /u/ in *jug*? I hear /u/ in the middle. Do you?

Write *jug* on the board. Point to each letter as you say the sound: /j/ /u/ /g/, *jug*. Continue the routine with the following words: *mug, dug, pup, tub, cup*.

Picture Card

Guide practice

Envision It!

Have children open *My Skills Buddy* to p. 56. Demonstrate using the blending arrows on *My Skills Buddy* p. 56 as you model blending the first word. Put your finger on the red arrow below the *t*. Say the sound that *t* stands for: /t/. Continue with the letters *u* and *b*. Now I run my finger along the blue arrow as I blend the letters quickly to read *tub*. Repeat with the word *pup*. Have children work with a partner to blend the rest of the words on the page.

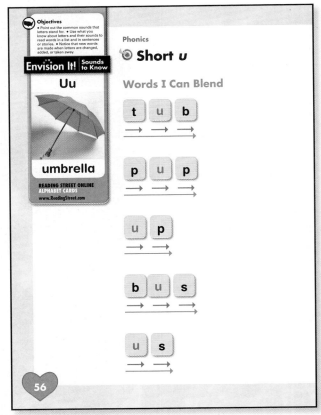

My Skills Buddy, p. 56

Blend

Use the following routine to review blending *u* words.

ROUTINE Sound-by-Sound Blending

① Connect Write the letter *u*. What is the sound we learned for this letter? The sound is /u/. Say it with me: /u/ /u/ /u/. When you see this letter in a word, what sound will you say?

② Model Write the name *Bud* on the board.

- Point to *B*. What is the sound for this letter? Say it with me: /b/ /b/ /b/. Repeat the routine for *u* and *d*.

- Let's blend the sounds together. Listen as I blend the sounds: /b/ /u/ /d/. Say it with me: /b/ /u/ /d/. Now say it without me.

- Listen as I use *Bud* in a sentence: *The puppy's name is Bud.* Say it with me. Have children use *Bud* in a sentence.

③ Guide Practice Continue the routine established in step 2 with these words:

pup	ruff	jump	sun	dug	mud	hug

Have children successfully read all of the words before reading Decodable Reader 27 on pp. 58–65 of *My Skills Buddy*.

Corrective Feedback If children have difficulty blending words, model blending the sounds to read the word. Then have children say it with you.

Routines Flip Chart

MONITOR PROGRESS ⟳ **Check Sound-Spelling /u/ Spelled *Uu***

Give each child a blank card. Have children write the letters *Uu* on the card. I am going to read some words. When you hear a word with /u/, hold your *Uu* card up in the air. Say: *umbrella, pit, mud, pup, can, bus, hug, bell, bud, run, tug.*

If... children cannot discriminate /u/ words,

then... use the small-group Strategic Intervention lesson, p. DI•36, to reteach /u/.

Continue to monitor children's progress using other instructional opportunities during the week so that children can be successful with the Day 5 Assessment.

Day 1	Day 2	Day 3	Day 4	Day 5
Check Phonemic Awareness	Check Sound-Spelling/ Retelling	Check Word Reading	Check Phonemic Awareness	Check Oral Vocabulary

Differentiated Instruction

 Advanced

Support Phonics Cut a large dog shape out of construction paper for each child. Have children look for words with /u/ as they read Decodable Reader 27. Ask them to write each word they find on their dog cutouts.

Success Predictor

241

Sound-Spelling

Succes Predicto

Objectives
- Write *U* and *u*.
- Read high-frequency words.

Handwriting
Write Words with *Uu*

Review

Write *Ursula* on the board. This is the name *Ursula.* I use an uppercase *U* for the first letter in *Ursula's* name. Watch me make an uppercase *U.* Write another uppercase *U* on the board using the instructional strokes indicated in the model. There is another *u* in the name *Ursula.* It is in the middle of the name. It is a lowercase *u.* Watch me make a lowercase *u.* Write another lowercase *u* on the board using the proper instructional strokes.

D'Nealian™   Ball and Stick

Guide practice

Have children use their Write-On Boards to make a row of uppercase *U* and a row of lowercase *u.* Circulate around the room, assisting children as necessary. Have children then write the following words: *fun, tub, hug.*

High-Frequency Words

Model reading

Have children turn to p. 57 of *My Skills Buddy.* Read the high-frequency words *what, said,* and *was* together. Then have children point to each word and read it themselves. Read the sentences on the *My Skills Buddy* page together to read the new high-frequency words in context.

Team Talk Pair children and have them take turns reading each of the sentences aloud.

High-Frequency Words

Words I Can Read

what
said
was

Sentences I Can Read

1. What can the pup do?
2. Gus said, "Pups run."
3. The pup was fun.

My Skills Buddy, p. 57

On their own

Use *Reader's and Writer's Notebook,* p. 349, for additional practice with this week's high-frequency words.

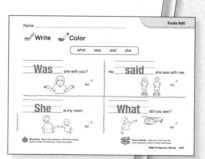

Reader's and Writer's Notebook, p. 349

Differentiated Instruction

SI Strategic Intervention

Handwriting Write letters *u* and *w* on the board. Point out to children that the letters can look similar if they are not careful. Have children practice writing a row of each letter to help them distinguish *u* from *w.*

ELL

English Language Learners

High-Frequency Words Have children write this week's high-frequency words. Then have them make up phrases or sentences using the words.

Decodable Reader 27
↻ /u/ Spelled *Uu* and High-Frequency Words

Review Review the previously taught high-frequency words. Have children read each word as you point to it on the Word Wall.

| is | a | said | what | see | the | was |

Have children turn to Decodable Reader 27, *Fun for Bud,* on p. 58 of *My Skills Buddy*. Today we will read a story about a puppy named Bud. Point to the title. The title of this story is *Fun for Bud.* What is the title? Point to the name of the author. The author's name is Judy Wienhouse. What does the author do? The illustrator's name is Gabrial Peterson. What does the illustrator do?

Use the routine for reading decodable books to read Decodable Reader 27.

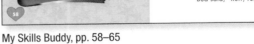
My Skills Buddy, pp. 58–65

 Reading Decodable Books

1. **Read Silently** Have children whisper read the book page by page as you listen in.

2. **Model Fluent Reading** Have children finger point as you read a page. Then have children reread the book without you.

3. **Read Chorally** Have children finger point as they chorally read the page. Continue reading page by page, repeating steps 1 and 2.

4. **Read Individually** Have children take turns reading aloud a page.

5. **Reread and Monitor Progress** As you listen to individual children reread, monitor progress and provide support.

6. **Reread with a Partner** Have children reread the book page by page with a partner.

Routines Flip Chart

Small Group Time

DAY 2 Break into small groups after reading the Decodable Reader and before the comprehension lesson.

Teacher-Led

SI Strategic Intervention	**OL On-Level**	**A Advanced**
Teacher-Led Page DI•36	Teacher-Led Page DI•40	Teacher-Led Page DI•43
• Phonemic Awareness and Phonics	• Phonemic Awareness and Phonics	• Phonics and Spelling
• **Reread** Decodable Reader 27	• **Reread** Decodable Reader 27, DI•40	• **Reread** Decodable Reader 27 for Fluency, DI•43

ELL Place English Language learners in the groups that correspond to their reading abilities in English.

Practice Stations
• Visit the Word Work Station
• Visit the Words to Know Station

Independent Activities
• Read independently
• Background Building Audio
• *Reader's and Writer's Notebook*

Differentiated Instruction

A Advanced

Support Reading Say the word *cat* and *pup.* Have children identify the medial sound in each word. Then ask them which letter spells each of these sounds.

English Language Learners

Frontload Decodable Reader Before children read *Fun for Bud,* have volunteers model the actions sat, run, jump, dug, and hug.

Objectives
- Practice compare and contrast.
- Preview and predict.
- Retell a selection.

Check Retelling
SUCCESS PREDICTOR

Listening Comprehension
🔄 Compare and Contrast

Review

Envision It!

Have children turn to pp. 54–55 of *My Skills Buddy*. Comparing is telling how things are alike. Contrasting is telling how they are different. Good readers **compare and contrast** settings, characters, and events to help them understand what happens.

My Skills Buddy, pp. 54–55

First Read—Big Book
Trucks Roll!

Concepts of print

Display the cover of *Trucks Roll!* Explain that the printed words tell us the title of the selection and who wrote and illustrated it.

Preview and predict

Think Aloud — The title of this book is *Trucks Roll!* Tell me what you see on the cover. I see a very big red truck. What do you think this book will be about? Let's read to find out.

Use illustrations

Take children on a picture walk through the book. Have children tell about what they see in each picture.

Introduce genre

A nonfiction selection tells information about something that is real, or not make-believe. This selection is rhyming nonfiction because it uses rhyming words to tell about real things.

Set purpose

Remind children of the question of the week: *What kinds of transportation help people do their jobs?* Have children listen as you read to see how the trucks in the selection help people do their jobs.

Model

Read *Trucks Roll!* with expression for enjoyment.

Read for enjoyment

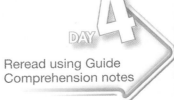

Reread using Develop Vocabulary notes

Reread using Guide Comprehension notes

Retell

Check retelling

Envision It!

Have children turn to p. 66 of *My Skills Buddy.* Walk through the retelling boxes as children retell *Trucks Roll!* Let's retell what happens in the first box—the beginning of the selection. Some trucks carry fruit or trees. They have to be cooled off with water in the desert. Let's retell what happens in the next box. Continue with the rest of the boxes. After children retell the selection as a group, have them draw a picture to retell a favorite part of the selection. Have them write or dictate a word or sentence to go with their picture.

My Skills Buddy, p. 66

Top-Score Response A top-score response identifies the topic and details.

Differentiated Instruction

SI **Strategic Intervention**

Frontload Main Selection Some children may not be familiar with the job of truck driver. Explain that many truck drivers only go short distances and are home every night. However, some truck drivers go very long distances and stay away from home many nights in a row.

Retelling Plan

- ☑ **Week 1** Assess Advanced students.
- ☑ **Week 2** Assess On-Level students.
- ☑ **This week assess Strategic Intervention students.**
- ☐ **Week 4** Assess Advanced students.
- ☐ **Week 5** Assess On-Level students.
- ☐ **Week 6** Assess Strategic Intervention students.

E L L

English Language Learners
Cognates Other languages have similar words for compare and contrast. The word for compare is *comparar* in Spanish and *comparer* in French. The word for contrast is *contrastar* in Spanish and *contraster* in French.

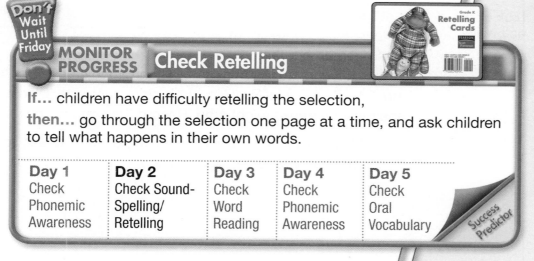

Don't Wait Until Friday
MONITOR PROGRESS **Check Retelling**

If... children have difficulty retelling the selection,

then... go through the selection one page at a time, and ask children to tell what happens in their own words.

Day 1	Day 2	Day 3	Day 4	Day 5
Check Phonemic Awareness	Check Sound-Spelling/ Retelling	Check Word Reading	Check Phonemic Awareness	Check Oral Vocabulary

Success Predictor

247

Retelling

Succes Predicto

Think, Talk, and Write

Discuss concept

We're learning about how transportation helps people do their jobs.

- What are some kinds of transportation you have ridden in?
- What do you think it would feel like to be in the cab of a big truck?
- What would you like best about being a truck driver? Why?

Confirm predictions

Have children recall the predictions they made before you read *Trucks Roll!*

- What did you think the selection would be about?
- Was your prediction correct?

Have children turn to p. 67 of *My Skills Buddy*. Read the questions and directives and have children respond.

Text to world

1. How do trucks help people do their jobs? How do trucks help people move things from place to place?

◉ Compare and Contrast

2. Look at the pictures. How are these trucks alike? (They carry goods from place to place and have cabs and trailers.) How are they different? (One truck is open and one is closed. One carries fruit and one carries books.)

Look back and write

3. Let's look back at our selection and write about it. We remember that trucks have to stop sometimes. Listen for why they have to stop. Read pp. 24–27 of *Trucks Roll!* Now let's write our ideas. Discuss with children the reasons trucks might stop. Record their responses on chart paper.

Possible responses: *for traffic lights, to pay tolls, to eat, to get weighed at weight stations, to get gas, to sleep.*

Think, Talk, and Write

1. How do trucks help people do their jobs? Text to World

2. How are these trucks from *Trucks Roll!* alike? How are they different?

◉ Compare and Contrast

3. Look back and write.

67

My Skills Buddy, p. 67

Conventions
Prepositions

Review

Remind children of what they learned about prepositions. A preposition is a word that tells us more about a noun in a sentence. It tells how the noun is related to the other parts of a sentence. Remember that we talked about the prepositions *on, in, over,* and *under.*

Guide practice

I am going to use a preposition in a sentence: *Trucks drive on the road.* Where do trucks drive? *On the road.* The word *on* is the preposition in the sentence. It tells where trucks drive: *on the road.* Repeat the routine with the sentence *The goods are in the trailers.*

Write the sentence frames below on the board and help children write the missing prepositions on the blanks.

> **Trucks drive _____ the road.** (on)
>
> **The goods are _____ the trailers.** (in)

On their own

Use *Reader's and Writer's Notebook,* p. 350, for more practice with prepositions.

Daily Fix-It

Use the Daily Fix-It exercise for more conventions practice.

Reader's and Writer's Notebook, p. 350

jectives

Write sentences comparing and contrasting jobs and vehicles.
Write *U* and *u*.
Identify and use words for jobs.

Writing
Respond to Literature

Discuss Display *Trucks Roll!* and *Mayday! Mayday!* Ask children to recall the jobs of truck driver and Coast Guard rescuer.

Model These two jobs are alike in some ways and different in other ways. The job of truck driver is like the job of Coast Guard rescuer because they both have to be done in all kinds of weather. They are different because a truck driver travels in a truck, and a Coast Guard rescuer travels in a helicopter or boat. For my sentence, I am going to write:

> **They work in bad weather.**

Guide practice Have children look at the truck on pp. 6–7 of *Trucks Roll!* and compare it to a photograph of a school bus. Have them tell how a truck is like a school bus. Then have them tell how it is different. Help children write two sentences comparing and contrasting the two forms of transportation.

Independent writing Have children write or dictate their own sentences about *Trucks Roll!* or copy one of the sentences from the board. Remind them to capitalize the first letter and use end punctuation. Then have children illustrate their sentences.

Daily Handwriting

Write *Uncle* and *pup* on the board. Review correct letter formation of uppercase *U* and lowercase *u*.

D'Nealian™   Ball and Stick

Have children write *Uncle* and *pup* on their Write-On Boards. Remind them to use proper left-to-right and top-to-bottom progression and proper spacing between letters when writing *U* and *u*.

Vocabulary
Words for Jobs

Model

Have children turn to p. 68 of *My Skills Buddy.* Use the first Vocabulary bullet on the page to guide the discussion. Direct children to the first picture. This is a *pilot*. A *pilot* is a person whose job is flying an airplane or helicopter. Direct children to the next picture. This is a *truck driver*. A *truck driver* is a person who drives a truck for his or her job. Direct children to the third picture. This is a *conductor*. A *conductor* is a person whose job is collecting tickets and calling out stops on a train. Direct children to the last picture. This is an *astronaut*. An *astronaut* is

My Skills Buddy, p. 68

a person who goes into outer space for his or her job. The words we learned about all name jobs. They name a person who does a kind of work.

Guide practice

Give each child a set of word cards with the job titles written on them. Ask questions such as the following and have children hold up the correct card:

- Who would take your ticket and help you down the steps on a train?
- Who would carry vegetables across the country in a truck?
- Who would test how seeds grow in outer space?
- Who would fly an airplane full of people across the ocean?

On their own

Have children take turns acting out something that one of the workers does. Other children can guess what job is being performed.

Wrap Up Your Day

✔ **Concept Talk** Remember our question of the week: *What kinds of transportation help people do their jobs?* How do trucks help people do their jobs in *Trucks Roll?* Help children list some answers to the question.

✔ **Phonemic Awareness** I will read a sentence. Tug on your ear when you hear /u/ words. *Bud the pup is under the umbrella with Uncle Jud.*

✔ **Vocabulary Skill** Tell me about our words for jobs. Which worker explores outer space? Which worker uses an airplane to do his or her job? Which worker takes tickets on a train? Which worker carries goods from place to place in a truck?

✔ **Homework Idea** Ask children to compare and contrast two things they have in their homes, such as a couch and a chair.

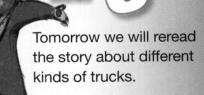

Preview

DAY 3

Tomorrow we will reread the story about different kinds of trucks.

Social Studies
Moving People and Things
Materials: crayons, construction paper

What Are Some Different Forms of Transportation? Different forms of transportation help us move people and things from place to place. Create a two-column chart on the board. Label the first column *Transportation* and the second column *Things Moved.* I want you to name all the different forms of transportation you know. Record their answers in the first column. Then point to each form of transportation and discuss what kinds of things it moves from place to place. Record these answers in the second column.

Transportation	Things Moved
school bus	children
car	families
ambulance	sick people

Forms of Transportation Have children draw and label their favorite form of transportation and what it moves.

Phonemic Awareness
Under the Umbrella
Materials: large umbrella cutout, paper raindrops (several for each student), crayons

/u/ Words Ask children to think of words that begin with /u/ or have /u/ in the middle. Record their responses on the board.

Give each child a paper raindrop. Have children copy and illustrate one /u/ word on each raindrop. Encourage them to fill the whole raindrop with their illustrations. Then display a large paper umbrella on a bulletin board with the title *Under the Umbrella.* Attach all of the raindrops around the umbrella to create a colorful display. Have children take turns reading the "raindrop" words.

Comprehension
Compare and Contrast
Materials: small boxes, transportation cards from the Teacher Resource DVD, pictures glued on cards

Transportation Circle Organize children into small groups. Give each group a box that contains transportation cards.

Begin the game by having one child pick two pictures out of the box. Then the child should tell how the two forms of transportation are alike and hand the pictures to another child in the group. The second child should tell how the forms of transportation are different. Return the pictures to the box, mix them up, and repeat activity.

bjectives

Share information and ideas about the concept.
Build oral vocabulary.

oday at a Glance

ral Vocabulary
ul, steering wheel

onemic Awareness
Initial and Medial /u/

onics
/u/ Spelled *Uu*

omprehension
Compare and Contrast

onventions
epositions

riting
em

stening and Speaking
scuss Literature

TRUCKTOWN
on Reading Street

Start your engines! Display p. 24 of *Truckery Rhymes.* Do you know the original "What Are Little Boys Made Of"? Recite it first, and then have children say it with you:

> Snips and snails, and puppy dogs tails,
> That's what little boys are made of!
> Sugar and spice and all things nice,
> That's what little girls are
> made of!

Truckery Rhymes

Concept Talk

Question of the Week
What kinds of transportation help people do their jobs?

Write and read the question of the week as you track the print. Talk with children about trucks and other kinds of transportation. Remind children to speak clearly and to take turns speaking.

Listen for Amazing Words

Let's Sing Display Sing with Me Chart 27B. Remind children that yesterday they sang "Trucks Are Rolling" and listened for the words *trailers* and *cabs.* Today we are going to listen for the Amazing Words *haul* and *steering wheel.* Sing the song several times to the tune of "Frère Jacques." Have children sing along with you, pretending to turn a steering wheel when they say the Amazing Word *haul* or *steering wheel.*

Trucks Are Rolling

Trucks are rolling.
Trucks are rolling.
What do you see?
What do you see?
Truckers' horns
a-blowing,
Early in the morning,
On their way,
on their way.

 Sing with Me Audio

Talk with Me/Sing with Me
Chart 27B

Oral Vocabulary
Amazing Words

Amazing Words

trailers	cabs
haul	steering wheel
truckers	headlight

Teach Amazing Words

Amazing Words Oral Vocabulary Routine

1 Introduce the Word When you carry something in a vehicle, you *haul* it. What's our new Amazing Word for carrying something in a vehicle? Say it with me: *haul.*

2 Demonstrate Provide examples to show meaning. *Trucks haul goods from place to place.*

Repeat steps 1 and 2.

Introduce the Word A *steering wheel* is a wheel you turn to steer a vehicle. What's our new Amazing Word for a wheel you turn to steer a vehicle? Say it with me: *steering wheel.*

Demonstrate *The driver sits behind the steering wheel.*

3 Apply Have children use *haul* and *steering wheel* in complete sentences. Have them illustrate their sentences.

Routines Flip Chart

Use Amazing Words

To reinforce the concept and the Amazing Words, have children supply the appropriate Amazing Word for each sentence.

I turned the _____ to make the car go right.
(steering wheel)

I use my car to _____ books to school. (haul)

E L L Expand Vocabulary
Use the Day 3 instruction on ELL Poster 27 to help children expand vocabulary.

E L L Poster 27

Differentiated Instruction

 Advanced

Build Vocabulary Have children draw a picture of their family's main form of transportation, such as the family car or a city bus. Have them include things that they often haul, such as people, groceries, or sports equipment.

E L L

English Language Learners
Visual Support Use the pictures on Talk with Me Chart 27A to help children complete the Amazing Word sentences.

bjectives
Isolate initial and medial /u/.
Discriminate initial and medial /u/.
• Blend syllables.

Phonemic Awareness
🔄 Initial and Medial /u/

Picture Card

Review

Initial /u/ Display the *up* Picture Card. This picture shows *up*. *Up* begins with /u/ /u/ /u/, *up*. What sound do you hear at the beginning of *up*? Continue with the *umbrella* Picture Card.

Practice medial /u/

Display the *duck* Picture Card. This is a *duck*. Listen to the sounds in *duck*: /d/ /u/ /k/. Where do you hear /u/ in *duck*? (in the middle) The /u/ in *duck* is in the middle. Continue the routine with the *bus, gum,* and *mug* Picture Cards.

Picture Card

Segment words

Listen to the sounds in *up*: /u/ /p/. How many sounds do you hear? (two) Where do you hear /u/? The /u/ in *up* is at the beginning. Continue the routine with the following words: *jug, mud, pup, cut, sun, rust.*

On their own

Have children think of a /u/ word that has three sounds or use one of the words from the previous activity. Have them draw a picture of the word and write or dictate a label.

Segment

Listen to the word *mug*. What sounds do you hear? Say them with me: /m/ /u/ /g/. How many sounds do you hear? There are three sounds in *mug*. Let's try some more words. **Continue the routine with the following words:** *pug, fill, bud, top, hut, bed, rug, pup, not, tip.*

Corrective feedback

If... children cannot segment the words, **then...** provide practice segmenting the words in chunks: /m/ -ug.

Blend syllables

Listen to these word parts: *bull/doz/ers.* Now I will blend the parts together to say the word: *bulldozers.* What's the word? The word is *bulldozers.* Now you try some. **Continue the routine with the following words:** *trailers, bookmobile, dispatcher, chocolate, puzzles, cinnamon, stations, sleepiness, headlight.*

Differentiated Instruction

A Advanced

Support Blend Syllables After you say a word in syllable parts, have children help you count the syllables in the word.

bjectives
- Practice /u/ spelled *Uu*.
- Read /u/ words.
- Read high-frequency words.

Check Word Reading
SUCCESS PREDICTOR

Phonics—Teach/Model
 /u/ Spelled *Uu*

Review — **/u/Uu** Display the *Uu* Alphabet Card and point to the *umbrella*. What sound do you hear at the beginning of *umbrella?* What letter spells that sound? Point to the letters *Uu.* What is the sound we learned for this letter? What are the names of these letters?

Review — **Letter Names and Sounds** Use Alphabet Cards to review the following letter names and sounds: *Aa, Bb, Dd, Ee, Jj, Mm, Oo, Pp, Rr, Xx.*

Blend sounds — Write the name *Bud* on the board. Point to each letter as you say the sound: /b/ /u/ /d/. When I blend these sounds together, I make the name *Bud.* Say the sounds with me: /b/ /u/ /d/. Now blend the sounds together: /b/ /u/ /d/, *Bud.* Repeat the blending routine with *box, pup, Mom, Jan, Rex, rug,* and *sun.*

B   u   d

More practice — Use *Reader's and Writer's Notebook*, p. 351, for additional practice with /u/.

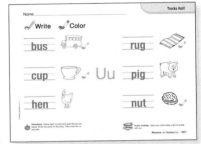

Reader's and Writer's Notebook, p. 351

Review **Sound-Spelling** Display the *Ss* Alphabet Card. What sound do you hear at the beginning of *salamander?* What letter spells that sound? Yes, the letter *s* spells /s/. Review the following sounds and letters with Alphabet Cards: *Gg, Jj, Mm, Nn, Pp, Rr, Tt*.

Review **High-Frequency Words** Write *what* on the board. This is the word *what*. What is this word? Continue the routine with *said, was, do, see, look,* and *with*.

Alphabet Card

Differentiated Instruction

SI Strategic Intervention

High-Frequency Words Have children work in pairs to review the high-frequency words. Write the words on flash cards. Have the first child display the flash card for his or her partner who then says the word aloud.

Don't Wait Until Friday

MONITOR PROGRESS   Check Word Reading   High-Frequency Words

Write *what, said, was, do, see, look,* and *with* on the board. Have children take turns reading the words.

Practice reading these words from Kindergarten Student Reader K.5.3, *Our Pup Bud*.

| **Bud** | **pup** | **fun** | **tug** | **rug** | **run** | **jump** | **sun** |

If... children cannot read the high-frequency words,
then... write the words on cards for them to practice at home.

If... children cannot blend sounds to read the words,
then... provide practice blending the words in chunks, /b/ -ud.

If... children can successfully blend sounds to read the words,
then... have them read Kindergarten Student Reader K.5.3, *Our Pup Bud*.

Day 1	**Day 2**	**Day 3**	**Day 4**	**Day 5**
Check Phonemic Awareness	Check Sound-Spelling/ Retelling	Check Word Reading	Check Phonemic Awareness	Check Oral Language

Success Predictor

Kindergarten Student Reader K.5.3
/u/ Spelled *Uu* and High-Frequency Words

Review

Review the previously taught high-frequency words. Have children read each word as you point to it on the Word Wall.

was	look	said	see	what	like	with

Read Kindergarten Student Reader K.5.3

Display Kindergarten Student Reader K.5.3. Today we are going to read a new book. Point to the title of the book. The title of this book is *Our Pup Bud*. The author's name is Peyton Walston. The illustrator's name is Hector Bolasca.

Use the reading decodable books routine to read the Kindergarten Student Reader.

Small Group

ROUTINE **Reading Decodable Books**

1. **Read Silently** Have children whisper read the book page by page as you listen in.

2. **Model Fluent Reading** Have children finger point as you read a page. Then have children reread the page without you.

3. **Read Chorally** Have children finger point as they chorally read the page. Continue reading page by page, repeating steps 1 and 2.

4. **Read Individually** Have children take turns reading aloud a page.

5. **Reread and Monitor Progress** As you listen to individual children reread, monitor progress and provide support.

6. **Reread with a Partner** Have children reread the book page by page with a partner.

Routines Flip Chart

Jem was sad.

"Look in the box, Jem," said Mom.
"See what is in the box."
It is Bud the pup.

"Come and see Bud the pup,"
said Jem.
"He is little and fun!"

Kindergarten Student Reader K.5.3

Jan and Rex like little Bud.
Jem likes Bud.
The pup is fun.

Look what Bud can do!
Bud likes to tug.
He likes to tug on the rug.

 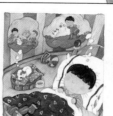

Bud can run and jump.
Bud can have fun in the sun.
Jem, Rex, and Jan have fun in the sun.

It was fun.
We had fun with Bud.
Jem likes Bud.

Differentiated Instruction

SI Strategic Intervention

Build Background Ask children what they know about puppies. Talk with them about the energy level of a puppy and what a puppy likes to do.

Small Group Time

DAY 3 Break into small groups to read the Kindergarten Student Reader before the comprehension lesson.

SI Strategic Intervention	**OL** On-Level	**A** Advanced
Teacher-Led Page DI•37	Teacher-Led Page DI•41	Teacher-Led Page DI•44
• Phonemic Awareness and Phonics	• Phonemic Awareness and Phonics	• **Read** Independent Reader K.5.3 or Kindergarten Student Reader K.5.3
• **Read** Concept Literacy Reader K.5.3 or Kindergarten Student Reader K.5.3	• **Read** Kindergarten Student Reader K.5.3	

E L L Place English language learners in the groups that correspond to their reading abilities in English.

Practice Stations
• Visit the Words to Know Station
• Visit the Let's Write! Station

Independent Activities
• Read independently
• Audio Text of Big Book
• *Reader's and Writer's Notebook*

Objectives
• Recall and retell a selection.
• Practice compare and contrast.

Comprehension

Retell the selection

Have children turn to p. 66 of *My Skills Buddy* and use the retelling boxes to retell the selection *Trucks Roll!*

My Skills Buddy, p. 66

** Envision It!**

Think Aloud Direct children to the first retell box. This part of the selection tells us that some trucks carry fruit and trees. Tell me what we learn about next.

Continue reviewing the retelling boxes and having children retell about the selection.

Review **Compare and Contrast** Display illustrations in *Trucks Roll!* Remind children that there are many ways to haul things from place to place. Use these questions to help children compare and contrast trucks and other forms of transportation.

• Besides driving a truck, what are some other ways that people can travel to deliver a package? (in a car, by airplane, on a bike)

• Which do you think is faster, driving a truck or flying in an airplane? (flying in an airplane)

• How is a truck like an airplane? (They both move things from place to place.) How are they different? (A truck drives on the ground while an airplane flies in the sky. An airplane moves faster than a truck.)

More practice Use *Reader's and Writer's Notebook,* p. 352, for additional practice with compare and contrast.

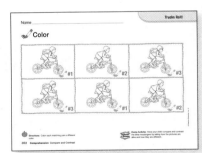
Reader's and Writer's Notebook, p. 352

Second Read—Big Book
Trucks Roll!

Reread *Trucks Roll!* Follow the Day 3 arrow beginning on p. 264 and use the Develop Vocabulary notes to prompt conversations about the selection.

Have children use the Amazing Words *trailers, cabs, haul, steering wheel, truckers,* and *headlight* to talk about the selection.

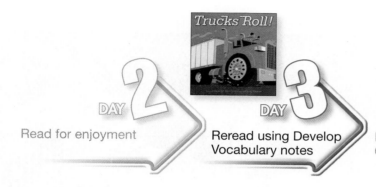

DAY **2**
Read for enjoyment

DAY **3**
Reread using Develop Vocabulary notes

DAY **4**
Reread using Guide Comprehension notes

Develop Vocabulary

DAY 3

Wh- question
What do truck do? (trucks roll)

• Trucks roll. What do you think that means?

Trucks' wheels
go 'round and 'round.
Trucks' pistons
go up and down.

Trucks roll!

6

7

Big Book, pp. 6–7

Guide Comprehension

DAY 4

Distancing
What goes up and down? (trucks' pistons)

• A piston is a piece of metal that goes up and down in a truck engine. What other things have engines?

Distancing

What are these trucks carrying? (rabbits and labs)

- These trucks are hauling rabbits and a kind of dog called *Labrador retriever,* or *lab* for short. Have you ever seen a lab?

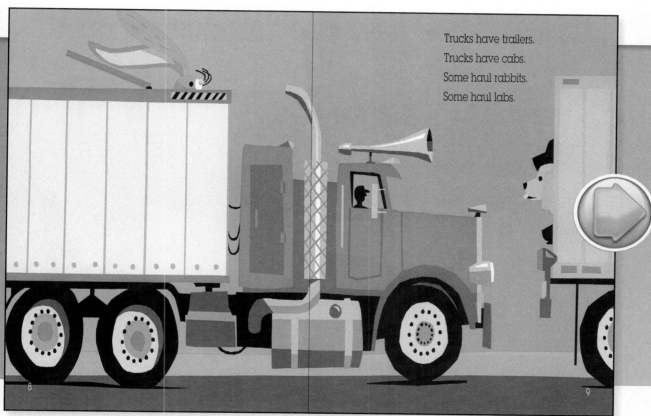

Trucks have trailers.
Trucks have cabs.
Some haul rabbits.
Some haul labs.

Big Book, pp. 8–9

Compare and Contrast

How are rabbits and labs alike? (They are both animals. They both have four legs.)

- How are they different?

Develop Vocabulary, continued

DAY 3

Distancing

Why is there a big waterspout on the side of this truck? (to water down the fruit and trees)

- It can be hot and dry in the desert, so the truck driver may have to put water on the fruit. How does water help you when you are hot?

Develop Vocabulary desert

Some haul apple juice.
Some haul trees.
Water them down
in the desert, please.

Trucks roll!

10   11

Big Book, pp. 10–11

Guide Comprehension, continued

DAY 4

Compare and Contrast

What kind of plants do you see on the ground? (cactus)

- There are cactuses on the ground. How are the cactuses different from the trees on the truck?

Inferential

Which truck is carrying something cold? (the
ice cream truck)

- The ice cream truck is made like the
  refrigerator in your house. It keeps the ice
  cream cold. Where do you think this truck
  is taking the ice cream?

Trucks bring ice cream.
Trucks bring blocks,
books and bulldozers,
dolls and clocks.

Big Book, pp. 12–13

Distancing

What are these trucks carrying? (ice cream,
blocks, books, bulldozers, dolls, and clocks)

- Which of these trucks would you like to
  drive most? Why?

Develop Vocabulary, continued

DAY 3

Distancing
Who tells the truck driver to start driving? (the dispatcher)

- The dispatcher is the person who tells the truck drivers where to take the things they are carrying. Would you rather be a truck driver or a dispatcher?

Expand Vocabulary dispatcher

Dispatcher calls,
says Get underway!
Chocolate chip cookies
have to travel today.

Big Book, pp. 14–15

Guide Comprehension, continued

DAY 4

Wh- question
What is this truck carrying?
(chocolate chip cookies)

- Do the cookies in this illustration look real or make-believe? Why?

Wh- question

Where are the puzzles? (on a little truck)

- Stacks of puzzles are on a little truck called a forklift. The forklift is lifting the puzzles up onto the truck that will carry them away. Why do you think they use a forklift to put things on the truck?

Develop Vocabulary stacks

Stacks of puzzles ready to load. Spaceships, toy trains— get them on the road!

Big Book, pp. 16–17

Open-ended

What is this truck carrying? (puzzles, spaceships, toy trains)

- This truck is carrying stacks of puzzles, spaceships, and toy trains. These are all toys. Where do you think the truck is taking them?

Develop Vocabulary, continued

DAY 3

Wh- question

Where is the truck driving in this picture? (**past a town, through a mountain and rainfall, over a bridge**)

- The truck is driving past a town, through a mountain pass, through rainfall, and over a bridge. Do

you think it would be fun to drive through a mountain?

Haul them through mountains, over rivers, past towns— around blue sky curves, through rain pounding down.

18

19

Big Book, pp. 18–19

Guide Comprehension, continued

DAY 4

Distancing

It says trucks drive "around blue sky curves." What do you think that means? (**in good weather**)

- Blue skies are a sign of good weather. Do you think it would be

easier to drive a truck in blue skies or in rain?

Completion

What do trucks do? (trucks roll)

• What other things do you know that roll?

Trucks roll!

ROLL

Big Book, pp. 20–21

Recall

What things have we learned about trucks carrying so far? (rabbits, labs, apple juice, trees, ice cream, blocks, books, bulldozers, dolls, clocks, cookies, puzzles, spaceships, toy trains)

Develop Vocabulary, continued

DAY 3

Distancing

Where is the TV? (in the bunk)

- The TV is in the bunk, or the place behind the seats where the truck driver can sleep. There is a bed in the bunk. What else do you think would be in a bunk?

Expand Vocabulary bunk

Steering wheel, radio, horn's deep beep. TV in the bunk where tired truckers sleep.

Trucks stop.

22   23

Big Book, pp. 22–23

Guide Comprehension, continued

DAY 4

Open-ended

This page tells about things inside the cab of the truck. What is the cab? (the front part where the truck driver sits)

- The cab is the front part of the truck where the truck driver sits.

What is the back part of the truck called?

Distancing

What are some things trucks might stop for? (traffic lights, tolls, pork chops, cinnamon rolls)

• Truck drivers have to stop at red lights, just like car drivers have to do. They also have to stop at toll booths to pay tolls. Tolls are money charged for using a road. Have you ever been through a toll booth?

Expand Vocabulary tolls

Stop for traffic lights.
Stop for tolls.
Stop for pork chops
and cinnamon rolls.

TRUCK STOP

24

25

Big Book, pp. 24–25

Distancing

What kinds of food does it say truck drivers stop for? (pork chops and cinnamon rolls)

• These truck drivers stop for pork chops and cinnamon rolls. What kinds of food would you stop for if you were on a long trip?

Develop Vocabulary, continued

DAY 3

Wh- question

Where and when does this part of the selection take place? (**at a gas station at night**)

- The setting of this part of the selection is at a gas station at night. What in the picture tells you it is night?

Stop for weigh stations.
Stop for gas.
Stop for the night
to let sleepiness pass.

Big Book, pp. 26–27

Guide Comprehension, continued

DAY 4

Recall

What do trucks do during the day? (**trucks roll**)

- Trucks roll during the day. What do they do at night?

Distancing

What do truckers travel? (rolling dreams)

- It says truckers travel rolling dreams. That means they drive through the night while other people sleep and dream. What do you dream about?

Stars above like headlight beams;
Truckers travel rolling dreams.

28   29

Big Book, pp. 28–29

Compare and contrast

How are the stars like the light from the truck's headlights? (They both shine in front of them. They both light up the night sky.)

- How are they different?

Develop Vocabulary, continued

DAY 3

Distancing
Where is the key? (in the slot)

* It says the key is "in the slot." That means the key is turned in the keyhole near the steering wheel. That's how the truck driver starts the truck. What else needs a key?

Expand Vocabulary slot

Then, key in the slot,
coffee in the cup,
trucker's at the wheel
when the sun comes up.

30

31

Big Book, pp. 30–31

Guide Comprehension, continued

DAY 4

Inferential
How do you think the truck driver feels at the start of a new day?
(I think the truck driver feels excited for the new day to start.)

Completion

What do trucks do? (trucks roll)

• Trucks roll. What do trucks do when the truck drivers are sleepy?

Continue with DAY **3**

Conventions p. 278

Big Book, p. 32

Inferential

We learned about a lot of trucks. Were they going just a short way or a long way from home? (long way)

• They were going a long way from home. How do you know?

Skip to DAY **4**

Conventions p. 292

bjectives
- Review question marks and uppercase letters.
- Write a poem.

Conventions
Question Marks and Uppercase Letters

Review   A sentence that asks something is called a question. A question begins with a capital letter and ends with a question mark.

Write *how are you today* on the board. Correct the sentence on the board as you explain the corrections. This question is *How are you today?* It needs a capital *H* at the beginning. It needs a question mark at the end.

Guide practice   Write the following sentences on the board:

> **What is your name?**
> **Where are you going.**
> **do you like dogs?**

Have AlphaBuddy read the sentences to the class. Point to each word as AlphaBuddy reads. Look at the sentences on the board, and listen as AlphaBuddy reads them to you. Raise your hand if you see a mistake in a sentence that AlphaBuddy is reading.

Team Talk Pair children and have the first child ask a question. Have the second child tell where the capital letter and question mark belong. Then have children switch roles and repeat.

On their own   Use *Reader's and Writer's Notebook*, p. 353, for more practice with adjectives for opposites.

Daily Fix-It   Use the Daily Fix-It exercise for more conventions practice.

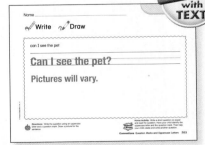

Reader's and Writer's Notebook, p. 353

Writing
Poem

Teach

A poem is often written in lines as well as sentences. It has rhythm, like clapping to a beat. The words at the ends of the lines can rhyme with each other.

Model

Write the following poem on the board.

> **Mary had a little lamb,**
> **Its fleece was white as snow,**
> **And everywhere that Mary went**
> **The lamb was sure to _____.** (go)

Have children suggest words to fill in the blank. Then recite the completed poem. Have children echo read the lines with you and identify the rhyming words. (*snow, go*)

Guide practice

Now let's write our own poem about a truck. What sound does a truck's horn make? (beep, beep) Let's write a poem using the rhyming words *beep* and *sleep.* Write the following poem on the board and read it aloud with children.

> **I drive a big red truck**
> **With a horn that goes "Beep, beep!"**
> **I fill my trailer up**
> **And hit the bunk to _____!** (sleep)

Independent practice

Have children turn to p. 354 of *Reader's and Writer's Notebook.* Have them copy the poem about the truck and then draw a picture to go with it.

Reader's and Writer's Notebook, p. 354

Daily Handwriting

Write *Uri* and *mud* on the board. Review correct letter formation of uppercase *U* and lowercase *u.*

Have children write *Uri* and *mud* on their Write-On Boards. Remind them to use proper left-to-right and top-to-bottom progression and proper spacing between letters when writing.

ELL

English Language Learners
Support Writing Pair English learners with children for whom English is the home language and have pairs write together.

Objectives
- Practice discussing literature.
- Face the speaker when listening.
- Ask the speaker questions to clarify information.
- Take turns and speak one at a time.

Listening and Speaking
Discuss Literature

Review

Remind children that when they listen, they should focus their attention on the speaker and ask questions if they don't understand something. They should take turns and speak one at a time.

Model

Display *If You Could Go to Antarctica.* Do you remember how scientists travel from South America to Antarctica? They ride on a boat. Let's name some other ways that people move from place to place. (cars, taxis, trucks, fire engines, helicopters)

Have children turn to p. 69 of *My Skills Buddy.* I see a picture from *Trucks Roll!* Let's talk about that book. Display *Trucks Roll!* Many companies use trucks to move the things they make to the people who want to buy them. Why do you think they use trucks? What makes a truck better than a car for moving lots of things? Ask children to use toy cars and trucks to act out how a truck could haul more products than a car. Use the Listening and Speaking bullets on p. 68 of *My Skills Buddy* to continue the discussion.

My Skills Buddy, p. 69

Independent practice

Display *Max Takes the Train.* Have pairs of children work together to discuss the story and list the modes of transportation it includes. Max and Uncle Bunny take many different rides to get to Zeke's Ice Cream Palace. What kinds of transportation do they take to get around the city? (bus, train, ferryboat, plane, subway train) Allow children to look at pictures from the book to help them remember all of the transportation. Refer children to their Rules for Listening and Speaking from pp. 1–2 of the *Reader's and Writer's Notebook.* Remind children to face their partner when listening and to take turns, listening and speaking one at a time. They should also ask questions if they don't understand.

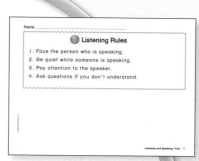

Name _____

Listening Rules

1. Face the person who is speaking.
2. Be quiet while someone is speaking.
3. Pay attention to the speaker.
4. Ask questions if you don't understand.

Reader's and Writer's Notebook, p. 1

Be a Good Listener

1. Face the person who is speaking.
2. Be quiet while someone is speaking.
3. Pay attention to the speaker.
4. Ask questions if you don't understand.

Differentiated Instruction

 Strategic Intervention

Support Retelling If children cannot recall a story or selection after looking at the pictures, then page through the book with them. Point out important words and remind them of key events in the story.

E L L

English Language Learners

Support Listening and Speaking Pair struggling children with more able children so that they can learn from each other's strengths.

Wrap Up Your Day

✔ **Concept Talk** Today we reread the selection about trucks. What are some things that the trucks carry?

✔ **Respond to Literature** Today we read about a happy surprise that Mom and Dad gave to Jem. Did you ever get a surprise that was fun to get?

✔ **Conventions** Instruct children to ask you a question. Write it incorrectly on the board. Have children correct the capitalization and end punctuation.

✔ **Homework Idea** Have children draw and label a picture of a word with initial or medial /u/.

Preview

DAY 4

Tomorrow we will read a story about two of our Trucktown friends, Max and Melvin.

Extend Your Day!

Social Studies
Deliveries

Materials: domestic and foreign food products or packages with labels, U.S. map, world map

Where Does Food Come From? Locate your community on a U.S. map. Talk about where people in your area get their food and how food gets from farms and dairies to stores. Explain that transportation, such as trucks, brings food and drink from far away.

Cross Country Display a domestic food product and locate on the map where it was produced. Have children brainstorm different ways the food might have been transported

from that location to your city. Trace a path between the product's origin and your city.

International Food Display a foreign product. Locate its country of origin on a world map. Discuss how it might have been transported to your area.

Math
Compare and Contrast

Materials: assorted shapes cut out of white construction paper, crayons

Shape Designs Give children three shape cutouts. Ask them to color each with a color or simple pattern, such as stripes or polka dots.

Alike Now it is time to play a game. When I say *go*, I want you to find someone with a cutout that is like one of your cutouts in some way. It can be the same shape or the same color or the same pattern. Go.

Different Have pairs find and explain a way in which their two cutouts are different.

Phonics
Connect /u/ to *Uu*

***Uu* Riddle** Write the following words on the board.

sun	fun	run	bun	cub
rub	under	grub	sub	tub
up	cup	pup		

Decode the words as a class, pointing out /u/ in each. Organize children into two teams. Take turns asking one member of each team to answer a riddle using one of the words on the board.

Objectives
• Discuss the concept to develop oral language.

Today at a Glance

Oral Vocabulary
truckers, headlight

Phonemic Awareness
final /ks/

Phonics
/ks/ Spelled Xx
Spell Words

Comprehension
⊙ Compare and Contrast

Conventions
Prepositions

Writing
Extend the Concept

Vocabulary
Words for Jobs

TRUCKTOWN on Reading Street

Start your engines!

• Display "That's What Trucks Are Made Of" and lead the group in saying the rhyme a few times.

• Have the group clap the rhythm as they recite the rhyme.

• When children master the rhythm, have them march around the room as they say the rhyme.

Truckery Rhymes

Concept Talk

Question of the Week

 What kinds of transportation help people do their jobs?

Build concepts

Write and read the question as you track the print. Tell children to respond in complete sentences. Display Sing with Me Chart 27B.

Listen for Amazing Words

We are going to sing this song again. Listen for the Amazing Words *truckers* and *headlight.* Sing the song several times with children to the tune of "Frère Jacques." Have them stand up when they hear the Amazing Word *truckers* or *headlight.*

Sing with Me Audio

Trucks Are Rolling

Trucks are rolling.
Trucks are rolling.
What do you see?
What do you see?
Truckers' horns
a-blowing,
Early in the morning,
On their way,
on their way.

Talk with Me/Sing with Me Chart 27B

ELL **Produce Oral Language** Use the Day 4 instruction on ELL Poster 27 to extend and enrich language.

ELL Poster 27

Oral Vocabulary
Amazing Words

Amazing Words

trailers	cabs
haul	steering wheel
truckers	headlight

Teach Amazing Words

> **Amazing Words** **Oral Vocabulary Routine**
>
> **1** **Introduce the Word** People who drive trucks for their job are called *truckers.* What's our new Amazing Word for people who drive trucks? Say it with me: *truckers.*
>
> **2** **Demonstrate** *The truckers stopped for dinner at the rest stop.*
> Repeat steps 1 and 2.
>
> **Introduce the Word** A *headlight* is a bright light at the front of a car, truck, or train. It helps the driver see when it's dark outside. What's our new Amazing Word for a bright light at the front of a car, truck, or train? Say it with me: *headlight.*
>
> **Demonstrate** *The snow fell in the light of our headlight.*
>
> **3** **Apply** Have children use *truckers* and *headlight* in sentences. Then have them illustrate their sentences.

Routines Flip Chart

Use Amazing Words

To reinforce the concept and the Amazing Words, have children supply the appropriate Amazing Word for each sentence.

The light from the _____ shows the way. (headlight)

The _____ took a break from the long drive. (truckers)

Differentiated Instruction

 Strategic Intervention

Build Background Remind children that headlights usually come in pairs, meaning that there are two headlights on the front of each car or truck. Show children pictures of cars and trucks to support this.

ELL

English Language Learners
Build Vocabulary If children need help completing the sentences, say a sentence using each Amazing Word and ask children to choose the sentence that makes sense.

Phonemic Awareness
Review Final /ks/

Picture Card

Review

Display the *fox* Picture Card. This is a *fox*. *Fox* ends with /ks/. What is this? What sound does it end with? Continue the routine with the Picture Cards *box* and *ox*.

I am going to say three words. Tell me which words end with /ks/: *fix, fan, box*. *Fix* and *box* end with /ks/. *Fan* ends with /n/. Let's try some more. Listen carefully. Continue the activity with these sets of words: *mix, Max, sun; Rex, sat, six; fox, dog, ox; fox, job, box.*

Picture Card

Corrective feedback

If... children cannot discriminate /ks/, **then...** have them say /ks/ several times, /ks/ /ks/ /ks/.

When you say /ks/, press the back of your tongue against the roof of your mouth, make a slight smile, and nearly close your teeth. **Have children practice saying /ks/, and then repeat the discrimination activity.**

Picture Card

Phonics
/ks/ Spelled *Xx*

Display the *six* Picture Card. This is the word *six*. *Six* ends with /ks/. What letter did we learn to spell the sound /ks/? Yes, the letter *x*.

Write the word *fax* on the board. Help me read this word. The sounds in the word are /f/ /a/ /ks/. The word is *fax.* Add the word *tax* to the board. What part of this word is the same as *fax?* What is the first sound in the new word? (/t/) Let's say the first sound and the word ending: /t/ *-ax.* The new word is *tax.* Repeat the routine with the following pairs of words: *mix, Max; box, fox*.

Don't Wait Until Friday

MONITOR PROGRESS | **Check Phonemic Awareness**

Phoneme Segmentation I am going to say a word. Tell me each sound in the word.

| bug | jump | cut | bus | up | mud |

If… children cannot connect segment the sounds,

then… use the small-group Strategic Intervention lesson, p. DI•38, to reteach segmentation skills.

Continue to monitor children's progress using other instructional opportunities during the week so that they can be successful with the Day 5 Assessment. See the Skills Trace on p. 224.

Day 1	**Day 2**	**Day 3**	**Day 4**	**Day 5**
Check Phonemic Awareness	Check Sound-Spelling/ Retelling	Check Word Reading	Check Phonemic Awareness	Check Oral Vocabulary

Success Predictor

Differentiated Instruction

SI Strategic Intervention

Support Phonemic Awareness Remind children that /ks/ is usually found at the end of words. If they see *x* at the end of a word, they should always pronounce it /ks/.

ELL

English Language Learners

Support Phonics Children who speak French may struggle with words with /ks/, as final *x* is often silent in French. Remind children that *x* is always pronounced /ks/ when it appears at the end of a word in English.

287

Phonemic Awareness

Success Predictor

bjectives
- Spell words.
- Blend and segment words.
- Read decodable text.
- Read high-frequency words.

Spelling
/u/ Spelled *Uu*

ROUTINE Spell Words

Spell words

1 Review Sound-Spellings Display the *Hh* Alphabet Card. This is a *helicopter. Helicopter* begins with /h/. What is the letter for /h/? (*h*) Continue the routine with the following Alphabet Cards: *Ee, Gg, Jj, Ll, Uu, Ww, Xx.*

2 Model Today we are going to spell some words. Listen to the three sounds in *rub:* /r/ /u/ /b/.

- What is the first sound in *rub?* (/r/) What is the letter for /r/? (*r*) Write *r* on the board.
- What is the middle sound you hear? (/u/) What is the letter for /u/? (*u*) Write *u* on the board.
- What is the last sound you hear? (/b/) What is the letter for /b/? (*b*) Write *b* on the board.
- Point to *rub.* Help me blend the sound of each letter together to read this word: /r/ /u/ /b/. The word is *rub.* Repeat the modeling with the word *hub.*

3 Guide Practice Now let's spell some words together. Listen to this word: /t/ /u/ /b/. What is the first sound in *tub?* (/t/) What is the letter for /t/? (*t*) Write *t* on the board. Now you write *t* on your paper. What is the middle sound in *tub?* (/u/) What is the letter for /u/? (*u*) Write *u* on the board. Now you write *u* on your paper. What is the last sound in *tub?* (/b/) What is the letter for /b/? (*b*) Write *b* on the board. Now you write *b* on your paper. Now we can blend the sound of each letter together to read the word: /t/ /u/ /b/. What is the word? (*tub*) Continue spell and blend practice with the following words: *Bud, run, can, hot, wet, hug.*

4 On Your Own This time I am going to say a word. I want you to write it on your paper. Remember, first, say the word slowly in your head and then write the letter for each sound. Listen carefully. Write the word *cub.* Give children time to write the word. How do you spell the word *cub?* Listen to the sounds: /k/ /u/ /b/. The first sound is /k/. What is a letter we learned for /k/? Did you write *c* on your paper? What is the letter for /u/? Did you write *u* on your paper? What is the letter for /b/? Did you write *b* on your paper? Name the letters in *cub. Cub is spelled c, u, b.* Continue the activity with the following words: *pup, hot, mud, had, did.*

Routines Flip Chart

Get Set, Roll! Reader 27
 Practice /u/ Spelled *Uu*

Review

Review the high-frequency words *the, to, a, is, of, see, what, said,* and *was.* Have children find each word on the Word Wall.

Teach rebus words

Write the word *tank* on the board. This is the word *tank.* Name the letters with me: *t, a, n, k, tank.* Look for the word *tank* in the story today. A picture above the word will help you read it.

Read Get Set, Roll! Reader 27

Today we will read a story about our friends Max and Melvin and a tank. Point to the title of the book. What is the title of the book? (*The Tank*) We will read some words with /u/ in this book.

Use the routine for reading decodable books found in the Routines Flip Chart to read Get Set, Roll! Reader 27.

Get Set, Roll! Reader 27

Small Group Time

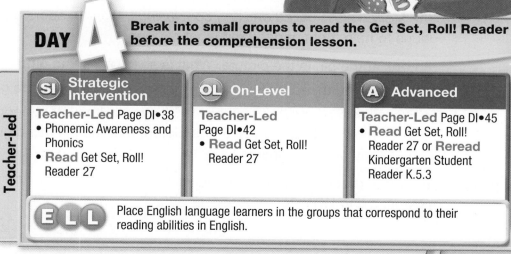

DAY 4   **Break into small groups to read the Get Set, Roll! Reader before the comprehension lesson.**

Teacher-Led

SI Strategic Intervention	**OL** On-Level	**A** Advanced
Teacher-Led Page DI•38 • Phonemic Awareness and Phonics • **Read** Get Set, Roll! Reader 27	**Teacher-Led** Page DI•42 • **Read** Get Set, Roll! Reader 27	**Teacher-Led** Page DI•45 • **Read** Get Set, Roll! Reader 27 or **Reread** Kindergarten Student Reader K.5.3

ELL   Place English language learners in the groups that correspond to their reading abilities in English.

Practice Stations
• Visit the Let's Write Station
• Visit the Read for Meaning Station

Independent Activities
• Read independently
• Audio Text of the Big Book
• *Reader's and Writer's Notebook*

 **ELL**

English Language Learners
Frontload Reader Do a picture walk with children to preview the reader before starting the routine.

Objectives
• Practice compare and contrast.
• Review and practice draw conclusions.

Comprehension
Compare and Contrast

Practice compare and contrast

Envision It!

Have children turn to the Compare and Contrast picture on pp. 54–55 of *My Skills Buddy.* As you look at the pictures, remind children that they can compare and contrast characters, events, settings, or ideas to help them understand a story or selection better.

My Skills Buddy, pp. 54–55

Team Talk Have children find any object in the classroom, such as a book or toy. Pair children. Have one child tell something that is alike about their two objects. Have the other child tell something that is different about their objects. Then have children switch roles and repeat the activity.

Draw Conclusions

Review

Direct children to the Draw Conclusions picture on pp. 114–115 of *My Skills Buddy.*

After we read a story, we think about what we have read. We use what we know and what we hear to make up our minds about what is happening in the story. This is called *drawing conclusions.* Good readers draw conclusions to help them understand what happens in a story.

• Look at the girl in the picture. What is she holding? (a gift)

• Why do you think she is smiling? (She is happy to have the gift.)

• How did you draw that conclusion? (I already know that people smile when they are happy. I see in the picture that the girl has a gift. She must be happy because she has a gift.)

More practice

For more practice with draw conclusions, use *Reader's and Writer's Notebook,* p. 355.

Reader's and Writer's Notebook, p. 355

Third Read—Big Book
Trucks Roll!

Guide comprehension

Display *Trucks Roll!* Let's use what we know and what we read to draw conclusions about *Trucks Roll!*

Display the pictures on pp. 10–11.

- Where are these trucks? (in the desert) How do you know? (The words say so.)

Display the pictures on pp. 14–15.

- Where is this truck? (in the city) How do you know? (I can see tall buildings in the picture. I know there are tall buildings in cities.)

Display the pictures on pp. 18–19.

- Where is this truck? (in the mountains, near towns) How do you know? (The words and pictures both say so.)

- Why do you think the trucks are in so many different places? (They have to carry their loads to all different places.)

Reread *Trucks Roll!* Return to p. 264. Follow the Day 4 arrow and use the Guide Comprehension notes to give children the opportunity to gain a more complete understanding of the story.

 DAY **2** Read for enjoyment

DAY **3** Reread using Develop Vocabulary notes

 DAY **4** Reread using Guide Comprehension notes

 Differentiated Instruction

 **Strategic Intervention**
Practice Draw Conclusions
If children struggle with drawing conclusions, provide simple classroom examples. Play some music or sing a simple song and have AlphaBuddy dance along. Ask children to draw a conclusion about why AlphaBuddy is dancing. (because there is music playing)

Academic Vocabulary

draw conclusions arrive at decisions or opinions after thinking about facts and details and using prior knowledge

English Language Learners
Proessional Development
Support Draw Conclusions
According to Dr. Lilly Wong Fillmore of the University of California at Berkeley, it is important to "teach children when the text calls for activation of prior knowledge. All children have such knowledge, but English learners need help in deciding where it is called for and how they should bring what they already know to interpret the texts they are reading."

Conventions
Prepositions

Review | Remind children of what they learned about prepositions. A preposition tells more about a noun in a sentence. It tells us how the noun is connected to the other parts of the sentence.

Guide practice | Do you remember the prepositions we have learned this week? We learned the prepositions *on, in, over,* and *under.* Write the prepositions on the board and read them aloud with children. Listen for one of those words in this sentence: *The rainbow is over the river.* Which word is the preposition? *Over* is the preposition. It tells where the rainbow is. It is *over* the river. Let's try another one: *The load is in the trailer.* Which word is the preposition? Right! *In* is the preposition. It tells where the load is. It is *in* the trailer.

Have children repeat one of the sentences after you and identify the preposition. Then have them write the preposition on their Write-On Boards.

On their own | Use *Reader's and Writer's Notebook,* p. 356, for more practice with prepositions.

Daily Fix-It | Use the Daily Fix-It exercise for more conventions practice.

Reader's and Writer's Notebook, p. 356

Writing
Extend the Concept: Text to World

Teach

We just read a selection about how trucks help truck drivers do their jobs. Let's think about other kinds of transportation that help people do their jobs.

Guide practice

Ask children to think about different jobs that use transportation. Use children's contributions to the discussion to make a two-column chart on the board.

Job	Transportation
firefighter	fire truck
police officer	police car
garbage collector	garbage truck
paramedic	ambulance
mover	moving van
pilot	airplane

Independent writing

Have children write or dictate a sentence about a job and form of transportation from the chart and illustrate it. Invite children to read their sentences to the class.

Daily Handwriting

Write *Uma* and *cut* on the board. Review correct letter formation of uppercase *U* and lowercase *u*.

Have children write *Uma* and *cut* on their Write-On Boards.

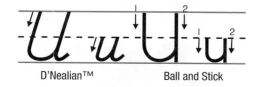

D'Nealian™   Ball and Stick

Remind them to use proper left-to-right and top-to-bottom progression and proper spacing between letters when writing.

Differentiated Instruction

 A **Advanced**

Support Writing Have children find a picture in a kid's magazine or book of someone using a form of transportation as they do their job. Help children cut out or make a copy of the picture and glue it to construction paper. Then have them write or dictate a label for the picture that includes the name of the jo and kind of transportation bein used.

Daily Fix-It

she likes to sing?
<u>S</u>he likes to sing<u>.</u>

This week's practice sentences appear on Teacher Resources DVD-ROM.

ELL

English Language Learners
Support Content-Area Writing If children have difficulty describing the details of the job and form of transportation they chose to write about, have them think about the things they already know about the job and vehicle. Then have them write one or two details before writing their sentences.

Vocabulary
Words for Jobs

Teach

Write the words *pilot, conductor, astronaut,* and *truck driver* on the board. Point to each word as you read it. These words tell about some jobs that people have. Have children turn to p. 68 of *My Skills Buddy.* Point to the picture of the truck driver. Which job is this man doing? Repeat for the other three pictures. Then use the last Vocabulary bullet on the page to guide a discussion about job preferences.

My Skills Buddy, p. 68

Team Talk Pair children and have them take turns describing one of the jobs. Have the other child guess which job is being described. Then have children switch roles and repeat the routine. Remind them to take turns listening and speaking.

Wrap Up Your Day

✔ **Oral Language** Sing "Trucks Are Rolling" with me. Pretend to drive a truck when you hear an Amazing Word—*trailers, cabs, haul, steering wheel, truckers,* or *headlight.*

✔ **Phonemic Awareness** Listen to this sentence. Clap when you hear /ks/ words: *An ox and a fox sat in a box eating bagels and lox.*

✔ **Homework Idea** Ask children to look on a package they have at home to find out where the item was made. Then have them find that place on a map and think about how it might have gotten from there to here.

Preview

DAY **5**

Tell children that tomorrow they will review some of the books and stories they have read this week.

Extend Your Day!

Social Studies
People and Their Jobs

Materials: 4-inch x 6-inch unlined index cards, Trade Book *Abuela*

What Do You Do All Day? Display *Abuela*. Rosalba and Abuela see people at work as they fly over the city. Let's see how many people we can find doing jobs that have to do with transportation. Page through the book and list jobs on the board. Add other jobs using transportation that children suggest.

Have children think of phrases that describe what specific workers do. Why do we need bus drivers? If you were an airplane pilot, what would you do at work?

Transportation Memory Game Give each child two index cards. Assign each child a job from the list (do not duplicate). Instruct children to write the worker's name on one card (*bus driver*) and the transportation on the other (*bus*). Have them illustrate each card.

Collect children's finished cards and place them face down in rows. Ask children one by one to turn over two cards, keeping any matches. Play until all the cards are gone.

Language Arts
Vivid Vocabulary

Materials: drawing paper, pencils, crayons

Another Word for... Remind children how the author of *Trucks Roll!* uses the word *bunk* for the truck driver's bed. Mention other descriptive words such as *shut-eye,* meaning *sleep,* and *flapjacks,* meaning *pancakes.*

New Words for Old Things Talk about alternative names you might make up for everyday things, for example, *wordwriter* for *pencil.* Make a list of these things on the board. Ask children to copy and illustrate one of the new words or create another one to illustrate.

Comprehension
Compare and Contrast

Materials: 4-inch x 6-inch unlined index cards, pencils, crayons

These Three Things Remind children that nouns name a person, animal, place, or thing. Give each child four index cards. Have the children write or dictate one noun on each card and illustrate their word.

Let's play a game with our nouns. We need to find things that are alike and things that are different. Collect and mix the cards; display three of them. Have children find something that is alike between two of the cards and something that is different.

Objectives
• Review the concepts.
• Build oral vocabulary.

Today at a Glance

Oral Vocabulary
trailers, cabs, haul, steering wheel, truckers, headlight

Phonemic Awareness
Initial and Medial /u/

Phonics
/u/ Spelled Uu

Comprehension
Compare and Contrast

Conventions
Prepositions

Writing
This Week We…

Check Oral Vocabulary
SUCCESS PREDICTOR

TRUCKTOWN on Reading Street

Start your engines!

• Display "That's What Trucks Are Made Of" and lead the group in saying the rhyme a few times.

• Have half the group recite the rhyme while the other half acts it out.

• Then have the groups change roles.

Truckery Rhymes

Concept Wrap Up

Question of the Week

What kinds of transportation help people do their jobs?

Listen for Amazing Words

Write the question of the week on the board. Track the print as you read it to children. Have them use the Amazing Words in their responses (*trailers, cabs, haul, steering wheel, truckers, headlight*) and answer in complete sentences. Display Sing with Me Chart 27B. Let's sing "Trucks Are Rolling." I want you to listen for the Amazing Words we learned this week. Remind children that the words *trailers, cabs, haul, steering wheel, truckers,* and *headlight* are in the song. Sing the song several times to the tune of "Frère Jacques." Have children pretend to honk a horn each time they hear an Amazing Word. Then discuss how the trucks in the song help people do their jobs.

Trucks Are Rolling

Trucks are rolling.
Trucks are rolling.
What do you see?
What do you see?
Truckers' horns
a-blowing,
Early in the morning,
On their way,
on their way.

Sing with Me Chart 27B

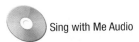 Sing with Me Audio

ELL Check Concepts and Language Use the Day 5 instruction on ELL Poster 27 to monitor children's understanding of the lesson concept.

ELL Poster 27

Oral Vocabulary
Amazing Words

Talk with Me/Sing with Me Chart 27A

Review

Let's Talk Display Talk with Me Chart 27A. We learned six new Amazing Words this week. Let's say the Amazing Words as I point to the pictures on the chart. Point to each picture and give children the chance to say the appropriate Amazing Word before offering it.

Have children supply the appropriate Amazing Word.

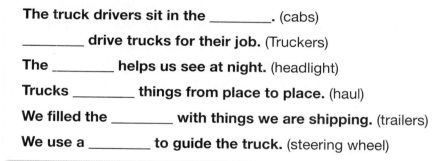

The truck drivers sit in the _____. (cabs)

_____ drive trucks for their job. (Truckers)

The _____ helps us see at night. (headlight)

Trucks _____ things from place to place. (haul)

We filled the _____ with things we are shipping. (trailers)

We use a _____ to guide the truck. (steering wheel)

Amazing Words

trailers	cabs
haul	steering whee
truckers	headlight

Differentiated Instruction

SI Strategic Intervention

Sentence Production Have children choose one Amazing Word. Ask them to say a complete sentence using that word.

It's Friday

MONITOR PROGRESS **Check Oral Vocabulary**

Demonstrate Word Knowledge Monitor the Amazing Words by asking the following questions. Have children use the Amazing Word in their answer.

- **What light helps truck drivers see at night?** (headlight)
- **What are the back parts of trucks called?** (trailers)
- **What is it called when trucks carry things?** (haul)
- **What helps a truck driver guide the truck?** (steering wheel)
- **What is another name for truck drivers?** (truckers)
- **What are the front parts of trucks where drivers sit called?** (cabs)

If... children have difficulty using the Amazing Words,

then... reteach the words using the Oral Vocabulary Routine on the Routines Flip Chart.

Day 1	Day 2	Day 3	Day 4	Day 5
Check Phonemic Awareness	Check Sound-Spelling/ Retelling	Check Word Reading	Check Phonemic Awareness	Check Oral Vocabulary

Success Predictor

297

Oral Vocabulary

Succes Predicto

Wrap Up your Week

10–15 mins.

bjectives
Review initial and medial /u/.
Review /u/ spelled *Uu*.

Phonemic Awareness Review

/u/

Isolate initial and medial /u/

Display the *up* Picture Card. What is the beginning sound in *up*? Say the word with me: /u/ /u/ /u/, *up*. Continue to review initial /u/ with the following words: *us, umbrella, umpire, under.*

Display the *mug* Picture Card. What is the middle sound in *mug*? Say it again: *mug.* The middle sound in *mug* is /u/. Continue to review medial /u/ with the words *sun, cup, truck,* and *bus.*

Picture Card

Segment words

I will say some words. I want you to say each sound in the word. Listen carefully. I will do the first one: *cup;* the sounds are /k/ /u/ /p/. I hear three sounds: /k/ /u/ /p/. Have children segment the following words into individual sounds: *bud, hug, tip, pup, rat, tub, mud, man, get, rug.*

Picture Card

Phonics Review
/u/ Spelled *Uu*

Teach /u/Uu

Display the *Uu* Alphabet Card. This is an *umbrella*. What sound do you hear at the beginning of *umbrella*? What letter spells that sound?

High-frequency words

Write the word *what* on the board. This is the word *what*. What is this word? Repeat the routine with *said* and *was*.

Apply phonics to familiar text

Have children reread one of the books specific to the target letter sounds. You may wish to review the decodable words and high-frequency words that appear in each book prior to rereading.

Alphabet Card

Decodable Reader 27
My Skills Buddy, p. 58

Kindergarten
Student Reader K.5.3

Get Set, Roll!
Reader 27

Differentiated Instruction

SI Strategic Intervention

Support Handwriting Have children use Decodable Reader 27, Kindergarten Student Reader K.5.3, or Get Set, Roll! Reader 27 to find a word with initial or medial /u/. Have them copy the word on a sheet of paper or on their Write-On Boards. Then have children read the word.

Small Group Time

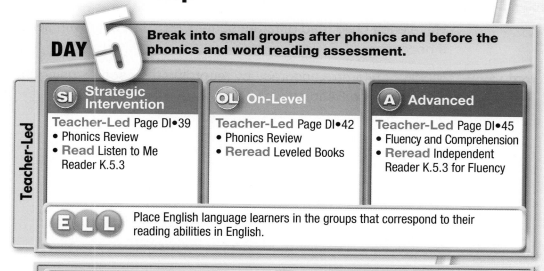

DAY 5 Break into small groups after phonics and before the phonics and word reading assessment.

Teacher-Led

SI Strategic Intervention
Teacher-Led Page DI•39
• Phonics Review
• **Read** Listen to Me Reader K.5.3

OL On-Level
Teacher-Led Page DI•42
• Phonics Review
• **Reread** Leveled Books

A Advanced
Teacher-Led Page DI•45
• Fluency and Comprehension
• **Reread** Independent Reader K.5.3 for Fluency

ELL Place English language learners in the groups that correspond to their reading abilities in English.

Practice Stations
• Visit the Read for Meaning Station
• Visit the Let's Make Art Station

Independent Activities
• Read independently
• Story Sort
• Concept Talk Video

ssess
- Read words with /u/.
- Read high-frequency words.
- Read sentences.

Assessment
Monitor Progress

/u/ Spelled Uu

Whole Class Give children a sheet of paper folded in fourths. Have children draw a picture of something that begins with /u/ or something that has medial /u/ in each section. Have them label the pictures with the word or the letter *u*.

MONITOR PROGRESS	Check Word and Sentence Reading

If... children cannot complete the whole-class assessment,
then... use the Reteach lesson in *First Stop*.

If... you are unsure of a child's grasp of this week's skills,
then... use the assessment below to obtain a clearer evaluation of the child's progress.

/u/ Spelled Uu and high-frequency words

One-on-One To facilitate individual progress monitoring, assess some children on Day 4 and the rest on Day 5. While individual children are being assessed, the rest of the class can reread this week's books and look for words with /u/.

Word reading

Use the word lists on reproducible p. 301 to assess each child's ability to read words with /u/. We're going to read some words. I'll read the first word, and you read the rest. The first word is *up,* /u/ /p/. For each child, record any decoding problems.

Sentence reading

Use the sentences on reproducible p. 301 to assess each child's ability to read words in sentences. Have each child read two sentences aloud. Have each child read different sentences. Start over with sentence one if necessary.

Record scores

Monitor children's accuracy by recording their scores using the Word and Sentence Reading Chart for this unit in *First Stop.*

Name _____

Read the Words

up ☐   jump ☐
rug ☐   drum ☐
what ☐   was ☐
tub ☐   club ☐
said ☐   dust ☐
cup ☐   plum ☐

Read the Sentences

1. Bud said he will hug Mom.

2. Was that a bump in the rug?

3. What will Bud do in the tub?

4. She said, "Mud is fun."

5. What bug will jump?

Note to Teacher: Children read each word. Children read two sentences.

Scoring for Read the Words: Score 1 point for each correct word.

Short *u* (*up, rug, tub, cup, jump, drum, club, dust, plum*) _____ /__9___
High-Frequency Words (*what, said, was*) _____ /__3___

MONITOR PROGRESS
- /u/ Spelled *Uu*
- High-frequency words

Objectives
- Recognize signs.
- Identify what signs mean.
- Discuss the purpose for understanding signs.

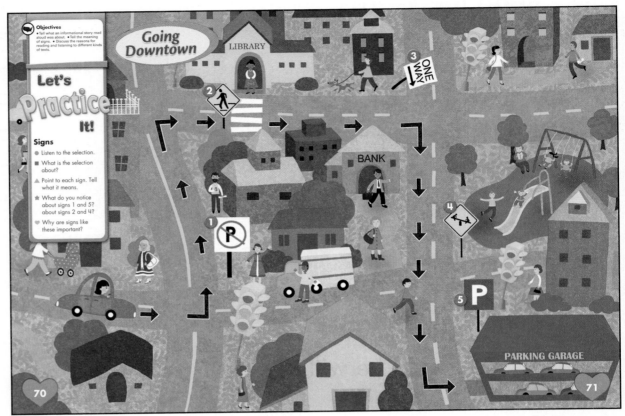

My Skills Buddy, pp. 70–71

Let's Practice It!
Signs

Teach

Today you will listen to a woman's trip downtown. She uses signs to help her find a place to park. **Review the features of signs with children.**

- Signs have specific meanings.
- Signs have letters, words, or pictures.
- Signs are put up in public places.

Have children turn to pp. 70–71 of *My Skills Buddy.* I am going to read a story about a trip downtown. Look at the pictures. Continue to look at the pictures as I read. **Read the text of "Going Downtown."** As you read, direct children to look at the appropriate part of the picture and to follow the arrows.

Guide practice

Discuss the features of signs with children and the bulleted text on p. 70 of *My Skills Buddy.*

- What is the selection about? Why is listening to this selection important?

- Signs have specific meanings. Look at sign 2, the yellow diamond-shaped sign. What do you think it means? (People are crossing the street there, so be careful.)

- Signs have letters, words, or pictures. Which signs in this picture have only letters? (signs 1 and 5) What do they mean? (no parking near this sign, and parking garage)

- Signs are put up in public places. What public place is the setting for these signs? (the downtown area of a town or city)

Going Downtown

Lucy is driving downtown. Listen as I read, and trace Lucy's route with your finger. Follow the arrows. Watch for signs along the way.

At the first corner, Lucy turns left. She is looking for a place to park. *Can she park on this block? How do you know?*

At the next corner, Lucy turns right. Then, as she drives down the block, she sees a yellow diamond-shaped sign. *What does it mean? What should she do?*

After she passes a bank on the right, Lucy turns right at the next corner. *Could she turn left there? What tells you that?*

Then as she drives down the street, still looking for a parking place, Lucy passes a playground. *Which sign warns her about the playground? Why does she need to know about it?*

Then Lucy drives past the next corner. Finally, she sees somewhere she can park. *What does she see that tells her that?*

Comprehension Assessment
Monitor Progress

Review

⊙ **Compare and Contrast** We can look at how things are alike and different to learn more about them. When we tell how things are alike, we compare them. When we tell how they are different, we contrast them. Good readers compare and contrast to help them understand and remember the story.

Read "Ready for a Ride!"

Tell children that you are going to read them a story about a girl named Sari and her grandma getting ready for a bike ride. Ask children to think about what is alike and different about how Sari and her grandma get ready for the ride. Listen carefully as I read the story. When I am done, I am going to ask you to compare and contrast how they get ready for the bike ride. Read "Ready for a Ride!" on p. 65 of *Read Aloud Anthology*.

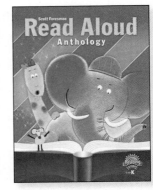

Read Aloud Anthology

Check compare and contrast

After you read, have children compare and contrast parts of the story.

- Does Sari's bike tire need air? **(yes)** Does Grandma's bike tire need air? **(no)** Is this alike or different? **(different)**

- Does Sari wear kneepads? **(yes)** Does Grandma wear kneepads? **(yes)** Is this alike or different? **(alike)**

- Does Sari wear a helmet? **(yes)** Does Grandma wear a helmet? **(yes)** Is this alike or different? **(alike)**

Corrective feedback

If... a child cannot identify similarities and differences,
then... reteach compare and contrast using the Reteach lesson in *First Stop*.

Assess compare and contrast

Use the blackline master on p. 305. Make one copy for each child. Have children color the things that are alike and cross out the things that are different.

Compare and Contrast

Color the things that are alike in the two pictures.
Cross out the things that are different.

Note to Teacher: Have children practice comparing and contrasting by coloring things that are the same and crossing out things that are different in the two pictures.

MONITOR PROGRESS   • Compare and Contrast

Conventions
Prepositions

Review   Remind children of what they learned about prepositions. A preposition is a word that tells us more about a noun in a sentence. It connects the noun to the rest of the sentence. We learned about several prepositions this week. Which prepositions did we learn about? (*in, on, over, under*) There are a lot more prepositions, but we started by learning about the words *in, on, over,* and *under.*

Model   Stand on a rug and say: I am standing on the rug. Which word tells where I am standing? *On* tells where I am standing. *On* is the preposition. It tells us where I am standing: on the rug.

Guide practice   Write the following sentences on the board:

> **The plane flies over the clouds.** (over)
> **Jose reads in class.** (in)
> **Tia camps under the stars.** (under)

Read each sentence with children. Then have them identify the preposition. In each sentence, help them understand how the preposition connects the noun to the rest of the sentence.

On their own   Ask children to choose an object in the room. Have them describe the object's position in relation to something else using the preposition *in, on, over,* or *under.* Ask children to write or dictate the preposition they use.

Daily Fix-It   Use the Daily Fix-It exercise for more conventions practice.

Writing
This Week We...

Review Display *Trucks Roll!,* Sing With Me Chart 27B, Phonics Songs and Rhymes Chart 27, Decodable Reader 27 from *My Skills Buddy,* Kindergarten Student Reader K.5.3, and Get Set, Roll! Reader 27. This week we learned about transportation that helps people do their jobs. We read new books, and we sang new songs. Which book or song was your favorite? Let's share our ideas with each other.

Team Talk Pair children and have them take turns telling which book or song was their favorite and why.

Model writing a list Today we will write a list of the things trucks carry in our songs and stories. In the song "Trucks Are Rolling," one of the trucks carries hay. I will write *hay* on our list.

Things Trucks Carry

1. hay

Guide practice Continue the list with children. Then read through the list and have children pretend to be one of the things trucks carry.

Things Trucks Carry

1. hay	5. toys
2. animals	6. bulldozers
3. food	7. clocks
4. trees	8. puzzles

On their own Have children write or dictate a sentence about a truck on the list carrying an item.

Daily Handwriting

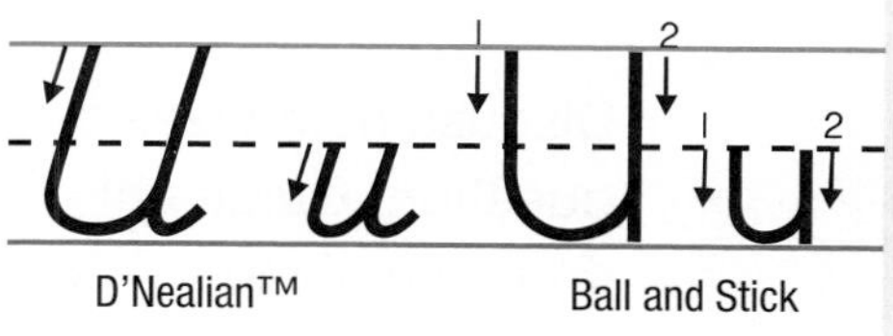
D'Nealian™
Ball and Stick

Write *Uncle* and *bun* on the board. Review correct letter formation of uppercase *U* and lowercase *u.*

Have children write *Uncle* and *bun* on their Write-On Boards. Remind them to use proper left-to-right and top-to-bottom progression and proper spacing between letters when writing.

Daily Fix-It

i fell down

I fell down.

This week's practice sentences appear on Teacher Resources DVD-ROM.

ELL

English Language Learners

Poster Preview Prepare children for next week by using Week 4 ELL Poster number 28. Read the Poster Talk-Through to introduce the concept and vocabulary. Ask children to identify and describe objects and actions in the art.

Objectives
• Review weekly concept.
• Review compare and contrast.

Wrap Up Your Week!

Question of the Week

What kinds of transportation help people do their jobs?

Amazing Words

You've learned
0 0 6
words this week!

You've learned
1 6 2
words this year!

Illustrate compare and contrast

This week we talked about kinds of transportation that help people do their jobs. Some people need several kinds of transportation to do their work.

• Make a word web like the one shown or use Graphic Organizer 18. Fill it with children's responses about the kinds of transportation people use to do their jobs.

• Have children compare and contrast two kinds of transportation from the web.

• Then instruct children to draw a picture showing how the kinds of transportation are alike or different.

• Ask children to explain to classmates how the picture shows a comparison or a contrast. Remind them to use complete sentences.

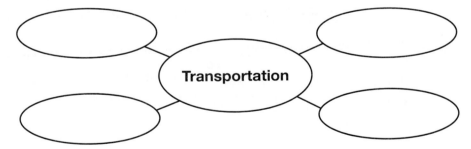

Transportation

Next Week's Question

What kind of work do trains do?

Discuss next week's question. Guide children in making connections between the work done by trucks and by trains.

Preview
NEXT WEEK

Tell children that next week they will read about a little train that was able to do big things.

Extend Your Day!

Social Studies
All Around Town

Materials: construction paper, drawing tools, length of butcher paper, glue

Transportation for a Town Tell children they will make a picture of a town and its transportation. Discuss the purpose of the places listed below and sketch them on a length of butcher paper, with labels: *hospital, police station, bus station, harbor, school, airport, fire station, supermarket*. Point out to students that the labels are signs that tell people what they will find inside each building.

Make a Mural Assign each child a different place in the town and have him or her draw, color, and cut out a picture of the transportation it needs. Have children attach their pictures in the appropriate place on the mural and tell why the transportation is needed in this place.

Near the hospital, draw a sign that has a large letter *H.* Ask children what information the sign gives. Then have children suggest and draw other signs on the mural that they think would be useful.

Social Studies
From Here to There

Materials: masking tape, construction paper

Giving Directions Make an outline of a set of streets with tape on the classroom floor. Make construction paper signs for *supermarket, bank, school, home,* and *hospital.* Tell children that they need to tell someone how to get where they want to go in town.

Have a child stand in the center of "town" and tell a partner where he or she needs to go. The partner uses words such as *left, right, behind, in front, near,* and *far* to direct the traveler. Repeat until all children have had a turn.

Reading
Book Fair

Materials: collection of familiar books

Sharing a Favorite Book Have children bring a favorite book from home or choose one from a display of familiar classroom books.

Pair children and have partners take turns telling each other about their books. Instruct children to show the following parts (model doing so before pairs begin):

book title
author
illustrator
table of contents

Weekly Assessment

Use the whole-class assessment on pages 300–301 and 304–305 in this Teacher's Edition to check:

✔ ◎ **Short *u* Spelled *Uu***

✔ ◎ **Comprehension Skill** *Compare and Contrast*

✔ **High-Frequency Words**   *what   said   was*

Teacher's Edition, Day 5

Managing Assessment

Use the Assessment Handbook for:

✔ **Observation Checklists**

✔ **Record-Keeping Forms**

✔ **Portfolio Assessment**

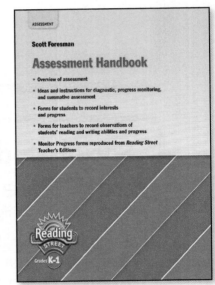

Assessment Handbook

Teacher Notes

acing Small
roup Instruction

5 Day Plan

AY 1
- Phonemic Awareness/ Phonics
- Decodable Story 27

AY 2
- Phonemic Awareness/ Phonics
- Decodable Reader 27

AY 3
- Phonemic Awareness/ Phonics
- Concept Literacy Reader K.5.3 or Kindergarten Student Reader K.5.3

AY 4
- Phonemic Awareness/ Phonics
- Get Set, Roll! Reader 27

AY 5
- Phonics Review
- Listen to Me Reader K.5.3

3 or 4 Day Plan

AY 1
- Phonemic Awareness/ Phonics
- Decodable Story 27

AY 2
- Phonemic Awareness/ Phonics
- Decodable Reader 27

AY 3
- Phonemic Awareness/ Phonics
- Concept Literacy Reader K.5.3 or Kindergarten Student Reader K.5.3

AY 4
- Phonemic Awareness/ Phonics
- Get Set, Roll! Reader 27

Day Plan: Eliminate the shaded box.

SI *Strategic Intervention*

DAY 1

Phonemic Awareness•Phonics

■ **Isolate /u/** Display the *up* Picture Card. This is *up*. Up begins with /u/. Say it with me: /u/ /u/ /u/, *up*. Repeat with *under* and *us*.

■ **Connect /u/ to Uu** I am going to say three words. I want you to tell me which word has /u/. Listen carefully: *bug, big, bag*. Say the words with me: *bug, big, bag*. Which word has /u/? *Bug* has /u/. *Big* and *bag* do not have /u/. Write the letters *Uu* on the board. The letter *u* can stand for /u/ in words. Write the word *bug* and underline the letter *u*. Follow the same procedure with these sets of words: *pig, peg, pug; rug, rig, rag; bad, bed, bud; cap, cup, cop.*

Decodable Story 27

■ **Review** Review the previously taught high-frequency words by writing each of the words and having children say the words with you.

the	was	from	to	have	what	he
do	for	see	they	said	go	we

If... children have difficulty reading the words,
then... say a word and have children point to the word and say the word. Repeat several times, giving assistance as needed.

■ **Read** Have children read *Fun for Jud* orally. Then have them reread the story several times individually.

Reader's and Writer's Notebook, pp. 347–348

Objectives
- Identify the common sounds that letters represent.
- Read at least 25 high-frequency words from a commonly used list.

SI *Strategic Intervention*

DAY 2

Phonemic Awareness•Phonics

■ **Discriminate /u/** Display Phonics Songs and Rhymes Chart 27. Sing "What Luck! Here Comes the Bus!" to the tune of "Here We Go Looby Loo" several times with children. Ask them to jump up when they hear /u/ in a word.

■ **Connect /u/ to** *Uu* Ask children to name words with /u/. List the words on the board as children say them. Have children echo read the list of words. Then ask children to take turns circling the *u* in the words on the board.

Decodable Reader 27

■ **Review** Review the high-frequency words by writing *said* on the board. *This is the word* said. *What word is this?* Continue with the following words: *is, a, what, see, the, was.*

> **If…** children have difficulty reading the words,
> **then…** say a word and have children point to the word. Repeat several times, giving assistance as needed.

■ **Read** Display the cover of *Fun for Bud* on p. 58 of *My Skills Buddy.* Ask a volunteer to read the first page of the story. Have children tell about the fun things Bud does. Continue through the story in this manner.

My Skills Buddy

Objectives
- Identify the common sounds that letters represent.
- Read at least 25 high-frequency words from a commonly used list.
- Retell a main event from a story read aloud.

More Reading
Use Leveled Readers or other text at children's instructional level.

SI *Strategic Intervention*

Phonemic Awareness•Phonics

■ **Isolate /u/** Display the *bus* Picture Card. This is a *bus. Bus* has /u/ in the middle. Say it with me: /b/ /u/ /s/, *bus.* Repeat the routine with the *duck* and *gum* Picture Cards.

■ **Connect /u/ to *Uu*** Write *Uu* on the board. These are the letters *Uu.* The letter *u* can stand for /u/ in words. Write the word *up* on the board. This is the word *up. Up* begins with /u/. Say it with me: /u/ /p/, *up.* When you hear a word with /u/, point up. Use the following words: *pup, cat, under, cup, bowl, rug, bun, tag, tug, tub.*

■ **Blend Sounds** Write *sun* on the board. Have children blend the sound of each letter to read the word: /s/ /u/ /n/, *sun.* Continue with *up, Bud, bug, run,* and *cut.*

■ **Review High-Frequency Words** Write *was* on the board. Have volunteers say the word and use it in a sentence. Continue with the word *what, said, blue, yellow,* and *green.*

■ To practice phonics and high-frequency words, have children read Kindergarten Student Reader K.5.3. Use the instruction on pp. 260–261.

For a complete lesson plan and additional practice, see the **Leveled Reader Teaching Guide.**

Concept Literacy Reader K.5.3

■ **Preview and Predict** Display the cover of the Concept Literacy Reader K.5.3. Point to the title. The title of the book is *What Carries Loads?* How does the wagon help the boy move the pumpkins? Have children tell about the picture and what they think the book might be about.

■ **Set a Purpose** We talked about the title of the book. Let's read the book to learn about what forms of transportation can carry loads. Have children read the Concept Literacy Reader.

■ **Read** Provide corrective feedback as children read the book orally. During reading, ask them if they are able to confirm any of the predictions they made prior to reading.

If... children have difficulty reading the book individually,

then... read a sentence aloud as children point to each word. Then have the group reread the sentences as they continue pointing to the words.

■ **Retell** Have children retell the content as you page through the book. Help them identify what the book is about. Also call attention to the how much each form of transportation can carry.

Concept Literacy Reader K.5.3

More Reading
Use Leveled Readers or other text at children's instructional level.

Phonemic Awareness•Phonics

■ **Segment** Listen to the word *cup.* I will separate the word into its separate sounds: /k/ /u/ /p/. Do it with me. How many sounds do you hear in *cup?* (three) Have children continue to segment: *dust, fuss, cut, bun, drum.*

■ **Hunt for *Uu*** Place various items around the room, including the following objects: mug, cup, rug, jug, umbrella, gum. Have children go around the room and hunt for objects with /u/. Have them put the /u/ objects in the center of the room. Hold up each object, name it, and write the word on the board. Have children repeat the names after you. What is the letter for /u/? Yes. The letter for /u/ is *u.* Circle the *u* in each word on the board.

Get Set, Roll! Reader 27

■ **Review** Review the following high-frequency words with children prior to reading the story *what, said, was, see, of, is, a, to,* and *the.*

Get Set, Roll! Reader 27

■ **Teach Rebus Words** Write the word *tank* on the board. This is the word *tank.* Name the letters with me: *t, a, n, k, tank.* The word *tank* is in our story today. There will be a picture above the word to help you read it.

■ **Read** Display Get Set, Roll! Reader 27. Today we will read a story about Max and Melvin and a tank. Max is a monster truck. What kind of truck is Melvin? The title of the story is *The Tank.* Look at the picture and think about the title. What do you think this story will be about?

> **If...** children have difficulty reading the story individually,
> **then...** read a sentence aloud as children point to each word. Then have the group reread the sentences as they continue pointing to the words.

■ **Reread** Use echo reading of Get Set, Roll! Reader 27 to model fluent reading. Use your oral reading to model for children where to pause, when to change pitch, and which words to stress. Then have children reread orally three to four times, or until they can read with few or no mistakes.

Objectives
- Identify the common sounds that letters represent.
- Read at least 25 high-frequency words from a commonly used list.
- Predict what might happen next based on the cover.

lore Reading

se Leveled Readers or other
xt at children's instructional
vel.

SI *Strategic Intervention*

DAY 5

Phonics Review

■ **Connect /u/ to *Uu*** Draw seven suns on the board. Gather about twelve Picture Cards, including the following *Uu* cards: *umbrella, up, tub, bus, drum, gum, mug.* Mix the cards and display them one at a time. Have a child name the picture. If the name has /u/, have the child write a lowercase *u* in one of the suns.

■ **Recognize /u/** Write uppercase *U* on the board. Name the letter as you write it several times. Give children a chenille stick and have them bend it into the shape of *U*. Have volunteers write lowercase *u* on the board.

Listen to Me Reader K.5.3

■ **Preview and Predict** Display the cover of the book. The title of this story is *The Mud Bug.* It is written by Alex Jordan. It is illustrated by Amy Loeffler. What do you think a mud bug is? What do you think this story will be about? Tell me your ideas.

Listen to Me Reader K.5.3

■ **Set a Purpose** Review children's ideas. Point out that after they read, they will know more about the bug. Tell children that you will read the story with them. Follow along with your finger as I read. Then we will take turns reading this page. Repeat this routine through all of the pages. Guide children to decode words.

■ **Reread for Fluency** Use echo reading of Listen to Me Reader K.5.3 to model reading fluently. Use your oral reading to model for children when to pause, when to change pitch, and which words to stress. Then have children reread orally three to four times, or until they can read with few or no mistakes.

Objectives
• Identify the common sounds that letters represent.
• Predict what might happen next based on the title.

 On-Level **DAY 1**

Phonemic Awareness•Phonics

■ **Discriminate /u/** Display the *umbrella* Picture Card. This is an *umbrella*. *Umbrella* begins with /u/. Say it with me: /u/ /u/ /u/, *umbrella*. Show children how to make an umbrella using your arms over your head. When I say a word with /u/, I want you to make an *umbrella* with your arms. Use the following words: *pup, dog, uncle, sister, over, under.*

■ **Connect /u/ to Uu** Display the *Uu* Alphabet Card. What is the name of this letter? What is the sound we learned for this letter? What is the object on the Alphabet Card? (an umbrella) Why is there an *umbrella* on the *Uu* card? (*Umbrella* begins with *Uu.*)

Objectives
• Identify the common sounds that letters represent.

Pacing Small Group Instruction

20–30 min

5 Day Plan

DAY 1	• Phonemic Awareness/ Phonics • Decodable Story 27
DAY 2	• Phonemic Awareness/ Phonics • High-Frequency Words • Decodable Reader 27
DAY 3	• Phonemic Awareness/ Phonics • Kindergarten Student Reader K.5.3
DAY 4	• Get Set, Roll! Reader 27
DAY 5	• Phonics Review • Reread Leveled Books

 On-Level **DAY 2**

Phonemic Awareness•Phonics

■ **Cut and Color** Give children a piece of paper. Have them draw six pictures, including the following /u/Uu pictures: *umbrella, mug, button, sun.* Have children cut out the /u/Uu pictures and color them. Give children construction paper. Have them paste their /u/Uu pictures on the construction paper, make a border of uppercase and lowercase *u*'s, and share their pictures with the class.

■ **High-Frequency Words** Display the following word cards: *said, what, was, green, yellow, blue.* Say the word *said* and select a child to point to the word. Have children say the word and use it in a sentence. Continue with the other words.

Objectives
• Read at least 25 high-frequency words from a commonly used list.

3 or 4 Day Plan

DAY 1	• Phonemic Awareness/ Phonics • Decodable Story 27
DAY 2	• Phonemic Awareness/ Phonics • High-Frequency Words • Decodable Reader 27
DAY 3	• Phonemic Awareness/ Phonics • Kindergarten Student Reader K.5.3
DAY 4	• Get Set, Roll! Reader 27

3 Day Plan: Eliminate the shaded box.

More Practice

For additional practice with this week's phonics skills, have children reread the Decodable Story (Day 1) and the Decodable Reader (Day 2)

OL *On-Level*

DAY 3

Phonemic Awareness•Phonics

■ **Recognize /u/** Tell children you will tell them a story and they should listen for /u/. When you say a word with /u/, children should jump up and repeat the word. Tell a simple story, emphasizing /u/ words and pausing to give children a chance to jump up and repeat the word. *Sunny* has a *rug.* She *rubs* the *mud* off the *tub.* She washes *mugs* and *cups* until the *sun* goes down. *But* she has *fun* with her *pup. Pup tugs* on the *rug. Sunny* gives *Pup* a *hug!*

■ **Connect /u/ to *Uu*** Write the letters *Uu* and the word *uncle* on the board. The word *uncle* begins with /u/. The sound /u/ is spelled *u.* Ask children to name other words with /u/. Write them on the board and circle each *u.*

Kindergarten Student Reader K.5.3

■ **Preview and Predict** Display the cover of the book. The title of this story is *Our Pup Bud.* Look at the cover and think about the title. What do you think will happen in this story?

Kindergarten Student Reader K.5.3

■ **Set a Purpose** Review the list of things children think might happen in the story. Remind children they will read to find out about Bud the pup.

■ **Read** Have children follow along as they read the story with you. After reading p. 3, ask children to tell who brings Jem a pup. Continue with each page. Ask the following questions:

- Who brings Jem a pup?

- What things do Jem, Jan, and Rex do with Bud?

- Why does Jem's mom look mad when Bud tugs on the rug?

■ **Summarize** Have children retell the story to a partner and tell what Jem dreams about at the end.

■ **Text to Self** Help children make personal connections to the story as they tell about something that makes them happy.

Objectives
- Identify the common sounds that letters represent.
- Predict what might happen next based on the cover.
- Respond to questions about text.

OL On-Level **DAY 4**

Get Set, Roll! Reader 27

■ **Review** Review the high-frequency words *the, to, a, is, of, see, what, said,* and *was* by writing each word on the board and saying the word with children.

■ **Review Rebus Words** Write the word *tank* on the board. This is the word *tank.* Name the letters with me: *t, a, n, k, tank.* A picture above the word will help you read it.

■ **Read** Display Get Set, Roll! Reader 27, *The Tank*. Point to the title of the story. What is the title of the story? *The Tank* is the title of the story. Look at the picture. What do you think will happen in this story? We will read some words with /u/ in this story. Let's read the story together.

Objectives
- Read at least 25 high-frequency words from a commonly used list.
- Predict what might happen next based on the cover.

More Reading
Use Leveled Readers or other text at children's instructional level to develop fluency.

OL On-Level **DAY 5**

Phonics Review

■ **Write a Letter** Divide the class into two teams. Have each team form a line. Put the *duck* Picture Card on the board ledge. Tell children you will say a word. If the word has /u/, the first person in each team line is to go to the board, write the letter *u* by the *duck,* and go to the end of the line. If the word does not have /u/, the person waits for another turn. Use the following words: *bunk, nut, bed, sung, must, hunt, cat, rug, net, thumb, sun, hat, bus, truck.*

Objectives
- Identify the common sounds that letters represent.

acing Small
roup Instruction

5 Day Plan

AY 1	• Phonemic Awareness/ Phonics • Decodable Story 27
AY 2	• Phonics • Spelling • Decodable Reader 27
AY 3	• Independent Reader K.5.3 or Kindergarten Student Reader K.5.3
AY 4	• Get Set, Roll! Reader or Kindergarten Student Reader K.5.3
AY 5	• Fluency/Comprehension • Independent Reader K.5.3

3 or 4 Day Plan

AY 1	• Phonemic Awareness/ Phonics • Decodable Story 27
AY 2	• Phonics • Spelling • Decodable Reader 27
AY 3	• Independent Reader K.5.3 or Kindergarten Student Reader K.5.3
AY 4	• Get Set, Roll! Reader or Kindergarten Student Reader K.5.3

Day Plan: Eliminate the shaded box.

More Practice

or additional practice with
is week's phonics skills and
develop fluency, have chil-
ren reread the Decodable
tory (Day 1) and the
ecodable Reader (Day 2).

A Advanced — DAY 1

Phonemic Awareness•Phonics

■ **Pass the Button!** Have children sit in a circle. Make a large button out of heavy paper or poster board. On one side of the button, write /u/*Uu.* Write /i/*Ii* on the other side. Choose one child to be "it." Have the child walk around the outside of the circle and place the button behind another child. The other child then grabs the button and names a word that has the appropriate sound of the side showing. This child now becomes "it" and repeats the routine. Continue until many children have had the chance to name a word.

Objectives
• Identify the common sounds that letters represent.

A Advanced — DAY 2

Phonics•Spelling

■ **Connect /u/ to *Uu*** Write the letters *Uu* on the board. Say the word *umbrella* and point to the letters. Tell children that the word *umbrella* begins with /u/ and the letter *u* can stand for that sound. Have a volunteer show the class the gestures for "thumbs-up." Have children give a "thumbs-up" if the word has an /u/. Say the following words to children: *fun, fin, hit, hut, button, tiger, uncle, under, rabbit, number, puzzle, rain.*

■ **Spell Sounds** Give each child the following letter tiles: *b, g, h, n, s, t, u.* Listen to the sounds in the word *hug:* /h/ /u/ /g/, *hug.* What is the letter for /h/? It is *h.* Place your *h* tile in front of you. Continue with the remaining sounds. Now let's make a new word by changing the first letter. Have children put a *t* tile in place of the *h* tile. What is this word? Say the sound for each letter and blend them together. The new word is /t/ /u/ /g/, *tug.* Then have children spell *bun* and *sun.*

Objectives
• Identify the common sounds that letters represent.
• Recognize that new words are created when letters are changed.
• Use letter-sound correspondence to spell consonant-vowel-consonant (CVC) words.

 Advanced | DAY **3**

For a complete lesson plan and additional practice, see the **Leveled Reader Teaching Guide**.

Independent Reader K.5.3

- ■ **Practice High-Frequency Words** Write *what* on the board. Have volunteers say the word and use it in a sentence. Continue with the words *said* and *was*.

- ■ **Activate Prior Knowledge** Tell children that a bike messenger is person who rides on a bicycle and delivers packages to people in the city. Picture walk through *Ming on the Job* and discuss Ming's journey. Why does Ming zip past the batters in the park? Why is Ann glad to see Ming?

- ■ **Compare and Contrast** After children read *Ming on the Job,* have children look at the picture on p. 3. This is when Ming starts his job. Display p. 8. This is when Ming is on his way home. How are these two pictures alike? How are these two pictures different?

Independent Reader K.5.3

- ■ **Reread for Fluency** After rereading with children, model reading fluently for them. I am going to read this book aloud. I will read the words with no mistakes. I want you to read it aloud with me. Try to read the words just as I do.

Use echo reading of Independent Reader K.5.3 to model reading fluently. Use your oral reading to model for children where to pause, when to change pitch, and which words to stress. Then have children reread orally three to four times, or until they can read with few or no mistakes.

- ■ For more practice with phonics and high-frequency words and to develop fluency, have children read Kindergarten Student Reader K.5.3. Use the instruction on pp. 260–261.

More Reading
Use Leveled Readers or oth text at children's instruction level.

Objectives
• Read at least 25 high-frequency words from a commonly used list.

ore Reading

e Leveled Readers or other
t at children's instructional
el.

A Advanced DAY **4**

Kindergarten Student Reader K.5.3

- **Revisit** Open to p. 2 of Kindergarten Student Reader K.5.3. Look at the picture. What are each of the characters doing? What do you think is happening on this page?

- **Reread** Use Kindergarten Student Reader K.5.3 to practice reading fluently.

- **Text to Self** Ask children to think about a pet they or would like to have. What kind of pet do you have or would want? What is your pet's name? What do you like to do with your pet?

Kindergarten Student Reader K.5.3

- **Read** Have children read Get Set, Roll! Reader 27, *The Tank.* Use instruction on p. 289.

Objectives
- Read at least 25 high-frequency words from a commonly used list.
- Predict what might happen next based on the illustrations.

A Advanced DAY **5**

Fluency•Comprehension

- **Reread for Fluency** Use the Independent Reader K.5.3 to model reading fluently for children. I am going to read this selection aloud. I will read the words with no mistakes. I want you to read it aloud with me. Try to read the words just as I do.

- **Comprehension** After children have finished reading, have them retell what happens in the selection. Then have children compare and contrast delivering packages on a bicycle or using a truck or car.

Independent Reader K.5.3

Objectives
- Read at least 25 high-frequency words from a commonly used list.

DAY 1

Concept Development

- **Read the Concept Literacy Reader** Read *What Carries Loads?* pausing to discuss each page. Model sentence patterns and vocabulary that describe how each machine carries a load. This is a train. It pulls many cars. A train can carry a huge load. On a second reading, invite children to talk about how different machines carry large or small loads.

- **Develop Oral Language** Revisit *What Carries Loads?*, reviewing the different modes of transportation used to carry freight. Then have children sing the following song with you to the tune of "I've Been Working on the Railroad":

> I've been loading up the train car,
> All the livelong day.
> I've been loading up the train car,
> Just to pass the time away.

Repeat the lyric using *airplane, trailer,* and *wagon.*

Phonemic Awareness/Phonics

- **Frontload Words with /u/** Have children look at the picture on pp. 52–53 of *My Skills Buddy.* This picture shows people doing different things. What work is being done here? What games are being played? Listen to the word *up.* What sound does *up* begin with? *Up* begins with /u/; *up,* /u/. Then use this Q & A exercise to introduce picture words with initial and medial /u/: *Up* begins with /u/ /u/ /u/. What things are going up? (The balloon is going up.) What people are going up? (The man is walking up.) Repeat the routine with *under, upset, unhappy, uphill, underground, truck, duck, umpire,* and *sucker.*

- **Connect /u/ to Uu** Use letter tiles to display the words *up* and *run* or write them on the board. Tell children that some words have /u/ at the beginning, and others have /u/ in the middle. This word is *up:* /u/ /p/, *up.* Say the word with me. Have children write the word *up* and circle the letter that makes /u/. Write and read aloud the following sentence: *Gus went up to the bus stop.* Point to the *u* in *Gus* and ask: What letter is this? Yes, this is *u.* Continue with *up* and *bus.*

Content Objective
- Develop content knowledg related to machines that help.

Language Objectives
- Understand and use grade-level content area vocabulary.
- Recognize the sounds of English.

Concept Literacy Reader K.5.3

Daily Planner

DAY 1	• Concept Development • Phonemic Awareness/ Phonics • Listening Comprehension
DAY 2	• Comprehension • Vocabulary
DAY 3	• Phonemic Awareness/ Phonics • Conventions
DAY 4	• Phonemic Awareness/ Phonics • Concepts and Oral Language
DAY 5	• Language Workshop • Writing

Support for English Language Learners

Content Objective
Understand cause and effect.

Language Objective
Learn and use academic vocabulary.

Use Learning Strategies

Preview To prepare students to compare and contrast details, have them preview the illustrations on pp. 54–55 of *My Skills Buddy.* Cover the bottom part of p. 55 What do you see? (a bike) What color is the bike? (purple) How many wheels does it have? (two) What do you see above the bike? (a cloud and rain) Now cover the top part of the page so that only the red bike is showing. Repeat the questions above to help children note contrasting details.

My Skills Buddy, pp. 54-55

E L L *English Language Learners*

DAY 1

Listening Comprehension: Compare and Contrast

- **Provide Scaffolding** Discuss the illustrations on pp. 54–55 in *My Skills Buddy* to frontload vocabulary. Explain the similarities and differences in the two bikes and the weather above them. Help children understand that both scenes show bikes that are the same size, but they are different colors. One bike has training wheels and the other does not. One bike is in sunshine and the other is in rain. Support your words with gestures or simple drawings.

- **Prepare for the Read Aloud** The modified Read Aloud below prepares children for listening to the oral reading "Two Vans" on p. 231.

Two Vans

Amy's dad is a mover. He packs boxes. He puts them in a van. He has a crew. They put furniture in the van. They drive to the new house. The crew unpacks everything.

Josh's dad is a carpenter. He has a small van. His tools are in the van. The van also carries boards.

Many people use vans to do jobs.

Their jobs are different, and so are their vans!

- **First Listening** Write the title of the Read Aloud on the board. This is about Amy's dad and Josh's dad. Each dad has a van. They use the vans for work. Listen to find out what kind of work they do. After reading, ask children to recall the names of the characters and the events. What job does Amy's dad do? What job does Josh's dad do? How do they use their vans?

- **Second Listening** Write the words *Amy's dad* and *Josh's dad* on the board. As you listen to the story, think about how their jobs are the same and different. After reading, point to *Amy's dad* on the board and ask children to tell what Amy's dad does in the story. Repeat the routine for Josh's dad.

Objectives
• Understand the main points of spoken language ranging from situations in which language is familiar to unfamiliar. • Demonstrate listening comprehension of increasingly complex spoken English by responding to questions and requests commensurate with content and grade-level needs.

 ELL English Language Learners

DAY 2

Comprehension

■ **Provide Scaffolding** Display *Trucks Roll!* Lead a detailed picture walk through the story, naming what you see in the illustrations and describing what is happening. Use gestures and facial expressions to convey meaning. Focus on the following:

• **Set the Scene** Use the cover of the Big Book to help children understand that this story is about trucks. A truck can be small or big. A truck carries a load. Big trucks have loud horns. What do you know about trucks? Allow children to use their prior knowledge to discuss trucks and what trucks do.

• **Frontload Vocabulary** Use the illustrations to introduce unfamiliar words in the text. Include prepositions, such as *on, in, over,* and *around,* as you discuss the text. A truck is on the road. The word *on* tells where something is. Where is the truck? The truck is on the road. Include other words such as *cabs* (p. 9); *stacks, load* (p. 17); *haul* (p. 19); *tolls, rolls* (p. 24); and *beams* (p. 29).

Vocabulary: Words for Jobs

■ **Frontload Vocabulary** Have children turn to p. 68 of *My Skills Buddy.* Talk about each picture, using the words *pilot, truck driver, conductor,* and *astronaut.* For example, point to the first picture. This is a pilot. The pilot flies a plane. Her job is to fly the plane. Then invite children to talk about the pictures using the words for jobs.

■ **Provide Scaffolding** Write the words *pilot, truck driver, conductor,* and *astronaut* on the board. Read the words aloud. These words are names for jobs people do. Point to the word *conductor.* Who can tell something about a conductor? Invite children to create and say a sentence about what a conductor does. Then say a sentence about the conductor and have children repeat it: The conductor takes your ticket. Repeat with the other words for jobs.

■ **Practice** Assign one of the job words (*pilot, truck driver, conductor,* or *astronaut*) to each child. Encourage children to think of something that the person does. For example, *The astronaut goes to the moon.* Have children draw a picture that shows what happens in the sentence. Then have children share with the class.

Objectives
• Use prior knowledge to understand meanings in English. • Share information in cooperative learning interactions.
• Use support from peers and teachers to develop background knowledge needed to comprehend increasingly challenging language.

Content Objective
• Develop background knowledge.

Language Objective
• Learn and use words for jobs.

Use Learning Strategies
Remind children that if they have trouble using job words, they can ask you or other children for help.

Big Book

Support for English Language Learners

Content Objective
Use learning strategies.

Language Objectives
Connect /u/ with Uu.

Use prepositions.

Transfer Skills
Pronouncing /u/ In Spanish, the letter *u* is pronounced /o/, as in *due*. If children experience difficulty producing short *u*, give them extra practice with words such as *yum, sum,* and *gum.*

Use Learning Strategies
Help children discover that many prepositions are used with position words. Explain that both tell where: where someone is or where something happens. On the board, write the position words *top, bottom, front,* and *back.* Stack several books and point out the top book. *This is the top book. Where is the book? The book is on top. On top* tells where the book is. Continue the exercise using *in front, in back, on the bottom, at the front,* and *at the back.*

Phonemic Awareness/Phonics

- **Isolate Initial and Medial /u/** Say *the pup is under the tub,* emphasizing /u/ as you read the words aloud. Model segmenting sounds in the word *pup:* /p/ /u/ /p/. Repeat for *tub.*

- **/u/ Spelled *Uu*** Write the word *mug* on the board. As you read it aloud, track the sounds and letters with your fingers. Let's write new words by changing the first letter. Write *tug* on the board. What is the new word? (*tug*) Segment and blend each sound as you point to the corresponding letter: /t/ /u/ /g/, *tug.* Continue with *bug.*

Conventions: Prepositions

- **Provide Scaffolding** Have children look at their chairs. Where is your chair? (on the floor) The chair is on the floor. The word *on* helps tell where the chair is. Is the floor under me? (yes) The floor is under me. *Under* tells where the floor is. These words are prepositions. They help tell where.

- **Practice** Look at the illustration on pp. 10–11. Read the first two sentences on p. 11. Where is the truck in this picture? (in the desert) The truck is in the desert. The word *in* tells where the truck is. Continue practicing prepositions with *on the road* (p. 17); *in the bunk* (p. 23); *in the slot, in the cup, at the wheel* (p. 30).

Leveled Support **Beginning/Intermediate** For appropriate prepositions, have a child demonstrate the action. While the child is acting out the preposition, explain what is happening: (Child's name) is *on the rug.* Have children repeat the sentences after you.

Advanced/Advanced-High For appropriate prepositions, have a child demonstrate the action. While the child is acting out the preposition, explain what is happening: (Child's name) is *on the rug.* For advanced learners, have children repeat the sentences after you, and then make up their own sentences using the prepositions.

Objectives
- Internalize new academic language by using and reusing it in meaningful ways in speaking activities that build concept and language attainment.
- Learn new expressions heard during classroom instruction and interactions.

ELL *English Language Learners*

Phonemic Awareness/Phonics

■ **Review Final /ks/** To review /ks/ in words, say the word *fox*. What is a fox? (an animal) What is the last sound in *fox*? Yes, it is /ks/. Next, say several word pairs and ask children to repeat the word that ends with /ks/: *ax, at; sip, six; fit, fix; Max, man.*

■ **/ks/ Spelled *Xx*** Hold up the *x* letter tile. What is this letter? What sound does it make? Remind children that the letter *x* at the end of a word is always pronounced /ks/. Use the tiles to form the following words: *fox, fix, six.* Read each word, tracking the sounds with your finger. Have children read aloud the words with you.

Concepts and Oral Language

■ **Revisit Talk with Me Chart 27A** Display the chart. Have children describe each image on the page. Help them by describing how trucks can help people do their jobs.

■ **Develop Oral Language** Introduce language patterns that help describe the pictures on Talk with Me Chart 27A. Write this sentence frame on the board: *The _____ is _____.* Let's use this sentence pattern to talk about trucks. *The truck driver is in the truck. The truck is on the road. The steering wheel is in the front.* Have children use the sentence pattern to tell about all the pictures on the page. Encourage them to use prepositions, or words that tell where.

 Leveled Support

Beginning Have children repeat the sentences that other children make up. Let them take a turn pointing to a picture on the chart.

Intermediate Ask questions to help children notice more details about the people and things in the pictures, such as: Where are the trailers? What is the truck carrying?

Advanced/Advanced-High Organize children into pairs and have them create their own sentence frames. Encourage pairs to use prepositions to complete their sentences about trucks.

Content Objectives
• Develop oral language.
• Use learning strategies.

Language Objectives
• Connect /ks/ with *Xx*.
• Learn English language patterns.

Use Learning Strategies
Work with children to create a Venn diagram titled *Cars and Trucks.* Label one circle *Cars* and one circle *Trucks.* Label the intersecting section *Both.* Help children fill in the diagram with information about cars and trucks. Help children by asking questions about the physical nature of cars and trucks and about how cars and trucks help people do jobs.

Talk with Me Chart 27A

Language Workshop: Talk About Jobs

■ **Introduce and Model** Turn to p. 12 of *Trucks Roll!* and read the sentences aloud. A truck can haul ice cream. A truck can haul books. A truck can even haul a bulldozer. Which of these loads would you like to haul? Allow children to give their opinions. What you think is called your *opinion.* Everyone has an opinion. People often have different opinions. Opinions are not right or wrong. They are just our thoughts. Then turn to the illustration on pp. 18–19. Read the sentence aloud and ask children where they would prefer to drive their trucks. Reinforce that what they prefer is their opinion.

■ **Practice** Think about how people use transportation to do work. Think about how these machines are alike and different. Which machines carry large loads? Which machines move loads the fastest? List answers in a T-chart with columns labeled *Alike* and *Different.* When the chart is complete, have volunteers share their opinions about which types of transportation are better for carrying loads. Restate that there is no right or wrong answer.

Writing: Write About Jobs

■ **Prepare for Writing** We have talked about ways people use transportation to do work. Now let's write about them. Have each child fold a piece of paper in half, creating two sections.

■ **Create Sentences About Machines That Work** Help children brainstorm sentences about how different types of transportation help people. Include sentences about how these machines are similar and how they are different. For ideas, encourage children to revisit the T-chart they made. Have children copy the sentence frame *I like _____ best.* at the bottom of the right side of the paper. Have them draw the mode of transportation they like best on the left side. Then ask children to write or dictate its name to complete the sentence frame. Have children share their papers with a partner.

Leveled LS Support

Beginning/Intermediate Write the sentence frame for children and have them write or dictate words to complete the sentence.

Advanced/Advanced-High Encourage children to write their sentence on their own. You might also have children help less-proficient partners complete their sentence.

Content Objectives

- Understand *Trucks Roll!*
- Practice compare and contrast.

Language Objectives

- Express opinions through speaking and writing.
- Write using grade-level vocabulary.

Monitor and Self-Correct

Remind children that if they don't know how to write the words, they can ask their partners for help.

Home Language Support

Invite children to share opinions and ideas in their home languages before creating their sentences.

Objectives
- Express opinions ranging from communicating single words and short phrases to participating in extended discussions on a variety of social and grade-appropriate academic topics.
- Write using content-based grade-level vocabulary.

Customize Literacy in Your Classroom

Table of Contents
for Customize Literacy

Customize Literacy is organized into different sections, each one designed to help you organize and carry out an effective literacy program. Each section contains strategies and support for teaching comprehension skills and strategies. *Customize Literacy* also shows how to use weekly text sets of readers in your literacy program.

Weekly Text Sets
to Customize Literacy

The following readers can be used to enhance your literacy instruction.

	Decodable Reader	Concept Literacy Reader	Below-Level Reader	On-Level Reader	Advanced Reader
Unit 5 WEEK 1	*On a Jet*	*There It Goes!*	*The Jet*	*Jan and Jem Win!*	*The Bus Ride*
Unit 5 WEEK 2	*Fox Can Fix It!*	*We Help*	*A Box for Rex*	*Our Boat*	*The Boat Ride*
Unit 5 WEEK 3	*Fun for Bud*	*What Carries Loads?*	*The Mud Bug*	*Our Pup Bud*	*Ming on the Job*

Customize Literacy in Your Classroom

Instruction in comprehension skills and strategies provides readers with avenues to understanding a text. Through teacher modeling and guided, collaborative, and independent practice, children become independent thinkers who employ a variety of skills and strategies to help them make meaning as they read.

Envision It!

A Comprehension Handbook

Mini-Lessons for Comprehension Skills and Strategies

Unit 1	Character, Setting, Sequence, Classify and Categorize, Predict and Set Purpose, Recall and Retell
Unit 2	Compare and Contrast, Setting, Main Idea, Realism and Fantasy, Sequence, Predict and Set Purpose, Recall and Retell
Unit 3	Compare and Contrast, Plot, Cause and Effect, Draw Conclusions, Main Idea, Predict and Set Purpose, Recall and Retell
Unit 4	Sequence, Cause and Effect, Character, Classify and Categorize, Setting, Predict and Set Purpose, Recall and Retell
Unit 5	Realism and Fantasy, Cause and Effect, Compare and Contrast, Plot, Main Idea, Draw Conclusions, Predict and Set Purpose, Recall and Retell
Unit 6	Compare and Contrast, Character, Main Idea, Plot, Setting, Draw Conclusions, Predict and Set Purpose, Recall and Retell

Envision It! Visual Skills Handbook

Author's Purpose
Categorize and Classify
Cause and Effect
Compare and Contrast
Draw Conclusions
Fact and Opinion
Generalize
Graphic Sources
Literary Elements
Main Idea and Details
Sequence

Envision It! Visual Strategies Handbook

Background Knowledge
Important Ideas
Inferring
Monitor and Clarify
Predict and Set Purpose
Questioning
Story Structure
Summarize
Text Structure
Visualize

Anchor Chart Anchor charts are provided with each strategy lesson. These charts incorporate the language of strategic thinkers. They help students make their thinking visible and permanent and provide students with a means to clarify their thinking about how and when to use each strategy. As children gain more experience with a strategy, the chart may undergo revision.

See pages 97–113 in the *First Stop on Reading Street* Teacher's Edition for additional support as you customize literacy in your classroom.

Good Readers DRA2 users will find additional resources in the *First Stop on Reading Street* Teacher's Edition on pages 100–102.

Contents

Pacing Guide

This chart shows the instructional sequence from *Scott Foresman Reading Street* for Grade K. You can use this pacing guide as is to ensure you are following a comprehensive scope and sequence. Or, you can adjust the sequence to match your calendar, curriculum map, or testing schedule.

Grade K

LANGUAGE ARTS

UNIT 1

	Week 1	Week 2	Week 3	Week 4	Week 5	Week 6
Phonological/ Phonemic Awareness	Rhyming Words	Syllables Sound Discrimination	Discriminate Sounds Segment Syllables	Discriminate Sounds	Isolate /m/ Discriminate Sounds	Isolate /t/ Discriminate Sounds Rhyme
Phonics	Letter Recognition: Aa, Bb, Cc, Dd, Ee	Letter Recognition: Ff, Gg, Hh, Ii, Jj, Kk, Ll, Mm, Nn	Letter Recognition: Oo, Pp, Qq, Rr, Ss	Letter Recognition: Tt, Uu, Vv, Ww, Xx, Yy, Zz	/m/ Spelled Mm	/t/ Spelled Tt
High-Frequency Words	I, am	I, am	the, little	the, little	a, to	a, to
Listening Comprehension	Character	Setting	Sequence	Classify and Categorize	Character	Classify and Categorize
Comprehension Strategies	Preview and Predict, Retell					

UNIT 2

	Week 1	Week 2
	Isolate /a/ Oral Blending	Isolate /s/ Oral Blending
	/a/ Spelled Aa	/s/ Spelled Ss
	have, is	have, is
	Compare and Contrast	Setting

UNIT 4

	Week 1	Week 2	Week 3	Week 4	Week 5	Week 6
Phonemic Awareness	Isolate /h/ Oral Blending Segment Phonemes	Isolate /l/ Oral Blending Segment Phonemes	Consonant Blends	Isolate /g/ Segment Phonemes	Isolate /e/ Segment Phonemes Discriminate Phonemes	Isolate /e/ Segment Phonemes Discriminate Phonemes
Phonics	/h/ Spelled Hh	/l/ Spelled Ll	Consonant Blends	/g/ Spelled Gg	/e/ Spelled Ee	/e/ Spelled Ee
High-Frequency Words	are, that, do	are, that, do	one, two, three, four, five	one, two, three, four, five	here, go, from	here, go, from
Listening Comprehension	Sequence	Cause and Effect	Sequence	Character	Classify and Categorize	Setting
Comprehension Strategies	Preview and Predict, Retell					

UNIT 5

	Week 1	Week 2
	Isolate /j/, /w/ Oral Blending Segment Phonemes	Isolate /ks/ Oral Blending Segment Phonemes
	/j/ Spelled Jj and /w/ Spelled Ww	/ks/ Spelled Xx
	yellow, blue, green	yellow, blue, green
	Realism and Fantasy	Cause and Effect

Are you the adventurous type? Want to use some of your own ideas and materials in your teaching? But you worry you might be leaving out some critical instruction kids need? **Customize Literacy** *can help.*

Week 3	Week 4	Week 5	Week 6
Isolate /p/ Oral Blending	Isolate /k/ Oral Blending	Isolate /i/ Discriminate Sounds Oral Blending	Isolate /i/ Discriminate Sounds Oral Blending
/p/ Spelled *Pp*	/k/ Spelled *Cc*	/i/ Spelled *Ii*	/i/ Spelled *Ii*
we, my, like	*we, my, like*	*he, for*	*he, for*
Main Idea	Realism and Fantasy	Sequence	Realism and Fantasy
Preview and Predict, Retell			

UNIT 3

Week 1	Week 2	Week 3	Week 4	Week 5	Week 6
Isolate /n/, /b/ Oral Blending Segment Phonemes	Isolate /r/ Oral Blending Segment Phonemes	Isolate /d/, /k/ Oral Blending Segment Phonemes	Isolate /f/ Oral Blending Segment Phonemes	Isolate /o/ Oral Blending Segment Phonemes	Oral Blending Segment Phonemes
/n/ Spelled *Nn* and /b/ Spelled *Bb*	/r/ Spelled *Rr*	/d/ Spelled *Dd* and /k/ Spelled *Kk*	/f/ Spelled *Ff*	/o/ Spelled *Oo*	/o/ Spelled *Oo*
me, with, she	*me, with, she*	*see, look*	*see, look*	*they, you, of*	*they, you, of*
Compare and Contrast	Plot	Cause and Effect	Plot	Draw Conclusions	Main Idea
Preview and Predict, Retell					

Week 3	Week 4	Week 5	Week 6
Isolate /u/ Oral Blending Segment Phonemes	Isolate /u/ Oral Blending Segment Phonemes	Isolate /v/, /z/ Oral Blending Segment Phonemes	Isolate /y/, /kw/ Oral Blending Segment Phonemes
/u/ Spelled *Uu*	/u/ Spelled *Uu*	/v/ Spelled *Vv* and /z/ Spelled *Zz*	/y/ Spelled *Yy* and /kw/ Spelled *qu*
what, said, was	*what, said, was*	*where, come*	*where, come*
Compare and Contrast	Plot	Main Idea	Draw Conclusions
Preview and Predict, Retell			

UNIT 6

Week 1	Week 2	Week 3	Week 4	Week 5	Week 6
Isolate /a/ and /i/ Blend Phonemes Segment Phonemes	Isolate /o/ Blend Phonemes Segment Phonemes	Isolate /e/ Blend Phonemes Segment Phonemes	Isolate /u/ Blend Phonemes Segment Phonemes	Consonant and Vowel Sounds	Consonant and Vowel Sounds
/a/ Spelled *Aa* and /i/ Spelled *Ii*	/o/ Spelled *Oo*	/e/ Spelled *Ee*	/u/ Spelled *Uu*	Consonant and Short Vowels	Consonant and Short Vowels
Review: *here, do, little, with, what*	Review: *where, is, go, that, come*	Review: *the, was, to, like, from*	Review: *for, of, my, we, yellow*	Review: *have, they, four, two, blue*	Review: *you, said, see, look, three*
Compare and Contrast	Character	Main Idea	Plot	Setting	Draw Conclusions
Preview and Predict, Retell					

Pacing Guide

Grade K — LANGUAGE ARTS

UNIT 1

	Week 1	Week 2	Week 3	Week 4	Week 5	Week 6
Speaking and Listening	Follow Directions	Drama: Respond to Literature	Listen for Rhyme and Rhythm	Talk About Me	Announcements and Messages	Drama: Respond to Literature
Grammar/ Conventions	Say Our Names	Write Our Names	What We Look Like	What We Can Do	Nouns for People and Animals	Nouns for Places and Things
Writing	Song	Invitation	Poem	Instructions	Caption	Personal Narrative

UNIT 2

	Week 1	Week 2
Speaking and Listening	Listen for Sequence	Listen for Directions
Grammar/ Conventions	Nouns for More Than One	Proper Nouns
Writing	Label	List

UNIT 4

	Week 1	Week 2	Week 3	Week 4	Week 5	Week 6
Speaking and Listening	Give Directions	Compare and Contrast	Listen for Sequence	Discuss Authors and Illustrators	Listen for Story Elements: Character	Listen to Poems
Grammar/ Conventions	Subjects (Naming Parts)	Predicates (Action Parts)	Complete Sentences	Telling Sentences	Capital Letters and Periods	Pronouns *I* and *me*
Writing	Directions	Poem	Description	List	Informal Letter	List

UNIT 5

	Week 1	Week 2
Speaking and Listening	Ask and Answer Questions	Drama: Respond to Literature
Grammar/ Conventions	Questions	Question Marks and Capital Letters
Writing	Caption	Rhyme

Week 3	Week 4	Week 5	Week 6
Discussions	Listen for Setting	Give a Description	Listen for Plot
Adjectives: Colors and Shapes	Adjectives: Sizes and Numbers	Adjectives: Opposites	Adjectives
Notes	Poem	Caption	Story

UNIT 3

Week 1	Week 2	Week 3	Week 4	Week 5	Week 6
Respond to Literature	Sequence	Recite Rhymes	Oral Presentation	Messages and Letters	Ask and Answer Questions
Verbs	Verbs for Now and the Past	Verbs That Add -s	Verbs for Now and the Future	Meaningful Word Groups	Sentences
Summary	Invitation	Persuasive Statement	Caption	List	Poem

Week 3	Week 4	Week 5	Week 6
Discuss Literature	Sequence	Oral Presentation: Description	Discuss Literary Elements: Plot
Prepositions	Nouns	Nouns in Sentences	Verbs
Poem	Formal Letter	Invitation	How-to Report

UNIT 6

Week 1	Week 2	Week 3	Week 4	Week 5	Week 6
Recite Language	Discuss Fact and Opinion	Interpret Information	Discuss Literary Elements: Character	Oral Presentation: Book Report	Discuss Literary Elements: Setting
Pronouns *I* and *me*	Prepositional Phrases	Telling Sentences	Questions	Exclamations	Complete Sentences
List	Song	Rhyme	Rhyme	Poem	Report

Teaching Record Chart

This chart shows the critical comprehension skills and strategies you need to cover.
Check off each one as you provide instruction.

Reading/Comprehension	DATES OF INSTRUCTION		
Predict what might happen next in text based on the cover, title, and illustrations.			
Ask and respond to questions about texts read aloud.			
Identify elements of a story including setting, character, and key events.			
Discuss the big idea (theme) of a well-known folk tale or fable and connect it to personal experience.			
Recognize sensory details.			
Recognize recurring phrases and characters in traditional fairy tales, lullabies, and folk tales from various cultures.			
Respond to rhythm and rhyme in poetry through identifying a regular beat and similarities in word sounds.			
Retell a main event from a story read aloud.			
Describe characters in a story and the reasons for their actions.			
Identify the topic of an informational text heard.			

" Tired of using slips of paper or stickies to make sure you teach everything you need to? Need an easier way to keep track of what you have taught and what you still need to cover? **Customize Literacy** can help. "

Reading/Comprehension	DATES OF INSTRUCTION		
Identify the topic and details in expository text heard or read, referring to the words and/or illustrations.			
Retell important facts in a text, heard or read.			
Discuss the ways authors group information in text.			
Use titles and illustrations to make predictions about text.			
Follow pictorial directions (e.g., recipes, science experiments).			
Identify the meaning of specific signs (e.g., traffic signs, warning signs).			
Discuss the purposes for reading and listening to various texts (e.g., to become involved in real and imagined events, settings, actions, and to enjoy language).			
Ask and respond to questions about text.			
Monitor and adjust comprehension (e.g., using background knowledge, creating sensory images, re-reading a portion aloud).			
Make inferences based on the cover, title, illustrations, and plot.			
Retell or act out important events in stories.			
Make connections to own experiences, to ideas in other texts, and to the larger community and discuss textual evidence.			

Realism and Fantasy

Mini-Lesson

Understand the Skill

My Skills Buddy K.5, pp. 14–15

Distinguishing **realism and fantasy** means to figure out whether a story could happen in real life. Children use clues about the characters, setting, and plot—along with their own experiences—to determine if it is realistic (could happen in real life) or fantastic (could not happen in real life).

Teach

Use the **Envision It!** lesson on *My Skills Buddy* K.5, pages 14–15 to visually teach realism and fantasy. Help children determine which fish is realistic and why.

Tell children that authors write different kinds of stories. One kind of story could happen in real life, and the other could not. Think aloud to model determining whether a story could happen in real life.

This story is about Max. He drums on a bucket and then on a garbage can with his two sticks. He makes music. I think this story could happen in real life because Max is a person. He lives in a neighborhood like mine. He likes to make music. I know people who like to make music.

Practice

Show children a familiar story. Recall the story with children. Ask questions to help children decide whether a story could happen in real life, such as: Do the people in this story act like real people I know? Are there things that could really happen in real life in this story? How do I know? Talk with children about clues they see in the pictures and hear in the story that help them determine if a story could happen in real life.

If... students have difficulty identifying whether a story could happen,

then... point to specific parts of the story (the characters, setting, or plot events) and ask pointed questions to connect prior knowledge to what happens in books, such as *Do I know people who _____? Do I _____?*

Apply

Tell children to listen carefully as you read a story and think about whether or not a story could happen in real life. As you read to children, pause to ask questions to help children think about whether the events, characters, and settings could happen in real life.

Writing

Children can write a sentence about their favorite story. Have them tell whether or not the story could happen. Give children the sentence frame: *This story could happen in real life because _____.* or *This story could not happen in real life because _____.* Record children's thoughts if needed.

Objectives:
- Children identify "what happens."
- Children identify "why something happens."

Texts for Teaching
- *George Washington Visits*
- *My Lucky Day*
- *Mayday! Mayday!*

Leveled Readers
- See pages CL16–CL17 for a list of Leveled Readers.

Cause and Effect

Mini-Lesson

My Skills Buddy K.5, pp. 34–35

Understand the Skill

A **cause** is why something happens. An **effect** is what happens. Children learn that things are sometimes connected to each other. Children think about what happens and why as they listen to stories.

Teach

Use the **Envision It!** lesson on My Skills Buddy K.5, pages 34–35 to visually teach cause and effect.

Tell children that some things happen because of something else. Talk about what happens when the dog puts paws on the table. Use simple physical examples to model cause-and-effect relationships, such as getting cold if you go outside without a coat on a cold day or a snowman melting on a warm day. After each example ask: What happened? Why did that happen?

Practice

Tell children that sometimes one thing makes another thing happen. Ask: Why might I have put on a coat? Together come up with reasons why you might have put on a coat. Continue with other questions, such as Why might I have eaten a snack? Why might I have opened the window? Why might I have spilled a glass of water? Write some of their responses on the board using a pattern: I _____ because _____.
If... children have difficulty explaining why something happened,
then... give them choices and have them choose.

Apply

Tell children to listen carefully as you read to find out what happens and why something happens. After reading, ask: *What is one thing that happened in the story? Why did it happen?*

Writing

Children can draw two pictures that show a cause-effect relationship.

Objectives:
- Children tell how things are alike.
- Children tell how things are different.
- Children make groups by identifying likenesses and differences.

Texts for Teaching
- *Flowers*
- *Little Panda*
- *Trucks Roll!*
- *Building with Dad*

Leveled Readers
- See pages CL16–CL17 for a list of Leveled Readers.

Compare and Contrast

My Skills Buddy K.5, pp. 54–55

Understand the Skill

Compare and contrast means to find the likenesses and/or differences between two or more people, places, things, or ideas. Children use the terms *alike* and *different* to talk about stories, characters in stories, their experiences, objects, and so on.

Teach

Use the **Envision It!** lesson on *My Skills Buddy* K.5, pages 54–55, to visually teach compare and contrast. Have children point out ways the bikes are alike and different.

Tell children that two books can be the alike or different. Model using two familiar books by the same author with the same characters. Recall the books with children. Talk about the two books using alike and different. Show which parts are *alike* and *different* using the pictures, author's name, and titles.

Practice

Show children two familiar books. Recall each book with children. After talking about each book ask questions to help children think about ways the books are alike and different. Ask: Do the books have the same characters? Do the books happen in the same place? Do different things happen in each book? Draw a Venn diagram (two overlapping circles) on the board. Record similarities in the center where the circles overlap. List differences in the outer circles. As children answer the questions and talk about the books, use these sentence frames: *The books are alike because* _____. *The books are different because* _____. Write down what children say.

If... children have difficulty finding likenesses,

then... ask leading questions, such as: *Is there a bear in both books? Do they look different? Is it the same bear?*

Apply

Tell children that sometimes books have the same characters, happen in the same place, or are about the same things. After you read a book with children, compare it to another familiar book. Help children talk about what is alike and different in the books.

Writing

Children can write their own sentence about how the books are the same or different. Supply sentence frames if needed. Post the sentences in the appropriate place on the Venn diagram.

Objectives:
- Children tell what they think will happen in a story and what will happen next in a story.
- Children preview a book and set a purpose for reading.

Texts for Teaching
- *Predicting and setting purposes is a strategy that can be applied to any selection. Encourage children to make predictions and set a purpose before they read.*

Predict and Set Purpose

Understand the Strategy

To predict means to tell what you think might happen next in a story or what the author may tell you next. Predicting goes hand-in-hand with previewing, which involves looking at text features and language to get an overview of a piece of writing. Before reading, previewing and predicting helps readers access what they already know about the topic and so **set a purpose** to guide reading.

Teach

Tell children that readers do things before they listen to or read a book. We look at the book inside and out. We think about what it might be about. Then we think about what we would like to find out as we read. Model predicting and setting purpose using the tips below.

Before We Listen or Read
- Look at the cover. What do you see?
- Look inside. What do you see?
- Think. What will this story will be about?

As We Listen or Read
- Listen or read carefully.
- Did you predict what would happen?
- Think. What will happen next?

After We Listen or Read
- Look back. Did you predict what would happen?
- Think. Do you like this story? Why or why not?

Practice and Apply

Use the strategy on a new story. Record some purposes children have. Record some predictions they make. After reading, return to them and talk about whether their purposes were met. How close were their predictions?

If... children have difficulty making predictions,

then... model the process using text clues and personal experience.

Anchor Chart

Anchor charts help children make their thinking visible and permanent. With an anchor chart, the group can clarify their thinking about how to use a strategy. You might make a chart of the strategy Predict and Set Purpose to hang in the classroom.

Glossary of Literacy Terms

This glossary lists academic language terms that are related to literacy.
They are provided for your information and professional use.

A

alliteration	the repetition of a consonant sound in a group of words, especially in poetry
animal fantasy	a story about animals that talk and act like people
antonym	a word that means the opposite of another word
author's purpose	the reason the author wrote the text
autobiography	the story of a real person's life written by that person

B

background knowledge	the information and experience that a reader brings to a text
biography	the story of a real person's life written by another person

C

cause	why something happens
character	a person, an animal, or a personified object in a story
classify and categorize	put things, such as pictures or words, into groups
compare and contrast	tell how things are the same and different
comprehension	understanding of text being read—the ultimate goal of reading
comprehension strategy	a conscious plan used by a reader to gain understanding of text. Comprehension strategies may be used before, during, or after reading.
context clue	the words, phrases, or sentences near an unknown word that give the reader clues to the word's meaning

D

details	small pieces of information
dialogue	written conversation
draw conclusions	arrive at decisions or opinions after thinking about facts and details and using prior knowledge

E

effect	what happens as the result of a cause
expository text	text that contains facts and information. Also called *informational text*.

F

fable	a story, usually with animal characters, that is written to teach a moral, or lesson
fact	piece of information that can be proved to be true
fairy tale	a folk story with magical characters and events
fantasy	a story that could not really happen
fiction	writing that tells about imaginary people, things, and events
folk tale	a story that has been passed down by word of mouth
foreshadowing	the use of hints or clues about what will happen later in a story

generalize   make a broad statement or rule after examining particular facts

graphic organizer   a drawing, chart, or web that illustrates concepts or shows how ideas relate to each other. Readers use graphic organizers to help them keep track of and understand important information and ideas as they read. Story maps, word webs, Venn diagrams, and KWL charts are graphic organizers.

graphic source   a chart, diagram, or map within a text that adds to readers' understanding of the text

G

historical fiction   realistic fiction that takes place in the past. It is an imaginary story based on historical events and characters.

humor   writing or speech that has a funny or amusing quality

H

idiom   a phrase whose meaning differs from the ordinary meaning of the words. *A stone's throw* is an idiom meaning "a short distance."

imagery   the use of language to create beautiful or forceful pictures in the reader's mind

inference   conclusion reached on the basis of evidence and reasoning

inform   give knowledge, facts, or news to someone

informational text   writing that contains facts and information. Also called *expository text*.

interview   a face-to-face conversation in which someone responds to questions

I

legend   a story coming down from the past about the great deeds of a hero. Although a legend may be based on historical people and events, it is not regarded as historically true.

literary elements   the characters, setting, plot, and theme of a narrative text

L

main idea   the big idea that tells what a paragraph or a selection is mainly about; the most important idea of a text

metacognition   an awareness of one's own thinking processes and the ability to monitor and direct them to a desired goal. Good readers use metacognition to monitor their reading and adjust their reading strategies.

monitor and clarify   a comprehension strategy by which readers actively think about understanding their reading and know when they understand and when they do not. Readers use appropriate strategies to make sense of difficult words, ideas, or passages.

M

M

moral	the lesson or teaching of a fable or story
mystery	a story about mysterious events that are not explained until the end, so as to keep the reader in suspense
myth	a story that attempts to explain something in nature

N

narrative	a story, made up or true, that someone tells or narrates
narrator	a character in a selection or someone outside the story who tells the story
nonfiction	writing that tells about real things, real people, and real events

O

onomatopoeia	the use of words that sound like their meanings, such as *buzz* and *hum*
opinion	someone's judgment, belief, or way of thinking
oral vocabulary	the words needed for speaking and listening

P

personification	a figure of speech in which human traits or actions are given to animals or inanimate objects, as in *The sunbeam danced on the waves.*
persuade	convince someone to do or to believe something
play	a story that is written to be acted out for an audience
plot	a series of related events at the beginning, middle, and end of a story; the action of a story
poem	an expressive, imaginative piece of writing often arranged in lines having rhythm and rhyme. In a poem, the patterns made by the sounds of the words have special importance.
pourquoi tale	a type of folk story that explains why things in nature came to be. *Pourquoi* is a French word meaning "why."
predict	tell what a selection might be about or what might happen in a text. Readers use text features and information to predict. They confirm or revise their predictions as they read.
preview	look over a text before reading it

Q

questioning	a reading strategy in which readers ask and answer questions to help make sense of what they read

R

reading vocabulary	the words we recognize or use in print
realistic fiction	a story about imaginary people and events that could happen in real life

repetition	the repeated use of some aspect of language	**R**
rhyme	to end in the same sound(s)	
rhythm	a pattern of strong beats in speech or writing, especially poetry	

science fiction	a story based on science that often tells what life in the future might be like	**S**
semantic map	a graphic organizer, often a web, used to display words or concepts that are meaningfully related	
sequence	the order of events in a selection or the order of the steps in which something is completed	
sequence words	clue words such as *first*, *next*, *then*, and *finally* that signal the order of events in a selection	
setting	where and when a story takes place	
stanza	a group of lines in a poem	
steps in a process	the order of the steps in which something is completed	
story map	a graphic organizer used to record the literary elements and the sequence of events in a narrative text	
story structure	how the characters, setting, and events of a story are organized into a plot	
summarize	give the most important ideas of what was read. Readers summarize important information in the selection to keep track of what they are reading.	
supporting detail	piece of information that tells about the main idea	

tall tale	a humorous story that uses exaggeration to describe impossible happenings	**T**
text structure	the organization of a piece of nonfiction writing. Text structures of informational text include cause/effect, chronological, compare/contrast, description, problem/solution, proposition/support, and ask/answer questions.	
theme	the big idea or author's message in a story	
think aloud	an instructional strategy in which a teacher verbalizes his or her thinking to model the process of comprehension or the application of a skill	
topic	the subject of a discussion, conversation, or piece of text	

visualize	picture in one's mind what is happening in the text. Visualizing helps readers imagine the things they read about.	**V**

Matching Books and Readers

Leveled Readers Skills Chart

Scott Foresman Reading Street provides more than six hundred leveled readers. Each one is designed to:

- Practice critical skills and strategies
- Build vocabulary and concepts
- Build fluency
- Develop a lifelong love of reading

Grade K

Title	Level*	DRA Level	Genre
Max the Duck	A	1	Fantasy
Fun for Us	B	2	Informational Text
Nick the Fix-It Man	B	2	Informational Text
Red and Blue	B	2	Realistic Fiction
We Have Fun Together	B	2	Fantasy
Two or Three?	B	2	Realistic Fiction
Buds for Mom	B	2	Realistic Fiction
A Walk in the Forest	B	2	Realistic Fiction
Looking for Animals	B	2	Realistic Fiction
Skip and Run	C	3	Fantasy
A Winter Home	C	3	Informational Text
A Yard for All	C	3	Fantasy
The Fawn	C	3	Realistic Fiction
We Can Do It!	C	3	Realistic Fiction
Fun with Gram	C	3	Realistic Fiction
They Will Grow	C	3	Realistic Fiction
What Can You Do?	C	3	Informational Text
Sad and Glad	C	3	Realistic Fiction
The Trip	C	3	Informational Text
Pigs	C	3	Informational Text
Frog's New Home	C	3	Informational Text
Five Bears	C	3	Fantasy
My Walk in Antarctica	C	3	Realistic Fiction
A Trip to Washington, D.C.	C	3	Informational Text
The Bus Ride	C	3	Realistic Fiction
The Boat Ride	C	3	Realistic Fiction
Ming on the Job	C	3	Realistic Fiction
The Big Train	D	4	Realistic Fiction
Get On the Bus!	D	4	Realistic Fiction
Catch the Ball!	D	4	Realistic Fiction
Homes	D	4	Informational Text
The Best Club Hut	D	4	Realistic Fiction
A Small Trip	D	4	Informational Text
The Box	D	4	Informational Text
Our Camping Trip	D	4	Realistic Fiction
Safe Places for Animals	D	4	Informational Text

* Suggested Guided Reading Level. Use your knowledge of children's abilities to adjust levels as needed.

This chart lists titles of leveled readers appropriate for children in Kindergarten. Use the chart to find titles that meet your children's interest and instructional needs. The books in this list were leveled using the criteria suggested in *Matching Books to Readers: Using Leveled Books in Guided Reading, Grades K–3* by Irene C. Fountas and Gay Su Pinnell. For more on leveling, see the *Reading Street Leveled Readers Leveling Guide.*

Comprehension Strategy	Target Comprehension Skill	Additional Comprehension Instruction	Vocabulary
Recall/Retell	Character	N/A	N/A
Recall/Retell	Setting	N/A	N/A
Recall/Retell	Sequence	N/A	N/A
Recall/Retell	Classify and Categorize	N/A	N/A
Recall/Retell	Character	N/A	N/A
Recall/Retell	Classify and Categorize	N/A	N/A
Recall/Retell	Compare and Contrast	N/A	N/A
Recall/Retell	Setting	N/A	N/A
Recall/Retell	Main Idea	N/A	N/A
Recall/Retell	Realism and Fantasy	N/A	N/A
Recall/Retell	Sequence	N/A	N/A
Recall/Retell	Realism and Fantasy	N/A	N/A
Recall/Retell	Compare and Contrast	N/A	N/A
Recall/Retell	Plot	N/A	N/A
Recall/Retell	Cause and Effect	N/A	N/A
Recall/Retell	Plot	N/A	N/A
Recall/Retell	Draw Conclusions	N/A	N/A
Recall/Retell	Main Idea	N/A	N/A
Recall/Retell	Sequence	N/A	N/A
Recall/Retell	Cause and Effect	N/A	N/A
Recall/Retell	Sequence	N/A	N/A
Recall/Retell	Character	N/A	N/A
Recall/Retell	Classify and Categorize	N/A	N/A
Recall/Retell	Setting	N/A	N/A
Recall/Retell	Realism and Fantasy	N/A	N/A
Recall/Retell	Cause and Effect	N/A	N/A
Recall/Retell	Compare and Contrast	N/A	N/A
Recall/Retell	Plot	N/A	N/A
Recall/Retell	Main Idea	N/A	N/A
Recall/Retell	Draw Conclusions	N/A	N/A
Recall/Retell	Compare and Contrast	N/A	N/A
Recall/Retell	Character	N/A	N/A
Recall/Retell	Main Idea	N/A	N/A
Recall/Retell	Plot	N/A	N/A
Recall/Retell	Setting	N/A	N/A
Recall/Retell	Draw Conclusions	N/A	N/A

What Good Readers Do

You can use the characteristics and behaviors of good readers to help all your children read better. But what are these characteristics and behaviors? And how can you use them to foster good reading behaviors for all your children? Here are some helpful tips.

Good Readers enjoy reading! They have favorite books, authors, and genres. Good readers often have a preference about where and when they read. They talk about books and recommend their favorites.

Develop this behavior by giving children opportunities to respond in different ways to what they read. Get them talking about what they read, and why they like or dislike it.

This behavior is important because book sharing alerts you to children who are somewhat passive about reading or have limited literacy experiences. Book sharing also helps you when you select books for the class.

Good Readers select books they can read.

Develop this behavior by providing a range of three or four texts appropriate for the child and then letting the child choose.

This behavior is important because children gain control over reading when they can choose from books they can read. This helps them become more independent in the classroom.

Good Readers use text features to help them preview and set purposes.

Develop this behavior by having children use the title and illustrations in fiction texts or the title, contents, headings, and other graphic features in nonfiction texts to make predictions about what they will be reading.

This behavior is important because previewing actually makes reading easier! Looking at features and sampling the text enables readers to predict and set expectations for reading.

Good Readers predict and ask questions before and while they read.

Develop this behavior by asking questions. After reading a passage, ask children what they think will happen next in a fiction text. Have them ask a question they think will be answered in a nonfiction text and read on to see if it is.

This behavior is important because when children predict and ask questions as they read, they are engaged. They have a purpose for reading and a basis for monitoring their comprehension.

" Want to improve your children's performance by fostering good reading behaviors? **Customize Literacy can help.** "

Good Readers use effective strategies and sources of information to figure out unknown words.

Develop this behavior by teaching specific strategies for figuring out unknown words, such as sounding out clusters of letters, using context, reading on, and using references.

This behavior is important because when readers have a variety of strategies to use, they are more able to decode and self-correct quickly. Readers who do these things view themselves as good readers.

**CH-
QU-
ST-**

Good Readers construct meaning as they read and then share or demonstrate their understanding.

Develop this behavior by having children retell what they read or write a summary of what they read in their own words.

This behavior is important because the ability to retell or write a summary is essential for success in reading. It shows how well a child has constructed meaning.

Good Readers make connections.

Develop this behavior by asking questions to help children make connections: *What does this remind you of? Have you ever read or experienced anything like this?*

This behavior is important because making connections helps readers understand and appreciate a text. Making connections to self, the world, and other texts supports high-level thinking.

Conversation Starters

Asking Good Questions Children want to read and listen to interesting and thought-provoking books! You can help them talk about these books. Use questions such as the following to assess listening comprehension and help children think about books. As you read longer books, pause often to ask questions about past and future events.

Cause and Effect

- What happens in this story?
- Why does it happen?

Classify and Categorize

- How are these things alike?
- Do these things belong in the same group?
- Is this thing like the others? Does it belong in the group?
- How do you know that it is like/not like the others?
- How would you group these things?

Draw Conclusions

- What happens in the story?
- What did the characters do to show you that they are kind/mean/strong?
- Which character do you like best? Why?
- Do you like this story? What makes you like it or dislike it?

Character

- Who is in this story?
- What does this character like to do?
- How did the character feel in this part of the book?
- What does this character think about what happens in the book?
- Does this character seem real or made-up? What makes you think so?
- What character would you like to be? Why?

Compare and Contrast

- How are these things/characters/stories alike?
- How are these things/characters/stories different?

Main Idea

- What is this story all about?

- What is the big idea of this story?

- What clues help you know what the story is about?

Plot

- In the story, what happens at the beginning? in the middle? at the end?

- What are other important things that happen in the story?

- What do you think is the most exciting/ important thing that happens?

- What is the problem that the character must solve/fix?

- How is that problem solved or fixed?

Realism and Fantasy

- Could this story happen in real life? Why do you think as you do?

- What things in the story could happen in real life?

- Do the people in this story act like people you know?

- How do you know if a story is make-believe or could really happen?

Sequence

- In this story, what happened first? next? last?

Setting

- What do the pictures tell you about when and where this story happened?

- What is this place like? What do you think it would be like?

- Does the place seem real or made-up? How can you tell?

- Do you want to visit this place? Why?

Connecting Science and Social Studies

Get Ready For Grade 1

Scott Foresman Reading Street Leveled Readers are perfect for covering, supporting, or enriching science and social studies content. Using these books ensures that all students can access important concepts.

Grade K Leveled Readers

Science

Earth and Space Science

Fiction Books

- *We Can Do It!*

Life Science

Nonfiction Books

- *A Winter Home*
- *What Can You Do?*
- *The Trip*
- *Pigs*
- *Frog's New Home*
- *A Small Trip*
- *Safe Places for Animals*

Fiction Books

- *A Walk in the Forest*
- *Looking for Animals*
- *Skip and Run*
- *A Yard for All*
- *The Fawn*
- *Fun with Gram*
- *They Will Grow*
- *Sad and Glad*

Physical Science

Fiction Books

- *Catch the Ball!*
- *The Best Club Hut*

Grade K Leveled Readers

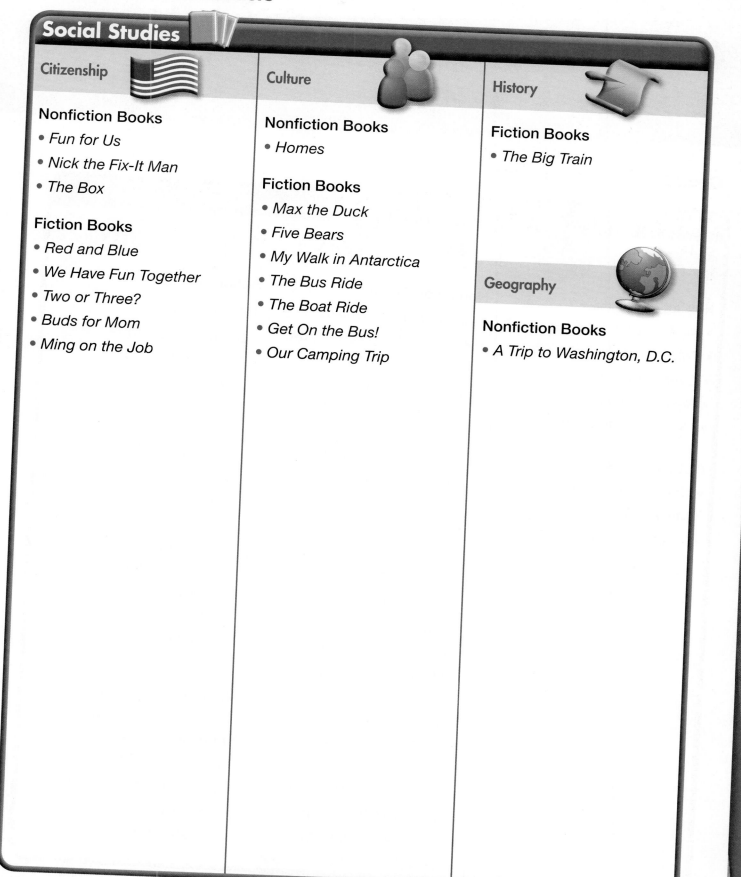

Social Studies

Citizenship

Nonfiction Books
- *Fun for Us*
- *Nick the Fix-It Man*
- *The Box*

Fiction Books
- *Red and Blue*
- *We Have Fun Together*
- *Two or Three?*
- *Buds for Mom*
- *Ming on the Job*

Culture

Nonfiction Books
- *Homes*

Fiction Books
- *Max the Duck*
- *Five Bears*
- *My Walk in Antarctica*
- *The Bus Ride*
- *The Boat Ride*
- *Get On the Bus!*
- *Our Camping Trip*

History

Fiction Books
- *The Big Train*

Geography

Nonfiction Books
- *A Trip to Washington, D.C.*

Connecting Science and Social Studies

Grade 1 Leveled Readers

Science

Earth and Space Science

Nonfiction Books
- All About the Weather
- The Communication Story
- Over the Years
- Ready for Winter?
- Using the Telephone

Fiction Books
- Cody's Adventure
- Marla's Good Idea
- What a Detective Does

Life Science

Nonfiction Books
- All About Food Chains
- Animals Change and Grow
- Around the Forest
- Around the World
- Baby Animals in the Rain Forest
- Bees and Beekeepers
- The Dinosaur Detectives
- The Dinosaur Herds
- Fun in the Sun
- Honey
- In My Room
- Learn About Butterflies
- Learn About Worker Bees
- Let's Go to the Zoo
- Let's Visit a Butterfly Greenhouse
- Look at Dinosaurs
- A Mighty Oak Tree
- Monarchs Migrate South
- People Help the Forest
- The Seasons Change
- Seasons Come and Go
- What Animals Can You See?

Life Science

Fiction Books
- Bix the Dog
- Britton Finds a Kitten
- Carlos Picks a Pet
- Cary and the Wildlife Shelter
- Mac Can Do It!
- Mack and Zack
- Plans Change
- Sam
- The Sick Pets
- Time for Dinner
- What Brown Saw
- Which Animals Will We See?
- Which Fox?

Physical Science

Nonfiction Books
- The Inclined Plane
- Simple Machines at Work
- Simple Machines in Compound Machines

Grade 1 Leveled Readers

Social Studies

Citizenship

Nonfiction Books
- A Class
- A Garden for All
- Great Scientists: Detectives at Work
- Here in My Neighborhood
- A New Library
- Puppy Raiser
- The Story of the Kids Care Club
- Ways to Be a Good Citizen

Fiction Books
- The Art Show
- At Your Vet
- Big Wishes and Her Baby
- Double Trouble Twins
- Fly Away Owl!
- Grasshopper and Ant
- Hank's Song
- Let's Build a Park!
- Look at My Neighborhood
- My Little Brother Drew
- On the Farm
- Paul's Bed
- A Play
- Rules at School
- Space Star
- Squirrel and Bear
- That Cat Needs Help!

Culture

Nonfiction Books
- Cascarones Are for Fun
- My Babysitter
- Special Days, Special Food
- We Are a Family
- What Makes Buildings Special?

Fiction Books
- Go West!
- Grandma's Farm
- Gus the Pup
- Jamie's Jumble of Junk
- A New Baby Brother
- A Party for Pedro
- A Visit to the Ranch
- Where They Live

History

Nonfiction Books
- School: Then and Now
- Treasures of Our Country

Fiction Books
- Loni's Town

Government

Nonfiction Books
- America's Home
- Our Leaders

Fiction Books
- Mom the Mayor

Planning Teacher Study Groups

Adventurous teachers often have good ideas for lessons. A teacher study group is a great way to share ideas and get feedback on the best way to connect content and students. Working with other teachers can provide you with the support and motivation you need to implement new teaching strategies. A teacher study group offers many opportunities to collaborate, support each other's work, share insights, and get feedback.

Think About It

A weekly or monthly teacher study group can help support you in developing your expertise in the classroom. You and a group of like-minded teachers can form your own study group. What can this group accomplish?

- Read and discuss professional articles by researchers in the field of education.

- Meet to share teaching tips, collaborate on multi-grade lessons, and share resources.

- Develop lessons to try out new teaching strategies. Meet to share experiences and discuss how to further improve your teaching approach.

Let's Meet!

Forming a study group is easy. Just follow these four steps:

1. **Decide on the size of the group.** A small group has the advantage of making each member feel accountable, but make sure that all people can make the same commitment!

2. **Choose teachers to invite to join your group.** Think about whom you want to invite. Should they all teach the same grade? Can you invite teachers from other schools? Remember that the more diverse the group, the more it benefits from new perspectives.

3. **Set goals for the group.** In order to succeed, know what you want the group to do. Meet to set goals. Rank goals in order of importance and refer often to the goals to keep the group on track.

4. **Make logistical decisions.** This is often the most difficult. Decide where and when you will meet. Consider an online meeting place where group members can post discussion questions and replies if people are not able to meet.

What Will We Study? Use the goals you set to help determine what your group will study. Consider what materials are needed to reach your goals, and how long you think you will need to prepare for each meeting.

How Will It Work? Think about how you structure groups in your classroom. Use some of the same strategies.

- **Assign a group facilitator.** This person is responsible for guiding the meeting. This person comes prepared with discussion questions and leads the meeting. This could be a rotating responsibility dependent on experience with various topics. This person might be responsible for providing the materials.

- **Assign a recorder.** Have someone take notes during the meeting and record group decisions.

- **Use the jigsaw method.** Not everyone has time to be a facilitator. In this case, divide the text and assign each portion to a different person. Each person is responsible for leading the discussion on that particular part.

Meet Again Make a commitment to meet for a minimum number of times. After that, the group can reevaluate and decide whether or not to continue.

" Have some great teaching tips to share? Want to exchange ideas with your colleagues? Build your own professional community of teachers. **Customize Literacy** gets you started. **"**

Trial Lessons

Use your colleagues' experiences to help as you think about new ways to connect content and students. Use the following plan to create a mini-lesson. It should last twenty minutes. Get the support of your colleagues as you try something new and then reflect on what happened.

Be Creative! As you develop a plan for a mini-lesson, use these four words to guide planning: *purpose*, *text*, *resources*, and *routine*.

- **Purpose:** Decide on a skill or strategy to cover. Define your purpose for teaching the lesson.

- **Text:** Develop a list of the materials you could use. Ask your colleagues for suggestions.

- **Resources:** Make a list of the available resources, and consider how to use those resources most effectively. Consider using the leveled readers listed on pages CL16–CL17 and CL22–CL25 of Customize Literacy.

- **Routine:** Choose an instructional routine to structure your mini-lesson. See the mini-lessons in Customize Literacy for suggestions.

Try It! Try out your lesson! Consider audio- or videotaping the lesson for later review. You may wish to invite a colleague to sit in as you teach. Make notes on how the lesson went.

How Did It Go? Use the self-evaluation checklist on page CL29 as you reflect on your trial lesson. This provides a framework for later discussion.

Discuss, Reflect, Repeat Solicit feedback from your teacher study group. Explain the lesson and share your reflections. Ask for suggestions on ways to improve the lesson. Take some time to reflect on the feedback. Modify your lesson to reflect what you have learned. Then try teaching the lesson again.

Checklist for Teacher Self-Evaluation

How Well Did I ...	Very Well	Satisfactory	Not Very Well
Plan the lesson?			
Select the appropriate level of text?			
Introduce the lesson and explain its objectives?			
Review previously taught skills?			
Directly explain the new skills being taught?			
Model the new skills?			
Break the material down into small steps?			
Integrate guided practice into the lesson?			
Monitor guided practice for student understanding?			
Provide feedback on independent practice?			
Maintain an appropriate pace?			
Assess student understanding of the material?			
Stress the importance of applying the skill as they read?			
Maintain students' interest?			
Ask questions?			
Handle student questions and responses?			
Respond to the range of abilities?			

Books for Teachers

Children aren't the only ones who need to read to grow. Here is a brief list of books that you may find useful to fill your reading teacher basket and learn new things.

A Professional Bibliography

Adams, M. J. "Alphabetic Anxiety and Explicit, Systematic Phonics Instruction: A Cognitive Science Perspective." *Handbook of Early Literacy Research.* The Guilford Press, 2001.

Adams, M. J. *Beginning to Read: Thinking and Learning About Print.* The MIT Press, 1990.

Afflerbach, P. "The Influence of Prior Knowledge and Text Genre on Readers' Prediction Strategies." *Journal of Reading Behavior,* vol. XXII, no. 2 (1990).

Armbruster, B. B., F. Lehr, and J. Osborn. *Put Reading First: The Research Building Blocks for Teaching Children to Read.* Partnership for Reading, Washington, D.C., 2001.

Bear, D. R., M. Invernizzi, S. Templeton, and F. Johnston. *Words Their Way.* Merrill Prentice Hall, 2004.

Beck, I., M. G. McKeown, and L. Kucan. *Bringing Words to Life: Robust Vocabulary Instruction.* The Guilford Press, 2002.

Biemiller, A. "Teaching Vocabulary in the Primary Grades: Vocabulary Instruction Needed." *Vocabulary Instruction Research to Practice.* The Guilford Press, 2004.

Blachowicz, C. and P. Fisher. "Vocabulary Instruction." *Handbook of Reading Research,* vol. III. Lawrence Erlbaum Associates, 2000.

Cunningham, P. M. and J. W. Cunningham. "What We Know About How to Teach Phonics." *What Research Says About Reading Instruction,* 3rd ed. International Reading Association, 2002.

Daniels, H. *Literature Circles.* 2nd ed. Stenhouse Publishers, 2002.

Dickson, S. V., D. C. Simmons, and E. J. Kame'enui. "Text Organization: Instructional and Curricular Basics and Implications." *What Reading Research Tells Us About Children with Diverse Learning Needs: Bases and Basics.* Lawrence Erlbaum Associates, 1998.

Diller, D. *Making the Most of Small Groups: Differentiation for All.* Stenhouse Publishers, 2007.

Duke, N. K., V. S. Bennett-Armistead, and E. M. Roberts. "Bridging the Gap Between Learning to Read and Reading to Learn." *Literacy and Young Children: Research-Based Practices.* The Guilford Press, 2003.

Duke, N. K. and C. Tower. "Nonfiction Texts for Young Readers." *The Texts in Elementary Classrooms.* Lawrence Erlbaum Associates, 2004.

Ehri, L. C. and S. R. Nunes. "The Role of Phonemic Awareness in Learning to Read." *What Research Has to Say About Reading Instruction.* 3rd ed. International Reading Association, 2002.

Fountas, I. C. and G. S. Pinnell. *Guided Reading: Good First Teaching for All Children.* Heinemann, 1996.

Fountas, I. C. and G. S. Pinnell. *Matching Books to Readers: Using Leveled Books in Guided Reading, K-3.* Heinemann, 1999.

Harvey, S. and A. Goudvis. *Strategies That Work: Teaching Comprehension to Enhance Understanding.* 2nd ed. Stenhouse Publishers, 2007.

Hiebert, E. H. and L. A. Martin. "The Texts of Beginning Reading Instruction." *Handbook of Early Literacy Research.* The Guilford Press, 2001.

Indrisano, R. and J. R. Paratore. *Learning to Write, Writing to Learn. Theory and Research in Practice.* International Reading Association, 2005.

Juel, C., G. Biancarosa, D. Coker, and R. Deffes. "Walking with Rosie: A Cautionary Tale of Early Reading Instruction." *Educational Leadership* (April 2003).

National Reading Panel. *Teaching Children to Read.* National Institute of Child Health and Human Development, 1999.

Pressley, M. *Reading Instruction That Works: The Case for Balanced Teaching,* 3rd ed. The Guilford Press, 2005.

Smith, S., D. C. Simmons, and E. J. Kame'enui. "Word Recognition: Research Bases." *What Reading Research Tells Us About Children with Diverse Learning Needs: Bases and Basics.* Lawrence Erlbaum Associates, 1998.

Snow, C., S. Burns, and P. Griffin, eds. *Preventing Reading Difficulties in Young Children.* National Academy Press, 1998.

Vaughn, S., P. G. Mathes, S. Linan-Thompson, and D. J. Francis. "Teaching English Language Learners at Risk for Reading Disabilities to Read: Putting Research into Practice." *Learning Disabilities Research & Practice,* vol. 20, issue 1 (February 2006).

UNIT 5 Acknowledgments

Acknowledgments

Illustrations

Cover Rob Hefferan
12, 59–65 Natalia Vasquez
15–25 Maria Mola
30 Julia Woolf
42 Paul Meisel
40–45 Cale Atkinson
50–51 Rob Hefferan
52 Mary Sullivan
70 Jan Bryan Hunt
72, 108 George Ulrich
78–85 Dani Jones
90–91 Ana Ochoa
92 Carol Koeller
99–105 Robbie Short
110 Leslie Harrington
112 Jamie Smith
119–125 Wednesday Kirwan
129 Anthony Lewis
130–131 Viviana Garofoli

Photographs

Every effort has been made to secure permission and provide appropriate credit for photographic material. The publisher deeply regrets any omission and pledges to correct errors called to its attention in subsequent editions.

Unless otherwise acknowledged, all photographs are the property of Pearson Education, Inc.

Photo locations denoted as follows: Top (T), Center (C), Bottom (B), Left (L), Right (R), Background (Bkgd)

10 (B) ©Tim Bird/Corbis
28 ©Alex Segre/Alamy Images, ©moodboard/Corbis, ©Randy Faris/Corbis, ©Corbis/Jupiter Images
29 ©JG Photography/Alamy
48 Getty Images
68 ©Peter Titmuss/Alamy Images, ©Picture Contact/Alamy Images, Brand X Pictures, Jupiter Images.

144

Teacher Editions

KWL Strategy: The KWL Interactive Reading Strategy was developed and is used by permission of Donna Ogle, National-Louis University, Skokie, Illinois, co-author of *Reading Today and Tomorrow*, Holt, Rinehart & Winston Publishers, 1988. (See also the *Reading Teacher*, February 1986, pp. 564–570.)

Understanding by Design quotes: Wiggins, G. & McTighe, J. (2005). *Understanding by Design.* Alexandria, VA: Association for Supervision and Curriculum Development.

Illustrations

Cover Rob Hefferan

Running Header Steven Mach

Photos

Every effort has been made to secure permission and provide appropriate credit for photographic material. The publisher deeply regrets any omission and pledges to correct errors called to its attention in subsequent editions.

Unless otherwise acknowledged, all photographs are the property of Pearson Education, Inc.

Teacher Notes

Teacher Notes

Teacher Notes

Teacher Resources

Looking for Teacher Resources and other important information?

In the First Stop on Reading Street

Teacher Resources

Looking for Teacher Resources and other important information?

In the **First Stop** on Reading Street